Living Martyrs

Living Martyrs

Individuals and Revolution in Nepal

James F. Fisher
with
Tanka Prasad Acharya
and
Rewanta Kumari Acharya

DELHI
OXFORD UNIVERSITY PRESS
CALCUTTA   CHENNAI   MUMBAI
1998

Oxford University Press, Great Clarendon Street, Oxford OX2 6DP

Oxford New York
Athens Auckland Bangkok Calcutta
Cape Town Chennai Dar es Salaam Delhi
Florence Hong Kong Istanbul Karachi
Kuala Lumpur Madrid Melbourne Mexico City
Mumbai Nairobi Paris Singapore
Taipei Tokyo Toronto

and associates in

Berlin Ibadan

ISBN 0 19 564544 8

Typeset by Print Line, New Delhi 110048
Printed in India at Saurabh Print O Pack, Noida
and published by Manzar Khan, Oxford University Press
YMCA Library Building, Jai Singh Road, New Delhi 110 001

For
Kim and Maya

Acknowledgements

Tanka Prasad Acharya expounded many times on the fundamental importance to a Hindu of extending hospitality to whoever needs it, and his wife, Rewanta Kumari, inconspicuously but unfailingly practised what he preached. All the Acharyas did so, including the daughters-in-law who served me countless snacks and cups of tea. This book is a family project in the fullest sense of the term. From the beginning I was made to feel at home, and by the end I had to remind myself occasionally that I was not really one of them.

If the recounting of their lives had been left entirely to Tanka Prasad and Rewanta Kumari and me, not much would have come of it. The initial round of taped interviews was all translated and transcribed (even the portions in English) by their youngest son, Bir Bhadra, and by their second granddaughter, Beena (the former is two and a half years older than the latter). In the case of Tanka Prasad, particularly, whose speech had become somewhat slurred with advancing age, this was a formidable task. I am greatly in their debt.

These interviews, invariably raising more questions than they answered, constituted only the first, halting step on the long march through their lives. Their answers were often elusive, partly because neither Tanka Prasad nor his wife were natural raconteurs, and partly because, Tanka Prasad's political ego notwithstanding, they were both genuinely modest people. On several occasions they tried to convince me, with notable lack of success, that there was nothing particularly interesting or unusual about their lives. Therefore it took many repeated conversations not just to put flesh and blood on their relatively skeletal narrations, but even to clarify the basic chronology and uncover the stubborn facts of what had transpired over the course of their multifarious lives.

I was extremely fortunate to have the active cooperation of two of the three compatriots who had spent a full ten years in prison with Tanka Prasad. Mr Ram Hari Sharma answered countless questions and reviewed the entire manuscript, with the assistance of the Acharyas' oldest son,

Angira, who read the text to him, because of Ram Hari's failing eyesight. Mr Govinda Prasad Upadhyay talked to me and provided me with scores of articles he had recently published in the Nepali daily, *Samaj*, on the life and times of the Praja Parishad (usually translated as 'Peoples' Council' or 'Peoples' Conference'), the political party founded by Tanka Prasad and his friends. Students of modern Nepalese political history owe Govinda Prasad an incalculable debt.

In addition, Mr Rishikesh Shaha generously shared with me not only his personal reminiscences but also relevant portions from what was then a pre-publication manuscript of his invaluable *Modern Nepal: A Political History from 1769 to 1955*. Such material, sometimes intercalated into the text (where it is fully acknowledged), supplements and enriches the Acharyas' own accounts. The resulting pastiche is only apparently less authentically first-person, since the end result has been checked and approved by various members of the Acharya family.

Tanka Prasad and Rewanta Kumari's eldest daughter, Meena, spent many hours with her mother clarifying details and coaxing out the minutiae of events, some of which had featured herself in a supporting role. She also employed her well-known powers to *gali garnu* (a species of verbal behaviour ranging from mild rebuke to harsh abuse) her father from time to time when his commitment to the project wavered. Nor did she hesitate to *gali garnu* me when progress on the book proceeded more slowly than she would have preferred. The youngest Acharya daughter, Pushpa, was extremely helpful in untangling myriad transliteration and spelling problems. The second daughter-in-law, Sushan, rendered superb assistance in translating documents.

The Acharyas' grandson, Umesh, sat innumerable times with me and Tanka Prasad, or his wife, or both. His translation skills, both oral and in rendering the documents we collected, were truly remarkable. He also never hesitated to indulge in the somewhat un-grandson-like behaviour of badgering his grandparents when they got fed up with our incessant queries. A large portion of what follows would never have seen the light of day without Umesh's unstinting effort. It is a source of great sadness to me that his tragically early death prevented him from seeing the fruits of our labours.

I hope I have made clear by now that without the assistance of many Acharya family members the project would have aborted early on or imploded at several points along the way. Since the Acharyas are both extremely hard of hearing, and I am totally deaf in one ear myself, without the good offices of many of their progeny the three of us would have spent a good deal more time shouting at each other than we did.

I thank Professor Merrill Goodall for generously making available to me material (including summaries of interviews with Tanka Prasad and others) his late wife, Betsy, collected for her dissertation on Tanka Prasad. A series of decreasingly crude versions of the manuscript have benefitted from comments and suggestions made by various students at Carleton College, by faculty and students at seminars at the University of Michigan, Ann Arbor, Reed College, and the University of California, Berkeley, where some of the material was presented, and especially from close critical readings by Krishna B. Bhattachan, Kim C. Fisher, Maya C. Fisher, Stephen Swan, Nancy C. Wilkie, and anonymous press reviewers. I also record my debt to Dr Laxmi Datta Bhatta for helping to convert Bikram era dates to Christian era ones. Uncredited photographs are my own.

Finally, I acknowledge the Social Science Research Council, the Ford Foundation, the PICAS Program (Inter-Institutional Collaboration in Area Studies) of the University of Michigan, and Carleton College for their support, through grants for field research, writing, and released time from teaching, for the work which has resulted in this book. Royalties from book sales will be donated to the Tanka Prasad Memorial Foundation, which has been created to promote the ideals and principles which Tanka Prasad stood by and fought for.

Contents

Illustrations

Figures

Maps

Main Characters

By virtue of their frequent appearance in the text the following names comprise the principal players in the Acharya drama. Those names (by far the majority) mentioned in the text merely for the sake of making the historical record as complete as possible have been omitted from the list below.

Tanka Prasad Acharya
Bua (father):

founder of Praja Parishad, Prime Minister, husband of Rewanta Kumari

Rewanta Kumari
Acharya *Ama*
(mother):

wife of Tanka Prasad, mother of the following seven children (in descending birth order; family nicknames in parentheses): Meena: eldest daughter, wife of Victor Sivyakov (divorced), mother of Beena; Shanta: second daughter, wife of Kalika Prasad Rimal, mother of Rita and Umesh; Mallika (*Babi*): third daughter, wife of Bishnu Sharma; Angira (*Thulo Bhai* or *Thulo Babu*): oldest son, husband of Sabita; Kushumakar (*Kanchhu*): second son, husband of Sushan; Pushpa (*Sanu*): fourth daughter, wife of Sanjay Koirala; Bir Bhadra (*Sano Kanchhu*): third son, husband of Leela

Sanima:

Tanka Prasad's second mother's younger sister

Mithi:

life-long servant of the Acharyas

Kancho Baje:

Tanka Prasad's youngest paternal uncle

Ram Hari Sharma:

Tanka Prasad's political ally and fellow prisoner in jail for ten years

Chuda Prasad Sharma:

as above (Tanka Prasad's older brother's wife's brother)

Govinda Prasad Upadhaya:	as above, and author of numerous newspaper articles on political events in which Tanka Prasad was involved
Ganesh Man Singh:	Praja Parishad member; escaped from jail in 1946; leader of Congress Party during and after the 1990 People's Movement
Mangala Devi Singh:	wife of Ganesh Man; active in women's organizations
Khadga Man Singh:	active in Prachanda Gorkha Movement; served nineteen years in prison, the last ten with Tanka Prasad
Chandra Man Sainju : (Chandra Man Compounder)	health specialist and confidant of King Tribhuvan; clandestine courier between Praja Parishad and the King
Dasarath Chand:	Praja Parishad member, executed by Ranas
Dharma Bhakta:	as above
Ganga Lal:	as above
Sukraraj Shastri:	social and religious reformer, active in Arya Samaj Movement; executed by Ranas
Rishikesh Shah:	political activist; first Nepalese Ambassador to the United Nations; author of important scholarly books on Nepalese history and politics
Prithvinarayan Shah:	founder of modern Nepal in 1769, and of present dynasty of Nepalese Kings; ruled 1769-75
King Tribhuvan:	collaborated with Tanka Prasad's group to overthrow the Ranas; ruled 1911-55
King Mahendra:	son of Tribhuvan; appointed Tanka Prasad Prime Minister in 1956; ruled 1955-72
King Birendra:	son of Mahendra; present King, ascended the Nepalese throne in 1972
Chandra Shamsher Jang : Bahadur Rana	Prime Minister, 1901-29
Juddha Shamsher Jang : Bahadur Rana	Prime Minister, 1932-45

Padma Shamsher Jang : Bahadur Rana	Prime Minister, 1945-8
Nara Shamsher Jang : Bahadur Rana	Army General, in charge of executing the four martyrs; interrogator of Tanka Prasad and Rewanta Kumari during the 1940s
Matrika Prasad Koirala : (M.P., 'Matrika Babu')	first non-Rana Prime Minister, 1951; one of Tanka Prasad's political rivals, whose son (Sanjay) married Tanka Prasad's daughter (Pushpa)
Bishweshwor Prasad: Koirala (B.P.)	leader of Nepali Congress and first popularly-elected Prime Minister, 1959-1960; younger half-brother of Matrika Prasad; older brother of Girija Prasad Koirala, Prime Minister 1991-4
K. I. Singh :	leader of Raksha Dal revolt in 1952; Prime Minister following Tanka Prasad, 1957

Glossary

achaar	any combination of spices, fruits, or vegetables, pickled or fresh, usually hot and sour, eaten as a relish
ama	mother
ayurveda	traditional South Asian medical system
Bada Hakim	governor
bartaman	sacred thread ceremony for high-caste Hindu boys
bhai-tika	part of Dasai Festival, when sisters worship their brothers
bhakti	devotional sect
bigha	unit of land (about 1 and 5/8ths acres) in the Tarai divided (like the Indian Rupee) into 16 *annas*, hence the 7/9 crop distribution referred to in Chapter 9.
bua	father
chakari	ritualized obsequiousness consisting of bowing and scraping and excessive, insincere flattery by lower, less powerful individuals towards those of higher rank or greater power
chhina	tin snips
chiura	beaten rice
dal	lentils
dasai	most important Hindu festival, organized around worship of goddess Kali
das dan	"ten gifts", given to someone of higher status
dharma	duty
dhoti	plain cotton loincloth worn by men
doko	funnel shaped wicker basket for carrying things on the back
dukha	suffering, pain

dulahi	bride
gagro	narrow-necked vessel for carrying water
ghate vaidya	traditional doctor at the *ghat* by the river who pronounces someone dead
gotra	exogamous section within Brahmin caste
jamindari	landlord system
jogi	Hindu ascetic
katoli	enclosed palanquin
kharpan	shoulder borne carrying device used by Newars
kuldeuta	household god
Mahottari	Tarai District where Tanka Prasad's father lived
maiti	wife's parental home
mantra	secret formula
manusmriti	traditional Hindu law code, codified in second century AD by Manu
moksha	release from rebirth
olinkath	open palanquin
pasne	first feeding of rice to infants
purohit	Brahmin priest
puja	worship ritual
rudrachha	prayer beads
sanyas	renunciation of the world
satyagraha	peaceful demonstration
shaligram	amonite fossil used in devotions
swasti	welcome
theki	wooden container for holding milk or curds
tika	mark on forehead, applied after doing *puja*

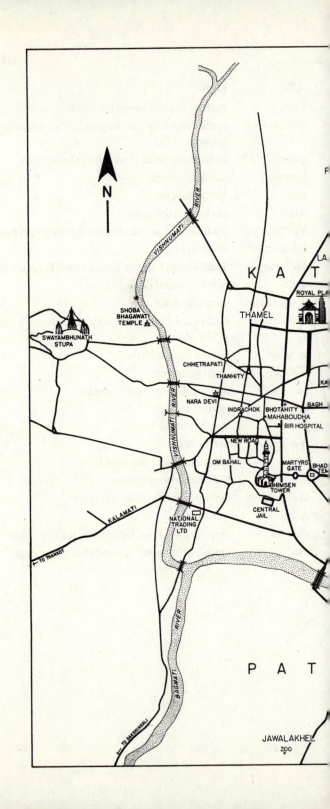

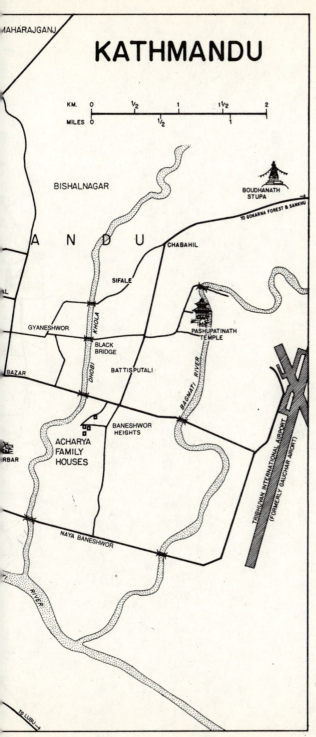

KATHMANDU

MAHARAJGANJ

BISHALNAGAR

BOUDHANATH STUPA

TO GOKARNA FOREST & SANKHU

A N D U

CHABAHIL

SIFALE

GYANESHWOR

BLACK BRIDGE

BATTISPUTALI

PASHUPATINATH TEMPLE

BAGMATI RIVER

DHOBI KHOLA

BAZAR

BANESHWOR HEIGHTS

ACHARYA FAMILY HOUSES

RBAR

TRIBHUVAN INTERNATIONAL AIRPORT (FORMERLY GAUCHAR AIRPORT)

NAYA BANESHWOR

RIVER

TO LUBU

Map 1 : KATHMANDU

Introduction

On 24 November 1986 some 10,000 people gathered in the heart of Kathmandu for a political procession—a very rare event in Nepal during the thirty years of the Panchayat era.[1] The procession included people from all over Nepal and from all walks of life—social workers, politicians, intellectuals, students, and common people. They included an eighty-eight year old man who had travelled all the way from the western Tarai just to be present. Though the event was extraordinary, it is all the more remarkable that most foreigners, including those living in Nepal, did not even hear about it, because it was not reported in the official English-language government newspaper, *The Rising Nepal*. Nor was it mentioned in the official government Nepali-language newspaper, *Gorkhapatra*, or on news broadcasts from the official government radio station, or on the fledgling government television station.[2]

The occasion was the seventy-fifth birthday (calculated precisely, according to the lunar calendar, from the scrolled, rice-paper horoscope that was prepared when he was born) of Tanka Prasad Acharya (frequently referred to in this book as *Bua*, the Nepali term for father).

[1] The so-called 'partyless Panchayat system' followed King Mahendra's incarceration of the entire cabinet of the first elected government in 1960. More accurately described as absolute monarchy, it became one more absolutist victim of the multi-party democratic movements that swept the world in 1989-91. The dramatic political events of February-April 1990 culminated in the drastically reduced power of the King and the introduction of western-style parliamentary democracy.

[2] All information concerning the seventy-fifth birthday celebration has been culled from non-government Nepali-language press coverage of the events. The government detected, correctly, anti-panchayat political activities in the celebration. Celebrating the seventy-fifth, 'diamond' anniversary of anything is a western innovation, and served as a convenient rallying point for dissident political interests. Traditionally, and particularly among Newars, one's eighty-fourth birthday is the subject of great fanfare; it may be celebrated a few years early in the face of doubts about one's lifespan, or even, as in Tanka Prasad's case, posthumously (see Appendix 7).

Tanka Prasad was President of the Nepal Praja Parishad, the first political party in Nepal, which he and a few friends founded in 1936. For their efforts, the Ranas (hereditary prime ministers of Nepal from 1846 until their overthrow in 1950—see Appendix 8) shot and hanged several of his friends—the four martyrs whose bronze busts are mounted, along with a (slightly larger) one of King Tribhuvan, in the marble memorial called Martyrs' Gate in the middle of the parade-ground (*Tundikhel*) in Kathmandu. Their deaths are commemorated annually on Martyrs' Day, a national holiday. In contrast to his executed friends, Tanka Prasad, who died on 23 April 1992, was often referred to as 'The Living Martyr'[3] for the suffering he endured. Although most Nepalese know at least superficially about Tanka Prasad's 'martyrdom', the equally great courage his wife Rewanti Kumari Acharya demonstrated, and the pain she bore, have never been acknowledged—hence the plural extension of the notion of martyrdom in the title of this book. The bulk of the book—the heart of it—relates the independent but interdependent stories of Tanka Prasad and his wife, Rewanta Kumari, in their own words.

Although he was the leader of the movement, Tanka Prasad could only be subjected to the humiliation of decasting[4] and a death sentence commuted to life imprisonment, because executing a Brahmin was both illegal according to the National Law (*Mulki Ain*) and a very great sin, which the Ranas could not bring themselves to commit. After serving ten years of his term, including twenty-seven months in the notorious *Golghar* cellblock, from which few prisoners emerged alive, the Ranas were overthrown, Tanka Prasad was released from prison, and King Tribhuvan, with whom Tanka Prasad had conspired to end the Rana regime, was restored to power. Five years later King Mahendra (Tribhuvan's son) appointed Tanka Prasad as Prime Minister. After his year and a half tenure in office (the longest serving Prime Minister

---

[3] The term often used in Nepali newspapers and other publications is 'jiundo shahid'.

[4] *See* Chapter 6 for details. The question of why he could not be executed after being decasted (since he was then no longer a Brahmin) is a profound one which goes to the very heart of caste identity. On the one hand, violation of caste rules is grounds for outcasteing, which excludes a person from functioning as a member of his caste group, for example, by terminating commensal relations and marriage matches. But the juxtaposition of traditional decasteing with a legal and moral system which includes capital punishment for some but not for others provides a litmus test for the constitution of identity. Tanka Prasad's case shows that a Brahmin by birth (the only way to become one) is a Brahmin forever.

after the fall of the Ranas until the autocratic Panchayat period, which lasted from 1960 till 1990), he spent the rest of his life actively promoting democratic and human rights movements in Nepal.

Meanwhile, Rewanta Kumari Acharya (often referred to in the text as *Ama*, the Nepali term for mother) held the family together in the midst of appalling difficulties, including the confiscation of their house and all their property, and ostracism by many friends, neighbours, and relatives. In later years she herself became politically active, as she smuggled Tanka Prasad's letters out of prison and carried them through the Himalayan foothills to Prime Minister Jawaharlal Nehru, the socialist leader Jaya Prakash Narayan, and others in India. Her determination and grit illustrate as well as expand the stereotypical image of the traditional Hindu subservient wife. To tell Tanka Prasad's story while ignoring hers (as Regmi 1950, Joshi and Rose 1966, and Kumar 1967, among others, have done) is to describe the sound of one hand clapping.

Western images of Nepalese bravery, self-sacrifice, and honour are derived exclusively from the heroic exploits of two deservedly well-known and admired ethnic groups. The Sherpas are renowned for displaying extraordinary strength, stamina, and selflessness under some of the harshest conditions on earth. They have often saved the lives (sometimes at the cost of their own) of the mountaineers who attempt to climb the world's highest mountains. The Gurkhas have exhibited sometimes suicidal bravery for the British on battlefields ranging from India in the nineteenth century to Europe in World War I, various theatres in World War II and the Faulkland Islands in more recent times. Impressive though the valour of both these groups is, they are informed by western tastes, executed according to western design, performed for Western purposes, and remunerated by western money. By contrast, Tanka Prasad and his friends put their lives and their fortunes on the line solely for the benefit of Nepal and their Nepalese compatriots. He and his friends were Nepali nationalists dedicated to the overthrow of the despotic Rana regime. Tanka Prasad was much influenced by western liberal and radical thinkers, but he had nothing to gain personally or monetarily—and everything to lose—from his actions. One aim of this book is to present a portrait of this very different, and little known and understood, variety of Nepalese courage.

Another aim of the book is to make sense of the Acharyas' political lives by rooting them culturally. Rather than attempt to follow the minute twists and turns of Nepalese political life, I try to show how Tanka Prasad and his wife, both from traditional urban middle class

Nepali Brahmin backgrounds, have simultaneously embraced their culture and recreated it. Unlike most other Nepalese politicians, such as B.P. Koirala (Prime Minister in the first elected government, before being jailed during the royal takeover of 1960), who lived much of his life, and received much of his education, in India, Tanka Prasad is an unadulterated Nepali. Having lived all his life in Nepal, where he received what little formal education he had, he was an unreconstructed nationalist, caught up in the uncertainties and contingencies of Nepalese politics in ways that many Nepalese democratic politicians following him were not. The ambiguities of the peculiar relationship between India and Nepal are expressed in his uncompromising nationalist position, which Indians never easily understood or accepted. He and his wife were political revolutionaries while simultaneously remaining staunch monarchists, committed both to Hinduism and to a modern democratic state independent of Indian control. These inherent contradictions and tensions produced a distinctive Nepalese point of view, politically innovative and socially conservative.

This book is emphatically not about Tanka Prasad's politics *qua* politics. I leave it to the legion political scientists to debate the merits and demerits of his political record, whether he made wise or foolish political decisions, and the place he will ultimately be accorded in the history of Nepalese politics. Rather than immerse the reader in the controversies that surround Tanka Prasad's political achievements, I let the record, or at least Tanka Prasad's version of it, speak for itself. I would parenthetically add, however, as an antidote to the frequently negative assessment of Indian and Western political scientists, that what seemed controversial in the 1950s often appears unremarkable by the 1990s. Making a state visit to a nation (China) with which one shares a 500 mile border, for example, seems, in retrospect, neither contentious nor far-sighted, but merely commonsensical. One sometimes wonders what all the fuss was about.

Why Tanka Prasad?

Partly through the strength of his own character and partly due to accidents of history, Tanka Prasad occupied a symbolically unique position in Nepalese political life. In many respects he was merely typical of revolutionary politicians of his generation—high caste, upper class, urban, educated—and an unlikely candidate for the extraordinary attention he commanded. Indeed, he could easily be compared unfavourably with other politicians of his time along a variety of dimensions: he was not blessed with the charismatic oratorical skills of some of his colleagues (e.g., B.P. Koirala); he lacked the formal education and even scholarly abilities of others (e.g., D.R. Regmi). The sophistication and polish of many politicians (e.g., M.P. Koirala) are notably absent from the personality of this basically simple, straightforward, unrelentingly honest man.

Like all post-1950 Nepalese politicians (except those who went into exile) before the successful 1990 democratic movement, he had to walk the narrow line separating civility towards the royal palace and open defiance of it. But he remained an outspoken critic[5] and refused to compromise his democratic principles—for example, he declined veiled offers of high office made to him during the Panchayat period because to accept them would have signaled his approval of the so-called partyless Panchayat system, which he always opposed. Such steadfast devotion to human rights made him a symbol of unyielding integrity behind which opposition politicians of all persuasions, who were otherwise involved in perpetual ideological internecine warfare, could rally. The last such occasion occurred when he was paraded around Kathmandu in a palanquin on his seventy-fifth birthday, to the enthusiastic reception of the thousands who lined the streets in his honour. Some newspapers described it as the most important mass political procession since his release from jail in 1951.

It is sometimes said that Tanka Prasad had many admirers and not so many followers. He was never very successful at the polls—he did not even carry his own neighbourhood in the 1959 election. He found it difficult to convert his revolutionary charisma into more conventional political form, partly because of his refusal to accept financial aid from non-Nepalese sources and partly because he was not a spell-binding orator on the stump. Like all politicians he had his enemies and detractors, but even his severest critics granted his unimpeachable character and incorruptible honesty. The grand old man of Nepalese politics, the 'living martyr', was a political singularity, an institution unto himself.

Since this book shows how a fundamentally radical political philosophy, and the life which it has informed, can arise out of a traditional, high-caste Hindu family background, one can see how and where his political, social, and cultural views are connected and consistent—and where they are not. Two dimensions of the motivation for the political tack he chose have indigenous roots: the core Hindu values of courage in following his dharma wherever it might lead, and outrage over the

---

[5] *See* Appendices 4, 5, and 6 for examples of his views during the last years of his life.

injustice his father, a medium-level bureaucrat, suffered at the hands of the Rana government.

But, like Indians active in the independence movement of their country, he was profoundly influenced also by liberal and radical western works, such as those of Voltaire, Rousseau, Marx, Shaw, Thomas Paine, Napoleon, Dickens, Lenin, and others—all smuggled into the country across the Indian border. His beliefs and deeds—in a word, his life—show how the juxtaposition of a liberal democratic philosophy with an essentially Hindu world view produces not a logical inconsistency but a mutually compatible, cognitively and emotionally coordinated, context-sensitive[6] ideology.

The political parts of this book are therefore not only about Tanka Prasad, but about a type and generation of politician in Nepal. There are others who thought and acted the way he did—many of them mentioned in the text. Nevertheless, as the man whose imagination and leadership in 1936 launched modern Nepalese political history, a history so recent that its entire development can be encapsulated in the life of this single individual, his story is unique. Politicians are not in short supply in Nepal, but he will always hold the distinction of having been first among equals, at least at the time of the political Big Bang described in his early political life.

Many westerners are familiar with the heroism of the Sherpas and Gurkhas, whose pictures appear in the guide-books and glossy, coffee-table volumes that line bookstore windows in areas frequented by tourists in Kathmandu. This book is about an entirely different type of Nepalese hero, a genre not well known even among Nepalese, many of whom have only the vaguest notions of the sacrifices Tanka Prasad and his generation made, and the suffering they endured. As a way of life, Hinduism is curiously without heroes, at least of the human sort. Those who do acquire heroic proportions tend to be elevated to divine or semi-divine status—a category already amply supplied with representatives in the Hindu pantheon. These pages record the lives of a few of the many authentic Nepalese heroes whose existence is rarely noticed and even more rarely acknowledged. This book provides the historical context for the political upheaval of 1990, and the equally

---

[6] Context-sensitive refers to treating people, especially morally or jurally, according to a variety of social or cultural contexts, such as caste, religion, sex, etc., Kant's categorical imperative exemplifies the opposite idea of context-free. *See* Ramanujan (1989) for a wide-ranging discussion of context-free and context-sensitive in Indian thought.

inspiring story of its martyrs. The democratic revolution of 1990 is the logical and moral fulfillment of what Tanka Prasad and his friends started in 1936.

Since Rewanta Kumari Acharya gets equal time for her own story, the project reveals her frequently crucial but hitherto publicly unacknowledged role even in the visible political events, not to mention other aspects of Tanka Prasad's life—for example, holding their family (including two infant daughters) together under extremely trying circumstances for the ten years he was in prison. During this time even relatives were fearful of befriending her, for fear of retributory persecution by the Ranas. Her account also stands by itself as a chronicle of marriage as an uneducated bride of eleven to mother, grandmother, and great-grandmother; as a chronicle of awakening consciousness from naivete to political activist; and as a chronicle of empowerment from passivity to advocate of women's education and rights.

Finally, these dual life-histories show how a common body of experience has been differently defined and evaluated by two forceful and articulate people: one male, husband, father, and grandfather; the other female, wife, mother, and grandmother. Their lives play out as counterpoint, for the life of Tanka Prasad—childhood, marriage, imprisonment, Prime Minister, religion, family—resounds contrapuntally with that of Rewanta Kumari. Focused together, the two accounts draw a sexually stereoscopic portrait of their more than sixty years of married life.

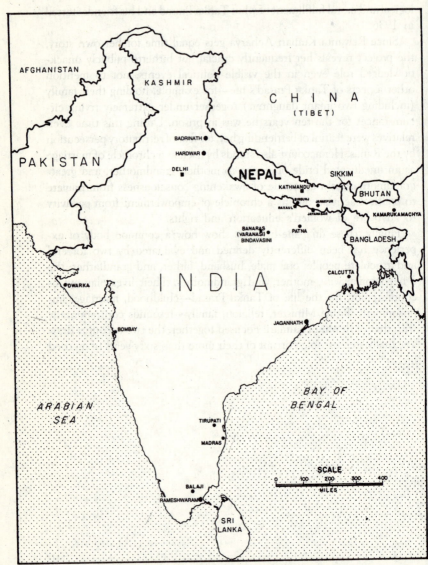

Map 2 : NEPAL AND NEIGHBOURING COUNTRIES

Chapter 1

Nepal
The Setting

Nepal is perceived by Nepalese, as well as by the rest of the world, as a very small country. This perception stems partly from the enormous size of the two countries which totally surround it: India and China. There are some ninety-three smaller countries in the world (out of one hundred-eighty, depending on how you count them), but even in absolute terms Nepal is not very big. It measures roughly 100 by 500 miles, about the same square area as Arkansas or Bangladesh. Its latitude—that of southern Florida or Egypt—gives the country its mild climate, except where altitude dictates the perennial snow and ice of the world's highest mountains, the Himalayas.

Over twenty million people, living on land consisting mostly of steep hills and frozen alpine wasteland (the flat and fertile extension of the Gangetic plain bordering India, called the Tarai, is an exception) contributes to the better-founded view that Nepal is very poor. Its per capita income of 180 US dollars is lower than that of all but four countries, but such stark and Western-derived GNP statistics exaggerate the poverty. The more comprehensive Human Development Index, which combines income figures with such quality-of-life factors as education, health, and sanitation, puts Nepal ahead of twenty-three other countries (Human Development Report 1995). The poverty would be even worse if several hundred thousand Nepalese were not forced to live and work in India, sending remittances home, because they cannot scratch a living from the steep hillsides of Nepal. With no railroads, few roads (and these subject to relentless erosion and landslides), but quite a few airstrips, the economy is still based overwhelmingly on hand-to-mouth agriculture. Revenues from the export of woollen carpets and textiles, tourism, and pensions drawn by soldiers serving in the Gurkha regiments of Indian and British armies constitute (in descending order of significance) the principal sources of Nepal's foreign exchange.

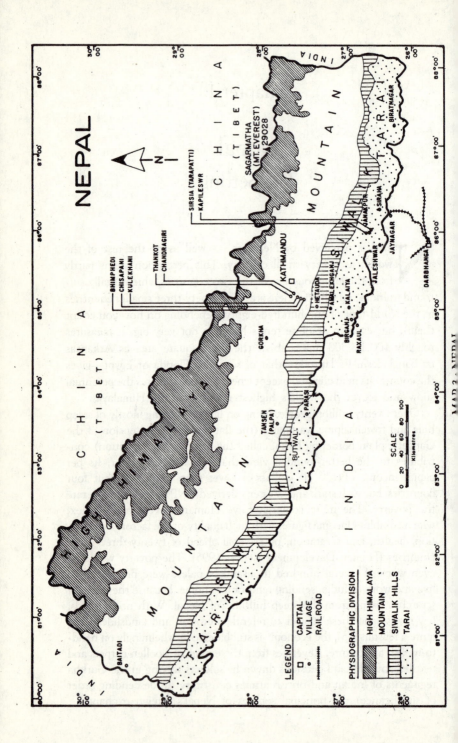

MAP 2 : NEPAL

Although the Himalayas are geologically young, thrust upward by the collision of the Indian and Eurasian tectonic plates, politically Nepal is an old country. It was united in roughly its present form by Prith-vinarayan Shah, a Hindu chieftain from the western hill town of Gorkha, who conquered the Kathmandu Valley and its indigenous Newar popula-tion in 1769. His eleventh dynastic successor, King Birendra, sits on the throne today. Strategic marriages have allied the royal family with a few elite families in Kathmandu and in far-flung hill centres. A courtier named Jang Bahadur Kunwar successfully liquidated most of his rivals for political influence in the Kot Massacre of 1846, and buttressed his false claim to Rajput descent by taking the surname Rana. He and his descendants (his nephews incorporated 'Jang Bahadur Rana' into their own names) ruled the country as hereditary Prime Ministers from the 1846 Massacre until they were overthrown in 1950, leaving the King a virtual prisoner in his own palace. It was against the rule of this Rana family that Tanka Prasad and his friends collaborated with King Tribhuvan Bir Bikram Shah Dev (Appendix 9 shows kin and marital ties between the Rana and Shah families.)

Socially, Nepal consists of a mixture of ethnic groups. Tibeto-Burmese speaking people such as Rais, Limbus, Gurungs, Magars, Tamangs, and Sherpas, are generally Buddhist or at least quasi-Buddhist and ultimately of northern or eastern origin. To these have been added over recent centuries, Hindu groups (conventionally, 'castes') speaking Indo-European languages (principally, Nepali) which have slowly migrated through the hills of Nepal from west to east. Prithvinarayan's movements were a high-profile political and martial dimension of this gradual eastward demographic expansion. Families with political and economic clout, including the Shahs (the Kings), the Ranas (the Prime Ministers), and semi-aristocratic or 'mid-dle-class' families like Tanka Prasad's and Rewanta Kumari's, (in their case, Brahmins), are mostly from this India-derived population (high-caste Newars, the indigenous people of the Kathmandu Valley, are an exception), and so the national social hierarchy has traditionally been tilted in their direction. These upper-echelon families, of the Brahmin and Chhetri (Kshatriya in India) castes, give the country its Hindu flavour. The con-stitutional requirement that the king be a Hindu is no accident. According to Hindu discourse the king is a reincarnation of Vishnu. To the annoyance of the Buddhist minority, so was the Buddha.

In Nepal, it is an ill wind that does not blow high-caste Hindus good. Hindus own most of the best land, tend to be better educated, and are employed in the best jobs, despite such occasional anomalies as the Tibetan-Buddhist Sherpas, who were exceptionally well-positioned to profit from the burgeoning mountain-climbing and tourist industries (Fisher 1990). Because the Rana Prime Ministership passed from brother to brother (an inherently unstable system, since impatient brothers waiting in the wings did not always wait for nature to take its course), this regime barely survived four generations—not enough time to establish a genuine indigenous aristocracy of cultivation and taste. Never part of the British empire, Nepal possesses neither India's intellectual and technological sophistication nor the ambivalent chip-on-the-shoulder resentment toward the West which lingers in some quarters there.

Each of these ethnic groups is endogamous, or is supposed to be—the example of Tanka Prasad's father's three non-Brahmin concubines shows how easily the rules can be bent, and concubinage among the Ranas and Shahs was rampant. People of high caste traditionally eat rice—the main staple for those who can afford it—only with those with whom they may intermarry. Hence Rewanta Kumari's initial Brahmanical reluctance—later abandoned—to eat with friends and political associates of various castes and groups.

Politically, Tanka Prasad had time on his side. By the 1930s a number of forces—virtually all from the urban Hindu center—were beginning to run against the tide of the Rana regime. Internally, the once influential families that had been deprived of the material rewards of power under the Ranas—among them the Thapas, Basnyats, and Pandes—were becoming increasingly restless. Newars in Kathmandu were unhappy with the short shrift they had received from the Ranas. The nominal rulers, the Shahs, chafed under their humiliating impotence. Even within the Rana family, from the beginning of their rule, various disaffected elements—including some of Jang Bahadur's own sons, tried to convert their discontent into joint conspiracies with the palace.

Moreover, by the twentieth century the Ranas themselves had been officially split into three differentially ranked branches: the 'A' Ranas married within prescribed circles; 'B' Ranas were born of mothers of otherwise high caste but not of 'A' status; and 'C' Ranas were products of concubines of varying ethnicity. The 'B' and 'C' Ranas, who were effectively disenfranchised from access to higher military rank, and from the Prime Ministership, became more and more numerous (the Ranas were notorious for their concubines) and disgruntled as time wore on. All these elements had strong interests of their own in bringing an end to the Rana era.

Externally, the Indian independence movement was gathering

momentum, together with its ideological offshoots such as the Hindu reformist Arya Samaj, to which Tanka Prasad refers. Although he insisted on a Nepalese movement entirely divorced from the Indian cause, he drew emotional and moral inspiration from the Indians, and especially from sympathetic Nepalese domiciled in India. All these components—the restless, dissatisfied internal ones as well as those inspired by external example—moved with concord of purpose but along tactically separate, splintered, and meandering routes against the existing regime.[1]

Into this essentially politically vacuous ideological setting stepped a small band of political warriors with Tanka Prasad at their head—the group that for the first time in the history of Nepal not only envisioned an explicitly political, democratic alternative for the country but mapped out a coherent plan of action to achieve it. Others, such as those involved a few years before in the Prachanda Gorkha ('Resurgent Gorkha') Conspiracy (including Tanka Prasad's prison mate, Khadga Man Singh, who had already served nine years of a life sentence when Tanka Prasad was sentenced), wanted to topple the Rana government through terrorist methods, but lacked any political organization to either effect their goals or to supplant the existing power structure. Unlike the exclusively Brahmin-Chhetri Prachanda Gorkha Movement, Tanka Prasad's Praja Parishad included members of different, urban-based middle-class castes. As was the case again in the democratic movement of 1990, the predominantly rural population at the periphery, whether Tibeto-Burmese or Indo-Aryan, was too remote, scattered, poor, and uneducated to launch an effective movement against the powerful groups which controlled the centre. Political agency in Nepal—whether of the establishment or in revolt against it—has always been confined to a small number of people who are relatively well-connected as well as interconnected in a distinctively Nepalese way.

Tanka Prasad tapped the suppressed discontent that had been surreptitiously festering in various quarters, but he and his group were the first to formulate a practical plan of attack and an ideological vision of what to do with the country if they were successful.[2] They were Nepal's first revolutionaries in the modern, organizational, and ideological sense of that term.

---

[1] *See* Uprety (1992) for a thorough discussion of political, social, and literary unrest throughout the first half of the twentieth century.

[2] *See* Joshi and Rose (1966) for a more detailed discussion of anti-Rana forces, as well as nineteenth-century political intrigue and the 1950–60 succession of democratic experiments culminating in the royal takeover of the elected Congress government in 1960.

Chapter 2

Anthropology, Life Histories, and Social Theory

Life histories can make anthropologists nervous—not so much collecting them, which they have done copiously (*see* Langness 1981 for an extensive bibliography) as incorporating them into their conceptual and theoretical toolkits. Barnouw (1963: 198) put the problem succinctly: 'At their best, life histories are fascinating documents. The main difficulty lies in knowing what to do with them.' Even now, in these postmodern times, when their use is undergoing one of the revivals that occur from time to time, a sense of unease lurks behind most discussions of them. Allowing 'others' to speak for themselves is one, partial solution to the 'crisis of representation' (Marcus and Fischer 1986) in anthropology, but giving a clearer, less muted voice to the people anthropologists study requires surrendering narrative power, making it much more difficult for the anthropologist to make things come out right analytically.

Those who write about life-history issues are often concerned with questions such as how this or that cultural theme is played out in the life of an individual, how a life-course is structured, how a self is formed, and a whole host of hermeneutical issues concerning modes of interpretation, inside/outside differences, phenomenological perspectives, interpretation, dialogue, narrative structure, intersubjective truth, epiphanies, and so on (*see* Mandelbaum 1973; Watson and Watson-Franke 1985; Denzin 1989, among others).

My primary aim, by contrast, is to view an important period of historical transformation—the emergence of a Nepalese polity informed by modern democratic ideas and institutions—through the somewhat unconventional prism of a person-centred ethnography. This device contrasts with such mainstream historical approaches as those which concentrate on the chronologies of the rulers (Regmi 1983), on economic history

(Regmi 1972; Mishra 1987), on political history (Stiller 1973), or on the history of specific institutions, such as land tenure (Caplan 1970), all of which rely on textual analysis.[1] In showing how history looks to those who are making it, these tandem life-histories show how political structure can be fundamentally unmade and remade by practice, and how history is always a combination, as Ricoeur says, of the system and the singular. I have attempted to make Tanka Prasad and Rewanta Kumari's world comprehensible to us by portraying their experience—an ostensibly transparent notion which Gadamer calls 'one of the most obscure concepts we have' (1975: 310)—as much as possible in their own words.

Life-histories conventionally bracket one of the larger question marks hovering over social theory today: human agency. But to talk of agency without looking at specific agents is like talking about poetry without examining specific poets. How better to deal with human agency than to see how it plays out in a specific historical transformation, in the life of particular agents who were present at the creation of a new social and political order, caught in the contingencies that informed the struggle with and against the cultural meanings with which they had to work? I concentrate on the crucible of power in which the self is created and recreated and emphasize the agent rather than the structure, not because structure is unimportant—it is, of course, indispensable—but because it is already relatively well-known. More precisely, I want to consider agents who played such a large role in transforming the structure into which they were born. Hence, the experiential, even anecdotal emphasis here is deliberate. At least I propose to take this substantive bull by these theoretical horns, if I may use that South Asian bovine trope.

Life histories have never had any pretense to quantification and the aura of reliable, no-nonsense, 'etic' science it evokes, so there is no place for them over on the 'hard' side of anthropology. Nor, focusing on individual actors instead of whole societies or cultures, are they amenable to analysis—whether structural, functional, evolutionary, symbolic, ecological, interpretive, or something else—of quite the same scope that can be applied to such macro-entities. And yet there is a paradoxical sense in which all anthropological data consist of life histories of some sort, since societies are composed of individuals who,

[1] For a lively discussion of disputes in Nepalese historiography, *see* Adhikari 1980 and Malla 1984.

at any point in time, have led concrete, historical lives. What is lacking is any conceptual apparatus, other than such obvious Parsonian notions of individuals with personalities in societies and cultures, designed to manage the transition from one level to the other. In the realm of both method and theory, then, if not of data, life histories have traditionally been assigned space somewhere out along the periphery of more respectable anthropological arenas, or in the occasional no-man's land between them.

One thing that can be done with life histories is to use them to tease out categories of native thought uncontaminated, in the first instance, by whatever theoretical angle may inform the anthropologist's analysis of social or cultural systems. Put less grandly, life histories allow 'others' to speak for themselves in a way they never quite do when the narrator is the anthropologist. This is one of the goals I set for myself as I began to elicit the stories of Tanka Prasad and Rewanta Kumari. Both had been born into traditional, middle-class, Hindu, Brahmin families; both remained middle-class and, in many respects, traditionally Hindu and Brahmin in their outlook. Yet both profoundly altered the culture they were born into and helped transform the society of which they were a part. My hope was that their own version of their lives would cast light on just what constituted their domains of politics, of religion, of power, of culture, and so on, and how these were related to each other.

Certainly Tanka Prasad and Rewanta Kumari speak for themselves, but their narratives did not result in the fine-grained 'emic' view of their world I had hoped for originally. That is why in some ways this book has turned out to be the opposite of the one I had intended to write. The Acharyas poured out neither their souls nor their indigenous categories to me. They wanted their stories told, but they were not very skilled at telling them. For example, before actual interviewing began I handed Tanka Prasad a list of questions which I suggested he might mull over before answering them orally when I returned with my tape recorder. One of the questions asked: 'Describe your *bartaman* [investiture of the sacred thread, a coming of age ritual required of all Brahmin boys] ceremony, and what it was like to go through it. Describe any other ceremonies you remember as a child (marriages, funerals, *bhai-tika*, *pasne*,[2] etc.) and what you thought about them at

---

[2] In *bhai-tika* ('brother worship'), sisters give their brothers *tika* and wish them long lives (the sentiments are then reciprocated). *Bhai-tika* occurs on the fifth day of Tihar. *Pasne* is the first feeding of rice to a baby, occurring six months after the birth of a boy and

the time'. When I returned for the first interview I asked him for his response to this question. He said, 'What? [he had not bothered to review the questions] Oh, yes, we had many such ceremonies when I was a boy; now, what is the next question?'

Even in the realm of politics, which was clearly Tanka Prasad's most valorized category, he sometimes preferred to rant and rail against Ronald Reagan and George Bush than talk about his past. He was a man of the present who generally regarded even his own past as only of antiquarian interest. This orientation to the present is an important part of his 'emic' mental makeup, and if that were all there was to say about his life I could have let it go at that. But his role in important historical events was too crucial to brush aside with a few truncated references to his past. Furthermore, at another level he agreed with me about the importance of making a detailed and accurate record of what had happened. The original impetus for the project had come from Tanka Prasad, who wanted to tell his version of the events in which he had been so centrally involved. If for no other reason, he felt he owed it to the memory of the martyrs whose fate he had escaped. The problem was that my passion for accuracy and detail occasionally overwhelmed and irritated them both. As Tanka Prasad once exclaimed to me in exasperation, 'Yes, I wanted to tell my story, but you want to look into every nook and cranny!' Also, despite their sometimes surprisingly candid assessments of others, both Mr and Mrs Acharya were sometimes reluctant, out of a sense of loyalty, to speak ill of their contemporaries.

I quickly became attuned to the difference between told and lived lives. As Bruner (1984) has put it: 'A life lived is what actually happens. A life experienced consists of the images, feelings, sentiments, desires, thoughts, and meanings known to the person whose life it is. A life as told, a life history, is a narrative, influenced by the cultural conventions of telling, by the audience, and by the social context.' To produce any kind of readable, coherent narrative at all, I had to piece together the scattered fragments of told lives I was given, frequently providing the chronological and substantive transitions myself. The 'told' result is a narrative arrangement of reality which is mine rather than theirs, and thus a third order derivative from their original 'lived' experience. Having followed a partly chronological and partly topical format, I share

---

five months after the birth of a girl.

the exasperation Rousseau expressed in his *Confessions* (1950: 107): 'But wait, I cannot tell everything at the same time!'

My textual meddling had the support of Tanka Prasad, since he insisted many times that what was important were the events, the changes that took place in the political system, not the details of his own experience. And when he could not remember details, or was bored by them, he often referred me to the fuller accounts of his friends. I suspect he would have even agreed with Levi-Strauss' anti-biographical view that 'what matters is the work, not the author who happened to write it; I would say rather that it writes itself through him. The individual person is no more than a means of transmission and survives in the work only as a residue' (Levi-Strauss 1990).

Use of the first person is always in some respects a ruse. By supplementing the Acharyas' accounts with recollections of others, I have tried to shrink what Crapanzano (1977) called the silent undersong of the dialogue, because in this case silence hides more than it reveals, if not about themselves, at least about the world of which they were a part. I have clearly marked sections of the text where the words or thoughts of others are used.

Thus, if ever there were an example of the biographical illusion (Bourdieu 1986), this is it. By providing the links between the lived and told lives, I am as implicated in their story as they are. Although the research was conducted in the form of dialogues, some formally recorded, others casual exchanges, for the sake of readability I have, unlike Crapanzano (1980) and especially Dwyer (1982), edited myself out of the text. The many silent prompts that the reader will discern throughout the text make clear that I was not a 'listener who understands passively' (Bakhtin 1986:69). I have tried to incorporate a third mediating party, namely cultural background in notes and parenthetical additions to the narratives. Thus the selves of this study are doubly oriented: inward towards the text, outward towards me (Ricoeur 1974: 256).

My defense of such heavy-handed editorial liberties is that I have remained faithful to the Acharyas' charge—to produce a narrative of their lives—and that their children and grandchildren have approved the final version. Indeed, various members of the family themselves suggested many features of the book, from substantive details to organizational format to interpretive significance of some events over others, so that the text is more than just nominally a family effort. The life histories take place not just in past actions, but also in their recounting to an anthropologist who 'stopped' the action by writing it down, or 'fixing' it, as in a photograph.

One reason the Acharyas were not particularly good story-tellers is the lack of models for this kind of thing in their cultural experience. There is scarcely any autobiographical or biographical tradition in South Asia generally, although story tellers such as the Rajput *charans* (genealogists and historians) produced biographical accounts, and occasional autobiographical works appear, such as that of the seventeenth-century religious leader Banarasi, or that of the wife of a Maharashtrian Christian convert, *I Follow After* (Tilak 1950). Even important historical figures such as Babur only rarely wrote autobiographically (Dale 1990), although modern leaders have shown no reticence in telling their stories (Gandhi 1940; Nehru 1962).

But there is also a cultural warrant for anonymity, as seen in the fact that authors of the most popular South Asian literary works of all time, the *Mahabharata* and the *Ramayana*, are nameless (Rudolph and Rudolph 1988). The Acharyas could not have been aware of what little Nepalese tradition of autobiography exists, such as that which undergirds *Four Lamas of Dolpo*, although they would have been casually aware of the genre of memoirs written mostly in Nepali, dating overwhelmingly from the post-1951 period.[3]

To the extent that any literary works could have been available as models to Tanka Prasad, they would have been such western works as the biography of Napoleon, which influenced him greatly as a young man. Rewanta Kumari was much influenced by a book, written in Hindi, called *Great Women of the World* (capsule biographies of women from Kasturba (Gandhi's wife) to Madame Sun Yat-Sen to Eleanor Roosevelt to Lady Mountbatten). But neither Tanka Prasad nor Rewanta Kumari see themselves in the heroic mould, despite my frequent protestations that they surely were. Thus another of the reasons they did not spin out detailed narratives about themselves is simply that they did not see anything particularly extraordinary about their lives.

I made many abortive attempts to get the Acharyas to tell me how they felt about the events they were describing, but like most Hindus they were hesitant to readily express their personal feelings publicly. This inhibition against the expression of affect is particularly strong in the case of women, who are expected to be demure in their life-long

[3] *See* Pradhan (1987) for a bibliography of such sources. I am indebted to Pratyoush Onta for this reference.

alien surroundings (their husbands' households), and this is therefore true of Rewanta Kumari. Of the things they did not tell me, the domain of feelings is the most sparsely represented. Finally, by the time I began this research the Acharyas' attention span, their capacity to hear, and their memories were already becoming marginal. Had we begun work even five years earlier, the entire project would have been easier for all of us.

The book does succeed in one experimental goal I had set for it. The traditional Hindu husband and wife, however disparate in background and education, often develop a relationship over the course of a lifetime so psychologically close, even if cognitively distant, that to tell the story of one while omitting the story of the other is to distort the ethnographic reality of both. I do not posit the existence of some mystical, dual-coded entity which cannot be dissolved into its component parts. I simply call attention to the fact that their lives were joined for over sixty years. I have therefore attempted to represent the life of Rewanta Kumari as fully as that of Tanka Prasad, even at the risk of occasional repetition. Equally long 'his and her' sections under each topical heading would have imparted an attractive but false symmetry to the narrative. Indeed, the lack of symmetry underscores the strong differences in their life courses. For example, in Rewanta Kumari's life there is no equivalent to the 'Political Agitation' in Tanka Prasad's, and his account of family life is bare-bones compared to Rewanta Kumari's. Tanka Prasad's life was consumed by politics; Rewanta Kumari's by concern for her family. Such contrasts demonstrate how differently constituted and valorized are the domains of each.

I start from Sartre's position that humans are not so much individuals as universal singulars. Much of the text describes the way both the principals, as part of universal human history, moved away from the singular traditions into which they were born towards empowering postures of change. Their lives recapitulate all of modern Nepalese political history and therefore inherently illuminate it. Their stories tell about Hindu society and politics from the vantage point of those who were in a position to profit from it but who chose to overturn it, at great personal cost.

The editing of these narratives was, as I have suggested above, enormously complicated by lapses, inconsistencies, and so on. My initial desire not to interrupt the text by intervening in it was later tempered by the realization that to publish demonstrably false historical information (dates, names, etc.) just to demonstrate how fallible memories can be only buttresses the view of scholarship as the perpetuation of historical error. On the other hand, the contrasts in perspective that each subject gives on the same set of events is invaluable, and I sought not merely to retain these contrasts but to underscore them wherever they could be detected. This male/female contrast is an important dimension of the book.

Capturing the flavour of the narrative in readable English while retaining the essence of the original also posed many translation predicaments. This was a problem even when Tanka Prasad spoke (or, in the few documents which were available, wrote) English, and the occasionally quaint turns of phrase—'gambols and frolics' to describe his childhood activities, for example—are a result of attempting to maintain the authenticity of his voice. Rewanta Kumari's way of speaking, using such rhetorical devices as repetition, I have also tried to render faithfully, to maximize her representation of self. I have also tried to resist the temptation to cast her in the guise of a modern western feminist. For example, at one stage her statement that Nepalese women 'suffer' (experience *dukha*, suffering) had inaccurately become a remark about women's 'oppression'. Another difficulty lay in giving a sense of the lightheartedness in which many of the responses, Tanka Prasad's particularly, were given. To indicate this spirit of levity I have simply inserted the word 'laughter' in brackets at the appropriate points. This is an important emendation, since the frequency and strength of the laughter seemed to vary inversely with the grimness of the topic under discussion, a frequent characteristic of Nepalese humor.

Life-histories constitute some of the most fascinating documents that anthropology can produce. Among their merits is the fact that they often make for interesting reading compared to the writings of anthropologists, which by contrast can be tedious and boring. I therefore eschew the frequently utilized approach in which the author or editor adds an explanatory section at the beginning or end of each chapter. Since such sections often merely repeat and summarize what the subject has already more than adequately expressed, I have chosen instead to leave the Acharyas to their own devices to make their own points to the maximum extent possible. My own contribution is a relatively mute and low-profile one, except at the beginning and the end. It lies primarily not so much in in-tandem theorizing explicitly about the narratives as in elucidating them through footnotes and explanatory chapters such as the next one, on the Acharyas' daily life.

As in interpretive anthropology generally, 'grand theory' in life-histories is 'suspended for the moment in favor of a close consideration of such issues as contextuality, the meaning of social life for those who enact it, and the explanation of exceptions and indeterminants rather than regularities in phenomena observed' (Marcus and Fischer 1986: 8). This present effort is decidedly in the 'cases and interpretations' tradition, rather than the 'laws and explanations approach' (Geertz 1983). What these lives illumine is the meaning and transformation of Brahminism, family life, politics, and religion from the perspective of two improvisational actors who, for a while, played the leads in the Nepalese social and political drama of their times.

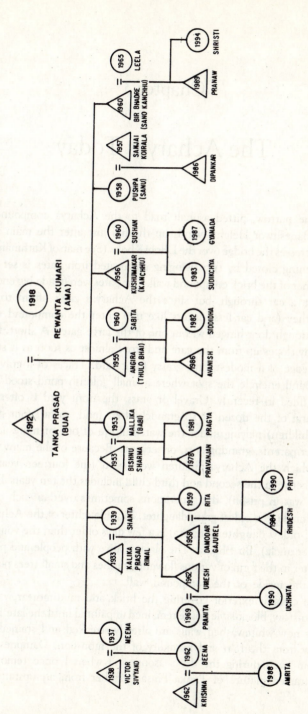

ACHARYA FAMILY (NICKNAMES IN PARENTHESES)

SONS AND THEIR FAMILIES LIVE WITH TANKA PRASAD AND REWANTA KUMARI.
DAUGHTERS LIVE ELSEWHERE, WITH THEIR HUSBANDS.

Chapter 3

The Acharyas Today

The narrow, pitted asphalt road to the Acharya compound in Baneshwor Heights winds up the hill just after the main road crosses the bridge over the Dhobi Khola. (See map of Kathmandu). An opening closed by two swinging corrugated iron gates is set into the corner of the brick compound wall. The gates were made big enough to drive a car through, but since the Acharyas can't afford to buy a car, they (and car-less visitors like me) enter the compound via a walk-through door hinged within one of the large gates. A short, brick driveway slopes up from the gate and stops almost as soon as it starts, at the edge of a modest, crab-grassy front yard. Traces of a gravelled turnaround encircle the spot where a small goldfish pond stood until it was filled in recently. Gravel or grass, the front yard is often full of several of the dozen or so grandchildren (and, so far, four great-grandchildren) playing under the watchful eye of one or more adults, whether parents, grandparents, or servants. Because of the many years over which the Acharya children were born (the fourteen year gap in age between the second and third child includes the ten years Tanka Prasad was in prison), the generations sometimes overlap each other. For example, the oldest granddaughter, Rita (daughter of the Acharyas' second-oldest daughter, Shanta) is a few days older than the youngest son (her uncle), Bir Bhadra. The place is alive with people and plants, the latter in the form of various flowering bushes and small trees planted along the inside of the compound wall.

The cement exterior covering the brick and mud-mortar walls of the two-story, block-style house remained unpainted until the late 1980s, but its now-whitewashed walls are already streaked and stained with mildew from the rain and humidity of the monsoon. Dampness is a problem even during the dry seasons, and when I once removed a large framed picture of Tanka Prasad's father from an upstairs wall (in order to photograph it), silverfish darted out from their hiding place behind it. Depending on the standard of comparison, I would describe the house as modest to substantial, but it is nowhere close to being one of Kathmandu's finer homes. A visitor looking for the residence of a former Prime Minister would pick one of the more fashionable, brick-facade, architect-designed houses to either side of the Acharya compound. But for a family whose only house and property was confiscated by the government fifty years ago, and for whom finding even a small, rented flat since then was often a major struggle, this house represents an impressive achievement. Despite Tanka Prasad's protestations that a roof over their heads should be enough, the Acharyas have been improving and adding to their house, piece-meal, ever since they started building it in 1966.

The front door is protected by a porch that juts into the yard from the centre of the house. Like most Nepalese, the Acharyas love flowers,[1] which are offered to gods or worn in women's hair, and potted plants line the cement drainage apron leading to the yard from the knee-high porch wall. The sides of the porch are open, but its roof supports the floor of the second story veranda. On wash-days, a sari or two might be hanging almost down to the ground from the iron veranda railing, drying in the sun. A flowering tree rises from the ground outside the porch to the veranda above; despite its arresting presence and its profusion of brilliant red flowers which seem to be always in bloom, nobody knows what it's called.[2] It was considered an inauspicious omen when it was uprooted during a storm a few days before Tanka Prasad died.

Positioned casually around the porch are a simple wooden bench, a wooden chair, two cane chairs, an earthenware pot holding a vine that creeps up the side of the house, and an occasional bicycle, protected here from the rain, from the envious eyes of a thief, or both. During the warm months people sit on the porch to stay out of the sun (Nepalese are as anxious to avoid the sun as Americans are to expose themselves to it), or to enjoy the coolness of the early evening, or just to bid welcome or good-bye to the constant parade of people coming from or going into the house.

In the side yard, Kanchhu, the second son, is building a small brick

[1] For aesthetic purposes, it does not matter much whether the flowers are natural or plastic.

[2] It is a bougainvillea plant; since it has no Nepali equivalent, only those with some command of English would have a name for it.

house—partly to relieve population pressure in the classical sense (not only more people, but children needing more space as they grow up) and partly to dissipate the tensions which result from trying to contain several distinct nuclear families under one roof. Familial fusion has its costs as well as its benefits. The new house has been only partially successful in providing a quiet refuge for Kanchhu's[3] wife, since it is a magnet for all the compound children who, intrigued by its novelty, now flock there to play. Behind the new house is a small garden planted mainly with large cauliflower plants lined up in neat rows, like soldiers in a parade—unless someone forgets to shut the gate and a hungry cow wanders in from the road. Tucked into a far corner towards the back of the compound is a squat-type latrine for the servants.

During the day the double wooden doors leading from the porch to the house are usually left open. A cheap, mass-produced brightly coloured picture of two snakes (*nag*, associated with Shiva) is glued above the screen door leading into the downstairs hall. Traditionally the picture was pasted above the door with cowdung, because of its purifying properties, but nowadays glue is added to attach it more securely. Every year the family priest replaces the picture with a new one, worshiping the snakes and asking them to protect the house from affliction. If the screen door is locked someone will answer the doorbell, because there is always someone at home.

The first room, off the hall to the left, is full of furniture and boxes of books that Meena (the oldest child) has brought back from her various jobs and consultancies abroad. Next to it is a small storeroom for the refrigerator (turned off during the winter, when the low room-temperature makes it superfluous) and a miscellaneous assortment of vegetables and fruits, occasionally-used kitchen utensils, and shoes worn outside the house (slippers are worn in the hallways and removed at the doorways before entering rooms). The next room, moving down

---

[3] 'Kanchha' (or 'Kanchhu' in its more affectionate form) is a common Nepalese family nickname meaning 'youngest son'. In the Acharya case, another son followed Kanchhu. Rather than transfer the title to the newly-arrived youngest son (a common technique for dealing with a common problem) to distinguish the two, the last-born became known as 'Sano Kanchhu' or 'small youngest son'. Variations on this theme are used by others according to their relation to him—for example, 'Sano Mama' ('small mother's brother') by his older sisters' daughters, who are both his age-mates and his nieces.

There are other names like 'Kanchha' and 'Kanchhi' ('youngest daughter'): *jetha* (for the first born), *maila* (second), *saila* (third), *kaila* (fourth), *thaila* (next to last). These are sometimes used outside the family context, but outsiders know the Acharya children only by their given names.

the central hall in a clockwise direction, is the dining room, much of it filled by a large, formica-topped table which will seat eight very comfortably and twelve at a pinch. The family eats in shifts following the traditional Hindu order: children first, men next, women last. There is a cold-water sink on the back wall, shelf space for serving-dishes, and a glass-door cabinet for storing plates and glasses, but the actual cooking is done over gas and kerosene stoves in a dark and dingy kitchen (there is talk about enlarging the single kitchen window to brighten it up) attached to the back of the house.

A small, cement patio behind the house gives access from the dining room to the kitchen. The gutter at its edge, open for years but recently covered, carries dirty sink and shower water from the house to the wall at the back of the compound. Out behind the kitchen there are a couple of galvanized iron holding tanks filled with water for cooking and washing (water for inside the house is pumped up every morning to a similar tank on the roof). Food preparation consumes much of the day, so at any given time there is likely to be someone—usually a servant or daughter-in-law—on the back patio winnowing and washing rice, peeling potatoes, or grinding dal on a hand-driven grindstone, while grandchildren run around, through, and on top of it all. A woman moves to her husband's house at marriage, but since the Acharya daughters all live nearby, they drop off their children each morning at the Acharya compound on their way to work. There they join their uncles' children in what becomes an impromptu day-care centre for those too young to go to school, and an after-school base for the others. All the grandchildren have spent major parts of their lives growing up in the house, when their parents were either away or renting out their own houses to help make ends meet.

Before the children began getting married, a ping-pong table, set up on the kitchen patio, saw almost continuous use from late afternoon until ten o'clock at night, but it has been in storage for many years now. There is speculation that when the grandchildren are older it might be brought out of retirement. A postage-stamp patch of ground off the back of the patio is planted with vegetables and two *bhogate* (a thick-rind grapefruit) trees.

Next to the dining room, at the end of the hall, are the bathroom facilities. First, a wooden door leads into a small sink-room. On a glass shelf above the sink an enamel cup holds a dozen or so toothbrushes. Beyond the sink another door opens onto the western-style toilet. In the room adjacent to the toilet and sink, but with a separate entrance from the hall, is a shoulder-high spigot and hot-water heater. A proper shower fixture installed above it has never worked properly, and it is low on the list of priorities of things to fix.

The last two rooms on the ground floor are bedrooms. Specific occupancy of bedrooms is always in flux, as daughters marry out of the house and daughters-in-law marry into it, or as someone goes to the Soviet Union, the United States, or India to study for years at a time. At present, however, the first of the two rooms belongs to the oldest son, Thulo Bhai,[4] and his wife Sabita and their two children. The second is Meena's room. Any formal entertaining of guests is done here, the closest approximation to a living room in the house. Meena moved her TV to this room after her youngest brother married, because it would make the new bride very uncomfortable if everyone flooded into the newlyweds' room every night to watch it (the Nepal station, which began broadcasting in the mid-1980s, operates only from 6 to 10 p.m.). Having the TV in Meena's room has similarly promoted it as a general family room, to her occasional annoyance.

Flush with the door jamb of Meena's room is the bottom step of the cement stairway leading to the second floor. Immediately at the top of the stairs, over Meena's room, is the doorway to Tanka Prasad and Rewanta Kumari's room. Following a clockwise floor plan parallel to that of the ground floor, the next door opens onto the veranda, which commands a fine view of Kathmandu and Swayambunath to the west and, when the sky is sufficiently free of clouds and smog, the summit of Himal Chuli and the shimmering white massif of Ganesh Himal. Then comes a room which doubles as a guest room (for visiting daughters, for instance) and as a sanctuary to which Ama ('mother', as Rewanta Kumari is called by everyone regardless of genealogical connections, just as Tanka Prasad is called Bua, 'father') can escape from the routine hurly-burly of the house. The remaining rooms are a storeroom for food-grains, cooking oil, etc.; a room for Kanchhu and his wife Sushan and their children; another small room which is used as a sleeping room for a variety of people, ranging from menstruating[5] females of the household to the family priest, when he has a particularly protracted

---

[4] 'Older (lit. big) younger brother' (from the point of view of his older sisters); alternatively Thulo Babu or 'older (lit. big) son/young boy'.

[5] A menstruating woman is considered so polluting that she must be separated from the rest of the family; she must sleep in a separate room, may not enter the *puja* (worship) room or kitchen, and must bathe before she can return to normal interaction with others in the house.

ritual schedule (such as occurs during Dasai, the biggest Hindu festival of the year) to fulfill; and finally a room for the youngest son, Sano Kanchhu (Bir Bhadre) and his recent bride, Leela.

Another, narrower cement staircase leads from the second floor to a cement roof (corrugated metal until it was renovated a couple of years ago) open to the sky and surrounded by a waist-high brick wall. The corrugated metal was Bua's idea. He didn't want it cast in reinforced concrete, for fear that it might collapse during an earthquake. Popping up out of the middle of the roof is the *puja* (worship) room. A simple wooden altar sits in one corner. Its whitewashed walls are covered with about forty pictures of various Hindu deities, particularly Narayan (an avatar of Vishnu), and the paraphernalia (incense, powders, rice, water vessels, etc.) necessary for their worship. Every morning Ama sits cross-legged on the cloth-covered straw mat she spreads in front of the altar where, after rising as early as 4 a.m., she spends an hour and a half in worship, and another half hour in the evening. Bua also spends considerable time worshipping here, though not as regularly or predictably as Ama.

Nowadays Tanka Prasad and Ama spend most of their time in their bedroom at the top of the stairs. This room, a little larger than the others, is about 19 feet by 13 feet. Built-in shelves in one wall hold a variety of books in English, Hindi, and Nepali—from the two-volume *Shorter Oxford Dictionary* to Steinbeck's *The Short Reign of Pippin IV* to *Patal Prabas* (*Underworld Journey*, an account of a trip to America by the literary scholar Taranath Sharma). One shelf is reserved for four pictures: of Parbati (Lord Shiva's consort); Tanka Prasad; his father; and Arjun and his charioteer Lord Krishna pictured in a battle scene from the *Mahabharata*. Hanging on the wall above the built-in shelf are two more pictures: one of Shiva, one of Hanuman (the monkey god), with a small corner inset of Ram and Sita (the hero and heroine of the Hindu epic, the *Ramayana*). A wall-hanging near the door, done up in the style of a Tibetan *thanka*, contains a statement celebrating and commemorating Tanka Prasad's lifetime of service to the nation (see Appendix 3), presented to him by well-wishers from all walks of life on his seventy-fifth birthday. On the opposite wall, between two more pictures of Hindu deities (and partially covering them), hangs a calendar showing both the Bikram[6] and Christian eras. Still more

---

[6] The Bikram era (Bikram Sambat, or BS) is based on a twelve-month year beginning fifty-seven years before the Christian era. Thus 1990 is usually (about two-thirds of the time, since the Bikram year begins in the middle of April) equivalent to 2047. Bikram

books (ranging from Marx and Engels' *Collected Works* to Gibbon's *Decline and Fall of the Roman Empire* to a volume of *Reader's Digest Condensed Books*) are crammed into a free-standing wooden bookcase-with-drawers along another wall; a small vase full of red and white plastic flowers is perched inconspicuously on top of it. Sunlight floods the room in the afternoons from the south and west, and it is lit at night by a bare, low-watt, non-frosted incandescent bulb on one wall and an uncovered fluorescent tube on another.

The windows, like all windows in the house, are covered by screens to keep out insects, as well as 'grills'—heavy-gauge metal lattice—to keep out thieves. The three strands of barbed wire strung along the top of the compound wall, and pieces of broken glass set in cement on top of the back wall, are designed to serve the same purpose. The broken glass also keeps out dogs, of which Tanka Prasad has had a pathological horror since the daughter of their longtime servant died of rabies many years ago. Within the house the door to each room is kept closed and locked, at least when no one is in it; the door may also be closed when people are in the room, to keep it warm, to keep out mosquitos, or to dampen the noise of children yelling and racing around. Within each room all cupboard doors and drawers are locked, as is the custom-made wooden cabinet in which the television is installed. All this is standard Nepalese procedure, intended not just to protect against outside thieves, but to remove temptation for live-in servants and the inquisitive and destructive tendencies of the numerous children constantly circulating in and out. The ultimate in security is represented by a free-standing, metal closet in Meena's room: inside its locked doors there is a locked safe, enclosing yet another locked safe, each with its own key.

Tanka Prasad's 'current-reading' books (*The Tao of Physics* is a recent favourite) are stacked on the far side of a large double bed (really two single beds pushed together) that fills an alcove created by a recently-completed bathroom. Mosquito netting suspended from a wooden frame is pulled back to open the side of the bed for sitting during the day. Two large framed pictures, one of Tanka Prasad's father and the other of his mother, sit on a cloth-covered table near the bed. A glittery plastic souvenir picture of Badrinath, in the Indian Himalayas, which Ama brought back from a recent pilgrimage there, is hung above

Sambat is used for official government purposes and holidays, but the Christian era is also widely known, hence the wall calendar showing both systems.

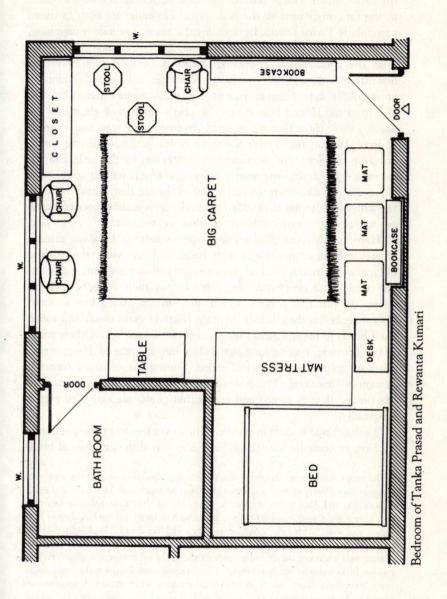

Bedroom of Tanka Prasad and Rewanta Kumari

the table, under a large mirror. The new bathroom behind the table, in the far corner next to the bed, makes life easier for both of them, particularly Tanka Prasad. By doubling the amount of indoor plumbing, it also makes life easier for everyone else, and has eliminated the lines (and the concomitant grumbling) formerly evident in front of the downstairs bathroom every morning. A wooden cabinet full of clothes, an upholstered, reclining easy-chair (a birthday present Meena brought Bua from the United States), a stool, and a small cane chair line the walls. Two or three thin, white-linen-covered sitting mats and a couple of wool Tibetan rugs lie on the more or less wall-to-wall jute carpet covering the floor. An electric space heater sits by the bed, ready to be turned on during the winter mornings, which remain chilly until about ten o'clock, when the sun burns off the fog that usually blankets the valley. A rotating electric fan sits under a protective piece of plastic on top of the wooden cabinet, waiting for summer.

Here in this room Tanka Prasad spends most of his days, reading whatever book or newspaper is at hand, and receiving relatives and old friends, journalists and scholars, pandits and ambassadors, and political cronies and neophytes who come to pay their respects, seek his advice, or just talk politics, which often means asking him to exert his influence on their behalf. Visiting relatives bend down and touch their heads to his and Ama's feet, a sign of filial respect.[7] Others pause at the doorway, waiting for a signal from him to come in. He generally gives it, unless he is in a bad mood. During the constant turnover of visitors Ama circulates in and out, keeping an unobtrusive but watchful eye on the flow of events and seeing that guests are extended proper hospitality.

Tanka Prasad is short in stature, a little over five feet tall—puckishly, he likes to compare himself to Napoleon. His thinning, tousled black

---

[7] The protocol governing this ritual obeisance is complex. The sons, and the sons' sons (or any other relative in such a classificatory relation) touch their foreheads to the feet of both Bua and Ama if they are leaving the house for more than a day, or returning to it after a night away, and on ritual occasions such as Dasai and the birthdays of both fathers and sons. Neither the daughters nor their children do so. The daughters-in-law touch Ama's feet, but bow to Bua from a distance, when the light is turned on in the evening and when coming to and going from the house other than casually. Ama also touches Bua's feet after she has completed her morning puja. Even a non-relative might touch Bua's feet (but not Ama's), as a sign of great esteem. The gesture both demonstrates respect and invokes blessings, which are given as Bua and Ama respond by touching the head of whoever is bowing to them. The general idea is that the feet and hands act as terminals for the flow of good-will between people.

hair sometimes falls over his forehead, partly covering the *tika* mark that he applies as part of his morning *puja*. He wears his glasses if he is reading; one lens is extremely thick, to compensate for weak vision due to a cataract which was removed recently. But even with a second pair of glasses for distance, when someone appears at the bedroom door he has to ask who it is, unless he can recognize the voice. He shaves only occasionally, so his more-salt-than-pepper stubble may be at any stage of growth. He is moderately overweight—even stout—and now slightly stooped. In the bedroom he is barefoot (all shoes and slippers come off before entering any of the bedrooms) and wears loose-fitting white trousers and a woollen shirt or sweater, unless it is very warm. A necklace of prayer-beads (*rudrachha*)[8] hangs around his neck.

Ama is even shorter than Tanka Prasad, only four feet ten inches tall. Her forehead always displays a *tika*, and there is a short, solid line of vermillion powder at the beginning of the part in her hair—both signs of a married woman. Her cropped black hair, now streaked with grey, is pulled back over her neck and held by a wide brown plastic barrette. She usually wears her glasses and a pair of diamond-studded earrings which match the nose ornament on her left nostril. Her sober, almost dour demeanour suggests a severe temperament, but this impression evaporates quickly when she breaks into her warm, broad, toothy smile, which she does frequently.

Like her husband she was always a little on the plump side, but perhaps because of the restricted diet required by her ulcers, she has recently lost about ten pounds. Ama always wears a sari (though she once posed for a photograph in Meena's dress, just to see how it would look), and bundles up in quilted cotton jackets and woollen sweaters in winter. In cold weather she pads around the room in socks. Whatever the season she is never without a key-ring full of keys (all doors have locks) hanging from her waist. Her high-pitched, almost falsetto voice contrasts with Tanka Prasad's deep-timbred speech. For a woman in her mid-seventies, Ama is very spry, alert, and energetic. For exercise she walks in circles around the house, because Tanka Prasad becomes anxious if she is out of earshot for long. She takes an afternoon nap only because Tanka Prasad wants her to join him during his, and because,

---

[8] *Rudrachha* refers to the rosary-type string of 108 beads often used in the devotions of Hindus and Buddhists.

now that her household contains a full complement of daughters-in-law to run it, she doesn't have anything more pressing to do.

Tanka Prasad is in generally poor health, suffering from high blood pressure and a variety of aches and pains which he treats with a large but haphazard collection of medicines that have accumulated over the years. Everyone in the house is trained to take his blood-pressure on the tonometer kept by his bed. His frequent coughs explain the small brass spittoon on the floor by the bed. He is increasingly feeble, slow in his movements, and addled about where he has put things, such as his glasses. He knows he ought to be on a low- or non-salt diet, but he shrugs off efforts to control what he eats. Nor does he engage in any kind of systematic physical exercise. His mind is on other matters—usually politics.

Despite his disabilities, he retains his enormous curiosity about the world of ideas and books, constantly asking to look at any book a visitor might mention or, better, have brought along. He still reads widely and voraciously, but not deeply; his poor eyesight prevents him from reading as much as he would like, and his energy and attention span are rarely sufficient to get him through an entire book. He is an avid newspaper reader, though, and I often found him sitting on the edge of his bed, leafing through the daily papers he tries to keep abreast of. Ama reads Nepali and Hindi, and she reads every word (or so Tanka Prasad complains) in the daily government newspaper, the *Gorkhapatra*, if she has time. Because of his poor vision, she frequently spends the afternoon reading a Hindi version of the great Hindu epic, the *Mahabharata*, to him. (See illustration 19.)

When Tanka Prasad goes out, as he does from time to time to see a doctor or visit friends or attend parties or weddings, two items he always wants to acquire more of are books and medicines. He also finds it hard to resist stopping at a vegetable stand. He loves to bargain, and the shopkeeper who refuses to accept the price Tanka Prasad offers is condemned to a brow-beating lecture on how outrageously expensive everything—including the hapless shopkeeper's wares—is these days.

Since neither of them can hear very well (Ama wears a hearing aid, and Bua ought to), he is often irritated by the fact that she cannot understand him, or vice versa. But as he is very skilled in seeing humour in adversity, he also is sometimes amused by their communication lapses. Once, when she misunderstood something he had said, he initially exploded in exasperation, but then broke into a chuckle, saying 'I say one thing and she hears another.' They both laughed.

His once intense interest in political matters is now muted. He played little part in the democratic movement of 1990, and although he is titular President of the resurrected Praja Parishad, the party and Nepalese politics have moved on. His relative political inactivity is due partly to poor health, partly to lack of access to financial resources, and partly to what he sees as the younger generation's abandonment of the principles for which he risked everything he had, including his life. He is frustrated, bored, and demoralized at not being able to continue to play a more active part in the political struggles that have occupied him so ceaselessly. When the first democratic elections in thirty-two years were held, on 12 May 1991, Tanka Prasad was too old, feeble, and dispirited to go out to the polls and cast his vote.

But he has not lost his sense of humour. Frequently he will begin to make a statement in a typically sombre, serious vein, and only near the end of it, when I hear his deep basso chuckle and see the twinkle in his eye, do I realize that everything he has just said is a joke. He also jokes fondly with his wife, at least in front of me. Once I asked him why he had shaved off several weeks of beard. When he replied, laughingly, that he had to because otherwise his wife would not kiss him any more, Ama laughed too. In anyone younger such an egregious reference to expression of physical affection would be scandalous, at least among middle-class Brahmins.

He and Ama both frequently demonstrate what strikes at least this foreigner as an extraordinary ability to laugh about things which aren't laughing matters. Examples include, in his case, the atrocious living conditions he endured during ten years in prison, much of it in solitary confinement; or, in her case, the equally difficult ten years when friends and relatives were afraid to speak to her, when it was hard even to find a roof to put over herself and the family she was struggling to hold together. Tanka Prasad is a deadly serious man who refuses to take himself too seriously. Like many strong personalities, his character lends itself easily to paradox. He is alternately autocratic and sensitive, imperious and sentimental, demanding and generous.

Although as a father he was always so embroiled in politics (or confined behind prison walls) that he was a remote figure for his children, he can be very affectionate towards his grandchildren and great-grandchildren. Tanka Prasad and Rewanta Kumari are Bua (father) and Ama (mother) not only to his children but also to his sons- and daughters-in-law, some of his grandchildren, and even outsiders like me.[9] After over sixty years of marriage the two, despite their occasional mutual irritations, are obviously very devoted to each other. They both maintain that the feelings they hold for each other go much deeper than the mere physical attraction that young people feel. This kind of affection grows gradually, they say, and they cite their own affectionate relationship as an argument for arranged marriages rather than love marriages, with their more passionate but less substantial and sustainable basis.

He has become extremely dependent on her psychologically—'I am she and she is me,' he says contentedly, quoting a line from the *Bhagwat* in which Krishna refers to his great love, Radha. They did not have such an emotionally close relationship before he went to prison. It is ironic that, although he lived without her for those ten incarcerated years, he cannot stand to be without her now for more than a brief period of time. If he is alone in his room for more than an hour or two he calls for her to come in order to simply be in the room with him. Once when she was about to leave for Delhi for medical treatment I asked if he wouldn't go to the airport to see her off. He said he couldn't, he was so shaken at the thought of her leaving him for a few days that he couldn't trust himself not to break down emotionally at the airport.

Whenever he needs something—say, a glass of water, or his glasses—he shouts, and shortly the bustle of swishing saris whispers the arrival of one of his three daughters-in-law, or Ama, or a servant, to do his bidding. (If no one responds to his call, he may become petulant and start addressing the wall in a voice loud enough to be heard anywhere in the house). He generally treats them all kindly, laughing and joking with them, or teasing them, unless he is impatient about what he wants. But he orders them about in the peremptory manner of one who has been used to giving orders all his life. He generally uses the lowest (or, one could alternatively say, the most familiar or affectionate) pronoun (*ta*) when addressing his own family, and the next most familiar (*timi*) for his daughters-in-law.

Issuing commands comes naturally to him not because he was once Prime Minister, but because it is the prerogative and position of the

[9] Since the younger Acharya children and the older Acharya grandchildren are about the same age and grew up playing together, the grandchildren adopted the same terms of address as the children. The grandchildren who address the senior Acharyas as 'Bua' and 'Ama' use English terms, such as 'Daddy' and 'Mommy', to address their own parents—a common affectation among western-educated Kathmandu families nowadays.

adult high-caste Hindu male to be served by women, whether of his own house or those who marry into it. His expectation of being served is accentuated not only by having been the youngest child, but also by having been, after the death of his older brother, the only son—both prime candidates in their own right in Nepalese society for pampering. He goes downstairs to eat the two major meals of the day, but the rest of the time he is brought tea, or snacks, or a glass of water, to his room, either when it is served in the normal course of events, or as he demands it.

Though his powers are failing, he is still indisputably the head of the household. Ama oversees the domestic routines, including what goes on in the kitchen, and she is in charge of the crucial area of family finances, handling and disbursing funds as they are needed. But the division of labour is not clear-cut. For instance, if an old friend-in-need asks Bua for a few hundred rupees, he will summarily, even whimsically, ask Ama to give out the money on the spot, having given no thought to the state of the cash-flow of the household. But Ama will insist on knowing for whom the money is needed, and why. She may resist dispensing such largesse even if it is for a good cause, because as it is she may not have enough to get the household through the end of the month. Thus are sown the seeds of financial disagreement, which have to be resolved, perhaps by giving some money, but less than that requested.

But if there are important phone calls to be made (to the Prime Minister, for example, to intercede on behalf of a qualified but un-employed associate) it is Tanka Prasad who makes them. It was he who took the primary role in arranging his youngest son's marriage (his last unmarried child, out of the seven) in 1988. If he thinks someone has lost weight, he worries about it. Anyone who has been out of the house for a while—even to spend the day at the office—reports to him upon returning home, to let him know they are back. And he is extremely concerned that everyone be home not long after dark. This applies, incongruously and annoyingly to those involved, to adult sons now in their late twenties or older, as well as to women. This solicitous concern contrasts with his attitude decades ago when his wife had to send him an invitation to come to the naming ceremony for their second son several days after he was born (on the day Tanka Prasad was appointed Prime Minister). It is as if the burning energy he used to pour into politics has been transformed into an obsession for the welfare of his family.

Ama's main concern in life also is for her family, and always has been. But whereas Bua is high-strung, irascible, and domineering, Ama is low-key, patient, and accepting. Because of an astrologer's prediction when she was young that she would not live to her seventy-fifth birthday, she believes in, and quietly accepts, her imminent death. Bua continues to command everything and everyone, and he is no more likely to go gently into the good night than he is to go gently anywhere else.

His jural ascendancy does not mean that his word is gospel. On the contrary, spirited discussion and hot disagreement over various matters, from the trivial to the political to the metaphysical, between Tanka Prasad and his family are not rare. Outsiders close to the family say it would seem anomalous not to hear heated, high-decibel ideological and political arguments wafting over the compound wall now and then. Emotional volatility characterizes him as well as some of the other members of his family: a firestorm of indignant wrath at one moment will be followed by freewheeling, rollicking laughter the next. Grudges are not part of the emotional makeup of the house. Through all the sound and fury shine the basic love and respect and concern they all hold for each other. When the chips are down, they all know that their surest source of bedrock support lies within the family.[10]

---

[10] I have attempted in this chapter to informally describe the Acharya household as I observed it in the late 1980s, with occasional updates into the 1990s. The resulting portrait of this living, growing household which is never the same even from day to day, is of course a montage.

Chapter 4

King or Saint

Childhood and Early Life of Tanka Prasad

I was born in the declining phase of the moon (*Krishna Pakchhay*), during the month of *Mangsir* in BS 1969. *Mangsir* is the eighth month in the Bikram calendar; it falls in the last two weeks of November and the first two weeks of December.[1] It was a Sunday. This was two years before the First World War. I was born in Parasi, then part of Taulihawa district but now under the jurisdiction of Lumbini Zone.[2] Parasi was the district headquarters, and my father, Tika Prasad Acharya, was posted there as the District Revenue Officer. He held the rank of Subba, so he was informally called Subba Saheb or Hakim [boss] Saheb. He worked there for about three or four years. The Ranas used to appoint someone to a place for a time, and then they would

[1] Tanka Prasad also gives his birthday as 31 December 1912, but this is only an approximation, accurate to within a few weeks, for the benefit of westerners. Birthdays are based on the lunar calendar, so while he was born in *Mangsir*, his lunar date would fluctuate back and forth between *Mangsir* and *Paush*, the ninth month of the Bikram calendar (BS, for Bikram Sambat), which like the Christian era is a solar calendar. Exact equivalences between the Bikram and lunar calendars on the one hand, and the Christian era on the other, are extremely difficult to calculate for times when the latter was rarely used. Tanka Prasad has subtracted the standard fifty-seven years to yield the AD date and guessed the month and the day of the month. 17 *Marg*, 1969 BS, was actually 1 December 1912. In 1986 his seventy-fifth birthday fell on 9 *Mangsir*, which was 24 November. In 1995 his eighty-fourth birthday (celebrated posthumously – see Appendix 7) fell on 3 December, always one year ahead of westerners, since Nepalese consider a person one year old at birth.

[2] Lumbini is one of 14 administrative Zones, which are subdivided into 75 Districts. Within Lumbini Zone, Parasi lies in Nawalparasi District, a few miles east of Lumbini, birthplace of the Buddha, in the plains of the western Tarai, near the Indian border. The current division of Nepal into Zones and Districts was put into practice in the early 1960s.

rotate him to another assignment. The house I was born in is still standing; it is now occupied by the Land Revenue Office.

My father had two wives. He married the second only about six months after being married to the first. Having a second wife was a matter of status, a way of showing how important and powerful one was. I addressed them both as 'mother'. My 'real' mother was a very good-hearted soul. She was the senior wife, but she did not object to the presence of a co-wife. She did not even object to my father's keeping concubines at the same house. But my stepmother strongly objected to his keeping these concubines. My brother had his own room, while my mother and I shared a room when I was small (we were joined there by my sister), and my father slept in another room with my second mother. When my father had concubines, he paid no more attention to my second mother. They often lived in a different place from where the rest of us stayed.

I was eighteen years old when my mother died. She was around forty-five at the time of her death. When my mother was on her death bed she called me and told me that, now that she was dying, I should consider my stepmother as my own mother, as she also loved me very much. My stepmother did love me very much, probably because she had no issue of her own.

Not all co-wives get along so well. Once I told a Secretary at the Russian Embassy that Juddha Shamsher had seventeen sons from his five wives.[3] The Russian said he thought that was remarkable, and

[3] Sir Geoffrey Betham, British Minister to Nepal at the time, described Juddha in rather uncomplimentary terms:

'There is no doubt that Sir Juddha Shamsher is a naughty old man and his way of life has left much to be desired and for all the number of his illegitimate children are said to have been a legion. A conservative estimate is one hundred sons and daughters spread all over the length and breadth of Nepal. Officially he claims nineteen illegitimate sons (daughters not mentioned). It has been and still is as far as I am aware his practice to pick up any damsel that takes his wayward fancy and then to return her, with a few rupees clutched in her hand, to her parents or her husband. Naturally this kind of behaviour does not earn him the respect or affection of the masses in Nepal. Like his predecessors, he has since his accession pocketed the whole of the surplus revenue of Nepal and he is now reputed to be an extremely wealthy man though his large family must cost him a pretty penny to support. I understand he supports any illegitimate sons that may be born to him but not many of the daughters. Although Sir Juddha is not peculiar in this respect, times have changed since the practice of pouching as much of the public money as possible by the reigning prime minister was started, and not only the people but also the royal family are complaining. His general universal behaviour has naturally antagonized the priesthood or at least given them a broom with which to beat him. This was not

then I told him a story about having multiple wives. Once the servants of the god of death (Yamaraj, who sends his sentinels to summon anyone whose time on earth has expired) brought two men before him. Yamaraj asked the first man how many wives he had. The man replied that he had two wives. Yamaraj sent this man to heaven. Then he asked the other man the same question. The other man replied that he had only one wife. The god of death sent him to hell. Yamaraj's servants were surprised by this and asked him why he had sent the first man to heaven and the other to hell. Yamaraj replied that the first man, being married to two wives, had already been through hell on earth itself, and the other being married to only one wife did not have the experience of hell on earth, so he was sent to hell [laughter].

Ours was a Brahmin family, and it is our custom for the family priest to give the newborn baby a name, and so our priest duly named me Tanka Prasad. Acharya is my surname. My gotra[4] is Kaudinya. We do not use our gotra name in daily life. I learned my gotra name because whenever we do certain religious rituals we have to recite it. There are seven gotras, each descended from an ancient rishi (sage). Ours is descended from Kaudinya Rishi. Members of this gotra are widely spread. A member of the Kaudinya gotra was the first disciple of Gautam Buddha after he returned to Banaras from Bodhgaya; he went to Cambodia many centuries ago and spread Buddhism there.

According to my china[5] I was born close to two zodiac signs in the same quarter. One was Sukra or Venus, who is the guru of the demons; the other was Brihaspati, or Jupiter, who is the teacher of religious devotees. The former makes me materialistic, while the latter makes me spiritual. It was predicted that I would either become a Raja (king) or a Jogi (saint). All my life both these influences have fought inside me, making me combative. Because of both these influences, I have never subscribed completely to either a materialist or a spiritual philosophy; I always waver between the two.

---

improved by his unfortunate shooting of a cow in the tarai last winter and his refusal to earn absolution by paying the enormous sum demanded by the priest.' (Shah 1990: pp. 127-8).

[4] Gotra is an exogamous section of a caste. Tanka Prasad's genealogy (see Appendix 11) shows nine different gotras represented among his and his wife's relations. The two extra gotras probably represent fission among the original seven gotras.

[5] The Hindu equivalent of a birth certificate, a china is a horoscope containing detailed astrological and calendrical information cast by the family priest and written in Sanskrit on a long parchment scroll of rice paper.

We belonged to the middle class and had no large property, yet we managed to live happily. Our family consisted of my father, my mother, my stepmother, and a brother and a sister—both older. Another brother, Ram Prasad, died of epilepsy at about the age of ten, before I was born. Later on my father also kept three concubines, one after the other. In those days keeping concubines was the fashion. All the big people kept concubines. If one wanted to be rated high he had to keep concubines [laughter]. We also always had three or four servants. Nowadays it is difficult to have servants, but formerly it was not [laughter].[6] With the end of the feudal system it became difficult to keep servants [laughter].

My father was a landlord. The salary he got from the Government was not sufficient to cover his expenses and had to be supplemented by the income that came from our land-holdings. He owned 101 *bighas* (about 164 acres) of land in Sirsia, in Janakpur district in the Tarai, and since my only brother died when I was young and my sister married into another family, I was the only heir of my father.

Although we were middle class, my father was of aristocratic bent of mind and liked the latest fashions. You could say he aspired to the aristocracy. His clothes were designed and made by one of the most expensive textile companies in India, and his shoes were manufactured by the famous Barret Company of Calcutta.[7] He preferred European things. He knew some English and was very proud of it. He was of imperious nature, himself a disciplinarian, and did not tolerate indiscipline among others, so the family members had to live up to his expectations of good discipline. I, being the youngest child, had some freedom, and I was pampered a lot. My father was kind-hearted and upright in his dealings, but he was quick-tempered and did not hesitate even to beat people, such as servants; but after beating them he would immediately show his sympathy for the person and give something as compensation for the beating. Although he was feared, he was also respected and loved by the people around him. He loved to tell stories about the good deeds he performed in his life. He was susceptible to flattery and praise.

He was a man of varied tastes. He had engaged a man on a monthly

[6] Unlike in the United States, labour in Nepal is extremely cheap, while goods are very expensive, so the Acharyas have three servants but no car. It is common for all but the poorest families to keep a live-in servant, often a teenage village boy or girl with no other prospects; the servant's basic living expenses are met, in addition to a small wage.

[7] The sartorial details are from Govinda Prasad Upadhyay.

salary who would tell him stories from the Arabian Nights in the evenings while he lay on his bed, before falling asleep. I also took advantage of this situation. My father retired late, whereas I went to bed early. But if there was sufficient gap in the time I used to avail myself of the opportunity to get Sena Lall, the story teller, to entertain me also. The stories seemed so amusing.

I cannot remember my early childhood too well. I had no childhood worries. I was much interested in reading, and therefore had few playmates. I played with others in my family, particularly with my sister, since my brother used to go to school everyday. I was a mischievous sort, and my mother used to tell me Vishnu's *chakra*[8] was always spinning, and that he would hurl it at me if I didn't behave. My brother, Chiranjivi, was senior to me in age by eight or nine years. He was shy in his behaviour at home, but he had a lot of friends outside. He spent most of his time in sports and games. He had a passion for kite-flying, which was considerably in fashion then. Even their Majesties took pleasure in kite-flying once a year during the early part of the winter.

During those days, being not yet in my teens, I could not participate with my brother in sports and games, and as a grown-up boy he, too, had no taste for the gambols and frolics I liked then. He was nine years older than I, so we had little opportunity of developing much intimacy and affection between us. But as far as I know he was of a genial nature, kind-hearted and generous, and bore no grudge or ill-will against anybody. He was loved by all those who were near him.

He loved hunting so much that he would pass several days at a time in the jungle. The climate being malarial, the excursions had their effect on him. Once when we were living in Biratnagar he went to the jungle and stayed there for nine or ten days. He contracted typhus[9] and died on the twenty-first day of the attack. It was very difficult to cure typhus in those days. My father didn't worry at all about health problems in the Tarai. It was said that there was no malaria in Bara when we were living there, but I frequently contracted malaria there. When I went to Biratnagar I didn't suffer from it, although Biratnagar, in the words of Toni Hagen,[10] had the 'malarial air'. My stomach was always weak. It is still weak.

[8] Lord Vishnu holds four items in each of his four hands. In the uppermost right hand is a discus (*chakra*) which when thrown will destroy anything in its path. Items in the other hands include a conch shell, another kind of weapon (*gada*), and a lotus flower.

[9] Tanka Prasad is not sure whether his brother died of typhoid or typhus.

[10] Toni Hagen is a Swiss geologist who explored the country for the government in the 1950s.

My brother was admitted to school, but did not take much interest in learning. It was not his fault; rather, the fault lay somewhere in the social system. In those days only a few people sent their children to school. The Ranas discouraged education in English, and despite a pretension of liberalism they permitted only one high school in Kathmandu, Darbar High School, where my brother studied up to the 8th or 9th class.[11] The aristocracy (more appropriately, the oligarchy) and the middle class had the false notion that their children should be taught at home by private tutors. Only those lacking the means to afford the luxury of private tutors sent their children to school.

On the other hand, to join the Government service one did not need to qualify oneself in such a higher type of education as is in vogue today. The aristocracy could obtain positions for their members in the Government service just by pleasing the Ranas. Moreover they regarded it as their right to claim such favours from them. The Ranas, having nothing to fear from the dumb masses of the people, also had to do little in order to please them. Their sole concern was to maintain themselves in power by keeping the aristocracy and the middle class satisfied, through the grants of such favours as the above. My father, who also came from the middle class, expected similar favours from the Ranas, so he did not care much whether his children were educated properly or not.

The other great reason for neglect in educating one's children arose from the fact that, the social system being feudalistic, one relied much on the income of land and interest from loans, and for that a little capacity for so much as reading and writing short notes, a little arithmetic and a capacity for attending to correspondence, was regarded as sufficient. There was no such thing as learning for learning's sake, and to the extent that there was such a thing, it was in the sphere of Sanskrit, which was limited to a few chosen people. My education also would have remained within the limits of reading and writing notes had I not, as I grew up, cherished an ambition to become something more than what circumstances had afforded me.

Before saying anything about my formal education and how I took up the career of a revolutionary, I think it would be better if I describe my informal education and the early beliefs that contributed to my mental makeup. Since our family was Brahmin, religiosity was inherent in us. My father devoted two to three hours a day to meditation and

[11] A Nepali-medium school, in which the curriculum included English.

worship. My mother also had religious duties to perform daily. She used to wake up before dawn, bathe and prepare the household shrine for my father. In the meantime she said her prayers, keeping track of them by fingering her beads. After that she would come to our room (she and I shared a common room), wake me up, sit down with me, and recite verses from the great Hindu epic, *Ramayana*. She was fair, graceful and had a beautiful voice. She had learned the whole of the epic by heart. My father liked my stepmother more than my mother, who therefore led a somewhat retiring life and passed her time reading religious books.

It was a delightful thing for a child to hear, in the sacred morning hours, holy verses recited in melodious tones by a loving and affectionate mother. The verses were composed in simple Nepali by the first and greatest of our national poets, Bhanubhakta Acharya, and even though I was a young child I could understand them. In order to make me fully understand their meaning, my mother would explain the verses in a very lucid manner, and with a ring in her tone that showed her full faith in the veracity of the story. The force of her conviction allowed me little room for doubt. I considered them to be as true as my mother believed them to be.

She would also recite verses from *Krishna Charitra* [a book containing stories of Krishna]. The exploits of Lord Krishna were a great source of inspiration and delight to me in my childhood. As she was well versed in many areas of Hindu mythology, she could tell the whereabouts of the various gods. One morning, I remember, she took me up in her arms, stood at the window facing east, pointing at the tallest mountain, and said that beyond that mountain lay the region where the sun resided, and the mountains lying around and further on were made of gold. For proof, she brought to my notice the golden rays of the sun that shone in the morning, with the explanation that they had taken such a hue as a consequence of their reflection against the mountains. The logic was irrefutable to a child. She said that the sun had a chariot in which he travelled from morning till night, and the chariot was drawn by a thousand horses, all very strong and stout, as certainly they should be as they had to cover the whole span of the sky in twelve hours. She also told me there were regions in the east that belonged to the Gods, such as Varuna and Kubera,[12] where angels lived in pairs and in great

---

[12] Varuna is the god of fire; Kubera is associated with wealth.

happiness.[13] In Hindu mythology there is no mention of angels having wings. Hindu angels travelled by means of some kind of celestial flying device, though it is not known whether they were propelled mechanically, or by magic or will power. I used to feel very romantic about all these stories and myths.

Such stories have their own effect on a believer. As I was a believer then, the accounts of the eastern region as stated by my mother completely captured my imagination. At times, I would wake up with my mother, stand by the window, and watch the dawn, filled with faith, curiosity, and romance. I came to know in my later years that the accounts were false, yet at that time they had a salutary effect upon my brain. They gave a new dimension to my imagination in place of the one provided merely by the surroundings of the household and the little I had seen outside it. I admired my mother for having knowledge of such magnificent things. Rising in the early morning and watching the heavens in a clear but bedewed atmosphere was in itself a rewarding act, not to mention its effect if it is inspired by romance. I still enjoy remembering those happy days.

My mother said many things about morals, associated with such accounts and stories, that constituted a body of ethics for me. Ethics change with changes in social patterns and in conformation to the philosophy emerging therefrom, and also according to their practicability under changed circumstances. Although I had to reject a good many of my beliefs in later years, yet they offered me a solid basis with which the new values could be compared with the old, thereby contributing substantially to the growth of my understanding and intelligence. I still retain a great deal of them.

I immensely enjoyed talking and conversing with my mother. Sometimes I would even give up playing in order to hear her recite the verses and tell stories. My ardent wish was to become capable of reciting the verses myself. So I asked my mother to teach me how to write the letters. She was so glad to hear my request, she took me in her arms and kissed me. As I had no slate or ink and paper then, she procured a wooden plank, on which she evenly laid out a coating of fine pink dust, and wrote the alphabet with a white chalk. The letters looked very nice, as if they were carved in marble by an artist. It did not take me long to get them by heart and reproduce them myself, though in very clumsy form. Immediately after undergoing

[13] This section is adapted from Goodall 1974.

training in deciphering joint letters I took up the leather bound book of the *Ramayana* and, fifteen or sixteen days after beginning to learn the letters, I started reciting the verses. I was five years old then, and to a child it becomes a matter of great delight as the letters he deciphers form words and begin to have meaning. My second mother was not as literate as my mother, but she could read and write basic Nepali.

In addition to Nepali I came to know Hindi. I learned it just by reading Hindi books. The first Hindi books I read were the *Chandra-Kanta-Samtati* mystery series, which were very popular. I also knew Sanskrit. I learned Sanskrit at my *bartaman*.[14] My *bartaman* had been delayed till I was six years old, because I had been sick a lot. At one point while the priest was doing some ritual to me I got up and ran away to suckle milk from my mother, even at that age! Afterwards I started reciting Chandi and Rudri, which all Brahmins are supposed to know. Chandi is a prayer for Durga which we recite during Dasai; we recite Rudri on many occasions. A *pandit* would come and teach me these texts, and in this way I gradually came to know Sanskrit.

I learned about the *Ramayana* and such things from my mother, but I learned other subjects from the teachers my father hired, and in high school. I had a tutor also, a Kayasta [an accountant caste found mostly in the Tarai] from Bara. In those days there were few educated Nepalese who could teach English, so my father brought a Madrasi teacher from Banaras for me when we lived in Biratnagar. When I enquired about him a few years ago, I found out that he was still alive. When he left us he went back to Banaras, where he worked as a clerk in some office. He taught me English. He didn't teach me anything else, just English. I am very sorry that I was deprived of learning mathematics at a young age. I am fond of reading books on general science, and the lack of mathematics stands in my way as an obstacle to understanding propositions presented in mathematical terms, which has been a matter of great regret in my life. I still think of learning that superb science. So, up until the age of fourteen I had formally studied only English.

There were few schools in Nepal. There was only one public high school in Kathmandu, called Darbar High School. I joined Darbar High School in Class Five, when I was fifteen, but the geography and mathematics teacher was very cruel. I was weak in both subjects, so he

[14] *Bartaman* (Sanskrit, *bratabandha*) is the coming of age ritual in which upper-caste males receive the sacred thread, thus making them 'twice-born' and full-fledged members of their caste.

used to beat me at every turn. I have already said that I did not know mathematics well. I was trying to learn and improve, but this teacher was devilishly wicked. He had all sorts of ways of punishing us, from making us stand up on the bench for hours, whipping and thrashing us, down to compelling us to wear monkey caps and parade through the long veranda that stretched from one end of the school to the other, in front of all the ten classes. I could not bear such treatment, and finally one day after about a year I quit the school and began to take private tuition.[15] In those days the national anthem was not sung at schools, perhaps the Prime Minister's anthem was sung (laughter).

My father had wanted to start a sugar mill in *muglan* [a term meaning any foreign land], on the Indian side of the border. Funds were collected, and everything was ready, but the Prime Minister, Chandra Shamsher, did not like the idea. Chandra Shamsher probably felt that if the people were allowed to build factories and all that, then they would become rich, and perhaps one day snatch power away from him. He knew that the industrial revolution had led to democracy in Europe, so he was against the idea of industrial development in Nepal. Even if the sugar mill was in India rather than Nepal, that was also not acceptable, because he thought it would attract still more Nepalis to India, where they would get bad ideas. So he was against Nepalese going to India for these purposes. The sugar mill that my father had planned was built and is still there. I understand it runs at a profit.

Another story illustrates Chandra Shamsher's character. When I was in my late teens in Kathmandu, we had an old grandfather's clock; it was running smoothly, but one day it broke down—something to do with the hands. I was trying to fix it, but my father stopped me, saying, 'if Chandra Shamsher finds out about it he will hang you.' He did not want people engaged in technical work which he thought might draw them eventually to politics, where they might start thinking about overthrowing the Ranas.

In Nepal, the Prime Minister could do anything. So his administration ordered my father to come back from Parasi to Kathmandu to work. I was only about four years old then, so I do not remember Parasi. After this assignment he was asked to become a collector again in

---

[15] Tanka Prasad is not exaggerating here. The teacher, an Indian named Amar Bahadur, later taught mathematics to Tanka Prasad's daughter, Meena, at Padma Kanya School (a women's school); she reports that he would tell students to place the text book on their heads and then pound it with a hammer, if they did not understand.

Bara.[16] A District Revenue Collector was a high post then. I was about seven or eight years old at that time; I was very small, and I was carried there in a palanquin. We stayed in Bara for about four years. We had no house of our own there, so we lived in government quarters, which were not so nice.

My father's last assignment was to the post of Bada Hakim [Governor] of Biratnagar. In those days the Bada Hakim had great power; all the District offices of the government fell under his domain, even the judiciary.[17] His salary was Rs 6,600 per year, plus a Rs 400 annual allowance. At that time you could buy sixteen *ser* [one *ser* is approximately two pounds] of rice for Re 1. Sixteen *ser* would last one person about fifteen days. I was about twelve or thirteen then. The house and compound there were big, but we never had electricity or tap water in the Tarai; we drew our water from a well in the compound.

Biratnagar was not as populated then, and there was not much trade. Jungles could be reached within a few miles, and you could hunt there and all. In Biratnagar we even kept two tiger cubs as pets. We used to take them to the market and for walks, on a leash. I was a brave man, you see, I was not even afraid of tigers! What happened was, once one of the cubs pounced upon a goat, and I realized that they were getting wild and dangerous. So we built two cages for them and kept one cage on each side of the gate to the government quarters, where we lived. But Chandra Shamsher was still Prime Minister then, and he claimed the cubs since they were from the jungle, which he claimed all for himself. He sold them to a circus company.

I was very fond of hunting also. I had a small gun, you see. The gun was the type where I could load a cartridge myself. Once I chanced upon a tiger, but the elephant I was on got frightened by the tiger and ran away. It panicked and ran out of control. I was looking for deer and encountered the tiger suddenly. I never had any interest in killing a tiger, which is the king of the forest and harmless, except for man-eaters. I used to like to ride horses and elephants. Although I was a little boy, even then I could drive elephants—very big, very tame.

I usually hunted birds, and I did not intend to eat the birds I shot. In theory, as a Brahmin I should not have killed all those birds and

---

[16] Bara District is in the central Tarai; its largest town is Birganj.

[17] Ama believes that Tika Prasad was the first Brahmin to be appointed to such a high post. Typically, Brahmins served other high Hindu castes as purohits [priests].

animals. But there is a difference between theory and practice. There was this *panditji* [term for a learned Brahmin] preaching from the scripture, and he said that Brahmins should not eat tomatoes. When he went home, his wife said to him, 'You preach in public that tomatoes should not be eaten, but at home you eat tomatoes. What is that?' And the Brahmin said, 'Theory and practice are not the same'.

Regarding my sister, she was about six years older than I was, and being a member of the womenfolk she used to spend more time with my mother. So, naturally, it afforded us ample opportunity to associate with each other and play together. I played with her, since my brother used to go to school every day. She was good and pretty, and looked after me with great care out of affection for me, and also because it was a task my mother entrusted to her. She was married while we were living in Biratnagar. In my later years, also, my sister extended help and assistance whenever I was in need. The assistance my brother-in-law gave me while I was preparing myself for politics will be referred to later on.

My life in Biratnagar lasted for two and a half secure, comfortable, care-free years. But then my father had a quarrel with the Ranas, and we returned to Kathmandu. It was an act of sheer injustice on the part of the then ruling Rana Prime Minister, Chandra Shamsher. I think it would not be out of place here to cite details of the case, which may serve as an instance of how justice was administered during the Rana days.

What happened is that one fine morning when my father was about to leave on an inspection tour of places within his territory, his things all packed and lined up neatly in the ante-room on the ground floor awaiting his departure the following day, he learned that the Chief Revenue Officer of Biratnagar had pocketed a large sum of money. As Bada Hakim my father was responsible for all government offices in Biratnagar, and it was his duty to investigate the case. Naturally, he cancelled his inspection tour for the next day.

My father's investigation proved that the revenue officer was the culprit. When he was interrogated they recovered Rs 400 from him, but he had embezzled a total of Rs 16,000. When this was reported to the Prime Minister, my father was called to Kathmandu. Though rigorously punishable by law, amazingly enough the revenue officer was acquitted. As Bada Hakim my father was his supervisor and therefore ultimately responsible, so the Ranas not only fired him but also fined him the amount of the missing funds.[18] The reason for such an act of gross injustice is obvious: the revenue officer was a relative of a high official in the Prime Minister's palace, Kazi Marich Man, so his punishment was merely dismissal from office. The courtier perhaps felt that my father should have hushed up the case and compensated the loss of the government secretly. My father did not know how to curry favour very well with the courtiers.[19] He was an honest, hardworking, and self-respecting man. He relied upon his own sincerity and hoped that if he did the right thing, the virtue of having done so would itself bring him rewards, which was a fallacy. I have also suffered much on account of the same mistaken idea, which I inherited from my father. Men are guided not by their sense of justice, but by their self-interest. Sometimes, when I reflect upon the drift of events in human life, I find myself siding with Thrasymachus rather than with Socrates. Thrasymachus said, 'I define justice and right as what is in the interest of the stronger party'. Another motive that prompted this injustice was perhaps the wish to humiliate my father. The spirit of self-respect among the people generally was considered a crime under the Rana regime. Absolute obsequiousness was the rule.

My father took the injustice bitterly, yet he did not feel humiliated, as injustice can humiliate nobody. Besides, everybody knew he was innocent. He neither waited nor begged for pardon or remission. Instead he busied himself to obtain the money to pay the fine. Although I was only a boy then I knew very well that he was innocent and penalized for the fault of some other official. This struck roots of hatred deep in my heart against the Ranas. That was not the only reason I hated the Ranas, but it was one of the reasons. I hated their injustice.

In order to pay the fine my father had to sell our Kathmandu house in Bishalnagar, which is the first house of our own I remember living in. My father had sold our ancestral home in Gairidhara, near where the Chinese Embassy now stands, and bought our house in Bishalnagar. As I recall the house was quite comfortable, and it was in a good neighbourhood. The house was in the middle of a Nepali aristocratic settlement near the house of Padma Shamsher, who later became one of the Rana Prime Ministers. My father and Padma Shamsher were

---

[18] Many of the details of Tika Prasad's troubles with the Ranas comes from Upadhyay.

[19] Tika Prasad may have been one victim of what Uprety (1992: 50-1) reports as a common practice: the posting of wealthy individuals to positions in the Tarai by the Rana Prime Minister, who would then charge them with 'misappropriation of their authority' and imprison them. Or, it would seem in Tika Prasad's case, fine them.

good friends. I used to play with Padma Shamsher's son when we were small. His name was Narendra, a son by one of his concubines. Padma Shamsher had appointed a teacher for his son. He asked my father to send me to his house to take tuition along with his son. There were two teachers—one taught us English and the other taught math. That way I became friends with his son.

My father had bought a bicycle at the age of fifty—I believe it was called a Humber. But he could not learn to ride it. I asked my father to let me learn to ride the bicycle, but he would not allow it. So I asked Padma Shamsher's son to teach me to ride his bicycle. He let me try it, and I learned to do it in one day. We used to take turns; one would ride while the other would chase after him on foot. Once my father saw me running behind Narendra on the bicycle and became angry. He told me he never wanted me to run along behind him like that again. It hurt his pride to see his son running after a Rana. After I explained to him that we took turns doing this, he permitted me to continue the game.

Our house was big, with twenty rooms. It had a garden and a stable. My father was fond of the garden and horses; we always used to have one or two horses and cows. The house didn't have electricity, which was very rare then. Only Ranas had electricity, not other people, so at night we used kerosene lanterns. Kerosene was available in Kathmandu, carried in on porters' backs from India.[20] Only the big Ranas had internal plumbing, and we had to draw our water from the well, the same way everybody else did. There was no water tap system except at public springs.[21] My father had to sell our whole compound—house, garden, and stable. He also had to sell 20 *ropanis* [about 2.5 acres] of his land in the Tarai. Later Juddha Shamsher pardoned him [*maphi*], and he no longer had to pay back all the money. He sold the Bishalnagar house for Rs 12,000, and the remaining Rs 4,000 he owed was forgiven. We then bought a smaller house near the Black Bridge in Sifale and moved there. It was located on eight *ropanis* of land, but the house was much smaller than our Bishalnagar house.

[20] Before a road connecting Kathmandu to the Tarai was completed in the late 1950s, any goods not made locally had to be carried by porters. Tuker (1957:211) reports that it took 120 porters eight days to carry a car over the Chandragiri Pass to Kathmandu from Bhimphedi, in the Tarai (unladen, one long day's march). His estimate of the automobile population of Kathmandu during Prime Minister Juddha's time is 400.

[21] Stone washing and bathing areas for public use have been built around many of the natural springs in the Kathmandu Valley.

In the beginning I did not like the new house, because it was located in an obscure quarter of town and had not the same open frontier and perspective as our former house had. Besides, it was a disappointing and humiliating experience to be forced to move there. But one thing happened to help dispel the gloom and rancor that had set in my consciousness since we had to sell our Bishalnagar house: I had a girl friend. In our Hindu society we could not really meet, except openly on the streets. We could only look at each other and smile. She was from our new neighbourhood, in Sifale. She was pretty and handsome. I wrote a poem about her. Owing to this new event in my life I began liking the house and its environment. I should say: as I embarked upon this novel enterprise, everything began to look bright, even the dark nights that hide. The spring looked nice and the summer likewise; every season spelled something that added delight; I did not know whether it was due to Aphrodite. Strangely enough, the whole mode of my perception was changed; even the dross began to look lovely—such is the power of love.

It was a tremendously exhilarating experience. But alas! not long after I had taken this path of peace and promise (promise in the sense that it opened the prospect of a heavenly life, as I then hoped) my father arranged my marriage with a Brahmin girl whom I had never seen. I was not willing to enter the relationship, but it was impossible to resist the wishes of parents in those days. Marriage to my girlfriend was out of the question, since she belonged to the Chhetri caste, while I was a Brahmin. The marriage my father arranged took place, and the love-affair ended then and there. The girl, being sensible enough to understand the situation and also being a member of a respectable family, completely avoided any further contact. When I went to jail I heard that she had married.

My parents arranged my marriage, of course. My father went to the girl's house and decided then and there. I had no idea what she was like. In my case I always liked her. When we were married, she was eleven years old and I was seventeen. She did not know how to make love with me. We slept in the same room together, but she was shy and would go over to the wall to sleep, and I would have to coax her to move nearer to me. She has turned out to be very, very helpful.

She was very interested to learn to read and write English, since she already knew Nepali, so I gave her homework to do in the morning, and she would have it all done in the evening. In this way I taught her some English, but not much. It's not that I didn't care, it's just that I had no time because of this damn politics. But I stopped teaching her because it was becoming a harassment. I regret now that I did not spend enough time to teach her more. If she had gone on becoming more educated she might have ended up even more useful for helping me in my work.

Even when I was in prison, she was working for me. Nobody's written anything about this lady, but she has made great sacrifices—to the husband living in jail and sentenced for life! Outside she remained true to me and supported me. She provided food for me on a weekly basis, out of her own money. And many other things she also did. She went to India and met with Jaya Prakash Narayan and even Prime Minister Nehru, and also Bisheswor Prasad Koirala,[22] and all that. The Nepalese rebels had become somewhat inactive, and she activated them. If you compare the sacrifices I have made and those she has made, she has made greater sacrifices. Somebody should write about her too. She must get credit for what she has done.

Political Awakening

My father, having been given the sack by the Ranas, was jobless for a long time and suffering serious financial problems. He and I therefore left for the Tarai to look for a way to earn some money. When he had been Hakim Saheb [informal title 'boss sahib' for any superior, in this case Chief Revenue Officer] in Bara he had become friendly with a man named Mohan Bikram Shah, who was noted for his generosity and kindness. Thinking that he might help us in our time of trouble, we visited him on his farm in a place called Barewa, near Kalaiya. It was near a jungle called Mahua Daha.

When we arrived we found that Mohan Bikram had gone hunting, and after a while a pleasant looking youth, riding an elephant, welcomed us and guided us to Mohan Bikram's camp site. He was the manager of the farm. In the evening, after Mohan Bikram had returned from his day's hunting, he and my father left this young man and me to ourselves. We talked about all sorts of things and became friendly. Later on, the more we talked the more we discovered that we had

---

[22] Jaya Prakash Narayan was leader of the Socialist Party in India. B. P. Koirala was a leader of the Congress Party and instrumental in its efforts to overthrow the Ranas; in 1959 he became the first popularly elected Prime Minister (see Appendix 2).

much in common, and we became the best of friends. We discussed human rights, democracy, industrial and educational revolutions, and the Indian independence movement. He was older than I was, had witnessed the Indian independence movement, and had precise ideas where mine were vague. We concluded that the autocratic Rana regime should be abolished.

That pleasant, easy-going youth was Dasarath Chand. He was a Thakuri from Baitadi.[23] He looked very striking in his white *khaki kurtha*,[24] a waistcoat like Pandit Nehru's,[25] and dark glasses. Whenever he smiled, his smile would begin very slowly from his lips, and after it was full would just as slowly leave them. He was devoid of selfishness and pride. He had an easy-going manner which made it hard not to like him.

After studying in Banaras he had enrolled in Tri-Chandra College [in Kathmandu]. The Commander-in-Chief, Rudra Shamsher, had gotten to know Dasarath and invited him to stay in a room above the stable in his compound during Dasarath's second year of studies. He admired the handsome, educated Thakuri from the far west and considered him a potential marriage partner for his daughter, Juliana. Bahadur Shamsher [son of Prime Minister Juddha Shamsher] had similar ideas, but before he could act on them Dasarath Chand and Juliana had fallen in love. In 1934 Rudra Shamsher was driven away from Kathmandu, and Dasarath went to live in Palpa, where he met Mohan Bikram, who offered him the job managing his farm.[26]

Meanwhile my father and Mohan Bikram decided that my father should open two hotels: one in Bhimphedi, which would also provide horses for people travelling to and from Kathmandu, and one in Thankot.[27] Mohan Bikram gave my father some of his best horses and

---

[23] Thakuri is a high Nepalese Hindu caste, usually regarded as a sub-caste of the Chhetris, ranked below only the Brahmins; the royal family are Thakuris. Baitadi is in far-west Nepal.

[24] Long-sleeved, almost knee-length men's pullover, open-throat shirt.

[25] Leader of the Indian independence movement and first Prime Minister of independent India.

[26] Rudra Shamsher, who was next in line on the 'roll' of potential Prime Ministers, was one of several C-class Ranas Juddha successfully purged in an intra-Rana family feud; he was exiled to Palpa, in west Nepal, where Dasarath apparently accompanied him (for details, see Shah 1990:86-101). It is tempting to speculate how history might have turned out if Rudra had become Prime Minister and if Dasarath had married his daughter.

[27] Before the road from Kathmandu to the Tarai was built in the late 1950s, all travellers to the capital had to walk from the jumping-off point in the Tarai, Bhimphedi, to Thankot, a village on the south-western side of the Kathmandu Valley, connected to Kathmandu

some financial support. The next year my father opened his one-story wooden hotel in Bhimphedi. His concubine, Indumati, accompanied him there, while the rest of us stayed in Kathmandu.

Having nothing much to do after my marriage, I started reading novels. I could not read novels written in English then, as I did not yet know the language well, so I read Hindi novels. In those days, good works or novels written in Hindi were few and far between, yet I read all that came my way: romantic, detective, historical, all sorts including all the volumes of the *Mysteries of London*.[28] I used to go to friends in search of such books.

In one of my quests I came across the life of Napoleon Bonaparte in Hindi. The story of Bonaparte fascinated me so much that I read the book several times. I found the story far more interesting than those written from imagination. The exploits of Bonaparte surpassed any fiction. Later, I thought of enlisting in the army, and underwent a training-course in physical exercise, but being short in stature (I am only 5'2"), I ultimately gave up the idea. From that time on I left off reading novels. The Napoleon book acquainted me with the French Revolution and its figures, and the great French authors. I was not satisfied with what little I found in the book. I wished to be more acquainted with the western world, and for that I had to learn English.

In Kathmandu my sister's husband, Ram Nath Sharma, helped me. My brother-in-law had been a student at Banaras Hindu University and knew English well. I requested him to give me lessons; he very willingly complied, and showed all earnestness to make me capable of reading books in English as soon as possible. Not only that, but he himself was interested in politics, and finding my own inclination also in that direction, he enlightened me with all that he knew. So he particularly taught me about two things: one was English, and the other was the Indian independence movement, which he was personally interested in. In a way he was my teacher in politics. He died early, at about the age of forty or forty-five. He contracted Black Fever when he went to Biratnagar, and died of that.

I laboured night and day, and my progress was rapid. In two years I became capable of reading newspapers and understanding their contents, which had been a cherished wish of mine. The movement for

---

by a motorable road.

[28] The *Mysteries of London* was a four volume series of mystery books by G. W. Reynolds.

independence in India was in full swing, and it was very interesting to read the Indian newspapers. There were four newspapers available then—*Amrita Bazaar Patrika*, *The Statesman*, *The Pioneer*, and *Vishwamitra*. There was no newspaper stand in Kathmandu. You had to order the newspapers by mail directly from the publisher in India. It used to take about three or four days, but it was refreshing to be able to read the news. Newspapers talked about the Indian independence movement, and I thought how it would be nice to have some kind of parallel movement in Nepal, too. Some Ranas seemed to support the Indian movement, but it wasn't real support. The Ranas themselves were not prepared to do anything. It was purely out of courtesy and self-interest that they acted pleased to hear about the Indian movement. That was their character, you see, not taking any risk. They tried to take advantage of any situation. For example, Chandra Shamsher [Prime Minister, 1901-29] maintained good relations with the British, but also made donations to Banaras Hindu University. But Juddha gave the independence movement no support at all. Later, he was enraged that Sukraraj Shastri had even visited Gandhiji.[29]

My mind was preoccupied with politics; I bought many books, and borrowed others. As I read, I came to realize the might of the British Empire. They were the masters of India and had some command over Nepal, too. They could dismiss even Kings as, for instance, they did in Afghanistan, at that time. Amanulla ruled, but he was overthrown by Bachha Sakkha with the help of the British. I felt bitter about that. That was why I became more interested in world politics and began to study more and more. I used to study mainly revolutionary books by Voltaire, Rousseau, Marx, Lenin, Thomas Paine, Napoleon, and others. Thomas Paine was famous at that time. He had written that if a land tax is managed properly, other taxes could be abolished. I read many other revolutionary works. We smuggled them from India, since such books were banned in Nepal, and would then share them with each other. We smuggled things via the Chandragiri Pass above Thankot.

Another of my favourite authors was Bernard Shaw. In *Arms and the Man*, Shaw said that hell is itself a fine place which people don't want to leave—that is America! One cannot claim to be an educated person without reading Shaw. I also liked H.G. Wells, and so many

---

[29] At his trial, Juddha Shamsher pointed at Sukraraj and said, *ta Gandhiji lai bhetna gaeko!* [you (using the lowest form of the pronoun) went to visit Gandhiji!].

other authors.[30] Bertrand Russell is also a very good writer. It is no wonder he got the Nobel Prize. I have read most of the books that are here in our house.

One particular book that I would like to mention here is the British history by Warner and Martin. At one level the book is just like any other history book, but when one starts to read it one finds many instances of revolutionary actions and self-sacrifice by the people and for the people. It influenced me greatly, particularly because we were familiar with only the British civilization at that time. I liked reading about King John and King Charles. The book explained that in all of British history, it was not just the king who was ruling. He was there, but the real rulers were others. And how the Industrial Revolution took place and how that Industrial Revolution brought about a democratic set-up and what is the meaning of democracy. All this is clearly explained in that book. The so-called liberal democracy is a political ideology of the bourgeoisie, according to my conception. I used to share books with my friends, and this book gave many of us inspiration. I still have that book.[31]

The only job I ever had outside of politics was as a bank clerk in Nepal Bank Ltd. My father recommended me to the manager, who hired me. I went to the office for only two or three days. Then I stopped going because I was already engaged in underground political activity and had no interest in such a job. So they just brought my salary—Rs 20 or 30 per month, I forget exactly how much—to my house every month anyway. I had the job for only about three months.

---

[30] Tanka Prasad kept his heavily underlined and badly dog-eared copy of Wells' *Outline of History* near him even late in life. Meena reports that if she borrowed it for only a couple of days her father would become testy and demand its return.

[31] Tanka Prasad retains his general admiration for things English. In a published interview after promulgation of the new constitution in November 1990, he indicated his general approval of the document, adding that he hoped the behaviour of Nepal's parliamentary representatives would measure up to the standards of the English.

Chapter 5

From Yageswari to Rewanta Kumari
Rewanta Kumari's Childhood and Marriage

I was born in the Thamel area of Kathmandu. I don't remember exactly which year I was born in. I only remember the month, because every year on your birthday you are supposed to make a donation to a Brahmin, such as your *purohit* (family priest), do *pujas*, etc. Therefore you remember the month, since it is the same every year; but there is no particular reason to remember the year. I know how old I am because I'm reminded of it every birthday, and then I remember my age for that year. Since I am seventy-one years old now, when was I born? It is now 2042 according to the *Bikram* calendar, so I must have been born in BS 1975. I can't tell you the exact date either, but it can be calculated from the *tithi*[1] of the lunar calendar. I believe it's the third of *Ashad*. The *purohit* knows all these things, such as my birth year, from my *china*,[2] and he calculates the exact day from the lunar calendar. He reminds me when my birthday is, and I do the *pujas* then. I remember that I was born on a Monday, although that fact has no significance, but not what year I was born.

The house I was born in is still standing. Some of my uncles' families, that is, the families of my father's brothers, are still living there. My father was the oldest of six brothers. The house was the joint property of my grandparents and their six sons, and ownership passed to those sons. When I was growing up the household was quite large, what with the families of all the six brothers being there. Then there were my grandparents too. I grew up in a household of twenty-five to twenty-six people, living in thirteen rooms.

[1] There are two, two-week *tithis* in the lunar calendar, one a period of waxing (*Sukla Pakshya*) and one a period of waning (*Krishna Pakshya*).

[2] See Chapter 4, footnote 5.

When my father and his brothers had all died, it was difficult to carry on the joint family. There was too little space for so many people. Everyone wanted their own place with their own kitchen, their own privacy to avoid quarrels, etc., so in the next generation, my generation, they all split up. My father had only one son, and my brother doesn't stay in that house anymore. Only the families of the children of my second uncle are still there. The children of the other uncles have all moved away. The third uncle's son has moved to Bombay, another brother's family is near the Ring Road. Others are nearby here in Baneshwor.

In all, my parents had ten children. My mother and father were each one of thirteen children, so ten wasn't so many. In those days you needed many children, because you didn't know whether they would live or not. My parents' first child was a daughter, but she died when she was very young, only two. I was the second child. Then there were seven more daughters after me, out of which only the youngest (born in 1934) survived. One of my other sisters died at the age of 11 months, and one died at a year and a half. They all just got sick and died, and we never knew exactly why. I don't know about any of the remaining sisters, except that one of them died when she was eight, just after I had gotten married. I used to play with her a lot, and I loved her very much. I was sad when she died. I also have a brother, who was born in 1939. There are eighteen years difference between me and my only surviving younger sister, Radha, which seems like a long time. So, out of the ten children, only three grew to adulthood, and all three of us are still alive. My father died on the 16th *Magh*, BS 2016 [29 January, 1960 AD], sixteen days after the birth of my last child. My mother died much later, in 1970.

I lived in that Thamel house until I was married off, and even after that I used to frequently visit the house. It was still a joint household when I was married off; it was partitioned only after the earthquake in 1934. My brother used to live there until 1975, so I continued going there often even after my parents had died.

Even now I still go there sometimes, when they invite me on special occasions. Although none of my uncles are alive now, my fourth uncle's wife is still alive and still there, and my second and fifth uncles' wives died only recently. They invite me, and once in a while I go.

Our house was, and still is, an old-style house, not like the one I live in now. It has a tiled roof and is three stories tall. We didn't have indoor plumbing, and we had to go to a public tap to fill our *gagros.*[3]The tap was about five or six blocks away. Sometimes I would fetch water, but others would also, including servants. I also had to take a bath at the outside tap, which was pretty uncomfortable during the winter months. We had no electricity; common people weren't allowed to have electricity, only the Ranas. We used kerosene lamps for light at night, just a simple wick lamp. We had a petromax [a kerosene pressure lantern], but didn't use it much because it used so much kerosene, which was quite expensive. All our cooking was done on a wood-fired mud *chulo* [cooking hearth].

To keep a proper kitchen we were supposed to wear clean clothes. That is, we were supposed to bathe before cooking, then put on clean clothes that had to be washed daily. We were supposed to wear only a sari, or you could call it a *dhoti* [plain cotton sari worn inside the house; men also wear *dhotis*]. Our kitchen was on the top floor. Some people in those days had a kitchen on the ground floor, but it was easier to keep children and dogs and cats out if it was on the top floor. There was also a place to wash the dishes and cooking pots with water which had to be carried from below.

The boundary of the kitchen was marked by a slightly raised platform, beyond which children couldn't cross, until after the sacred thread ceremony (*bartaman*) for the boys, or marriage for the girls, because neither observed caste rules until then. So I didn't really go into my own family's kitchen until after my marriage. There were also servants to help with the household tasks. Formerly all of us cooked and ate in one room on the top floor. Then more *chulos* were built on the top floor, when the brothers started eating in separate kitchens. There were one or two servants for each of the brothers and their families when they cooked their own food.

I only learned how to cook after I was married, in Bua's house. Young girls weren't expected to know how to cook until they married and lived in their husband's house. I was married at eleven, and once when I was twelve I had trouble lifting a pot of *dal* from the fire, so that it spilled and burned my legs. After I was married, when I went to my *maiti*[4] for a visit I would help cook for my parents.

The house is near that new hotel, the Kathmandu Lodge I believe it's called. There are so many foreigners in Thamel nowadays—lots

---

[3] A *gagro* is a narrow-necked earthenware (or *gagri* if metal) container used for carrying and storing water in the Kathmandu Valley.

[4] *Maiti* is an extremely important concept in Nepalese family organization; it refers to the wife's natal home, with which she maintains important links after marriage.

and lots of them. Our house is now surrounded all around by new buildings; formerly it was clearly visible, but now you can barely see it from the main street.

When I was a little girl growing up, they used to say that daughters shouldn't go out, daughters shouldn't study, etc. From a very early age, daughters were supposed to stay indoors or close by, and we were scolded if we stayed in the presence of a male visitor for a long time. We didn't play much outside. We used to go see friends in the neighboring houses, that's all. I didn't mind the restrictions and didn't blame society. I just took it all for granted. I had no regrets about it. I just played in our own yard, or with the kids next door. Boys and girls all played together when we were little.

But I did play a lot. I didn't have any studying to do, so what else do you do except play? If you had younger brothers and sisters, you played with them and looked after them, that was the household work we were assigned. We played all sorts of things. We played with dolls, played at cooking. Sometimes we married dolls, sometimes we played dancing, sometimes this, sometimes that. All sorts of things. We played marbles, we played hide-and-seek in the different rooms of the house, we played *paya* [a kind of gambling game], but we gambled with pieces of broken bangles, not money. Later too I gambled for money, when I went back to my *maiti* for festivals, like Dasai. I had no brothers or sisters close to me in age. The closest people in age to me were two of my aunts, my father's younger sisters. After my marriage I was best of friends with my *taili ama* (the wife of my fourth uncle) and my *sainli ama* (the wife of my third uncle). Both called me *manche* [man], and I called *taili ama manche* too (I called *sainli ama sainli ama*). That is how we addressed each other because it was awkward for us to call each other 'mother' and 'daughter', since they were my age. We also used *timi* to address each other. My youngest uncle was much younger than I. I used to carry him around when he was a baby, and I called him *babu*, not *kanchha ba* [youngest paternal uncle]. As long as he lived I always called him babu.

Once my mother's brother and I were at his house, my *mamaghar* [mother's brother's house]. We were about the same age, and we were the best of friends. We were sitting together by the window on the second floor. There were some pickled foods on the window sill, which had been put there to cook in the sun. We both decided to steal some of those pickles. My mother's brother urged me to be quick and pushed me, with the result that I fell out the window all the way down to the ground, from the second storey. I didn't have any external injury, except that the back of my skull was swollen, but I was unconscious for 24 hours. I was about five or six years old at the time, and ever since then I've been able to hear very little in my right ear. Actually, at the time I could hear alright in my left ear, and I didn't realize my right ear was gone. Long afterwards, when Bua became Home Minister, I began getting pains in my right ear. The doctor told me my right ear was not functioning properly. I think the ear drum had collapsed. He said that if my parents had taken care of it at the time I fell it could have been fixed, but that now it was too late. When I got still older, I began to lose the hearing in my left ear; I tried different hearing aids in my left ear for a long time, but the kind I have now works better than any that I had before.

Once when I was little my mother's brother and I were carried in a *kharpan* [5] to his house during Tihar [or Laxmi puja, the festival of lights, occurring shortly after Dasai, emphasizing worship of Laxmi, goddess of wealth]. They were doing their *kuldeuta puja* [worship of their household god] at Bhaimal, near where the airport is now. Lots of cows grazed there. They had sacrificed a goat and roasted it, and to balance the load they put one portion of the cooked goat meat in each side. But by the time we had returned home there was no meat left!

My mother's *maiti* was in Kathmandu itself, in Maha Boudha. It's a place near New Road, behind Bir Hospital. My mother didn't know Newari [Tibeto-Burmese language spoken by Newars, indigenous people of the Kathmandu Valley]. Daughters weren't allowed to go out much then, so she didn't mix with the neighborhood kids. She just played in her own courtyard, and didn't learn Newari. My grandmother, my first uncle's wife, my other aunts (my father's sisters), and I knew Newari. My father also knew Newari, but my mother, even though she grew up around a lot of Newars, never learned the language.

Some of my friends were Newars, so I picked up the language from them, and I learned to speak Newari very fluently. When I was little I was allowed more freedom and learned it by playing with other kids. I have forgotten most of it now, although I can still speak it a little. I also know Hindi. I learned it just by reading Hindi books. It has a lot of similarities to Nepali, so if you work at it it comes pretty easily.

[5] A *kharpan* refers to the characteristic Newari method of carrying two equally-balanced loads suspended from each end of a pole borne across the shoulders.

Education

I didn't go to school, but I was taught a few things at home. I learned to read Nepali at home. When I was little, my grandfather and father taught me to read and write Nepali. My father didn't have much land. He was a *pandit* [scholar or learned man; used loosely to refer to any Brahmin man] of Sanskrit and used to teach in a Sanskrit school. He taught Nepali and Sanskrit there. I learned a little Sanskrit from him, but I don't know very much of it. In my natal home I just learned to read Nepali a little, write it a little, and count up to a hundred. Then I was married off.

I had a great wish to learn, but I only managed to learn how to read and write Nepali before I was married. When I first got married, I was just a kid, not interested in much besides playing. But later I developed a strong desire to study. I asked my husband so many times to teach me, but he taught me only a little bit. When I was seventeen or eighteen, I begged him to teach me English. I used to obstinately insist on learning. Once in a while he would write down a few things in English for me to learn. He would give me my homework in the morning, and I would be ready with it, all done, by evening. For nineteen or twenty days he did this, and then he didn't want to do it anymore. He taught me the English alphabet. I learned the A-B-C-D's[6] from him, so the little bit of English I know is because of him. I wish he would have taught me more. Since I was not very educated, he thought I could not learn and, therefore, didn't teach me much. Maybe if he had believed that I could learn, he would have taught me, but he was already so heavily involved in politics then. I never had a chance to study properly.

At that time there were so few educated people. When my uncle and one of his friends who had studied Ayurvedic medicine [traditional herbal medicine], and another two friends who had studied English, arrived back in Thankot from Banaras Hindu University, Prime Minister Chandra Shamsher sent some people to welcome them back with honours and presented them with an expensive *doshala* [shawl]. When I was married, my second uncle could not be present at the wedding because he was taking his I.A. [Intermediate Arts, taken after two years of study] exams in India. When my fourth uncle was twenty-eight, he

---

[6] The normal Nepali phraseology Ama uses here—referring to the A-B-C-D's rather than the A-B-C's—is modelled on the Nepali equivalent: the Ka-Kha-Ga-Gha's.

died of TB, but later on my grandfather decided he had died not because of disease, but because he had studied English [new things were considered inauspicious], so after that nobody else in the family was allowed to study English. In general, nobody in my family was very educated in English. They were mostly *pandits* of Sanskrit.

My grandmother was against the idea of my learning to read and write. She was illiterate herself, and she thought I might run off and elope with someone if I were educated, and that would disgrace the family. She even got angry at my uncles' wives for reading such books as the *Ramayana* and the *Mahabharata*. But my grandfather argued that in order to take care of a house a woman should know at least a little bit of mathematics, and he taught me simple arithmetic. Since he was quite encouraging I had more scope than most girls my age. But I never had a chance for a formal education.

When I was about eight or nine years old, Chandra Kanta, Sukra Raj Shastri's younger sister,[7] opened a girls' school with the approval of the government. I went there quite often—not to learn to read and write, which I already knew how to do, but to do needle-work.

Afterwards, when I was staying with my parents in Thamel while *Bua* was in prison, I used to teach a handful of neighbourhood kids; I taught them the Nepali alphabet. Later on I did the same thing in Janakpur in the Tarai, seven miles from my father-in-law's place in the village of Sirsia. I had rented a small room in Janakpur, where I lived with my daughters, Meena and Shanta. Congress had an office across the Indian border, in Jaynagar, but they couldn't open an office in Janakpur, so I rented a house there which informally served as a Congress [the political party organizing to overthrow the Ranas] office. They asked me to start a Mahile Sangathan [women's organization]. For outward appearances I was there to put Meena and Shanta in school. People were put in jail nearby in Jaleshwar, the District headquarters for Mahottari District. Their relatives used to come to see them, that's where I met some of those political people. In the evenings I gathered the neighbourhood children to our house and taught them whatever I knew, along with Meena and Shanta. It was just a voluntary service.

When I was little nobody would send girls to school. They used to say that you shouldn't send a daughter to school. For one thing

[7] Sukra Raj Shastri is one of the four martyrs executed by the Rana Government; see Chapter 6.

there were no schools just for girls (Chandra Kanta's was the first), and people were reluctant to send their girls to school with boys—they might run away with some boy and bring disgrace on the family. So, it was easier not to send them to school than to take this risk. If we went out we wore a *bhoto-suruwal* [double-breasted blouse and baggy pants tight at the ankles] and covered ourselves with a shawl. We wore the *suruwal* because girls were not supposed to show their legs, and we wore the shawl to cover our breasts. The outfit was somewhat like the *punjabi* clothes [pants covered by a knee-length shirt] worn by girls today.

Nevertheless, I have read a lot, little by little. By my own effort I started reading Hindi books. I barely know English, just names here and there. I can read the headings in the newspapers, that's all, nothing else. But I read Hindi and Nepali books and newspapers.

I read anything that comes in sight. I have read story books, the *Mahabharata*, the *Ramayana*, *Krishna Charitra*, the *Bhagvat Purana*. I have read the autobiography of Gandhi, the autobiography of Nehru and his letters from prison, the autobiography of President Rajendra Prasad, and Hindi or Nepali translations of the great authors, such as Tolstoy, Gorki, Shakespeare, plus whatever philosophy and literature I happen to come across.

I haven't read more about other countries and other subjects, because most of the time those books are in English, and I can't read English. But whatever I can find written in Hindi or in Nepali, I read. History or whatever else it may be, I read.

With my own children it's been different. I sent all my daughters to school.

Marriage and Married Life

I was married off when I was eleven years old. It was arranged in a very short time by my father, my mother, grandfather and grandmother, everybody. I never met my husband before my marriage. At such a young age, what do you know anyway? When you are ten or eleven, you don't even know what marriage is all about. So, what are you supposed to feel? Sadness, happiness, or what? I don't remember how I felt when I came to the Acharya household. All the girls were getting married, so I wasn't scared. I didn't know what it was. All I knew was that you went to another house to live.

I was a little kid then, so of course I cried when I left home. After all, I was brought to a new house where I did not know anybody. I didn't have too much work to do, since there were already a couple of cooks there. They always treated me well. My mother-in-law was sick, but my second mother-in-law[8] also treated me very well. I didn't know anything. Who? Where? What? It's difficult to say what I felt.

My name was changed when I got married. When I was little, everyone used to call me Magarni. It seems that I used to be very chubby and looked like a Gurung or Magar [two of the many Tibeto-Burman, mongoloid groups living all over the hills of Nepal] when I was little. So, they used to call me Magarni. My grandfather [father's father] gave me my official name. He was the head of the household and gave names to all his sons' children. My real name written on my birth *china* is Yageswari.

In my horoscope the constellation that went with my name, it seems, was *Jesth* (Scorpio) constellation. This constellation was believed to bring disaster to one's older siblings. *Bua*'s sister-in-law, his older brother's wife, had the same Scorpio constellation. My *jethaju* [husband's older brother] died after his marriage, and at that time they said it was because of his wife's Scorpio constellation. So to prevent something like this from happening again, they changed my name at the time of my marriage. My grandfather was confident that although I had the same constellation as Bua's brother's wife, nevertheless it would surely bring no harm on those in the household I had married into, since my only older sibling had died before my birth. Even then, just to avoid any suspicion of possible disaster, my name was changed and my *china* was forged. So I had two *chinas*, one accurate and one faked. The groom's side didn't know about it; Bua heard about it only much later. My name before marriage was Yageswari, but when I was married off they changed it to Rewanta Kumari.

Not everyone had their names changed at marriage. You had to first take the *chinas* of both the boy and the girl to an astrologer and have the astrologer see whether things matched or not—constellations, planets, etc. In our case, there were thirty-two points, out of which twenty-eight were compatible, and four were incompatible. It

[8] Tanka Prasad's father had two wives simultaneously and three concubines serially. Tanka Prasad was the son of his 'first mother'. Since the two wives got along well with each other and were both 'mother' to him (see Chapter 4), I refer to the second wife as 'second mother' or 'second mother-in-law' rather than 'step-mother', with its less affectionate connotations.

didn't matter if only about three or four points didn't match. That's why my constellation and name was changed.

At home—my new home, that is, not the *maiti* I had come from—they formally called me by my new name, Rewanta Kumari, but the term used to address me was *sano dulahi* [little bride], to distinguish me from my older sister-in-law, *sainli nani* [third little girl; she probably had been sainli before marriage]. Mithi [a household servant for 40 years] still calls me *dulahi* [bride]. In my *maiti* they still called me by my old name. These days, nobody really calls me by any name, whether here, in my *maiti*, or anywhere else. People call me either mother [Ama], or sister, or grandmother, or, in Mithi's case, bride, or something like that [Nepalese often address others—even strangers—by kinship terms, whether fictive or authentic]. Nobody calls me either Rewanta Kumari or Yageswari anymore.

I didn't feel anything about the name change then; I didn't know anything about it. I didn't know anything about anything. I was 11 years old when I got married. My parents did everything that was necessary. I found out only later about what had been done. At the time of my marriage I didn't know anything.

After I was married off I lived at my husband's house. I only rarely went back to my *maiti* to stay with my parents. I needed *Bua*'s permission to go to my *maiti*, but if I asked him he would say to ask his father. When I asked his father he would say to ask my mother-in-law, and when I asked her she would say to ask *Bua*, etc. In this way they gave me the runaround and made it hard for me to go. I was needed there since I was the only child in the house, and they liked having the presence of a child.

But during the first *Purushotam* month[9] after your marriage you can't stay with your husband; that occurred during the first year I was married, so I spent that time at my *maiti*. Also during the month of *Shrawan* [July-August], the first time it occurs after your marriage, you can't drink from the same tap as your husband, so I went to my *maiti* then too. Then during *Jesth* [May-June], you can't drink from the same tap as your husband's older brother, so then too I went to my *maiti*. The same restriction applies during *Bhadra* [August-September] to drinking water from the same tap your father-in-law drinks from, so I spent that month at my *maiti* too. On the other hand, during *Chaitra* [March-April]

[9] The *Purushotam* month is the extra 'leap' month added every three years to the lunar calendar.

you can't drink water from the same tap as your parents, so at that time you cannot visit your *maiti* at all. After these occasions I would go to my *maiti* only occasionally.[10]

After marriage, they put Bua and me up in the same room. I slept in my husband's room, they let the two of us sleep together. My menses began when I was 14, I had a miscarriage when I was about 16, and I gave birth to my first child when I was 19. I was sexually active before my menses began. Men don't have enough patience to wait.

After we had been married for three or four months his mother became bed-ridden, and so I went to sleep in her room, to help take care of her. During the night she would moan and groan, or ask for help, because she was sick. Although I heard her and knew she was in distress, instead of getting up and helping her, I would pretend I had not heard her and turn over on my side and go back to sleep. Now I regret not taking better care of her, but I wonder how they could entrust the care of a sick old woman to me, when I was only a child and a newcomer to the family.

She died a year after we got married. She had been ill even when our wedding took place. In fact she had been complaining about how she would not be able to see her son's wedding and a daughter-in-law. That is why my marriage was arranged and over within a week. And then a year later she died.

Domestic Difficulties

When I was married, Bua's sister's daughter, Mana, was two and a half years old, and she was left with us because her mother was pregnant again. So I took care of her, and neighbourhood boys also played games with us, such as hide- and-seek. Once we were playing dolls, which in those days were made from china. One day Bua came and broke them all one by one, because he thought I was too old to be playing with such things. I was very annoyed but I didn't cry, although his sister's daughter was very upset and cried a lot.[11]

[10] A woman always gives birth in her husband's house and must stay there through the naming ceremony on the eleventh day, after which she normally pays a visit to her *maiti*.

[11] Much later Mana married, and her husband went to Calcutta to study. Her husband's family wrote that she was no good, etc., which distracted him. When he came back, he brought another wife with him, so Mana had to leave; her husband and the second wife went to the U.S., where they have remained.

Once about three or four years after I got married I was late getting up in the morning. To make matters worse, the servants were all sick or were having their periods, so we were short-handed. The first thing that should be done after getting up in the morning is to sweep out the house. That is because the house should be clean so that the gods can enter it and bless it. But since I was late getting up, I opened the door and found Bua's father sweeping. I was embarrassed and tried to take the broom from him, but he pushed me into a corner and said I should go back to sleep. My second mother-in-law also tried to take over the sweeping, but he pushed her away too. Then I went to cook, but again Bua's father was cooking, so he lifted me in his arms, patted me on the back, like a baby, and told me to go back to sleep. This was his diplomatic way of dealing with my bad behaviour— letting me know that I was remiss in my duties, but not complaining to my *maiti* about me.

When I was married, Bua's father was keeping the second of the three concubines he had. Her name was Ganga. She died the same year his first wife died. After her death he acquired another concubine, Indumati, who was only twenty-two years old. She was nasty and made everybody miserable. She would tell my father-in-law that I had not cooked well, or had stolen things, or talked badly.

Indumati had been an entertainer in a Rana palace belonging to a son of Bir Shamsher [brother of Chandra Shamsher and Juddha Shamsher]. She had lived and worked there for eleven years. She had also trained newcomers. Then she got fired, and was staying at her *maiti*. In the meantime Bua's father sent someone to look for a concubine for him; he found Indumati and brought her to Bua's father.

When I was married I had an eighteen-year old sister-in-law; her husband, Bua's older brother, had already died. She was nasty to me and my mothers-in-law, but made it a point to be on good terms with whatever concubine was there. So she was very friendly with Indumati, the third concubine, but when my father-in-law was in Birganj, she found another concubine and wanted to send her to him there. Indumati found out about it from a letter father-in-law wrote to my sister-in-law, which caused a big fight between Indumati and my sister-in-law. Then Indumati left in a huff and went to my father-in-law. After Indumati left, my sister-in-law went to her *maiti* and stayed there. In 1938 she went to Janakpur with her father, and while on her way back to Kathmandu she died. My father-in-law came to Kathmandu for her mourning. After Indumati left with father-in-law my sister-in-law told us all the stories about Indumati attempting to poison my second mother-in-law. This poisoning attempt took place sometime before 1933, in Kathmandu.

Indumati asked the cook to get some poison, and while the cook was poisoning my second mother-in-law, Indumati would arrange to be away visiting her *maiti,* so she wouldn't be suspected. The cook asked Indumati why she wanted to kill her, and she said it was because the second mother-in-law was the only problem in the house. If she could be gotten rid of, she could run the house the way she wanted to. If Bua and I didn't like it, we would just have to leave, and then she would have the place to herself and could do whatever she wanted. Indumati was very close to Bua's sister-in-law, and I think they might have been co-conspirators, but after they quarrelled the sister-in-law left the house. Bua heard about the poison incident only after he got out of prison and Indumati started visiting us. Bua's father never knew about it. After the incident Indumati went to Birganj to be with Bua's father, and he probably never heard about it.

Indumati used to give us a lot of trouble, creating misunderstandings between us and Bua's father, who would then be angry with us. I was angry with her at those times, but as a daughter-in-law I had to suppress my feelings. My second mother-in-law and I sympathized with each other, but we couldn't complain to Bua's father since he wouldn't have believed us. Nevertheless, many years later we took Indumati in when she had no place to go.

When my sister-in-law's second daughter was born (sometime before 1933), the mother and baby were under a big mosquito net. I made some milk for her, because she didn't have enough. We had no electricity, so I was holding the milk in one hand and a candle in the other. One thread from the net was hanging down, and I thought I could get rid of it just by burning it, but to my surprise the whole net caught fire. Instead of putting down the candle and the milk, we started yelling until Bua and his father came and put out the fire. A *palang* [bed with four legs and a headboard] was a luxury then, so we slept on the floor, on a *charpate* [thick straw mattress], covered by three or four cotton mattresses. The mosquito net was hung from the ceiling. A *khat* [plank raised on legs off the floor] was necessary on the damp ground floor, for anyone sleeping there, such as soldiers who would stay there (there were few barracks then) in exchange for a little help around the house.

After 1933 my father-in-law never came to our house in Sifale to stay. He lived most of the time in the Tarai; at first Indumati didn't go with him. She spoke badly to him about my mother-in-law and me, so when he did stay in Sifale the two of them kept a separate kitchen. Since Indumati was a Chhetri, he couldn't eat any food cooked by her either, so he cooked himself on the balcony. Then they went away together. They came back for Meena's *pasne* [12] for a week or so. He stayed in the Tarai, and bought one hundred *bighas* of land in an auction.

After he left we had a hard time economically. When he left for Sirsia in the Tarai in 1933, he left us no resources to live on. Also Indumati was with us then. But we got food from the eight *ropanis* of land we had by the Sifale house. Sometimes we would cook rice only for Bua, and the rest of us would eat corn and beans (soybeans, black-eyed peas, etc.). When he ate rice, he would ask if there were enough for us; we would show him a covered pot and say it was full of rice, and then when he was finished we would eat whatever we had cooked. When Shankar Mani's [son of Bua's sister] older sister got married, Bua went in one pair of clothes, came back in the evening, and I washed them right away so he could wear them again the next day, because that's all the clothes he had.

At home we wore *chitphuriya sari*, made of very thick cloth. They were worn like a *sari*, but they were very long—about eleven yards long. We wore them without petticoats. The *gaun* [another kind of cloth] *sari* was worn over a *suruwal* [pants], rather than petticoat. Then in about 1933 or 1934, thinner saris came on the market, and that's when we started wearing petticoats. We never wore bras; instead we wore those tie-up blouses, which to some extent serve the same purpose. I started wearing bras and underwear sometime after Bua's father's death, when I was about thirty. This was after I started associating with the Congress people and more modern people. I didn't buy bras but made them myself. I made all my own clothes, and those of my children. We made them all together, with the daughters making their own too when they were old enough. My sons can also do minor sewing.

In 1933 Bua and his father went to Tribeni, between Chitwan and Butwal, where the Gandaki, Narayani, and another small river meet. I was staying with my parents in Thamel when the big earthquake struck in January 1934. Our house was slightly damaged, but the quake

---

[12] *Pasne* is the first feeding of rice; it takes place five months after birth for girls, and six months after birth for boys.

didn't strike all at once, it kept going for a couple of days. We couldn't stay inside the house as long as the tremors lasted, so we stayed under a tent in a neighbour's yard. Our house had no yard where we could put a tent. After that we began to sleep outside on the ground floor veranda. Then they sent me back to Sifale, where everyone stayed in a tent, because there we had plenty of room for it. Bua's sister and her husband and their children also spent many nights under that tent.

Political Awakening

At first I didn't know anything about Bua's political activities. Sometimes he said that one day he would be the Commander-in-Chief, and I would have to come and salute him. When he was writing those pamphlets in the beginning, I didn't know what he was doing. Afterwards he asked me to help write them, but since I couldn't write very well I didn't do it. When they started duplicating the pamphlets on that machine they told me not to tell anyone, but I didn't know what they were doing. He would run the machine under the mosquito net.

I understood about his political activities only after he went to prison, when I started reading about what was going on in India, etc. Before he went to prison, Jeev Raj, Ram Hari, and Chuda Prasad used to come to our house and talk and talk and talk, but I didn't know what they were talking about. Dharma Bhakta and Dasarath Chand also occasionally visited, so I met them too. I never met Sukra Raj Shastri or Ganga Lal.

They hanged Sukra Raj Shastri on 10 *Magh* [Upadhaya's date is 13 *Magh*], and there was a rumour that they would kill Dharma Bhakta on 12 *Magh*. My second mother-in-law's sister, Sanima, who stayed with us, and I took a goat to Dakshin Kali to sacrifice, in the hope it would prevent their killing him. We left two small servant boys overnight in the house when we went. In those days you had to walk there, so it was a two-day trip. We stayed the night at Dakshin Kali, and when we came back the next evening, we saw many people coming by. We asked where they were coming from, and they said they had gone to see where Dharma Bhakta was hanged. The executioners had asked people in that area to close their windows that night. The two boys we had left in the house were very scared. We felt very bad about it.

Once Bua brought some things and put them in a hole which he dug under a *haluabed* [persimmon] tree behind our house. He told me to guard them very carefully, not to let anybody tamper with them. I didn't know it then, but they were three bombs.[13] Later he told me what they were. At Shankar Mani's older sister's marriage, I wanted to stay at Shankar's house, because his sister was my friend. But Bua wouldn't let me, because he wanted me to come back to guard the bombs. When Bua left for Banaras, Ram Hari took the bombs to Godavari and left them with his father's brother's wife, who was very old, saying that they were medicines. They stayed there until everyone was caught; their existence became known after the confessions that came out from the torture. The police went there and wanted to bring the old lady to the police station. She was too old to walk, so they carried her all the way from Godavari to Singha Darbar in an *olinkath* [an open palanquin].

Bua's father told me that when Bua brought the cyclostyle machine to Sirsia he realized that his son was getting involved in politics. My father-in-law asked him not to. He said to Bua, 'I am old and you are my only son, do you want to leave me in tears?' Bua replied, 'All over Nepal there are thousands of fathers crying whose tears I want to wipe'. Instead of staying with his father Bua left Dasarath Chand there to help him look after the land.

When I got married I was less concerned about my husband than I was about the rest of the household, there were so many of them. I gradually got to know them, and this facilitated growth of the affection that developed between us. In an arranged marriage, at first you don't know the other, but slowly you get to know each other. Tanka Prasad treated me like a child at first. All my ambitions and desires were connected with him and his household. In time the interests of his family grew intertwined with mine and a genuine affection developed. That affection [*sambandha*, relationship] is very deep now. These days, in love-marriages people only know each other, not their families, and therefore they have a narrow base for their relationship. Modern young people have love, but not affection.

---

[13] The 'bombs' were four sticks of dynamite for fishing, smuggled from Darjeeling by Dharma Bhakta. Ram Hari told interrogators he had thrown the dynamite in the Dhobi River near his house. He revealed its location when Dasarath Chand asked him to, following intense interrogation about their location.

Chapter 6

The Thousands of Mangoes Have Been Distributed
Tanka Prasad's Early Political Agitation

About the time I met Dasarath Chand I began to hear of others talking against the Ranas, but such conversations took place only within a very closed circle. That was both in the Tarai and in Kathmandu. We talked about how the Ranas were taking away the riches and money of the country to India or other places. They did not care one bit about the welfare of the people. Everywhere I sensed dissatisfaction among the people. The treatment of the Ranas towards the common people was like master and slave. I resented it very much. I thought all men should be treated as equals. I committed myself to Nepalese politics and vowed to overthrow the Ranas and bring a parliamentary system like that of Britain to Nepal.

Chakari was the rule in those days.[1] Talk about *chakari!* All of Kathmandu's gentlemen had to be at the gates of the Rana Prime Minister's palace when he came out. If somebody did not appear there and the Prime Minister noticed him missing, he would want to know why he wasn't there and what he was doing. People were scared! These gentlemen would sit on the wall around Bhadra Kali,[2] and as the Prime Minister passed by, the Chhetris and Newars would salute and say *salam*, while the Brahmins would extend both hands forward, palms up, and say

---

[1] *Chakari*, a form of ritualized obsequiousness, inscribed on peoples' bodies and postures, consists of bowing and scraping and excessive, insincere flattery by lower, less powerful individuals towards someone of higher rank or greater power.

[2] A shrine to the goddess Kali, near Singha Durbar, a 1,000 room palace which was the private residence of the Rana Prime Ministers, and now serves as the seat of the government.

swasti.[3] Then after he returned to his palace they would return home. That was how it was—*chakari.*

Things like *chakari,* and the sheer injustice of Rana rule, drove me to want to overthrow them. The Ranas were autocratic; they considered the common people as sub-human and treated us accordingly—that included even aristocrats and semi-aristocratic people like us. Their attitude infuriated me. No one was happy with the Ranas' treatment. I was of a recalcitrant bent of mind, and I refused to accept whatever was said and done. I thought, something different must be done, and I acted on that belief. Here the question of courage came in. God gave me the necessary courage to go against the Ranas [laughter]. My father had some inkling about my political mind and activities. He tried to dissuade me from politics. But I did not heed his advice and came to Kathmandu.

A few months after meeting Dasarath Chand for the first time, we met again in Kathmandu. We were taking a stroll along the road in front of Phora Darbar when we saw an elegant, graceful, powerfully built man in typical Nepalese dress walking towards the palace in our direction on the other side of the street. He was an athlete who Dasarath Chand knew. Dasarath asked me to wait for him there, and he went to meet that athlete and chatted with him for a while. After he came back I asked him who that big man was. Dasarath told me that he taught exercise to King Tribhuvan every day, and that he was on his way to the palace at that moment. I thought it was important to our plans to overthrow the Ranas that we establish contact with the King. So I asked Dasarath to make contact with the King through this man.

Dasarath Chand was not very enthusiastic about this idea, because the athlete was the son of a highly reputed citizen, and the grandson of Bhagwat Kazi, a wealthy courtier during Bir Shamsher's regime. He had a contract to import salt from India, and he also owned a *kothi*[4] in Calcutta. His son, Adi Bhakta, had been appointed a Subba the moment he was born. He inherited his father's salt business, but got entangled in some shady dealings regarding the contract. When Juddha Shamsher heard about it, Adi Bhakta fled with all his possessions to Calcutta before Juddha could do anything. Therefore his son, Khardar

---

[3] *Swasti* is Sanskrit for 'Be well'. The practice of greeting by saying *namaste* (Sanskrit, 'I bow to you') did not become widespread until after 1950. Information about the salutes is from Ram Hari Sharma.

[4] A *kothi* is a business establishment, in this sense a place where men can find female entertainment such as singers and dancers.

Dharma Bhakta (for that was the name of that athlete), spent his childhood in luxury and style in Calcutta and Kalimpong.[5] Dasarath Chand was not sure if a man who had grown up in comfort and luxury would take such risky steps as we were contemplating. Discussing all this, we went home. But all the time I was wondering how we could make contact with the King.

Later I talked to Dharma Bhakta in Bhimphedi. The hotels my father had opened there and in Thankot were the first in Nepal. My father always wanted to do new things. He had also opened a horse service from Thankot to Bhimphedi. We had about eight or ten horses there. Well! Once when I was staying at Bhimphedi, it so happened that Dharma Bhakta (the athlete) was coming back from India with his wife. Dharma Bhakta's father, Adi Bhakta, and my father were friends. He came to Bhimphedi and stayed at a Dharmashala. I sent our hotel manager to enquire about them—i.e., whether they needed food and horses to take them to Thankot. He replied that, yes they needed food and horses. While they were staying there I also visited them. The next day as he was leaving I also took a horse and accompanied Dharma Bhakta up to Chisapani Gadhi [hilltop site of the district head-quarters and a police checkpost; this was the major route through which traffic to and from Kathmandu Valley passed]. On the way, I very cautiously started to tell him about the Rana's atrocities and how we should do something about it. He agreed with all of this. He had stayed in Calcutta, so he also had these liberal thoughts. Our talk ended when we reached the checkpost. He went towards Kathmandu, and I returned to Bhimphedi.

Two months after I saw Dharma Bhakta in Bhimphedi I came to Kathmandu. I went to see Dharma Bhakta at his house, and then I started visiting him every three or four days, or even more frequently [Dharma Bhakta's younger brother, Dhruba, relates how they were at first a little suspicious of Tanka Prasad, because he was a Brahmin and therefore perhaps not entirely trustworthy. They would say things to provoke him, as a kind of 'acid test', to see how he would respond. But Tanka Prasad talked so much and so openly that they quickly decided to take him into their confidence]. He and his family members had requested permission from the Ranas to start a school for the neigh-bourhood children, who had nothing to do. They were given permission,

<hr/>

[5] Details concerning Dasarath Chand and Dharma Bhakta are from Govinda Prasad Upadhyay.

provided there was no school uniform for the children and no name for the school. They used to take the parents of the children aside and try to convince them of the need for reform, to advance our cause. At that time most people thought that since Nepal was an independent country, there would not be any problems.

We used to gather at Dharma Bhakta's house in Jhoche Tole, to talk and make plans. Finally, Praja Parishad, as we called our party, was born on 22 Jesth 1993 [4 June 1936 AD], in Dharma Bhakta's drawing room. I got the idea for the party name while I was in Calcutta with Dasarath. It was the name of a political party active at that time in Jammu [a state in northern India]. We started the party with only five members: myself, Dasarath Chand, Ram Hari Sharma, Dharma Bhakta, and Jeev Raj Sharma. Ram Hari I had known since he was eleven, when his father (a friend of my father's) sent him to me to learn his ABC's. We read books and began talking about politics together. Jeev Raj was a friend of Ram Hari's at Tri-Chandra College. We met in Dharma Bhakta's house because for one thing his house was centrally located. Dasarath Chand lived in Thamel, Ram Hari and I lived in the Black Bridge area, and Jeev Raj lived in Gyaneshwor, so Dharma Bhakta's house was convenient for us. It also provided some safety. Since it was in the middle of the city, we could go there without attracting attention.

The five of us vowed, touching the *Bhagavad Gita* [an important Hindu text] with our heads, to serve the nation sincerely. It was not only a dream of something for the country, it was also a dream of something for myself, for self-realization. We entered into all this in a spirit of martyrdom; we didn't know what would happen. Similarly, the architects of the French Revolution were not conscious of what the result of their revolution would be.

Dharma Bhakta recruited Ganesh Man Singh, Ganga Lal, and Hari Krishna Shrestha into the party. They had been active in his wrestling centre. At first he told Ganesh Man that his organization was composed of Newars who were working for the liberation of Newars from the domination of the Parbates, because in general Newars resented the Shahs for taking over their valley.[6] Only later did Dharma Bhakta reveal the true nature of Praja Parishad, but when he found out about it Ganesh Man nevertheless joined our movement.

---

6 Newars are the indigenous people of the Kathmandu Valley, speaking a Tibeto-Burmese language; Parbates ('hill people') speak Nepali (an Indo-European language). The royal family and the Ranas, as well as Brahmins such as Tanka Prasad, are Parbates. See Chapter 1.

At that time it was very difficult to speak out against the Ranas, even within a closed circle, because there was always the possibility of someone spying for them. Since our work had to be carried out in secret, we invented a secret language. For instance, the code word for the King was 'Mukhiya' [village headman], 'Jamdar' [sergeant] for the Prime Minister, 'Prakash' for me, 'Sewa Singh' for Dasarath Chand, 'Basant' for Jeev Raj, 'Hare Gopal' for Ram Hari, and 'Ajab Bahadur' for Dharma Bhakta.[7]

Members of Praja Parishad were from all castes. The Vice-President of the Party, Dasarath Chand, was from the Thakuri caste. Dharma Bhakta, Ganga Lal, Hari Krishna Shrestha, and Ganesh Man Singh, were Newars. To me everyone was equal. Our aim was to provide food, clothing, shelter, education, and health for all Nepalese. There was no question of Brahmans, Chhetris, Vaisya, Sudra, Magar, Tamang, etc. They all are the children of Nepal [The first eighteen Praja Parishad members included eight Brahmins, one Thakuri, four Chhetris, and five Newars].

I still felt that the King was also in prison, and that we should establish contact with him and take assistance from him. But I had not been able to act on this thought. I did not know anyone who had access to the palace, other than Dharma Bhakta.

I took a big risk and told him to talk to the King about us. He said that the King might not agree. I insisted that he try once, and he agreed to try. But since the king was surrounded by Rana bodyguards even when he was exercising, Dharma Bhakta was unable to communicate our talk to the King. His appointment as the King's athletic instructor had already come to an end. He could still join in other physical activities in the palace, but only in the presence of other people. He had to look for someone else with more confidential access to the King. This was difficult, because all the employees of the royal palace were appointed by the Ranas, were therefore loyal to them, and could be assumed to be spies for them.

After observing many people Dharma Bhakta finally decided to sound out Chandra Man Sainju, who lived in Chhetrapati. After a few days he brought him to meet me and told me to talk to him. So I talked with him for a while. He was a somewhat plump, jolly man of dark complexion. He also proved to be reliable. Being a compounder [Nepalese

---

[7] Most of the information in this paragraph is paraphrased from Jeev Raj Sharma's 'A Brief History of Nepal Praja Parishad', *Daily Diary*, 29 August 1988.

use the English word, compounder, to refer to one who mixes and dispenses medicines; a pharmacist] he could visit the King any time the King wasn't feeling well.

After many friendly talks he and Dharma Bhakta became close friends. During Nava Ratri of Dasai[8] in 1936, Dharma Bhakta asked Chandra Man to go to Shobha Bhagwati temple to offer prayers and do *puja* [worship]. After the prayers and *puja* had been offered to the goddess, they both walked along the bank of the Vishnumati River. The atmosphere was peaceful and serene. They walked and then sat in total isolation and tranquility, chatted about various things, and finally Dharma Bhakta ended up on the subject of politics. They discussed the history of Nepal, current politics, the hopelessness of the King's situation, and finally the autocracy of the Ranas.

When Chandra Man agreed with Dharma Bhakta's conclusions, Dharma Bhakta, his voice shaking with emotion, asked Chandra Man if he could keep a secret. Chandra Man said yes. He plunged his hand into the holy waters of the Vishnumati, and feeling the presence of the divine mother, Shobha Bhagwati, Chandra Man said, 'Let the divine mother bring her wrath down upon me if I reveal to anyone what you tell me today!' Dharma Bhakta said, 'Compounder *Saheb!* The Ranas have taken our country as their private property; the people are oppressed and unhappy; there is no industrial development; they have seized power from the king and confined him to his palace as if he were a criminal in a jail. You know about all these things and have seen them with your own eyes. Therefore, some friends of mine and I have been preparing to bring a democratic system of government, like that of England. If we can bring democracy to this country, the King will be the King, and we his subjects. There will be no Ranas in between to spoil everything. Therefore join us! Our organization is secret, and we have been carrying out our work in secret till now'.

Chandra Man, although illiterate, was sensible and educated enough to join us in our work. Moreover, he was a patriot and loyal to the King. It was no joke to get involved with an anti-Rana organization. One had to think seriously and have a lot of guts to endanger one's life by joining a party of that sort. However, on reflecting upon the King's hints of support for an anti-Rana organization, Chandra Man finally said he was ready to join.

[8] Dasai, in which the goddess Durga is worshipped, is the biggest Nepalese Hindu celebration of the year; it occurs in October-November. Nava Ratri refers to the first nine days of the ten day Dasai festival.

Dharma Bhakta told Chandra Man that a party named Praja Parishad had been born to bring democracy to the country under the constitutional leadership of His Majesty, the King. He needed to convey that message to the King. The King was so closely watched that Dharma Bhakta had not been able to give him the message. Chandra Man had easy access to the King, and because he could cleverly act like a simpleton he did not arouse suspicion. Accordingly, one morning Chandra Man went to the palace to seek an audience with the King. He saw the King taking a stroll in the garden with his dog.

'What is it, Chandra Man?', the King asked.

'My lord, we are your subjects and you are our King. But instead of you, the Ranas have become the King. Development has accomplished much in other countries, while there is no sign of it here. Some people have formed an anti-Rana organization here, and I have agreed to work with them'.

After listening to this, the King's lips betrayed a faint smile. He did not say anything but continued his walk with his dog. Chandra Man was left standing there confused, with a cloud of nervousness hanging over his simple mind. After a half hour's confused waiting the King returned. Chandra Man stood there, his head bowed low in total surrender and respect. Finally Chandra Man was asked to be seated, and the King asked, in Newari, '*Aie*, Chandra Man.....' His voice shaking with emotion, Chandra Man said, 'Lord, whatever I have said is from the bottom of my heart.'

'If it is so, then who else is involved?'

'Dharma Bhakta, Tanka Prasad, Dasarath Chand, Ram Hari, and Jeev Raj.'

'Do you trust Dharma Bhakta?'

'I do, my lord!'

'Absolutely?'

'Absolutely!'

'Have you already talked to them?'

'I have only talked to Dharma Bhakta, my lord.' Dharma Bhakta's joy knew no bounds when Chandra Man related every detail of his conversation with the King.

The following day Chandra Man was welcomed to the party and introduced to the other members, at Dharma Bhakta's place at Om Bahal.[9] After Dharma Bhakta lit the kerosene lamp in his room, which

---

[9] Originally a Buddhist monastery, *bahal* now refers to a courtyard with a Buddhist image

was quite modest and tidy, the real talk started. I said to Chandra Man, 'We had been waiting for you to come. Now since you have finally come, allow me to say that we are individuals all dedicated to the same cause. The aim of our organization is to abolish the autocratic and cruel Rana regime in order to serve the country and the King, and this is the reason for the birth of Praja Parishad, which of course Dharma Bhakta must have already told you about. Now all we need is your dedication and selfless service.' Chandra Man assured me, 'Your wish shall certainly be fulfilled'. All of us welcomed Chandra Man's reply with applause. In that moment of mutual trust and friendship Jeev Raj added hope and confidence by singing a song. Then we discussed writing articles in Indian newspapers, arousing the people from their slumber or ignorance, and many other things. Ram Hari, Dharma Bhakta, Jeev Raj and I (Dasarath Chand was not present) swore Chandra Man in as the sixth member of Praja Parishad.

After about a week Chandra Man related everything that had happened at Dharma Bhakta's place to the King. 'What do you think of them?' asked His Majesty. 'I believe Tanka Prasad's words from the bottom of my heart. Ram Hari and Jeev Raj are enthusiastic and dedicated'. King Tribhuvan indicated his approval, and from that day onwards, the King asked Chandra Man to keep him informed of all of Praja Parishad's activities. But, what was the proof that the King supported us? Chandra Man Compounder also brought us proof.

Chandra Man had to be very circumspect, because everything sent to the King was carefully inspected. The King would hide smuggled political books and newspapers over the mosquito-netting of his bed. Nothing was supposed to be presented to him directly. Once someone presented a carpet to the King out of sheer respect, and when the Ranas heard about it they immediately fired him. So Chandra Man used to carry the letters that we wrote, as well as the King's replies, in the sole of his shoe, where they were safe and sound. He used to hide a small knife, needle, and thread in his pocket. He hid the letters in-between the two layers of the sole of his shoe. He would cut open the sole of the shoe upon entering the King's private chambers, hand him the letters, and after replacing our letter with the King's reply, he would sew and stitch back the sole with perfect workmanship. In this way we exchanged four letters with the King.

---

at its centre, and the residences surrounding it in which many contemporary Newars in Kathmandu, Bhaktapur, and Patan live. Om Bahal is thus the name of the particular *bahal* where Dharma Bhakta lived.

We wrote a letter to the king asking him what view we should have towards him. He wrote back that we could consider him as one of the members of the party. Then I again asked him, after the Ranas, what? We also wrote to him about our future plan, i.e., a British pattern of democracy. We asked about his views on this. He replied back that he accepted our plan. This gave us encouragement.

Gradually our organization grew. I recruited my brother's widow's brother, Chuda Prasad. I went to see him in Banaras, where he was studying. He was involved in the Revolutionary Socialist Party led by Jogish Chatterjee. Chuda Prasad believed that in order to overthrow the Ranas it was necessary for India to be free first. Over a month of discussions with him I argued against that view, and that in any case the Nepalese movement against the Ranas must start from within Nepal and under no circumstances be foreign based. I told him that while he was only talking about radical political activity, the Praja Parishad was actually doing something, so why didn't he join us? He accepted membership enthusiastically.

Meanwhile, the King had been making his own attempts to overthrow the Ranas. In addition to joining Praja Parishad, Chandra Man and two others were also members of Raktapat Mandal (Nepali for Bloodshed Group). I and other Parishad members did not learn of the organization's existence until Chandra Man told me about it in jail, but Govinda Prasad Upadhyay has described it as follows:

'It was 1993 (1936 AD), and twenty-five years had passed since King Tribhuvan had ascended the throne. Juddha Shamsher, in order to please the King and gain his confidence, arranged to celebrate the twenty-fifth anniversary of his coronation lavishly, because he had to marry his grand daughter [Chandra Laxmi] to the Crown Prince [Mahendra] and great grand daughters to the other two princes [Princep and Helen to Himalaya and Basundhara, respectively; see Appendix 9]. Beginning on 25 Phalgun, the celebration would last for seven days, and all the courtiers, of both the Ranas and the King, were to participate in it. Mukhiya Ganesh Raj, who worked in the main treasury section, was assigned to make the necessary arrangements, and to welcome the guests.

'The second prince, Himalaya, told Ganesh Raj not to go to where the courtiers gathered. He was taken aback, and without thinking, fearlessly replied, 'Your Highness, why do you order a man not to go to a place where other people get together? Besides, I am not going there out of my own choice, but because I was assigned to go. Your Highnesses are prisoners inside the white house, while prisoners of the black house are west of the Bagh-Khor. [Bagh-Khor refers to the area east of the Central Jail where a tiger was formerly kept. It is now a petrol station]. You have to do what Singh Darbar beckons you to do. We, the sons of serfs, have no choice but to do what the officers order'. The prince, at a loss for words, said nothing and walked away. The next day the King sent for Ganesh Raj and asked him, in total privacy in the drawing room on the ground floor, what he had said to the second prince. Ganesh Raj was too frightened to say a single word. The King was smiling and very calm. Again he asked him to retell what he had said to the prince. Ganesh Raj then told the King everything he had said to the prince. The King did not get angry, but listened with interest. After hearing him, the King told him to go back to his work and to do his duty properly.

'After several days, during *Krishna Pakshya* [the declining phase of the moon] in *Bhadra* [August-September], when football and other sports were finished, Ganesh Raj was about to leave for home when the King told him to wait. He waited till midnight, when he was finally called to the garage. The King, General Agni Shamsher, Lieutenant Ramdas, Chandra Man Compounder, Mukhiya Ganesh Raj, Katak Bahadur, Marich Man (the last two drivers and mechanics), and the three sons of the King, altogether ten of them were there. Then they drove the car to Gauri Ghat. There the King told them they should fight to abolish the Rana regime and stake their lives to struggle for people who bring democracy. Taking the holy water in their hands, the King made them vow to carry on the work, with the Divine Mother Guheshwori and Lord Pashupatinath as witnesses. They returned to the palace, had dinner, and each went back to his own house.

'After that there were some seven meetings in the ground floor drawing room of the Royal Palace, and these conspirators named their secret group the 'Raktapat Mandal' [Shah (1990) states that King Tribhuvan was in direct control of it, and that Ram Das Khawas was its immediate supervisor]. In order to carry on their work and pull the wool over the Ranas' eyes, the King and the two princes [younger brothers of the Crown Prince] would act as if they were not on good terms with each other. The Crown Prince was supposed to convince the Ranas that they were not getting along. Accordingly, rumors spread and they started behaving in strange ways.

'The members learned to shoot, and a plan was devised stipulating which positions they would take to shoot the Ranas in that drawing room, and a trial run was made. They then planned to invite the Prime Minister and other important Ranas to the palace, but one day prior to the invitation Juddha Shamsher came alone at night. Because nothing had been prepared for that day, they were taken by surprise and the plan could not be executed. Other successive attempts also failed, and the Ranas started smelling something fishy. Hence they decided that each time the Prime Minister visited the King he would go alone, without the Commander-in-Chief and Military Lord [Jangi Lath, the third in command after the Prime Minister and Commander-in-Chief] and vice versa. The plan to overthrow the Ranas would not succeed unless all three were killed simultaneously. The Ranas kept a very strict watch on every activity which took place in the palace, and detectives followed most of the Raktapat Mandal. Then, the Praja Parishad came into existence, and after Chandra Man told the King about it, all the activities of the Raktapat Mandal collapsed, and it faded out of existence.

'A dance hall was being built in the palace. In 1940 the Crown Prince married Indra Rajya Laxmi. The King thought of inviting all the Ranas for a party in the dance hall, where they could be electrocuted. Driver Katak Bahadur's son was a very good electrician, and he was asked to make the necessary arrangements. But for some unknown reason, that plot also failed and the electrician was kicked out of the palace by the Ranas. Later, he would have been imprisoned or given the death sentence, but he died before the Ranas found out about the Raktapat Mandal. Another group of disgruntled associates of the King was called the Nava Ratna [Nine Pearls; Shah (1990) refers to it as the Navagrahas, or nine planets]; it consisted mostly of junior courtiers, such as Tribhuvan's valet, who entertained the King, but included Agni Shamsher [also a member of Raktapat Mandal], one of Juddha's own sons.'

Now, we had to get to work. But we had no money. The King had sent some money to Dharma Bhakta, but he thought it was given to him personally; it was just a misunderstanding. I don't know how much it was, but we did not get any money sent by the king. I went to Calcutta and met Dasarath Chand there. Dasarath introduced me to Mahendra Bikram Shah, another Nepali who wanted to overthrow the Ranas. Mahendra Bikram Shah bought us a duplicating machine and some paper to make pamphlets. Then Dasarath Chand and I went back to Nepal to my village in the Tarai [Sirsia, where Tanka Prasad's father owned land, is about eighteen kilometers northeast of Janakpur, the legendary city of the Hindu epic, the *Ramayana*]. Dasarath Chand stayed with us for a week and left. But I could not leave the village if I could not find a person who could accompany me and carry the duplicating machine to Kathmandu. My father always asked me what it was. I always said it was nothing. But even then he had some suspicion— i.e., my boy is going to do something (laughter) against the Ranas. He had once been made a high official by the Ranas, but he was not happy with their behaviour.

Well, there was the question of how to bring the machine with me. So I dismantled the machine part by part, and got the assistance of Govinda Prasad Upadhyay. Ram Hari had introduced me to Govinda Prasad—he was his cousin [Govinda's mother was Ram Hari's father's sister]. When his father was transferred to Biratnagar, long after my father's time, Govinda Prasad enrolled in Krishna Prasad Koirala's school there [Krishna Prasad Koirala was the father of Matrika Prasad and Bishweshwor Prasad]. Govinda Prasad had gotten excited about politics after reading about Gandhi in the Hindi newspaper, *Bishwamitra*. In Biratnagar they had an annual procession to the Bada Hakim's house, and a public meeting with speeches. Even though the event was in honor of Juddha's birthday, such a public event was unheard of in Kathmandu, and he had only heard and read about such things in India.

One day Ram Hari took Govinda Prasad to the far corner of a field where there was no possibility of being overheard, and told him about the work of the Praja Parishad. Govinda Prasad was progressive-minded and immediately wanted to be involved. The next day I met him. Dasarath Chand went to Nepalganj and met him there. Govinda Prasad's father had been transferred there, as Assistant Bada Hakim, from Biratnagar.

Govinda was a student in Kathmandu, and he had a big trunk to carry his books and clothing to Kathmandu from Nepalganj. Actually, he had two of those trunks. Anyway, I put the dismantled machine into one of the trunks. Then we came up to Bhimphedi together. It was a difficult job. We halted at Bhimphedi. Now, there again arose the question, what to do? I bought some cigarettes there, and early the next morning we started with our porters towards Kathmandu. We reached Chisapani Gadhi, a gateway to Kathmandu, which was strictly guarded. We had to show our passports [all Nepalese needed passports to enter or leave the Kathmandu Valley] to get through Chisapani Gadhi. We had been issued our passports in Birganj, so we showed them. It was early in the morning.

At Chisapani Gadhi, all persons and belongings used to be thoroughly checked before they could pass through. There were two people. One was a clerk who checked the belongings, and another a subedar [subordinate commissioned officer] who kept an eye on the clerk. The subedar, with his big moustache, was from the military. I started talking with the subedar. I also offered him a cigarette. I found out from him that he was involved in a case in the Kathmandu court. I told him that when I reached Kathmandu, the first thing I would do would be to help him win his case, by pulling strings. He had been a guard at Padma Shamsher's Darbar [palace] in Kathmandu. I used to study with Padma Shamsher's son at his Darbar, so I gave him every detail of the area and of Padma Shamsher's Darbar. I told him not to worry about his case. Finally he was convinced that I was who I claimed to be. At that moment, our trunk came in front of him. He opened it to check it. I told him it was my trunk. So he just peeped in and passed it saying, 'Oh! There is nothing here. You can take it.' It was a great relief. My heart began to throb heavily after that.

Then we walked on and came to the second of the two checkpoints at Chisapani Gadhi. The first was for customs, the second for security. But once the first was passed, the second, where our passports had to be checked once again, didn't pay such close attention. There was another subedar here called Chandra Kanta. He asked us whether our trunk had been examined, saying 'what have you poor Brahmins bought?' I said, of course our trunks had been inspected. But he sent a man to enquire about whether they had been inspected or not. At that time, you cannot even imagine how we must have felt. To our relief, the man came back and said it had been checked. So we walked on once again to Thankot, just inside the Kathmandu Valley, where we answered enquiries by a final police checkpost. When we arrived in Kathmandu we reassembled the machine. That much about mechanics I know [laughter].

After I reassembled the machine I took it to Govinda Prasad's house, where it was stored in a long wooden box. For three or four months, I would go there every two weeks or so just to get it out and look at it. We brought the machine in February, and in the summer I began writing the pamphlets. I wrote at night, by the light of a small earthen-ware kerosene lamp, so I did not make drafts, I just wrote them out. I wrote the pamphlets and reproduced them on that duplicating machine at my house. Then we took the machine to Ram Hari's place in Maligaon, near Gyaneshwor.

Although I wanted us to write and distribute pamphlets against the Ranas, Dasarath Chand hatched a different plot, yet it was a plot only in name. He was a brave Thakuri, and he was for blowing up the Ranas. He used to say that pamphlets could be of no use in overthrowing the Ranas, and that we have to use force against them. But I did not agree. We had a discussion on this for a whole month. I told him that, supposing we could not blow the Ranas up and were caught in the act, we would then be branded as conspirators. Others also had tried it, but they had failed and were branded as conspirators. Although they were not killed, these early conspirators had been treated very badly. They were tortured and beaten; it was worse than being killed. One of those conspirators, Khadga Man Singh, was in jail. He had served nine years in jail when we arrived, then he served another ten with us, for a total of 19 years in jail. I argued that we are not conspirators, and our work is just to arouse the people. After one month of heated arguments and counter-arguments we compromised. We agreed to both tactics—i.e., on the one hand we would do pamphleteering, and on the other we would prepare for the assassination of the Ranas. This was agreed to by a majority of the party, but I was not interested in the assassination idea. I do not rate conspiracy very high. It is a simple and ordinary thing. On my part, I started to write pamphlets, but since it was very hard to procure materials for the assassination of the Ranas, nothing could be done at that end. Some explosives were acquired, but we never had an opportunity to use them.

The Ranas were very powerful, and almost everything worked against us, but the annual Machendranath festival unwittingly facilitated us in our activities. Machendranath's *rath* [chariot] comes to a stop at a public plaza in Jawalakhel. People gather there to see Machendranath's *bhoto*[10] from the four sides of the *rath*. People from all three cities of the valley [Kathmandu, Patan, and Bhaktapur] and all castes, ranging from peasants to top officials, go to get a glimpse of the *bhoto*. On that day of the festival, Juddha Shamsher would lift the ban on gambling (in that location only), and also the curfew. (At that time there was a permanent curfew, at 9 p.m. in winter and 11 p.m. in summer, except for one night a week). We chose that very day to distribute the pamphlets. Without a curfew, we could distribute as many pamphlets as we wanted.

[10] Machendranath is the god of rains; just before the onset of the monsoon, his image is pulled through the streets on a chariot (*rath*) so that the public can view his brocade jacket (*bhoto*). The Patan Machendranath is called Red Machendranath; the Kathmandu Machendranath is known as White Machendranath.

We glued pamphlets on the trees, on walls, on houses; we even threw them over the walls of the Ranas' palaces.

We had already written five different pamphlets [*see* Appendix 1]. The first contained my appeal to the people to fight against the Ranas, to abolish their autocratic rule once and for all. The others focused on urging the Ranas to give the people their birth-right, freedom. I was very blunt and did not hesitate to speak my mind. Even though we merely printed some leaflets against the Ranas and distributed them among the people, to the Ranas this was a big crime.

The Ranas were so arrogant that they thought no one could do anything against them. They never guessed boys like us could work against them, or that any man could do anything against them, so they never suspected us. Once we started to distribute pamphlets, the whole detective machinery of the Ranas was directed at us. But they could not trace us. We used to work at night, before the curfew sounded.

We were very careful. Because I had gone to see Mohan Shamsher previously to suggest reforms, the Ranas may have been watching me. Also, since all those pamphlets were in my handwriting, my friends persuaded me to leave Kathmandu and stay in Banaras, lest I be arrested which could endanger the whole party. I left three days before the pamphleteering began, and I emphasized to Govinda Prasad, who saw me off in Kalimati, how concerned I was that the pamphlets be distributed. He assured me that the work would be done. When I left Kathmandu I was sick and feverish and had seven rupees in my pocket. That was enough to get me to Banaras, since the fare from Raxaul to Banaras was Rs 3. I met Dasarath Chand in Godhasan (a town on the Indian side of the border), and got more money from him. He was in India carrying on our work, writing articles in Hindi for *Janata*, etc.

Ram Hari and Govinda Prasad and the others divided up the city among themselves so that pamphlets would be scattered in every street and lane. They worked all night, and met at Ram Hari's house at four in the morning. When he left for home at 7:30 a.m., Govinda Prasad walked through several of the places he had left pamphlets and found that people had taken all of them. Near the hotel in front of the Ganesh temple in Kamaladi he had tossed some thirty or forty pamphlets. They got wet in a sudden shower, and the hotel keeper set them out to dry. The letters produced by the cyclostyle machine were bloated and magnified by the water, making them more clear and distinct.[11]

[11] All the details of the pamphleteering are from Govinda Prasad Upadhyay.

After the first round of pamphleteering, Ram Hari sent Dasarath Chand a coded telegram informing him of their success. The message was:

My Dear Chand,
The thousands of mangoes which you sent me I have distributed among our friends and relatives properly, and they are all satisfied.

Yours,
Hari Gopal

The appearance of the pamphlets was so unexpected that the whole valley remained mum for three or four days. After that my friends started hearing rumours about the pamphlets. They enjoyed listening to those rumours. One response to our pamphlets was that some people put up some other pamphlets on the *khare ko bot*[12] on the Tundikhel. We never knew who did this.

It was very difficult to find a newspaper in British-controlled India to publicise our work. One Indian paper called *Janata* used to report our activities (its address was Khudabaksh Library, Patna).[13] The writer of the articles was Dasarath Chand, but he signed his code name, Sewa Singh, to them.

Our membership kept on increasing, and on 18 *Bhadra*, 1997 [2 September, 1940], a meeting of Praja Parishad was held in Dharma Bhakta's drawing room. The meeting started after Dharma Bhakta returned from the wrestling match he had organized (General Nara Shamsher came to see the match). The conference adopted a party manifesto which set down rules, aims, and objectives of the party. The aim of Praja Parishad, which had already been written down by Dasarath Chand and shown to the King, was 'to establish a democratic Kingdom like that of England, under the constitutional leadership of the King'. Then Ram Hari suggested that I should be the President of the Party (in absentia, since I was in Banaras), and Dasarath Chand and Dharma Bhakta supported him. Everybody agreed, and thus I was made President.

---

[12] *Khare ko bot* (*Celtis australis*) was an enormous tree in the middle of the Tundikhel, a large parade ground in Kathmandu; it was cut down in the 1960s to make way for construction of a band shell.

[13] The Ranas responded by persuading the British to suppress publication of *Janata* (the original correspondence on this matter is reprinted in Gautam 1989). Other Nepalis living in India wrote anti-Rana articles in the newspapers *Agragami* and *Naya Hindusthan* (Shah 1990).

Dasarath Chand was made Vice-President, which was hard for Dharma Bhakta to accept, for when Ram Hari had suggested this, his face betrayed his disappointment. But when the others had no objection, Dharma Bhakta had to accept it in the end. Then Ram Hari was made Secretary, and the rest were made members. Dasarath Chand wrote everything down and everybody signed their names to it. The written record was given to Dharma Bhakta for safe keeping. Our manifesto made it clear that we wanted to hand over power to the people and not to a small group such as ourselves. Later, when Dharma Bhakta was caught and his house raided by the Ranas, they found this document and the letters written by the King, and all the documents were destroyed.

After that meeting, party members resumed the pamphleteering. The second time pamphlets were distributed they concentrated on the areas where educated people lived and gathered. They distributed our subsequent pamphlets any night they chose, but they had to do so before the curfew.

The Ranas were shaken by the pamphlets, and they increased the number of their CID [Criminal Investigation Department] agents, male and female, some of them even dressed as *sadhus* and *yogis*, to find out who we were. They announced a Rs 5000 reward[14] and a high government post to anyone who could catch us.

Unfortunately one of our own colleagues betrayed us, and we were caught. He was Ramji Shastri, the brother of Sukra Raj Shastri. The traitor was a *pandit* and very good in Sanskrit grammar. Some of us objected to him on the grounds that mentally he didn't seem quite normal, but Dasarath Chand liked him and recommended him. Even though he was a learned fellow I had told Dasarath not to take him into the party, but Dasarath wanted to take him into the party, so we did.

Like his brother he was also active in Arya Samaj [a reformist Hindu organization active in India]. We in Praja Parishad had little interest in Arya Samaj. They just wanted social reforms, whereas our main objective was political reform. They did not believe in icon worship or caste, whereas we did worship icons. We accepted people of all castes, but we didn't specifically disavow caste as such, the way they did. Somehow we could not develop any attachment towards Ramji and always felt uneasy in his presence. Anyway, he reported us to the

[14] The size of the reward offered shows that the Ranas took the activities of the Praja Parishad with the utmost seriousness. A teacher's annual salary at the time was Rs 180; Re 1 would buy about 13 pounds of rice.

Ranas, and that was that. We found out about him because everything came out in our trial at the Ranas' court. He was put in jail with us for some time, for six months. He was put with me, in the same compartment as me [laughter]. He turned traitor for the Rs 5000 reward the Ranas offered for information on who was behind the pamphleteering. Sometimes he would be apologetic about what had happened, and at other times he would simply say that in informing on us he was only guilty of speaking the truth. I understand he is still living. We should have just shot him [laughter].[15] Chandra Man Compounder did want to kill him.

So, on 2 *Kartik* 1997 [18 October, 1940], the news spread that the police had raided Dharma Bhakta's house, and General Nara Shamsher himself went there to search it. Then they raided Dharma Bhakta's uncle's house and Ganga Lal's house. Dharma Bhakta and Ganga Lal were arrested and taken to Singha Darbar for interrogation (Ganga Lal had joined the party only two months before being arrested). Only two weeks before, Dharma Bhakta had left me in Calcutta to return to the valley to direct and guide the party's activities. He said to me, 'Friend, I am leaving for Kathmandu, perhaps never to return!' When they heard that Dharma Bhakta had been arrested, they tried to hide the duplicating machine by burying it in a cowshed, but the Ranas found it and took it to Singha Darbar.

On that same day, Ram Hari, Chuda Prasad, and Govinda Prasad were sitting in Gyaneshwor around four in the afternoon, discussing what to do next. They decided to write more pamphlets opposing the arrests and house raids, rather than escape or go underground. That

---

[15] Tanka Prasad's casual reaction to the man whose perfidy cost him the lives of his friends and resulted in a life sentence for himself is typical of a common live-and-let-live attitude towards politics and among politicians in Nepal (cf. Chapter 7, footnote 12). This is reflected in the following inscription under the bust of Prime Minister Juddha Shamsher in the National Museum in Kathmandu: 'Ojaswi Rajamya Prithuladhisa His Highness Maharaja Joodha Shamsher Jang Bahadur Rana, Prime Minister and Commander-in-Chief of Nepal—A man of high integrity, scrupulous veracity, indomitable moral courage, irrepressible spirit of nationalism; and, last but not the least, an all round reformer who throughout his long and eventful life has been working to give a proper orientation to everything concerned with Nepal and the Nepalese nation;—this art gallery is named after him as the founder and this tablet inscribed as a work of heart-felt gratitude and deep appreciation of the nation.' Whereas elsewhere statues of tarnished heroes such as Lenin, Stalin, and Mao have come tumbling down, the fulsome praise of this inscription, prominently displayed in the entrance hall of the National Museum, has drawn no attention from the Nepalese public. By contrast, the Raktapat Committee referred to Juddha as *Joota* ('shoe'), a leather, and therefore highly polluted object (Uprety 1992:31).

would have aroused the Ranas' suspicion, as well as shown them to be faint-hearted. But on the next day Ram Hari was arrested in Asan Tole, on his way to his office; he worked as a sanitary inspector for the city of Kathmandu. Most of the others were also arrested, one of the last being Govinda Prasad, who refused to run away even when he knew it was only a matter of time before they came for him.

Chapter 7

The Prison Years: Views From Inside
Tanka Prasad

Arrest, trial, and executions

After the others had been arrested and our documents discovered, they knew that I was also involved. The Ranas sent a telegram to me in Banaras, saying that my father was very ill and that I should hurry home to see him before he died. It was sent by Ram Shamsher, the district head, whom Juddha had exiled to Janakpur [at the same time Rudra Shamsher had been similarly exiled to Palpa; both were C class Ranas]. Since he was a friend of my father's I didn't suspect anything, so I returned and was arrested just over the border from Jaynagar, on 29 October, 1940. I was put in heavy chains and carried to Kathmandu in a *khatoli* [a kind of enclosed palanquin]. About a dozen men took turns carrying it, and another dozen or so were armed guards.

I was brought into the prison at Singha Darbar with my hands cuffed, my legs in irons, and a thick iron chain that went round my neck, down my calf and locked to my leg irons. We were all chained in this way for three months. (See illustration 9.) In winter it was very difficult for us to sleep with those chains on, because the ice-cold chain had to get warm before we could fall asleep. But later on when we were in jail, as time passed we made a rock hammer from the stones lying around our cell, and used it to beat the chain until it bent. Then we could unhook one link of the chain from where it was linked to the next one, and thereby remove it.

About five hundred people were arrested, not just Praja Parishad people, but also palace employees who had conspired against the Ranas, including members of the King's Nava Ratna group, and any others interested in cultural or religious reform. Some had just wanted to open a library or a school, and one person's crime was that he listened to the radio (which was illegal) and read newspapers published mostly in India. We Praja Parishad people were first kept in the barracks near the main gate, and later moved to the School House, along with some of the Nava Ratna group. The School House was built for the education of Chandra Shamsher's sons. It had nine rooms, one for each of his sons. Later it housed Radio Nepal. Others were kept in several small tents erected on the football field. There were sentries on duty all over the place. For the first fifteen days we were very strictly supervised; although we were all together, we were forbidden to talk to each other.

There were four guards in our room in Singha Darbar. They slept in the same room with us, and they rotated so that at least one of them was always awake. The rumour started going around that I had great power, such as the ability to fly or become invisible. These rumours arose because it was so unheard of for anyone to challenge the authority of the Ranas that it was thought that anyone who did so that brazenly must have supernatural powers. Because of these rumours I was watched very closely, and two guards were assigned to me even when I went to the toilet.[1] But the guards later became sympathetic to us and did whatever they could for us, so that whenever an official visited the jail, a guard would inform us beforehand, and we would then put our chains back on before those officers or jailers reached us. In this way we were never found out. The guards became sympathetic for two reasons. One is that we used to tell them that our revolution was meant to benefit everyone, including them. The other is that they had heard that King Tribhuvan had also been implicated with us, and they were extremely loyal to the King.

Some of us were severely tortured while we were staying in Singha Darbar during the trial. They would use shock treatment, by attaching electric wires to our ankles and turning on the current. It made us nauseous. But I wore rubber shoes, so it didn't harm me [laughter]. Ram Hari and I were beaten a little, but Ganga Lal was beaten badly; they would tie us to a bamboo frame and beat us with a horse whip. I used to joke about our beatings, to cheer up my companions. I would chuckle and say, 'Do you see how cruel they are? They are trying to kill their anger by beating and torturing us!' Or I would say to the torturers, 'Today it is we who are being tortured, but tomorrow it will be you!' Because Brahmins should only be beaten by other Brahmins, they sometimes couldn't find any other Brahmins to beat me. One

---

[1] Most of the details about Singha Darbar, including the story of Tanka Prasad's supernatural powers, are from Govinda Prasad Upadhyay.

day one of the Rana officials said to me, '*Baje* [a term sometimes used to address Brahmins], how come you are wearing jewellery (referring to my iron chains)?' I replied, 'Yes, I am wearing jewellery. Autocrats and tyrants wear your kind of jewellery, and patriots and freedom fighters wear jewellery like this'.

General Shankar Shamsher told Prem Raj that 'There is a guy called Tanka Prasad being interrogated who can not be bought and who can not be forced to tell what we want him to tell'. I did not know what fear was then. I had expected my friends to be brave, bold, lively, and in high spirits in Singha Darbar, but when I arrived there my heart sank as I saw the expressions of hopelessness and doom in most of their faces. I felt my heart sinking in a bottomless cold ocean when vigorous and lively people like Jeev Raj, Phanindra Raj Hamal and Dhrubanath Dubedi said, 'Tanka Prasad, you have brought a huge catastrophe in our lives'. (Dhrubanath eventually settled in America, with his three sons). They had already thrown away their membership in Praja Parishad. Because the Praja Parishad activities had been conducted so secretly, many active in the movement had never actually seen Tanka Prasad.[Because of his audaciously courageous behaviour, they assumed he must be a man of physically gigantic proportions. Perhaps the disappointment which Tanka Prasad describes was partly a reaction to his very short height.] However, there were others like Ram Hari, Dasarath Chand, Chuda Prasad, Ganga Lal, Govinda Prasad, and Ganesh Man who were brave and maintained their vigour and spirits till the end, always smiling and never complaining. To tell the truth, if we had united in Singha Darbar and really fought till the end, they would have put all of us to death and democracy would have followed. What use is there in living a life like this now? What purpose can it serve? I got married, fathered children, married them off, and that's all. What's the use of this kind of life?[2]

On 17 *Kartik* 2 November 1940 I was taken before General Nara Shamsher[3] for interrogation. He asked me if King Tribhuvan was involved in our organization.

[2] Many of the details here and in the pages following immediately are from Govinda Prasad Upadhyay. Tanka Prasad was erratic in his assessment of his own accomplishments; at times he was proud of what he had done, but in his last years he increasingly despaired that all his efforts had been in vain. When I visited him once in 1991, he said he had just offered prayers to Ganga Lal and Dasarath (whose pictures were on the wall), and that he was sorry he had not been able to honour their memory with a better record of achievements.

[3] Nara Shamsher, a grandson of Juddha and son of Bahadur, was responsible for the

'No, he is not,', I answered.

'You deny it, but we know everything from the papers we confiscated from Dharma Bhakta's house. You can go now, but tomorrow after force is applied you'll know everything'. He used *ta*[4] to address me.

The next day I was taken to the terrace of the School House, where Nara Shamsher was seated.

'Tell me, who else is involved in this affair?', he implored.

I said, 'Government is the heart of a society. If it is infested with germs and rot, what will happen? You deposit the country's money in foreign banks, when people here don't have enough to eat, they don't even have the freedom to speak and write. Are we not citizens, or what? We should get our rights'. I had barely finished speaking when Nara Shamsher got up from his chair and slapped me hard. I then told him that the time of ruling by beating and force had already gone, and that he could beat me as much as he wanted. Nara Shamsher told Mahat Subba [Mahendra Bahadur Mahat, a judge], who was standing there with some papers in his hand, to relate Dharma Bhakta's tale to me. He did so, and I then realized that they had found out everything, and there was no sense in denying it anymore.

They started writing my confession then. Nara Shamsher would sometimes come between me and the interrogator, telling me not to include Mahendra Bikram's name (he had bought me the duplicating machine in Calcutta), and to say that Gunja Man was involved. I said we had no connection with Gunja Man. 'He, a Sardar himself, and the son of a Kazi,[5] how could he be involved with us? I am not going to tell you what is not true'. Then Shankar Shamsher (Chandra Shamsher's son) used to drop by now and then and say, 'Isn't it true that Mahendra Bikram bought that cyclostyle machine for you? Write that also'. It was very obvious that Juddha Shamsher's people were trying to implicate

---

execution of the four martyrs (see Appendix 9.)

[4] Nepali employs five second-person pronouns of address, and four associated verb forms, depending on the status of the person addressed. *Ta* is the 'lowest', or most familiar, and is used to address small children, lowly servants and animals; *timi* is used to juniors such as children, servants, and wives; *tapai* is the 'democratic' form, used among social equals; *hajur* is used to superiors, such as bosses and husbands; *sarkar* is used to address members of the royal family. Spousal forms vary according to class and education, but are typically asymmetrical.

[5] Sardar and Kazi are both titles; sardar is, roughly, 'chief', and kazi may be rendered as 'ruler' or 'governor'.

Chandra Shamsher's people.[6] Later on, under the direction of Juddha Shamsher, Subba Mahat again tried to force me to say that Gunja Man was also involved.

The Ranas thought it was not really the Brahmins and Chhetris who were against them. They thought the Newars must have led them astray, exploited them, tricked them, and turned them against the Ranas to seek revenge. So, during the interrogations, Judge Mahendra Bahadur Mahat would say, 'Tell me the names of those who told you to get involved in affairs like this. We know that the Newars have misled you. Tell me the name of the man who misled you, and you'll be set free'. They would hint that Gunja Man was the culprit, and they tried to get me to mention his name. Once they said, 'Why are you frightened to mention his name? Gunja Man is also involved, isn't that true? Tell us the truth. Nobody will do anything to you if you speak the truth. After all, you have been misled by Newars, we already know about this, so what difference does it make whether you tell us or not?'

I told them repeatedly that was not true. Gunja Man was not at all involved, and the Newars had not misled anybody. I said I myself was solely responsible for what had happened. But they were bent on hearing Gunja Man's name from my lips and again and again tried to force me to speak his name. I told them, 'I will not tell you what is not true no matter what you say and do. I am not ready to implicate those who had no connection with Praja Parishad. If that's what you want from me, write whatever you want in my confession, but I'll never sign it. Otherwise forget this nonsense and write whatever I say. I'll tell you the whole truth'. Even after I told them all this they said, 'These Newars, inspired by feelings of revenge, have led you astray, tell us that clearly and you'll be set free'.

After hearing them continue speaking this way I couldn't restrain my feeling of repugnance towards them, and I said, 'It's me who is totally responsible for all this, and the others, who have helped me, they know nothing about democracy; I have led them astray, they didn't know what they were doing or what my motives were. So you can let the rest of them go. As for the other things, like the Newars seeking revenge, and Gunja Man being involved, that's not true. If you write whatever I have said, I'll sign it. Otherwise you write whatever you

---

[6] Tanka Prasad is correct in asserting that he was being used in a power-play between two opposing lineages of the Rana family. For details, see Shah 1990.

want and sign it yourself.[7] I got annoyed and said I would speak the truth only and nothing else.

We were kept in Singha Darbar for three months. We were tried during that time. There were no lawyers at the trial. As prosecutors, there were four Rana commanding generals, one for the west, one for the east, one for the north, and one for the south. One of them also served as Commander-in-Chief. We were our own defence. It was not a court at all, it was purely a military trial. But even in a court martial one should be able to bring his advocates with him. But here, whatever the prosecutors wanted they could have. We defended ourselves anyhow (laughter). Our defence was to admit everything. We said we had not just violated some law, we were against the entire Rana system and wanted to overthrow it.

Some of us were given three-year sentences, some were given six years, some twelve, some eighteen, some life imprisonment, and six of us (Ganga Lal, Dharma Bhakta, Dasarath Chand, Sukraraj Shastri, Ram Hari and I) were sentenced to death. Others were fined varying amounts. Mahendra Bikram Shah, who bought the cyclostyle machine, was fined Rs. 500, while three people were fined Rs. 50, and twenty-eight were fined just Rs. 10 each.[8] Among the thirty-two of us who were imprisoned, about half were Praja Parishad members. Our total membership was about twenty-five, but some had fled to India, some were banished to their villages and not allowed to return to Kathmandu for as many as sixteen years, and two were released in the care of their guardians because they were underage, being only about fifteen or sixteen years old. I myself was twenty-eight; Ram Hari was twenty-four; Dasarath and Dharma Bhakta were about thirty-one; Ganga Lal was just twenty-one. There were also some prisoners who had merely taught social reform at the Mahavir School, which had been started in 1935-6. Some of them received jail sentences, others were fined ten rupees and one anna [one anna = four pice; the fine was increased by the

---

[7] The paragraphs about the Ranas suspecting the Newars is from 'Half an Hour with Tanka Prasad', by Mani Raj Upadhyay, in *Samaj*.

[8] These statistics are from *Swarnajayanti-Smarika* (edited by Sharma), page 41. According to Shah (1990: 130), 'Out of the forty-three persons who were arrested in 1940, three were hanged, fourteen given life sentences, twenty received sentences between three and eight years, and four were banished from the capital.' As Shah himself points out later on the same page, one was hanged and two were shot (the fourth, Sukra Raj Shastri, was also hanged). He also says the ten rupee fine was ten rupees and one anna (one anna = one sixteenth of a rupee).

odd amount, because an even number, especially one ending in zero, is considered inauspicious].

When the trial was over we were sent to jail, and our friends went to the gallows. After we heard our sentences, we went for a last visit with our friends who were given the death sentence, to say good-bye to them. (They could not carry out death sentences in the case of Ram Hari and me, as I will explain later.) Dharma Bhakta said that death meant nothing to him if it were for the sake of the country, and we told him that his name would be immortal in the history of our country. Dasarath Chand said, in English, 'The Nepal Praja Parishad is our life. As long as the Nepal Praja Parishad remains, we remain'. Sometimes he would speak English so that the guards could not understand him. He assured us that we would definitely see the fall of the Rana regime and the dawn of democracy. Then Ganesh Man, representing all of us, said, 'We will definitely fight to bring democracy as long as we are alive'.

After we had said good-bye to our doomed friends we were told to carry our luggage and march all the way to the jail. We had been prepared to bear all kinds of trouble and torture, but carrying our luggage, full of winter clothes, blankets and mattresses, kitchen utensils, etc., was too much for us. We didn't even have any rope to tie things up with. We were left to rest for a long time on the front porch of Singha Darbar and were finally told to move along, carrying our own luggage. I raised my voice against this. Although it was very heavy, it wasn't the weight we objected to, but the lack of any way to tie it all up into one or two bundles. I said we were not ready to carry our luggage, and we had a long argument with the Rana officials. Then they made us wait a long time again, maybe to let the Prime Minister know about our demands and to wait for his instructions. Finally at around 3 o'clock in the afternoon we were told to move, but we didn't have to carry our luggage. We marched to the jail in a kind of procession with me in front, Ram Hari behind me, then Chuda Prasad, then Govinda Prasad. Although people were not allowed to gather around Singha Darbar and Bhadrakali, quite a number of young people gathered there to catch a glimpse of us, in spite of the risk they thereby incurred.

Sukra Raj Shastri had been arrested a couple of years before us. He was not a member of our party; he was arrested for simply preaching a discourse on the *Bhagavad Gita* in Indrachok [the main bazaar in the old section of Kathmandu]. After the Ranas arrested him they offered him release on their terms. But he told them that he wouldn't even consider their terms unless they first apologized for arresting him.[9] The Ranas were suspicious of him because he had been to see Gandhi in India, and was associated with the Arya Samaj [a reformist Hindu organization]. A few days after going to the jail we could see from our window on the top floor of the Number two barracks a number of people gathering on the road to the south. Then a guard came and told us that they had hanged Sukra Raj Shastri. For preaching about the *Gita*, he was hanged from a tree on the road from Tripureswar to Kalimati, on 24 January, 1941. Till then I had been prepared to accommodate the Ranas to a limited extent, but after they hanged Sukra Raj I was determined not to make any compromise in our demand to end Rana rule.

Two days after Sukra Raj was hanged Dharma Bhakta was hanged in Sifale. Govinda Prasad Upadhyay has researched and described this in detail: 'On 13 Magh, 1997 [24 January, 1941, the same day Sukra Raj was hanged], Dharma Bhakta was brought to the Central Jail from the School House at Singha Darbar. The Ranas gave his relatives their permission to visit him that day in the afternoon. At the Ranas' request, his father had been imprisoned by the British in Calcutta, and his brothers were also there. So only his father's sister's daughter, Surya Laxmi, was here, and she and some of Dharma Bhakta's friends went to visit him in the jail.

Dharma Bhakta, handcuffed and bound in chains, was taken to meet them in front of the temple of Jagannath, right across from the prison. Surya Laxmi said, 'They say you'll be released if you ask for mercy. Why don't you beg for a pardon?' He answered, 'We worked for democracy and the King. What have we done to be pardoned for? We should not ask for mercy from such tyrants. I have decided to sacrifice my life for the nation. The future generation will avenge the Ranas of my death'. He added, 'I have troubled you too much; from tomorrow I'll trouble you no more'. He said this because it was his sister who had sent meals to him, done his laundry, and cared for and worried about him while he was imprisoned in Singha Darbar. When the jailer told him it was time to go, he said to Surya Laxmi, 'They are injecting me with drugs to make me frail and weak, but don't worry, everything will be finished soon'. Then he left.

That same night all the shops from Dilli Bazaar to Gyanehswor were ordered shut. At 10 o'clock Dharma Bhakta was put in a truck

[9] Shah 1990.

and taken through Kamal Pokhari and Gyaneshwor to Sifale.[10] Capt. Krishna Bahadur Thapa said, 'Around 7 o'clock I was ordered to take some twenty guards with me and tie the knot in the rope which was to hang the prisoner. I took the necessary things and the guards and left for Sifale at 9 o'clock. Dharma Bhakta was brought at around 11 o'clock, accompanied by some guards and two executioners. He was wearing a blue shirt, white *suruwal*, and a woollen vest. He was blind-folded and his hands tied, crossed, behind his back. General Nara Shamsher then asked him his last wish. Dharma Bhakta retorted, 'My last wish is to see the end of the Rana regime'.

Then he was made to stand on a small brick platform above which the rope had been tied to a tree branch pointing south. The noose was put around his neck and the wall kicked down. But the noose was improperly tied, and because of his weight, the branch sagged and his feet touched the ground. Then they tied another noose on another south-pointing branch. But when the support under his feet was removed, the rope was unable to support the struggling heavy body and broke.

Nara Shamsher was very nervous and agitated and went to cut the rope with a knife. Being in a hurry, to get it done quickly, he accidentally slashed a deep cut across Dharma Bhakta's cheek, up to his chin. Dharma Bhakta flew into a rage and kicked Nara Shamsher, who tumbled and landed some six feet away. Nara then ordered the guards to beat him. He was beaten to unconsciousness, and in that state some eight guards lifted him, put the noose around his neck, and hanged him. This was described by the famous poet, Bhimnidi Tiwari.

The next day people going to Pashupati saw his body, his eyes half-closed, an ugly wound across his face, mouth smeared with blood, his feet almost touching the ground. A message written on a piece of cardboard hung on his chest, which read 'This person has been active in conspiring against the Sri Tin Maharaja and the Rolewala[11] Generals, and to rule himself, and has thus been given such punishment'.

[10] According to Uprety (1992:81) General Nara's motorcade was stopped in Maharajganj by Mohan Shamsher, who feared being haunted by Dharma Bhakta's ghost if he was hanged near his residence; hence the last-minute change of venue to Sifale. In 1948 Mohan Shamsher became the last of the Ranas to accede to the Prime Ministership.

[11] As used today, *Sri* is equivalent to 'Mister', but with greater honorific connotations than the English term carries. The Prime Minister was addressed as *Sri Tin* (roughly, 'Sir three times over'), whereas the King is *Sri Panch* (as above, but 'five times'), while the royal priest is *Sri Chha* ('six times'), reflecting the supremacy of the Brahmin over the Thakuri/Chhetri. In addition, when addressing one's parents formally (as in a letter) 'six times' should be

When Dasarath Chand heard his death sentence he showed no reaction of fear. Laughing, he said, in Hindi, 'What is the stuff of life after all?' He had been educated in India and often spoke Hindi even to us. When Ganga Lal heard that the rest of his friends had gotten only life imprisonment, he had cynically said, 'Throughout Juddha Shamsher's life' (implying that Juddha would be assassinated soon enough).

Dasarath Chand and Ganga Lal were kept in Singha Darbar till 14 Magh [25 January]. There was a sweeper named Ram Maya who swept and cleaned their room. Dasarath's lover, Juliana, had died of tuberculosis in Palpa. One day he told Ram Maya, 'Ram Maya, my friends have many relatives and friends to weep for them after they are executed, while I do not have a single person in this world to weep for my dead body. Ram Maya, will you weep for me after I have been put to death?'

On 15 Magh [26 January], Dasarath Chand and Ganga Lal were taken to Shobha Bhagwati late in the evening. As they passed near Ganga Lal's house, he shouted to his wife, 'Hasina! Hasina!' at the top of his voice. Her name means 'always joyful and cheerful', and he had written poems about her.

When they reached Shobha Bhagwati, they both washed their hands and mouths in the holy water of the Vishnumati River. When they asked to pray and offer homage to the holy mother, Nara Shamsher, who had gone there with two executioners, had no objection. They prayed, saying 'we have lit an eternal flame for the motherland, don't let it be extinguished.'

Then they were led to two posts erected at the confluence of the Vishnumati and Bhatakhusi Rivers. Dasarath Chand was tied facing north, and Ganga Lal was tied facing west. Nara Shamsher asked Dasarath Chand for his last wish, which was 'to see the end of the Rana regime and the advent of democracy'. Then General Nara asked Ganga Lal to beg for mercy. He replied that he would never beg for mercy since he had done nothing to be pardoned for. Rather, the Ranas should ask for pardon for committing unjust slaughter. Nara Shamsher, shaking with nervousness and his mouth running dry, remained silent.

used. Other enumerations of *Sri* are possible, up to 108 in the case of a very few extraordinarily revered saints, such as the philosopher Sankaracharya. While in theory the numbers between six and 108 are available to designate individuals of various degrees of veneration, I know of no such actual cases. 'Rolewala' refers to someone on the 'roll' of those eligible to become Prime Minister, listed in descending order of succession. Often bitterly contested, the ordering of the 'roll' was the source of much dissension among the Ranas.

Dasarath and Ganga Lal then talked about who should be shot first. Dasarath wanted Ganga Lal to be shot first, but Nara wanted to shoot and torture the older prisoner, Dasarath, first, so as to terrify the younger Ganga Lal into begging for mercy, thereby robbing him of his dignity. He wanted to show the people that Ganga Lal was devoid of any principles. Nara must have been ordered to do so by his father and grandfather, Juddha, and Dasarath was aware of this. Therefore Dasarath requested them to shoot Ganga Lal first. Ganga Lal, understanding what was in Dasarath's mind, said, '*Dai* [older brother], set your heart at rest, I'll never beg for mercy, never, no matter what happens'.

Two strong Podes [a low Newar caste] had been specially trained to shoot them, and that day they had been given large amounts of liquor to drink, so they were quite drunk. One of them was told to shoot at Dasarath's knees first. He went close and shot him. Dasarath grimaced but did not cry out in pain; instead he shouted 'Down with the Rana regime'. Ganga Lal also joined in, so that their slogan echoed into the distance. Nara Shamsher flew into a rage and ordered the Pode to shoot at Dasarath's thigh. The pain was unbearable, and Dasarath struggled violently. Unable to bear Dasarath's torture any more, Ganga Lal screamed at them, 'If you have the guts, kill your father [*tero bau*; *tero* is the derogatory form of 'your'] with a single bullet!'

Nara, literally shaking with anger, took aim at Ganga Lal's knees and shot. Ganga Lal just shouted back at him, 'You unjust and cruel wretch!' The Pode then shot Dasarath in the side. Nara wanted Ganga Lal to see that. Ganga Lal, in a frenzy, shouted all sorts of abuse at Nara, and then Nara fired again, hitting Ganga Lal below his knee joint. Dasarath was still struggling. After some time, the Pode fired his fourth bullet in Dasarath's chest, finally killing him.

Then Nara himself aimed his third bullet at Ganga Lal's thigh and fired; Ganga Lal struggled. The second Pode, who had only watched silently till then, was asked to take final aim at Ganga Lal. He started to weep and refused to shoot. They tried to mollify him and to persuade him to shoot, but he still refused. Then the first Pode was told to do the dirty work instead, but he also lingered and started making all sorts of excuses, saying that it was impossible to shoot at close range, and that he could not hit the target from a distance, he also refused to shoot. He was literally shaking with fear at the ghastly sight. They finally persuaded him to shoot from a distance, and Nara Shamsher himself helped him hold the pistol steady in his hand. Two bullets were fired successively, hitting Ganga La in the stomach and the side.

And so, two days after Dharma Bhakta was hanged, Ganga Lal and Dasarath Chand were shot on the bank of the Vishnumati River near the temple of Shobha Bhagwati.[12] Another man, Nayab Subba Purna

[12] Govinda Prasad based his description of the executions on interviews with General Nara Shamsher and with a man who had talked with General Nara's *hajuria*, Bed Bahadur Silwal. In a letter to the Secretary to the Government of India in Delhi, dated 7 February, 1941, Sir Geoffrey Betham, the British Minister in Kathmandu, took a highly critical view of the executions: 'It is my considered opinion that the public executions carried out as they have been are a very grave political mistake and His Highness was ill advised to order them. From observations made of reactions of people to the public display of those executed it was apparent that the people of the valley—mainly Newars—although afraid openly to express their feelings are very bitter against the Maharaja [Prime Minister] for the degradation of fellow Newars and the sullen expression on their faces boded ill towards those responsible for the executions. Large crowds went to view the dead bodies and many were observed surreptitiously to pay respect to them. The refusal of Ganga Lal to appeal for mercy had been secretly applauded and I fear that rather than having the effect of stamping out the movement, these gruesome spectacles will have entirely the opposite effects, for feelings against His Highness in particular have been heightened and extended. Active agitation may die down for a time, but it is my opinion that it will break out again and will not be easily suppressed. I would not be surprised if desperate attempts are made at some time on the life of His Highness'. Quoted in Shah (1990: 132).

Indeed, Shah (1990: 133) reports two public reactions which gave expression to the bitter feelings which Betham reports: first, a placard was found on 27 January on a tree from which Sukra Raj was hanged, which read: 'Please carry out the other death sentences as soon as possible as the authors of this placard wish to carry out the sentences which they have imposed on those responsible for awarding death and other sentences to their friends'.

The following day the second incident took place: 'There is a statue of H.H. Juddha in Juddha Road, the main road into Kathmandu City. It is situated close to the Fire Station and also not far from the Nepal Bank ... Four men drove to the statue in a closed car. They got out and draped a sari round the statue. They then smeared the sari in certain places with blood. Further explanation in official and decent correspondence is unnecessary. They then drove away. Some men of the Fire Brigade saw them but have been definitely unable to name them'. (Betham, quoted in Shah 1990: 134). The explanation that Betham delicately chose to omit may be necessary for Western readers: in Hindu society menstruating women are treated as untouchables; they are banned to a separate room in the house and must refrain from all normal interaction with others. Since menstrual blood is the most polluting substance imaginable, draping the blood-stained sari over the statue was the most insulting and desecrating gesture that could have been perpetrated against it (see Chapter 3, footnote 5.) It is a small irony that three of the four streets converging on Juddha's statue (which is still in place) are now named, incongruously but unsurprisingly in live-and-let-live Nepal, for three of the four men he executed. The national sports stadium (Dasarath Ranshala) is named for the fourth. (Cf. Chapter 6, footnote 15.)

Shah goes on to relate that the official Rana version of the Praja Parishad was that it was a violent, anti-King organization committed to the establishment of a Republic run

Narayan Pradhan, was spared capital punishment by Juddha's command at the last minute.[13] He was not a member of our party; some said his crime was that he had gotten a radio (radios were outlawed) and listened to it. They were all set to hang him on the Tundikhel, the rope and platform were ready, but at that moment the Prime Minister happened by, asked what was going on, and commuted his sentence to life imprisonment.

King Tribhuvan was also taken to trial at Singha Darbar. Two of Tribhuvan's sons, Himalaya and Basundhara, were also taken with him. Some say Mahendra was also taken with them; but so far as we heard only Tribhuvan, Himalaya, and Basundhara were there. The Ranas had tried to win Mahendra to their side from the very beginning. The Ranas made sure that all of Mahendra's aids were their well-wishers.

King Tribhuvan was strongly against keeping a matrimonial relationship with the Ranas, but the Ranas were keen on it. Tribhuvan could do nothing about it, and Hari Shamsher's daughter, Indra Rajya Laxmi Devi was married to Crown Prince Mahendra. (Later, after his wife died, Mahendra married Indra Rajya's sister, Ratna Rajya Laxmi, in 1952.) The Ranas were trying to win Mahendra to their side. That might be the reason why only Tribhuvan and his other two sons were taken to the trial. I don't know if it's true, but I have heard that the Ranas had a quarrel with Basundhara. After the trial, the Ranas made preparations to banish King Tribhuvan and his two sons to Gorkha and declare Mahendra the king. When they were brought to Singha Darbar they were shut up there until 9:00 p.m. We heard all this from the talk among the guards who used to guard our cell.

The same day at around 8:30 p.m. the British Ambassador, Sir Geoffrey Betham, came to Kathmandu. The Ranas consulted him about banishing Tribhuvan from Kathmandu, and the British did not agree with this plan. The Ambassador told the Ranas that Gurkha troops were stationed in India, and if they heard about mistreatment of the king they might revolt. Therefore, they advised that Tribhuvan not be deposed or banished.

Later I asked Tribhuvan about it. I asked, if the Ranas were ready to banish you to Gorkha, why didn't they go ahead and do it? Then he told me about the British Ambassador's visit. In that way, Tribhuvan was saved from banishment.

---

by Newars.

[13] Shah 1990.

Later King Tribhuvan told us, 'You said you stayed in prison for so many years, but I did not suffer any less. I was also shut up in my own rooms. My queens used to cook food for us'. King Tribhuvan gave us his support, he did indeed.

After about six days in jail, during which all the executions took place, Ram Hari and I were taken back to Singha Darbar. We were singled out for capital punishment because we were the leaders. But Ram Hari and I were Brahmins, so the Ranas could not carry out the death sentences they had given us. In *Manusmriti* [the book of Hindu laws codified by Manu in the second century AD] it is written that Brahmins should not be given capital punishment. Since to kill a Brahmin was considered the greatest sin of that time, the *Mulki Ain* [the National Law of Nepal] stipulated that the severest punishment a Brahmin could receive was to have his caste taken away and be banished from the country. They could give us the death sentence, to show how seriously they regarded our crimes, but they could not carry it out.

The procedure for decasting or outcasting was as follows: first our heads were shaved down the middle and across the middle, in the shape of a cross, which was then painted with four different colours [*char pat mudne*, literally, cut in four parts; the shaving is critical because it necessitated cutting the tuft of hair (*tupi*) a Brahmin should always have on the back of his head]. The colours didn't mean anything, it was all meant just to insult us. Then our sacred thread [a simple cotton thread worn over one shoulder and under the opposite arm; after a Brahmin boy receives it at puberty, in the *bartaman* ceremony, he is considered twice-born and expected to observe caste rules] was taken away from us. A Brahmin should always wear a sacred thread, so after we got to prison our families sent us sacred threads to replace those which were taken from us. We should also have been given a pig to carry, but for some reason we were not [in Hindu culture, a pig is a very polluting animal]. It was all up to the whim of the Ranas.

They had wanted to take us around in public in chains to further humiliate us, but the Ranas did not dare to have us go around the city. The Ranas did not want people to see us, because they might become aroused, so they arranged that when we were taken to jail from Singha Darbar there would be a military parade going on at the Tundikhel, which no one was allowed to enter. So we walked in chains from Singha Darbar to jail in that manner.

Unfortunately the Ranas did not carry out the part of the punishment about driving us away from the country. They did not banish us from Nepal because they were afraid that if they did so it would be a golden opportunity for us to work against the Ranas from India [laughter]. Instead they put us in jail for life. In addition, not only did they confiscate all our property, but they also confiscated the shares that we would have inherited from our fathers. In my case, they calculated that there were four shares, one for me, one for each of my father's wives, and one for him. So one-fourth of my father's property was confiscated. This included our house in Sifale and the land that it stood on.

The Ranas sent their representatives many times to tell us that if we asked for their forgiveness we would be given full pardon. But we did not. Why should we beg pardon? They were wrong and we were right, so why should we apologize? We might have asked for a pardon, but when they hanged Sukra Raj Shastri in full view of our cells, we were so enraged that we vowed never to compromise with the Ranas by asking for a pardon. The four of us—Ram Hari, Govinda Prasad, Chuda Prasad, and I—sat together and pledged that even if we had to rot and die in jail, we would never ask for a pardon from the Ranas. We promised each other never to ask for forgiveness, and afterwards we were very glad we had done that. We would accept only an absolutely unconditional release. Once they wanted to release Ram Hari, but he put his chains back on and refused to leave. (We wore leg irons for ten years in jail). And in the end, after ten years, they did have to release us without any conditions. When we went to jail, we never dreamed that the Ranas would be deposed of so quickly.

Life in prison

Memories of my ten years in prison are pleasant and short; that is, we tried to make our time in jail seem pleasant and short. Nature gives you the ability to endure. When a person lives in one place for so long repeating the same thing everyday, he gets so used to his environment that even years pass by without his being aware of it. We had a calendar, and we kept track of time, but otherwise we were not conscious of it. Our ten years in prison passed like ten months. Every day it was the same routine, from morning till night. Mostly we passed our time in religious activities—prayer, yoga, meditation, and reading religious books. Ram Hari says life in prison was partly romantic and partly torture, but for me it was all torture. [Tanka Prasad's views on prison life here and in the following paragraphs are not very consistent; he alternately complains about and minimizes the difficulties he experienced.]

Our life in jail included some colourful activities. Among the prisoners were included Siddhi Charan, a poet who was imprisoned for writing some kind of revolutionary poem; Chandra Man, who carried messages to the King for us, was also an artist; Bhupal Singh, a musician; Ganesh Raj, a Raktapat Mandal member who was also a dancer; Jyoti Prasad, a devotee; and Ganesh Man, who loved sports and physical exercise. Since the Ranas kept us in such sordid conditions, depriving us of even a glimpse of our families, we had to make an effort to maintain healthy attitudes. We used to play *Pasa*[14] or recite the *Bhagwat* [an epic containing the *Bhagvad Gita* and other stories about Krishna], and some played the harmonium, tabla, or guitar. Ram Hari Sharma and Kedar Man Singh used to play the harmonium as an accompaniment to prayers they would sing. I did not have a voice for singing, so I used to just listen to them. Sometimes we played chess, or wrote poems and essays. We would arrange a seminar on literature once a month, and twice we staged dramas based on religious books. We would fast on days like Shiva Ratri, Ram Navami, Krishna Asthami, etc., and offer prayers and *puja* to god.

Although these activities helped kill time, the mental depression and anxiety that afflicted us from not being able to speak, touch, and see our wives, children, parents, relatives, and friends, and to hear so little news of them were difficult to throw off. The desires that burned inside us, the emotions that swept us, the longings that remained unfulfilled, who could understand them but ourselves? Some people, who were emotionally weak and sensitive, became melancholic and depressed. Sometimes they got sick and became bed-ridden. One of our party members, Bala Bahadur Pandey, eventually went mad. He would answer calls of nature in front of everyone and then eat or sleep in the same place. This caused some prisoners to panic, as they feared the same thing would happen to them. Some of them begged for the Ranas' pardon and release. Pandey was sent to the jail hospital, which was hopeless, where he eventually died without proper care or treatment.

The jail consisted of two parts: Central Jail, where serious criminals

---

[14] *Pasa* is a dice game in which red, white, green, and black pieces are advanced on a marked piece of cloth called a *tharki*; *pasa* is mentioned in the Hindu epic, the *Mahabharata*.

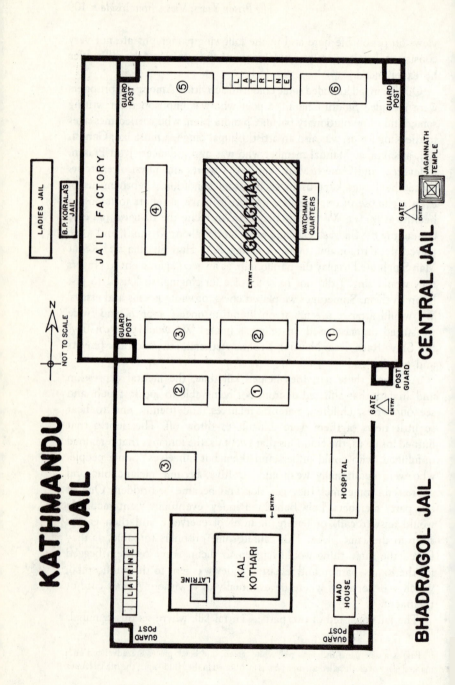

like murderers were kept, and Bhadragol Jail, for political prisoners and lesser offenders. (See map of Kathmandu Jail.) *Bhadragol* means miscellaneous, or different things mixed together. For the first six months all thirty-two of us political prisoners were kept in a two-storey barracks in Bhadragol Jail. About half of us were Praja Parishad members, and the rest were only political in the sense of being non-criminal. They were poets, social reformers, etc. There were four rooms on the second floor, so we were eight to a room. We were not allowed even to mix with the prisoners on the first floor. We went out a door and down a stairway to use the public toilet, which was located down a sloping hill from our barracks. That toilet was sheer hell, the most foul and stinking place imaginable. So that we wouldn't associate with other prisoners, a guard accompanied us to the toilet.

Then, after six months they completed a building inside an entirely separate compound (within the main compound of Bhadragol Jail), just for us thirty-two political prisoners. This we gave the nickname of 'Kal Kothari' [*kal* means both black and death, so the term could be translated as Death Chamber or Black Cell]. It was a locked compound with a door that was opened only if food, etc. arrived to be sent in. Because of escape attempts, they later raised one of the walls from six feet to eight feet in height. Our barracks in this new building also consisted of two stories. It consisted of eight small rooms, four to a room, with no ventilation. We had to do everything there—sleep, cook, eat, etc. At first we had no beds and just slept on the floor. But the ground floor was damp, since it was just dirt, so all thirty-two of us slept on the second floor (eight to a room) and used the first floor for cooking. Later Juddha Shamsher ordered four wooden beds to be made for each room. Since the main prison wall was beyond our compound wall, we were actually in a prison within a prison. The Kal Kothari has now been demolished.

I have seen the prisons of the United States in some American movies. There is no comparison between those modern, western prisons and our Nepalese jail. Our room was twelve feet by twelve feet. All eight of us were kept in the same room. There was a small court-yard outside our rooms. We were allowed to go only up to the courtyard. We had to live our lives in a very limited space. It was like hell. No one would voluntarily stay in that place for one hour. Nowadays when people come to me and urge me to do something against this political system, I ask them if they want to put me in jail once again [laughter].

They reply that I am an old person with only a short life to live, so while dying I would be doing something good for the people (laughter).

I was imprisoned again for a short while many years later, in 1951, the same year I was released, and the conditions were still the same. I never went back to that jail after I was released the second time. When I became Prime Minister I sanctioned four lakhs [one lakh = 100,000] of rupees for the improvement of the jail. But I was in office for only one and a half years, and my successors never carried out the improvements I had authorized.

Our daily routine started with getting up at four o'clock in the morning. Then we would take our bath and meditate for three to four hours. In the beginning we cooked in big groups, but as they were unwieldy and we had different tastes (for example, some of us were vegetarian and some were not), we broke down into smaller groups. Ram Hari or Govinda Prasad would cook our food. I used to help by doing such jobs as getting water. Chuda Prasad sometimes ate with us and sometimes cooked for himself. We were provided one and a half manas of rice per day per person by the government, half milled; we had to dehusk the other half [one mana of rice is about one lb.]. The rice smelled so bad we had to devise an instrument to polish it, which we did with the help of some pieces of tin, the only material we could find for that purpose. The rest of our rations consisted of two chilli peppers and a pinch of salt, but no *dal*. Because the government ration was so meagre we could not live only on that, so our families had to send us more food. Our families brought us food in jail from the very beginning. The Ranas thought, why should they spend money to feed the prisoners? So they felt that if the prisoners could get their food from their own houses, so much the better (laughter). We also had a small garden in jail and occasionally even sent out vegetables to our families to show them what we were growing.

In the beginning, when we were still in Singha Darbar, our families sometimes brought meat for us. When we moved to the jail, some of us became strict vegetarians. We observed what is called in Sanskrit a *satwik* diet—that is, no meat, no spices, oils, garlic, or onions. We did this so that our sexual urges would be depressed. I remained a vegetarian for two more years after I was released. We used to eat rice, *dal*, and curry. I was used to having three or four varieties of curries in my home at every meal. Therefore, I sometimes insisted to Ram Hari that he cook two or three varieties in prison too. He used to get angry at me over this, but he would make them anyway. For our fuel they used to provide us with a thin bundle of firewood. We usually ate our meal at ten or eleven o'clock in the morning.

The government also provided us one pice [=0.01 rupee] per day. We could buy five things with one pice inside the jail (laughter). There was a shop inside our jail, and the ancestor of the shopkeeper had made a contract with Jang Bahadur [the first Rana Prime Minister, who came to power in 1846] to supply five items of daily necessities to the prisoners for one pice. The original agreement was that he was required to give us those items for one pice, and the contract still held. The five items were salt, chillies, turmeric (*besar*), cooking oil (*tel*), and spices (*masala*). The quantity of things that we could buy for one pice was very little. We used to save our one pice allowances and then once a month use it, along with the food our families sent us, to have a special feast. Then all thirty-two of us would eat delicacies such as *puri* (deep-fried flat bread), *achaar* (relishes), and other vegetables.[15]

We also had razors to shave ourselves, and we could call for a barber if we needed a haircut. After eating we used to read books. Only spiritual books were allowed inside the prison. Even the papers that wrapped the medicines prescribed for us had to be returned. Therefore, we used to read *Kalyan*,[16] a spiritual book published in Gorakhpur, India, after our morning meal. Only such books were allowed. I reflected much on religion in jail, and I was convinced of the existence of god. I had heated discussions with another prisoner who was an atheist in search of some other belief to help him face the hardships of jail and to maintain hope for the future. I believed in the Hindu theory of rebirth, which meant that the desires and wishes unsatisfied in this life will be fulfilled in the next one. These thoughts made me optimistic and kept my morale up. I was solely dependent on Pashupatinath.[17]

At the end of the day we would have our evening meal. Since we had no lantern or electric light in our cell, we used to burn a kerosene

---

[15] Details of the prison feast are from Govinda Prasad Upadhyay.

[16] *Kalyana* is a non-sectarian but generally Hindu-oriented journal devoted to religious topics; it is published in forty-eight-page monthly issues. The volume to which Tanka Prasad refers is a 307 page 'Annual Number', subtitled the 'God Number', vol. 1 number 1, January 1934.

[17] Pashupatinath, a form of Shiva, one of the three deities which compose the Hindu trinity: Shiva the destroyer, Brahma the creator, Vishnu the preserver. Pashupatinath is also invoked as the protector of Nepal.

lamp (*tuki*) and read books for one or two more hours, and then go to bed.

Our daily necessities had to be provided by our own families, but we were not allowed to say hello to them, or even to see each other. The only news I heard about my two children was that they had joined a school. Once my wife tried to show my two daughters to me in jail, but the authorities would not allow it. I never saw anyone from my family for those ten years.

We were able to keep track of the outside world by smuggling letters in and out. We smuggled letters through a wooden pot (*theki*), which contained the curd our families would send for us. There were two such wooden pots (incoming and outgoing) in which we had hollowed out some space on the bottom, where we could conceal our letters under a layer of *ghee* and ashes. Our families also used the same technique when they brought us curd in that pot. Ram Hari's wife first did it (she became known as the Number One Smuggler), and Ram Hari discovered the letter by telepathy. He just suspected something, and looked and found the letter in a small hole. Then I enlarged the hole so that the *teki* would hold three or four pages.

At the outside gate of the prison the food had to be submitted for inspection to the jailer, who would thoroughly check the contents of the pot before bringing it to us or taking the empty pot from us. They did not detect our smuggling technique for a long time. When they found out (from a letter B.P. Koirala was carrying when he was arrested), the jailor came shouting at us because he was afraid he would lose his job (since he had failed to detect the letters). After that, we made false bottoms in two small tin suitcases (*kantur*) and started to do the same thing once again. The suitcases held food, such as rice and vegetables, that our families would send us. The jailer used to bring that suitcase to us, and we used to take out the letters from under his nose and sneak our own letters into the suitcase. They never suspected it. I sent letters to Nehru, Jaya Prakash Narayan (the socialist leader), etc., through this technique. The jail authorities would have never guessed it if somebody had not informed them about it. They knew we were smuggling letters from the prison, but they could never guess how, so they bribed someone inside or outside the prison and learned our secret. The Ranas were very angry when they discovered that we had corresponded even with Nehru and Jaya Prakash Narayan.

Other non-political prisoners inside Bhadragol Jail were taken outside to work everyday. Some were taken to Singha Darbar, and some were taken to other places. Through intermediaries, such as prison-guards, we could have contact with them, so we instructed our women to send money, books, or other necessities that we might need, through those prisoners. The prisoners would then smuggle those things to us. The guards would also help us get things. They were poor, and sometimes they would charge us Rs 3 for a newspaper, while at other times they would just give it to us for nothing. There was no fixed rule. We even had our secret library inside the prison consisting of all sorts of political, historical, philosophical, and other types of books. We read so many great things about other countries, e.g., about France, England, and authors, e.g., Charles Dickens, Scott, Thackeray, Shaw, Marx, Engels, and such books as Tom Paine's *Rights of Man*, and Harold Laski's *Grammar of Politics*. And we pictured in our mind the things they had written. We tried to compare those pictures with our conditions [laughter]. These authors were great reformers, particularly Dickens. His writings had great impact on the people. He could clearly depict peoples' character in his writing. There are no such authors in Nepal.

The only outside noise that we could hear was the human cry of other prisoners in pain. There was a *chowkidar's* [guard's] quarter where criminal prisoners were beaten, usually from problems arising from gambling and stealing inside the prison. Sometimes someone would even steal another's rice when he went to wash his hands after cooking it! But that never happened among us political prisoners. Not guards, but other prisoners and employees came and beat the prisoners. They got new shoes and clothes as a reward for giving beatings. They beat us severely in Singha Darbar, but once we were in Central Jail they didn't beat us political prisoners. They came to beat us once or twice, but we convinced them that we already had life sentences and there was nothing more they could gain by beating us, and things of that sort. After a while they left us alone.

My prison mates used to write letters to their wives, but at first I rarely did. One day my wife wrote to me asking why I was not writing letters to her. She wrote to me that all other prisoners' wives were getting letters from their husbands except herself. I wrote back to her, telling her that since I was there in prison for life I did not want her to develop deep affection for me which would make us both wretched. I thought, why should I just tie her to me in such sad correspondence? I thought to myself that a bond between us would develop even without letters. So, I stopped writing to her. But she replied that she was prepared to follow me into politics and was not afraid of any harm that might befall her because of it. She wrote saying that I should write and tell her what to do and she would do it. Only then did I start to write to her regularly like my other cellmates. She did so well. Her contribution was a great one. She was so devoted to me that when she washed my clothes while I was in prison, she would go to sleep with them on our pillow.

After that she also started to take an active part in politics: meeting with people, persuading and convincing them to go against the atrocities of the Ranas. She even went to India carrying my letters to Jaya Prakash Narayan, Nehru, and other Nepali leaders, including B.P. Koirala. I wrote to them because, since they called themselves socialists, I thought maybe they would help us in our struggle. But Jaya Prakash Narayan knew B.P. Koirala from his childhood and considered B.P. as his own son, so he was all for helping B.P., but not us. He did not even write back to me. So we did not depend on anybody, but still we had some hope for help from the King.

It is very difficult to live in jail for ten years without having anything to resort to. When one is cornered one does all sorts of things. Some took refuge in gambling, some in smoking marijuana. Marijuana relieves worry and depresses the sexual urge. But to deal with these problems we refused to either gamble or smoke hemp. I didn't gamble in prison because it was pointless, especially later when there were just four of us left to gamble. Instead we took refuge in religion and adopted an austere diet. For us, when we got books we read them, and when we did not have anything else to do we would pray to God, conduct *puja*, and recite our religious books. Inspired by my mother, I had been religious from my childhood.

When people live so close together for a long time, naturally there will be some quarrelling. Once I declared, out of frustration, that I would die in two days, and the others all quarrelled with me, arguing that I wouldn't [laughter]. But I never thought of committing suicide— no! Our religion forbids us to commit suicide. Never! There will be retribution and God will give it. The Ranas will go—with that conviction we endured.

I never had any regrets about what we had done, about our tactics, or about going into politics. No, no regrets! We used to scatter the pamphlets on the streets, which I think was an appropriate tactic for those times. I think what we did was not sufficient; we could have done more. But because the Ranas were such undesirable elements, whatever we did against them was very small. We should have done more. But living in jail and all that, I had absolutely no regrets about that.

There is one thing I missed or regretted the most during my ten years in prison. The day before I fled to India it was the fourth day after my wife's menstrual period. We believe that copulation on that day is the most favourable time for conceiving a child. Yet I did not sleep with my wife on that day, and when I was in prison I always regretted that I had not, because if I had we might have had another child, and that child might have been a son. As it was, I was condemned to life imprisonment with no possibility of ever having a son.

We were many castes living together in the jail. I had never felt that Newars were different from us, but in jail I had found that some of them were still resentful of being conquered by King Prithvinarayan Shah. Some of them even had soft corners for the Japanese. They said that if the Japanese come they will favour Newars more than others. The idea behind their belief was that since the British supported the Shahs and the Ranas, who had conquered the Newars, the Newars would have some natural affinity with the Japanese, who were enemies of the British.

It's a long story about the Newars. You see, Newars thought that Prithvinarayan Shah had usurped their kingdoms. In some quarters the resentment still continues, and they have numerous grievances against us. I told them that no country has been unified without a conqueror. England was unified by William the Conqueror. In America Lincoln fought the Civil War to preserve the union. The overwhelming majority of Newars understand that Prithvinarayan Shah unified us. Without this unification the tiny principalities of Nepal would have had little chance of preserving their independence from the British empire. They should not hold any grudge against him. Newars actually invited Prithvinarayan Shah into the Kathmandu Valley. Prithvinarayan made an alliance with the King of Bhaktapur in a dispute among the quarreling Newar kings of the three cities of the valley. Prithvinarayan Shah's father, King Nara Bhupal Shah of Gorkha, had developed a very close bond of friendship with the King of Bhaktapur. While he was the crown prince King Prithvinarayan spent three years with his father's friend at Bhaktapur Darbar where he had the opportunity to study the culture and political situation of the principalities of Kathmandu Valley in depth. Before leaving for his home in Gorkha, he developed a close friendship with Prince Bir Narsing of Bhaktapur.

Soon after becoming King of Gorkha, Prithvinarayan conquered

Nuwakot district northwest of Kathmandu. He then annexed Makwanpur principality and other regions surrounding the valley. His principal aim was to unify the hilly regions from the far west to the far east before the British could advance from the south to the north. Therefore, he had to conquer the Kathmandu Valley early on.

Someone wrote that when the subjects of one country are dissatisfied, then they call people from other countries to rule, so that they might enjoy a better life. It is also written that together with the conquerors come other people, who also have to be given something, whereas those who called the unifier get very little. The same thing happened here. They called Prithvinarayan Shah here, but he didn't come alone, he came with numerous higher caste courtiers, such as Thapas, Basnyats and Pandeys. Prithvnarayan had to share power with them. In spite of these obligations he also adopted and encouraged the cultural practices of the valley. Newars were placed in high official posts in his palace and continued to be given high posts in subsequent administrations, even during the Rana period. We have no objections to Newars making a big celebration out of rituals such as Mha Puja [worship of the body, a major annual Newar ritual]. Let them do it. If they want to maintain their rituals, that's welcome. But if they also want to have the Newari calendar replace the Bikram calendar, that is impratical.

In 1944 Ganesh Man escaped from the jail, but we never tried. He escaped by climbing to the top of a wall with a hook he had fashioned from an iron rod. Because Ganesh Man was quite short he stood on Chandra Man's shoulders. Then he used a rope that we had made out of cloth to lower himself to the other side. Every six months we were each issued four and one half yards of course white khadi cloth. We could have asked Damai [tailor caste] prisoners to sew clothes for us from that cloth, which they did in the prison workshop [karkhana], but our families sent us the clothes we needed. We used the cloth for bed sheets, and in this case we used that cloth to make Ganesh Man's rope. Chandra Man was supposed to follow him, but he could not get over the wall by himself. For his escape attempt Chandra Man was taken before the Prime Minister, who ordered him to the Golghar (which I'll describe later) for some months.

There were many secret passes from the Kathmandu Valley to the outside world which someone who wanted to pass undetected by the Ranas could use. Ganesh Man utilized one of those secret passes while escaping. He went over the Thori Pass, from Mankamana near Gorkha, to Chitwan, and then on to India. Some others also tried to escape but failed. Once Ram Hari's wife assisted in an escape attempt by Chuda Prasad, Govinda Prasad, and Khadga Man Singh. She made a rope out of cloth, painted it black so that it wouldn't be so visible at night, and brought the rope as far as Bhimsen's Tower [the tall minaret-type tower just north of the prison; in Nepali, *dhrahara*]. At that time there were only three prisoners in the Kal Kothari, and outside the Kal Kothari compound, barrack Number Three was also empty. Three of our party workers carried the cloth rope to a point just outside the prison wall in the middle of the night. Meanwhile, the prisoners climbed over the compound wall to the Number Three barrack and threw a fine cord over the prison wall from a third floor window. The men outside tied one end of the cloth rope to a tree, while the prisoners pulled up the other end of the rope by the fine cord which had been attached to it, and tied the rope to an iron bar on the ceiling of the barrack room. The idea was that the prisoners would go one by one laterally from the window to the tree, as if they were in a cable car. However, the rope sagged too much, and a man attempting to cross it would be left hanging inside the big prison wall, so the attempt was abandoned.[18]

In 1946 B.P. Koirala and other Congress members exiled in India wanted a picture of the four politicians still incarcerated in jail in order to publicize and promote the anti-Rana cause. Govinda Prasad's brother loaned his camera for the effort. To smuggle it into the prison was a formidable task. During her frequent visits to the jail Ram Hari's wife carefully observed the guards and tried to analyse their psychology—i.e., under what conditions they tended to be lax in their examination of food shipments, when they were thorough, etc. The strategy was to hide the camera beneath a pile of green soybeans at the bottom of a tin suitcase full of food. To her considerable relief the guard did not detect it.

After Khadga Man Singh took the picture, the camera was thrown over the two south walls (the Kal Kothari wall and the outside prison wall) to Ram Hari's wife who, by prior arrangement, was waiting on the other side. Through smuggled letters we had arranged for her to be at a particular place at a specific time (of day, not night) to receive the camera. When it came flying over the wall, it hit the ground but did not break. Govinda Prasad's brother developed the film himself, and sent it to the magazine. (See illustration 10.) After the picture

---

[18] Details of the unsuccessful escape attempt are from Ram Hari Sharma.

was published, the prison officials were angry and asked us how we had managed to smuggle a camera in and out of the prison. We replied that the Ranas had their own CID agents and should make their own investigation to find out how we had accomplished it.[19]

Jail conditions were so poor that once we collectively protested against our meagre rations and against other policies, such as the complete denial of any family visitation rights. That was in 1946, when there were only five of us political prisoners left in jail—the four of us in Praja Parishad plus Khadga Man Singh. We shut the door of our cell against the jail officials and declared a hunger strike. We had amassed soybeans and other dry foods secretly, so as a matter of fact we did not go hungry, but the jail authorities did not know this [laughter].

One day a jail official came to us and told us that the government authorities had agreed to our demand, and some government official had asked us to come to the jail office. We were suspicious; nevertheless we went. But when we came out of our cell, Ram Hari and I were separated from the other three and taken to another cell. This was in the Golghar, located on the other side of the wall, in the Central Jail, where murderers were kept. Golghar literally means 'roundhouse', but in fact the Golghar was square, not round.

The Golghar was built during Chandra Shamsher's time as a kind of death row. In those days criminals were executed by decapitation with a *khukri*, along the small stream where they shot Ganga Lal and Dasarath. Anyone who had received a death sentence was first sent to the Golghar for about two years. Few could survive the conditions there, so there were not many who actually were executed. Most of the time we were the only two people in Golghar, although there was an occasional criminal, such as a Damai [low-caste tailors] dacoit [robber] who was there for a while. A Rai and a Chhetri were also there. We were sent there because of our *satyagraha* [civil disobedience strike] for basic rights, such as the right to visits by our families and better food.

There were a number of cells on the outside of the Golghar, but Ram Hari and I were placed in two of the eight cells facing the inner courtyard. (See Golghar map.) The cells were about five feet by eight feet and had no windows. There were walls on three sides, and an iron gate on the fourth side. We were kept within four locked doors. There was no toilet, just a bowl, which was emptied every day. Our

---

[19] Details of the camera episode are from Ram Hari Sharma and Govinda Prasad Upadhyay.

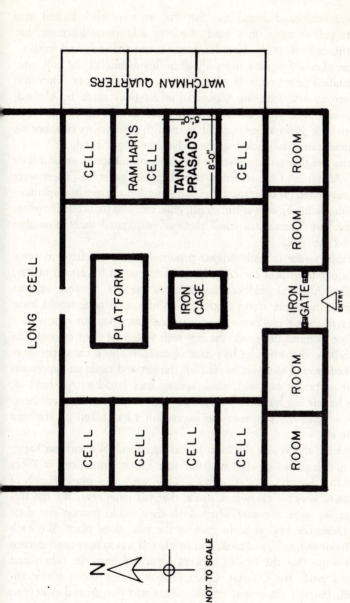

GOLGHAR

Note : The 'iron cage', a kind of Golghar within the Golghar, was
reserved for the most violent prisoners.

cells were unlocked during the day, but we were each locked in a separate cell at night, in a kind of partial solitary confinement, but since the cells were so dilapidated, we could go back and forth.

Then after a few days the jail authorities rebuilt all the cell gates and installed new iron rods where they seemed necessary. They also put a strong new lock, an *Alighad ko talcha* [lock made in Alighad] on the door. The same day Ram Hari came down with dysentery, so we were in a difficult position. They tried to separate us two, but we were determined to stick together whatever might befall us.

In the Golghar jail there was a big *chhidi* (uninhabited ground floor room). All types of prison scraps were kept in that room. There were some corrugated tin sheets as well. I had smuggled all types of carpenter's tools like a hammer, *chinna* [tin snips], glue, etc. into that cell. Therefore the next day I brought a small piece of corrugated sheet from that *chhidi* to our cell.

A *naike sardar* (a high-ranking prisoner) of the jail used to come twice a day to inspect the cells. He used to carry a big bunch of keys with him. After he unlocked our cells for the day, he went upstairs to inspect the upper storey of the jail. While upstairs he would leave the key ring on a platform. I had watched him open our prison door and kept in mind the particular key with which he used to open the door. So one day when he had gone upstairs to check the upper story I sneaked around to where he had left the key and made an impression of that particular key with some sealing wax I had gotten hold of. When he left our building I started to work on that corrugated sheet. Finally I made the key from the impression I had taken on the wax [laughter].

We tried the key in the lock. It was successful. We were so happy I can not describe our elation. After that I took impressions of every key of that bunch, on wax. After a while we had a whole bunch of alternative keys for every lock inside that jail [laughter]. We did this because we were not sure which lock they would put on our door next. Using the keys at night gave us the run of the place. We each slept in our own cells, and cooked in another. It was solitary confinement in the sense that the two of us were separated from the others and confined inside the Golghar. Other prisoners knew about our arrangement, but not the prison officials. That was our general policy: to please those closest to us, while deceiving authorities farther away.

In 1947 Ram Hari contracted double pneumonia, but he survived. I took care of him and emptied his bedpan, etc., but I got another prisoner to do the cooking. Dr. Indra Bahadur Mali saved his life with a sulfa drug and coramine. He also used to smuggle Indian newspapers to us.[20] My health had never been good, and it was always bad in prison.[21] From the time we were put in jail it became very hard for us to stay healthy.

There was more access to contraband literature inside prison than outside! Once I was corresponding with B.P. from the Golghar, while he was underground in Kathmandu and staying at Ram Hari's wife's house. When the Ranas caught him they discovered my letters, because he was carrying them on him at the time. Early the next morning the Inspector General of Police came to the Golghar and asked me how on earth I had managed to send B.P. Koirala so many letters. I told him that he had his own intelligence network, so he should ask it to investigate. Then they searched my cell and found eighteen copies of the magazine *Voice of the Age*.[22] That was a Nepali magazine published in Banaras and strictly banned in Nepal. Mere possession of a single copy was punishable by six months imprisonment, yet we had eighteen copies inside the Golghar! We also had copies of a magazine published in India about jail life, with articles about Gandhi, etc.

While we were in the Golghar, Ram Hari and I used to worship at a shrine for Krishna that Khadga Man Singh had built earlier in the open area outside the cells. (Khadga Man Singh, who had been jailed nine years before us, had had a plan to assassinate the Ranas in a parade.) I used to sit in front of that shrine and do *pranayam* meditation. I had no choice but to practice yoga without the guidance of a *guru*. Once when meditating I felt that I was picked up and thrown three metres away. This frightened me, and I felt it would be too dangerous to continue this meditation without a *guru*. But then after a while I started meditating again, and the same thing happened. This time I got really scared and gave up any further meditating.

While we were in the Golghar, Chuda Prasad's father and brother (both trusted officials of Prime Minister Mohan Shamsher) visited Chuda, Govinda and Khadga, and spent two and a half hours trying to persuade them to sign a statement that if they were released they would serve the Ranas the rest of his life. They refused to sign. When the visitors

---

[20] The discussion of Ram Hari's illness is from Ram Hari Sharma.

[21] The general consensus among Tanka Prasad's friends and family is that Tanka Prasad has always been prone to exaggerate the extent of his pains and illnesses.

[22] *Yuga Bani*. Information in this paragraph is from Ram Hari Sharma.

tried to change their minds, they answered that they would sign only if the statement were amended to read that 'they would serve the motherland'. This the Prime Minister never agreed to.

Ram Hari and I went back to the Kal Kothari after twenty-seven months in the Golghar, and then only because they needed the space for other political leaders who had been arrested and were causing trouble in Bhadragol. There were more than three hundred political prisoners from the Praja Panchayat [another party which had formed to support the constitution Padma Shamsher had proposed; many of these people later joined the Praja Parishad] movement in Bhadragol. A quarrel arose between them and jail authorities, who sent more than sixty criminals from the Central Jail to beat them all with iron rods, etc. They were beaten heavily without mercy. Then the authorities branded about twenty of the political prisoners as trouble makers and punished them by sending them to the Golghar. That's when Ram Hari and I were taken back to our three friends in the Kal Kothari.[23]

Of the thirty-two of us who were imprisoned, some were later released, and some were taken to other places. Those with three-year sentences were let out after three years. At the end of five years, Juddha Shamsher resigned from the Prime Ministership [the only Rana Prime Minister to resign from office] to try to become a kind of saint. As part of this retirement he released all the nineteen people who were still left, except for the four of us—Govinda Prasad, Chuda Prasad, Ram Hari and me — plus Khadga Man Singh. So, during my last five years of prison life (out of a total of ten) only four of us who were arrested in 1940 were left.

Ram Hari and I believed that if we stayed in jail with our firm resolution one day the Ranas would be defeated, and they would be bound to release us without any condition (laughter). If we were in jail today we might not be able to stand so uncompromisingly on our beliefs; then we were young and strong and determined, but now we are old and weaker. We had no political accomplices outside, and we were completely dependent on God.

B.P. Koirala's situation was different. In 1948 B.P. was also put into prison; his prison was a third one, adjacent to Bhadragol and Central Jails, but separate from them, next to the women's prison. The Ranas' policy was to keep political forces separate, so we could not communicate with each other and perhaps hatch further plots. So he sent a letter

---

[23] Details on leaving the Golghar are from Ram Hari Sharma.

to us through my wife, telling us that he was going to observe fasting in prison and that we should also fast along with him in sympathy. Ram Hari and I did not personally fast, but we supported eight others who wished to do so. He was soon released, due to Indian pressure (B.P. had strong contacts with powerful Indian politicians, such as Jaya Prakash Narayan), and he went to Patna without informing us that he had been released. We were still fasting on his behalf without knowing that he had been released and was already in Patna!

After a few days we came to know of his release, and then we broke our fast. In our jail the jail officials were treating the prisoners very badly. One jail official had even poured boiling water over the prisoners' heads and had beaten the prisoners badly. But when B.P. Koirala reached Patna he gave a statement to the effect that the prisoners were kept very well and the Ranas were quite conciliatory towards the prisoners. We started distrusting that fellow from that time. B.P. Koirala was always treated well in prison. That was because he had many friends in India. But we had no friends and were treated roughly.

The Praja Parishad couldn't carry on in Nepal after 1940 because all members were jailed. After Ganesh Man escaped from the jail he tried to activate the party in India. But because B.P. and others favoured a party that would be well-received in India, Ganesh Man helped B.P. and others to establish a new party, the Nepali National Congress. He raised donations from the public and gave it to Congress people. In 1947 I was nominated and elected President of the Nepali National Congress at their first convention. Ganesh Man was there and insisted that I should be President, to give a kind of symbolic unity to the struggle. At the convention B.P. Koirala and others proposed to merge Nepal with India (I still have the booklet they wrote).

Nepalese students in Banaras were dominant in forming a political party there, while Calcutta was dominated by 'C' class Ranas, whose sole objective was to take revenge against the 'A' class Ranas. Students in Banaras had participated in the 'Quit India Movement' in 1942, which drew them closer to the thinking of the Indian National Congress. They said that Nepalese independence was maintained by the British in collaboration with the Ranas just to divide the people of the Indian subcontinent in order to safeguard British rule. Consequently the Nepali Congress leaders lacked nationalist thinking. They were very pro-Indian, but now they are crying for patriotism. Having little experience in India myself, I was always purely nationalistic in outlook.

We were all alone. When we were in jail we read a book, a course book, you see, and it contained a piece by James Jean, a scientist, called 'Dying Sun.' He described the universe as such a vast thing, and said that this earth is like a grain of sand in the immensity of the universe. We consoled ourselves very much with the thought that in a grain of sand there is Nepal, a little country on a little planet, with little people. And here was the arrogant Juddha Shamsher pompously proclaiming, 'I'm the lord of all'. [laughter]. We consoled ourselves by reading that book, saying 'Forget Juddha Shamsher' [laughter].

One day I was looking out the jail window, and a fly flew from the outer jail wall, twelve feet away, and came to rest on our windowsill. After some time, it flew away again, beyond the boundary wall. That day when I reflected upon that insignificant fly, I came to realize the great power of the fly, and I thought, if we only possessed the power of that fly![24]

[24] This story appeared in the newspaper *Samikchha*.

Chapter 8

The Prison Years: Views From the Outside
Rewanta Kumari

When Bua was caught by the Ranas, I didn't know about it until he was brought to Kathmandu. That was in 1940. I knew he was in trouble after Dharma Bhakta and Dasarath Chand were caught. They were caught on the full moon day of Dasai, and Ram Hari was caught one day later. When that happened, I had my father write a letter warning Bua, and I sent it to him in Banaras. I sent it to Bua's sister's husband's father's address, because that's where Bua was staying. Later I found out that just minutes before my letter arrived, Bua had moved to another place, and since his sister's husband's father wasn't sure exactly where he had gone, Bua never received my letter warning him of the danger. I felt bad that there had been no other way to get in touch with him. But with censorship of the mail, even if I had sent it earlier it might not have reached him. I felt bad and sad about it, but there was nothing I could do.

Somebody came to tell me that he had been caught and brought to Kathmandu. Bua was brought to Kathmandu on the evening of *bhai-tika* [the day during Tihar, or Laxmipuja, when sisters wish their brothers prosperity and long life by placing elaborate *tika* marks on their brothers' foreheads]. People told me that same day, they told me that he was being kept at Singha Darbar. What could I do? I went to visit him, to see him. There was a long barrack, with military men sitting on *charpoys* [stringed cots] lining both sides of the barrack. At the end of the barrack Bua was sitting on the floor on a woolen blanket eating *chiura* [parboiled, beaten rice, usually eaten as a snack] and brown sugar on a leaf plate. He was covered all over with heavy chains, from his neck to his feet. Every time he raised his hand to eat, the chains rattled and made a sound. It was very upsetting to see, but I didn't cry. I cried after I returned home, because I didn't know what was going to happen to him or to me. I didn't realize he would be wearing those chains, so I felt very bad when I saw it. I said, 'Meena is crying to see you, so can I bring her to see you?' He said, 'Bring her after we go to jail, not now'. He asked me to bring things the next day—bedding, food, blankets.

They brought him to Singha Darbar on 16 *Kartik* [1 November 1940 AD] and took him away from there on 6 *Magh* [18 January 1941]. For those three months they kept him in the School House in Singha Darbar. The lawsuit was tried there, and they took him to prison after the sentence was finalized. During those three months I brought him both his morning and evening meals. I did this every day. We had to bring prepared food to him from home, and we were allowed to take the food to him in person. We could see him and talk to him. It was only when they took him to the Central Jail that we weren't allowed to see him. Then, for ten years I never saw him.

They locked him up in Singha Darbar in the month of *Kartik* [October-November], but even before that, twelve policemen patrolled around our house in Sifale. Until the time they took him to prison those policemen stayed at our house; they cooked there and they slept there. They provided their own food and bedding, but having them there in the house made me feel as if I had been put in prison too. I felt helpless and insecure, because I didn't know what the policemen might do. I felt desperate and didn't know what to do, or what they might do to us. My second mother-in-law understood even less about the situation and was even more upset.

They took him to jail in *Magh* [January-February], and the house was auctioned in *Chaitra* [March-April]. When we knew the house and everything in it and the land around it would be auctioned, we started taking some of our things to another house, to try to save something. We would throw things we wanted to save out of the window to other houses, and the guards would turn a blind eye to it. Even though the policemen saw what we were doing and knew what was going on, they took pity on us and didn't stop us or report us. They just watched and smiled. The guards used to buy vegetables and run other errands for us too. They showed sympathy for us, and even affection. Then everything was confiscated, and the house and everything in it was auctioned.

When Bua went to prison, naturally my parents were worried too, not just me. Most of their own children had died. There was one daughter surviving still at home, one daughter grown-up (that was me), and now their only son-in-law was in prison. Anybody would have been worried. It was the time of the Ranas. My parents were old-fashioned and they were not politicians, so they could neither think about nor perceive the future. Actually, my grandfather would sit there and forecast the future, but not my father. My grandfather would say, 'I won't be able to see it, but it will be successful, my son-in-law's work will be successful'.

The night before he was to go to prison I went to Singha Darbar to take him food. That is when he told me that they were being taken to prison and that I did not have to bring meals anymore. That was the last time I saw him for ten years.

I returned from Singha Darbar that last time at 9 o'clock at night. We were still staying at the house in Sifale then. Meena was with my father in Thamel, but Shanta was very little and so she was with me. Well, that same night I tied Shanta on my back, and together with Bua's second mother the three of us went to see his sister and brother-in-law. Their house was in Kamal Pokhari. Their children, Shankar Mani and his brothers and sisters, were all little then. I went to see them to tell her, his sole sister, that her brother was being imprisoned, but she did not even let us into her house. She did not even meet us, out of fear. Nine o'clock at night, I walked in the dark from Sifale to Kamal Pokhari with Shanta on my back, but they were too scared to even talk to me. A servant came to the door and said my sister-in-law would not meet us. My feelings were hurt, but I knew she was acting out of fear. And so, I had to turn around and leave. That's how it was. That's how friends and relatives behaved. Out of fear! I didn't see him go from Singha Darbar to the prison the next day. For one thing, I didn't want to watch it, and for another the Ranas didn't want anybody to see them. Originally they had thought of parading them around the city, in public disgrace. But then they became afraid of public reaction, so they abandoned that plan. People whose houses were along the way weren't even allowed to look out their windows. I had a relative who lived near Bhadrakali, and he was able to look through a hole at the procession as it passed by. He told me that Bua walked proudly by, with his head held high.

After he left Singha Darbar to begin serving his life sentence in the Bhadragol Jail, they allowed us to go there only twice a week. They would not allow us to meet him or see him, but we could bring food for him. I would take the food up to the gates of the prison, where the guards would turn everything upside down to check for forbidden material and then take the food to him. They would rummage through the goodies to see if it was cooked food; they would make us taste it before they sent it to him. They would even peel the oranges to be sure there was nothing hidden inside them, and they would tear open the *puri* [deep-fried bread] to be sure nothing was in them either. Then they would bring back the emptied pots and pans to the gates.

I took many kinds of food to the prison—lentils, rice, beans, *ghee* [clarified butter], salt, pepper, turmeric powder—everything! We—that is, the wives of the prisoners—used to bring a month's supply of these staples at a time, once a month. Then, on the two times a week they allowed us to take food, we would bring green vegetables and such. Once in a while we would also take cooked vegetables, bread, pickles, etc. I didn't take him any meat because he became a vegetarian for the entire time he spent in jail. He and the other Brahmins didn't like the idea of eating meat in jail, because the Newar prisoners ate buffalo, and the Brahmins were worried that their meat might accidentally get mixed up with the buffalo meat. So they ate separately. He still didn't eat meat for a year or two after he got out of jail.

During all my visits to the prison to take food to Bua, they would never let us see him or meet him. We would take the food to the prison gates, and then they would take it to him in his cell. One time, Meena wept bitterly, saying that she wanted to go see her father. I then took her to the prison gates and asked them to take her inside and let her see him once. They would not allow it. Even when I told them that I would take off all her clothes and they could take her in naked, they refused to let her see him. I then took her all the way around to the back of the prison and pointed out the Golghar to her, telling her that that's where her father was staying. After that she was satisfied, asking me whether seeing the building her father was staying in wasn't the same as seeing her father himself. She was three and a half years old at that time.

For the ten years he was in prison, the Ranas not only wouldn't let me see him, they would not even allow correspondence between us. Just the letters we were able to hide and smuggle in and out. Even the wrappers that medicines were wrapped in had to be returned once the medicine was taken. That's how suspicious they were about papers! The only things that were allowed in were religious books and scriptures.

For two years Bua didn't write to me. I wrote him that I had never known what *dukha* [suffering, pain] was when he was with me, but now that he was gone I had discovered what *dukha* was. He wrote that I should concentrate my mind on God, not on him. He wrote about transcendental kinds of things. He said that since he was locked up in jail for life he couldn't give me happiness. I wrote back, and slowly he started explaining about politics, and I began understanding.

I saved all our letters, and at one point I gave them to Ram Hari's wife for safe keeping. Once when I was away, after they got out of prison, Ram Hari's wife burned all our correspondence (along with her own), because she thought that once our husbands were out of prison the letters were no longer of any use.

The prisoners used to get sick quite often, because of the bad living conditions. The room was damp and cramped, especially when they were in solitary confinement. Dr Indra Bahadur Shrestha was the jail doctor; when he examined a patient, he was not allowed to talk about anything other than the illness, and a guard was always present. Dr Shrestha saved Ram Hari from pneumonia. Sometimes the jail had medicines, but if they didn't have it, or it was too expensive, I had to get it outside. Mostly I got traditional ayurvedic medicines.

Ram Hari's mother and his wife and I used to meet together and talk about the injustice of it all. We had a lady cook at our house at that time. After Bua was taken to prison, the neighbours started telling her not to stick around, otherwise she too would be sent to prison, and so they scared her away. That's how friends and relatives and neighbours were. It was difficult!

I never met with any of the Ranas. Anyway, why would they see us? Our own friends and relatives would not meet us, not to mention the Ranas. Bua had worked for the nation, and was sympathetic to anyone working for democracy, and had gone to prison for it. Now, people would not talk to me because they were scared that if they did, they might lose their jobs, they might be ruined. Relatives and others used to be scared to talk to us. If I walked on one side of the street, they would cross over and walk on the other. Most of the people I met with while he was in prison were those who were involved in politics, and a few friends. Most of the time I would meet with those working underground.

As I said, our house before Bua went to prison was in Sifale. There were eight *ropanis* [approximately one acre] of land with it. Once the government auctioned that house I had no place to stay. My

father-in-law's share from the Sifale auction was sent to him (Rs 2300
in Indian currency), but he didn't give us any of that money. Later,
when we visited him, we thought he would give us some, but instead
he said we had come not to see him but just to ask for his money.
At that time it was the Rana's order to exempt only the brothers'
and father's shares and confiscate the rest of the property without even
leaving behind children's shares. They confiscated even pots and pans,
beds and sheets—everything!

A Nomadic Life

So that's the way it was in 1941: my husband was taken away to prison
for life; my home was auctioned away; nobody would let us stay anywhere.
How could I feel?

Actually, Kanchho Baje [Bua's youngest paternal uncle] took us
in and let us stay in his house after our house was auctioned, three
or four days after we moved out of it. He also lived in Sifale then.
Later, we couldn't even find a place to rent. Nobody would agree to
rent out a place to me, for fear that they would lose their house and
property. But Kanchho Baje took pity on us and took us in.

When we went to live with Kanchho Baje, he put Meena and Shanta
on his lap and cried out of pity for our plight. They had a huge family.
He ate *masino chamal* (a type of high-quality rice), and the rest of
them ate ordinary brown rice [a courser and cheaper variety]. But Meena
couldn't eat parboiled rice, it upset her stomach, so he would keep
her beside him and give her whatever he was eating. Even the cook
was very sympathetic to us. She used to put white rice on the bottom
of Meena's plate and put parboiled rice on top of it, so the others
wouldn't see what she was eating.

Kanchho Baje was very sympathetic to us, but we had a different
experience with his son. He was trying to find a job and evidently
could not find one. He came back and shouted in the open courtyard
that because of *Tanke* [a derogatory form of Tanka] he couldn't get
a job. He was very mad at him. Later, when Bua was Prime Minister
the son came to him and said how proud he was that he had kept
up the good name and honour of the Acharya family and *gotra*.

I was very close to my second mother-in-law. She used to say that
I was her neck through which she swallowed water [*pani khaera, nilne
ghanti*; the sense is that she was completely dependent on Ama, whom

she trusted and relied on implicitly]. People tried to create a rift between her and me by telling me how nasty and hard-hearted she was. Even her younger sister, *sanima* (literally, 'small mother'), used to envy me, because my mother-in-law entrusted all the money to me, and I took care of all expenses. But my mother-in-law was always kind-hearted to me.

When Bua went to prison, my father-in-law was living with his third concubine, Indumati, in Janakpur. He was under a lot of pressure from her not to take back his second wife; he didn't want the second wife around. I wrote to my father-in-law and asked if we could come visit. One detail that had to be dealt with was the problem of who would take food to Bua in prison, if I left Kathmandu. My father-in-law asked who would feed him? I said that my mother could do that. He wrote back that, yes, I could come, but I shouldn't bring my second mother-in-law with me. But I said if I came the second mother-in-law also had to come. So he never invited us.

Nevertheless, in *Jest* [May-June] of 1941 I took Meena, Shanta, and Bua's second mother to visit Bua's father. When we went to the Tarai that time, I was the only one who walked. Shanta, Meena, and my mother-in-law, because she wasn't well, went in *dokos*.[1] Other times my mother-in-law and Shanta were carried together in an *olinkath*, while Meena went in a *doko*. When we arrived in Janakpur Meena told father-in-law that at Kanchho Baje's house they gave her '*kalo bhat*' ['black rice', her way of referring to parboiled brown rice] and that this gave her stomach aches. That's when my father-in-law said to leave her with him. Meena agreed to stay, so I left her with him. The rest of us came back to Kathmandu three months later, in *Bhadra* [August-September].

Then Bua's father took Meena with him to Banaras. He stayed there for two or three years. He had 100 *bighas* of land in Sirsia; he kept twenty-one and sold the rest of it and used the proceeds to go live in Banaras. When he was in Banaras, he wanted to start a jewellery business. He had unfinished stones brought from Nepal to Jaipur, in Rajasthan, where they were cleaned and polished. He wanted to start a business with the Maharaja of Darbanga, but it didn't work out.

So the way we ended up is that Meena went to stay with her grandfather in the Tarai, Shanta and I basically stayed with my parents

[1] A wicker basket carried on the back and supported by a leather band passed under the basket and around the forehead.

in Thamel, while my second mother-in-law and her sister [Sanima] stayed with Kanchho Baje in Sifale. Because of his big family they had to stay on the ground floor, which in old houses tends to be damp. My father lived in a big household with his parents and six brothers and their families. Nevertheless, they didn't resent my being back there in my *maiti* while Bua was in prison. There were just the normal small family squabbles, but not about Bua. I also visited back and forth often between my *maiti* and Kanchho Baje's place for almost six years. From the time the house was auctioned in 1941 until 1967, we rented rooms or houses, sometimes here and sometimes there. By the time this house was built, the one we live in now, I had moved ten times.

My father-in-law sent me a picture from Banaras of Meena dressed as a boy. I didn't like it, but later when I saw her in shorts and a shirt I didn't mind. I was worried about how Meena was getting along though, so in *Mangsir* [November-December] I went with Kanchho Baje and his family and Shanta to Banaras to see how she was doing. I stayed there four months. When I arrived in Banaras, my father-in-law was doing *pujas*, and Meena was playing nearby. I bowed to him, and then he asked Meena who I was, and Meena said I was her *bhaujyu* [elder brother's wife]. I didn't like that, and I asked her rather sharply, 'who are you calling *bhaujyu?*' Then Meena ran off, and I had to go get her for lunch. Later I slapped her for something, and she said, 'Did my mother [meaning Indumati, the concubine] give birth to me so you can scold and slap me?'

Until she was about three and a half years old Meena had called me Ama [mother]. After she went to stay with her grandfather she started calling his concubine, Indumati, Ama. After that she didn't call me anything, she avoided using any term of address. She did this for quite a long time after we started living together again. It was only much later, in Kathmandu, that she started calling me 'Shanta's mother'. I felt bad about this, and I regretted leaving her with my father-in-law. That was my fault. At the beginning it hurt, but later on I got used to it and didn't mind. Then later still, when she came back after a long separation while studying in India, she stopped calling me 'Shanta's mother' and started calling me Ama.

In *Kartik* [October-November], 1946 I went to Sirsia again with Bua's second mother and Shanta. He didn't want his second wife to come, but we took her anyway. Shanta was sick and couldn't seem to be cured in Kathmandu. My parents didn't want me to take her with me because they were afraid she might get worse. I thought she might get better with a change of climate, and if she died, at least she would die in Janakpur, a holy pilgrimage place. I was glad I took her, because my father-in-law treated her with homeopathic medicines and herbs, and she got better.

When I went back to Sirsia with Shanta, Meena received her very well. She wasn't jealous of her. I used to let Meena give *tika* to Shanta on *bhai-tika*, when she cried because she had no brother to give *tika* to. But Meena would be partial to the people there. For example, if we washed clothes and put them out to dry, Meena would take Indumati's clothes in and leave ours out. Once my father-in-law and mother-in-law ran after some mangoes that had fallen on the ground of our house in Janakpur, but Meena got there first and pushed my mother-in-law out of the way.

In 1947 I was ready to leave for Kathmandu, to enroll Meena and Shanta in school there, and my father-in-law said I should go and say good-bye to some friends in a nearby village, so I went and stayed overnight there. The next morning someone came to call me back to Sirsia. My father-in-law was seriously ill. When I got there I found him laid out in the courtyard, because Hindus believe you should not die inside the house. He was dying. We think it was a stroke or heart attack. In the morning he had sat in the village panchayat to discuss an issue in which he was involved. He had hit a neighbour's horse with a metal-tipped long stick (*bhala*) because the horse was always grazing in our rice fields. It belonged to a Maithili Brahmin, who had been warned many times before, but he continued to let the horse graze freely in the village. So my father-in-law was much agitated about it in the panchayat, which lasted till about 10:30. Then he took his daily bath and did puja and suddenly collapsed over the tray holding the *puja* materials. Meena and Indumati were nearby; Meena had a doll house in the *puja* room, and was supposed to stay there till he finished his *puja*. That's why she made her doll house there—so she could play while he did his *puja*.

After he collapsed Meena was sent to get some lemon from the garden, so he could be given lemon water, which was supposed to be good for him. But by the time she arrived with the lemon, he was already unconscious, and some white foam was coming out of his mouth. My mother-in-law and the Brahmin cook and Indumati had carried him outside. He never recovered. At about 3 o'clock we had his body carried to a sacred pond, Parshuram Talau, and had his body cremated there. His frontal lobe [*astu*; since it is difficult to burn it is taken from the remains of the fire and taken to pilgrimage places] was taken to the Ganges River afterwards. Since Bua was not there, a Brahmin had to light the funeral fire in his mouth. Mourning lasted for thirteen days. During this time Indumati and my mother-in-law wore white *dhotis* [no sewn cloth can be worn during the thirteen days], were secluded, and given a special diet (only rice, *ghee*, and sugar). They weren't supposed to touch anything, or wear clothing that had been sewn. I also didn't eat salt, and the children didn't eat salt for five days. Less serious mourning lasted for one year, during which there was a monthly *shradha* [mourning ritual], and other *shradhas* after forty-five days, six months, and one year. We also gave away bedding, cooking utensils, etc. to a Brahmin on each of these *shradha* days. You should also give away a cow if you can afford to. You can't eat meat for a year, and some other things.

In the meantime, when my father-in-law collapsed, Indumati transferred much of the valuable jewellery when she realized he was dying. I wasn't there, and she had the keys to the trunks which held the jewellery and land papers. My mother-in-law sat with the body. We didn't know anything about the property or money, and we had to borrow money for the death ceremonies. Bua observed the mourning in jail. We sent a telegram about Bua's father's death to my father, who communicated the news to Bua through the jailer. Puskarnath had been allowed out for his father's *kirya* (thirteen days strict mourning period), but they said they wouldn't let Bua out because he had been decasted.

So instead of returning to Kathmandu as I had planned, I stayed behind and performed all the death rituals. I came to Kathmandu in Shrawan [July-August], alone, to take care of things here, and to pick up Sanima who was alone here. Then we went back to Sirsia after about three weeks. I also brought along Ram Hari's wife, who had been sick. Bua wrote from prison that it might help her, so I took her along. Across the border from Janakpur at Kapileswar, in India, Congress people heard we were travelling, so they met us at Jaynagar, and took us to Kapileswar to spend the night.

Since I was in mourning for my father-in-law I could not eat rice unless it was cooked in a particular way, so I ate some dry food. Ram Hari's wife and Sanima ate a regular meal. Ram Hari's wife is very fussy and didn't eat much rice. The next day we had to walk seven miles, with nothing more to eat, so we ate *chiura* along the way. Ram Hari's wife was hungry and complaining. After one month Ram Hari's wife and I went to Darbanga to send her back to Kathmandu. There we met Ganesh Man for the first time, and also Rudra Prasad Giri and Kedar Man Bethit. Ram Hari's wife went to Kathmandu with another woman, and I returned to Sirsia. In *Baisakh* (April-May) of 1948 I returned to Kathmandu.

In Sirsia we had trouble with thieves from time to time. Our *shaligram* [black ammonite fossil representing Narayan[2]] was stolen from Sirsia when father-in-law was alive. The thieves took everything in the puja room, but about one kilometre away they discarded the box with the *shaligram*, so we found it and brought it back. After father-in-law died, a neighbouring Brahmin was asked to come worship it, since there was no male Brahmin at our house then. Another time it was stolen by one of our relatives. On the fourth day after he stole it his wife suddenly lost her sight; she just woke up blind. Within six months he fell off a horse and broke his elbow in such a way that they couldn't fix it. Between then and 1948 he had a series of mishaps, including losing his job. In 1954 they went to Banaras to try to find out why he had had so much bad luck, and he was told it was because he had stolen a *shaligram*. Bua was then Home Minister. The thief said that my second mother-in-law, who was dead by then, had given it to him in my absence, but I knew he had stolen it. Since then we have had it with us.

Once after Bua's father died, robbers came at night. They dug seventeen holes in the mud floor in the house, thinking we had money that Bua would have gotten after his father's death, but they didn't find anything. Also they couldn't get in the room where we were sleeping, because they would have awakened us while cutting a hole in the wooden floor [from the crawl space under the floor].

I was almost robbed another time after Bua came out of prison. I had gone to Sirsia with Shanta and Mithi, our servant who has been with us for forty years. I had sold paddy from the land during the day, and that night robbers, thinking the money from selling rice must be in the house, came to rob us. Mithi was sleeping in front of the door, and Shanta and I were in the bed. The room had two doors, one on the north side and one on the east side. There was a half-barrier dividing the room. There was also a *puja* room on the west side. The robber broke into the *puja* room, climbed over the barrier, got into my room and opened the east door. I awoke because of the sound of the door opening, and I saw him. He was a huge, dark man standing

---

[2] See Messerschmidt 1989 for details on *shaligrams*.

by the door. I was very scared. I tried to yell and clap my hands. I was so frightened that sound wouldn't come out of my mouth, but I clapped my hands so loud the neighbours on the other side of the pond heard it, and they came asking, 'Ki Bheli, Dulahan?' ('What happened, daughter-in-law?', in Maithili).

While in Sirsia I had established connections with the Congress office across the border in India. They asked me to start a Mahile Sangathan [Women's Organization] in Janakpur, seven miles from Sirsia. I put Meena and Shanta in a Janakpur school for three or four months. Congress was supposed to pay the rent on the house, but they never paid it. So I locked it up and returned to the village and then to Kathmandu.

When I arrived in Kathmandu, nobody would even rent out a place to me. The first night I went and slept at Ram Hari's. His youngest paternal uncle had built a small house made of unfired brick for him in Battisputali. They couldn't afford wooden beams, so they used bamboo to support the tile roof. There was a big room and a small room, and the big room was divided into two. His two daughters, his wife, his mother, his wife's brother, and a servant were there when we came. Even though they had no space we spent the night there. The next morning we went to the temple in Battisputali and stayed at the pilgrim's shelter (patti) there. I stayed there for one night. On the ground floor the patti was just an open, covered veranda. We stayed upstairs, under the roof. It was dark and dirty up there. Meena and Shanta didn't like it, so they went back to Ram Hari's place to sleep.

Then, the next morning I went to the house of a childhood friend of mine who lived in Battisputali. Her husband had already died, and she was also in a difficult economic situation. Her house was in Battisputali on the main road to Pashupati, very near Ram Hari's house. I asked her if she would rent out two rooms to me and she did, seeing how difficult it was for us to stay in an open pilgrim's shelter. Her children were small too, and they later became my childrens' playmates. The house had four stories; the first floor was rented to some other people, and we stayed on the second floor. We got our water from a public tap down the street. We stayed there from April-May 1948 until July-August 1950.

At that time, six months before Bua's release, my second mother-in-law died. She died of a heart attack. After she died, there was just her sister (Sanima), myself, and my two daughters remaining. I then went with Meena and Shanta back to stay at my parents' place in Thamel, while Sanima went and stayed with Bua's sister and her family.

While Bua was in prison, everything was equally difficult. The financial situation was not that good. I also got typhoid fever while he was in prison. It was a serious case and took between a month and a half and two months for me to recover. There was no place that I could call a home! I stayed with my parents, they gave me refuge. It was from my parents' place that I carried out all my operations. It was from there that I used to take all the food to prison. I left Meena at her grandfather's in Mahottari and Shanta stayed with me at my parents'. It was only in 1948, after my father-in-law's death, that I rented the place in Battisputali and moved from my parents'. Before my father-in-law died we didn't have enough money to afford a separate place, but after he died we had a little money. I thought, why shouldn't I spare my parents the problem of staying in their crowded house. They had only two rooms, one for cooking and one for sleeping. The sleeping room was subdivided by shelves and their bed, and we (my sister and I, plus Shanta and my brother, who were both still young) slept on mattresses on the floor which had to be rolled up every morning. In Battisputali we could also be together with my second mother-in-law. So when I could afford it we finally moved to a place of our own.

Still, we didn't have much money to live on. I would give Meena two paisa for her afternoon snack. In those days you could buy one *mana* [pound] of beaten rice for seven paisa, so two paisa was enough to buy some beaten rice or soybeans for a snack. When I was little I was given one pice to go buy something, and that was enough.

I sent Meena and Shanta to a coeducational Gandhian school in Gaushala, near Pashupati. Things were beginning to change, and the Ranas allowed this kind of school now. Meena and Shanta would walk to the school from Thamel. After Bua was released in January 1951, we all went and stayed at Bua's sister's house.

Friends and relatives were scared to talk to me. Some of them were afraid that I would corrupt them. People like Chuda Prasad's father and Ram Hari's mother used to say that Bua had corrupted their sons. They used to say that they shouldn't associate with me either, that I would ruin them too. They would prevent Ram Hari's wife and Chuda Prasad's wife from meeting me, warning them that I would taint them. Evidently Ram Hari's wife wrote to Ram Hari about this not long after they went to prison, and then he sent a letter to his mother from prison saying that she shouldn't treat me like this, that she should let me visit them. After that, Ram Hari's wife started visiting me and meeting with me. As for Chuda Prasad's father, he would hide his daughter-in-law if I went to pay a visit at his house.

In 1949, one year before the release of Bua and the others, I met Chuda Prasad's father. During my conversation with him, he said to me that Bua had corrupted his son. When I asked him how this might have happened, he replied by saying that Bua had gone to Banaras, where his son was studying, and had converted him. He also added that the Ranas were a mountain, and we have a saying that you can't move a mountain with an elbow [*kuinale pahar phutaune khojne?* (Can you try to move a mountain with an elbow?)] The Ranas were the mountain, and Bua was the elbow. Only a year later, the prisoners were freed.

But when Bua got out, everybody came to see us! I didn't say anything against them. Well, I smiled to myself. What could I say? Why get angry? There was no point in getting angry with them, or saying something to them. These are the ways of the world. Besides, how many people could you get angry at anyway?

Well, the families of Bua's political friends went through the same kinds of difficulties. The same problems happened to Ram Hari's family, they confiscated all his property too. It was the same with Chuda Prasad's and Govinda Prasad's people, and many others, including the families of those who were executed. That year (1940-1) they did that to everyone who was politically involved. The difference between me and the others was that the others' wives had parents-in-law here in Kathmandu who gave them refuge, whereas I didn't have anybody. The house in Sifale was auctioned, my father-in-law was in Mahottari with a concubine, and I had my daughters, my second mother-in-law and, later, her sister dependent on me. As I've said, I moved around a lot.

Chuda Prasad's father and second mother were here in Kathmandu, and so his wife stayed with them. Ram Hari's mother had inherited the house with a large garden as her share of the family property when he went to prison. His wife and two daughters lived with her; the older daughter died afterwards. Govinda [sentenced to life imprisonment] was not married.

Other people who weren't in jail with Bua had problems too. Saroj Koirala [Congress activist later killed by the Panchayat regime while he was in India; his wife won a seat in the 1991 election], D.N. Pradhan, D.P. Pariyar [both Congress activists], and one more person had been locked up in Jaleshwar Prison. They had organized some demonstrations and political activities. So, D.P. Pariyar's mother and some others came to Janakpur from Calcutta to visit the prisoners. They stayed where I was staying in Janakpur at the time. They got up early in the morning and went to Jaleshwar. That same morning, at 10 a.m., I went to bathe in Ganga Sagar and on my return found two policemen sitting on the porch of the house I was staying in. I asked them why they were there, and they told me that they had come to find D. N. Pradhan's wife, Hemlata Pradhan, and D.P. Pariyar's mother, Dhanakumari. I told them that they had left that morning, and they went away.

In 1947 we all—Bua's second mother, Sanima, Shanta, Meena, and Mithi—went back to Sirsia. Then I took Shanta and Meena with me and told everyone we were going to Kathmandu, but really I left them at Janakpur, at Saroj Koirala's house, while I went to Banaras to attend the first Congress meeting there.

Bua was still in prison then, and the Congress people told me that I should attend the session. Therefore I went to the meeting as his representative. The Nepali Congress chose Bua as the President of the Congress, although he was still in prison, and B.P. was named the Vice-President. Since Bua was in prison, B.P. was the acting president, and it was he who headed the session. I attended as Bua's representative.

I went from Mahottari to Banaras with ten others who were also attending the session. Rudra Prasad Giri [who later became a minister], Ram Babu, Baccha Jha, and Saroj Koirala were among those who went. They asked me to make a speech, so I did. I spoke without notes, and I can't remember now what I said, but I said something about freedom, liberty, and women's rights. I quoted from Indian women leaders I had read about, like Laxmibai.

When I came back the children were not where I had left them at Saroj Koirala's house. They had gone back to Sirsia, so I had to go back there and explain where I had gone. My second mother-in-law told me that Meena and Shanta had just arrived out of the blue, wearing saris. Meena and Shanta didn't know where I had gone, and after a week they just left for the village, on their own.

Smuggling

The next year I made another trip to India. This time I went to India to deliver some letters to Nehru and Jaya Prakash Narayan that Bua had smuggled to me from prison. Because I was going back and forth so much, they assigned a special woman to search my body at the checkpoint in Chisapani Gadhi. Everyone had to show their *radhani*, or passport [during Rana times Nepalese citizens needed a passport to enter or leave the Kathmandu Valley] there. They also searched everyone's luggage. So when I had to carry letters, I tied them around Sanima's legs and thighs, because they didn't suspect her. I smuggled not only these letters to Nehru and Jaya Prakash Narayan, but I also often smuggled letters between prison and political workers in the Tarai and in India. With a house and land in the Tarai I had a good excuse for going there.

Smuggling the letters was difficult. It wasn't just letters that were prohibited—we were not allowed to send any kind of paper into the prison. We had to bring back even the medicine containers. They wouldn't let us take those in. They would also check food containers inside and out for paper products. Even then, we were successful in hiding papers and sending them in, first in a metal cylinder (*goltin*), which we used to send in tobacco, spices, etc. The prisoners made a false bottom in it and put letters under it, and glued it on. Noticing that it seemed different, we were suspicious, so we looked and found the letter. Once the glue didn't hold and the letters fell out, and we were exposed. Even though we were caught, they didn't do anything to us. After that we used a tin box, like a small suitcase; we bored holes in the lid and inserted papers between the lid and the false lid, screwing on the latter tightly and painting it so it would match. Bua had written to get a box made in Tahity, by people of the Kau caste, but the prison officials captured that. After that we tried a similar tactic with a *theki* [a big wooden yogurt or milk pot]. The bottom part of it had been made very very thick. We would put letters and papers in there, cover them with a lid, smear the lid with red mud, then use *ghee*, sugar, and oil to smear it further and make it black. Then we would take it to the prison. Since it held liquid, it was difficult to examine what was in its bottom. Somehow they discovered that too, but I don't know how because I wasn't here then. That's how they found out about the letters to Nehru and Jaya Prakash. I used the box to smuggle letters, while Ram Hari's wife used the *theki*. She also smuggled letters inside the lock on the box, and she sewed letters into the cuffs of shirts.

Anyway, this time when I was taking letters to Nehru and others, I got into trouble with the CID [Central Intelligence Department]. After I put my mother-in-law and Sanima and Mithi and Shanta on the train in Raxaul [Indian town just across the border from Birganj], I met a man loitering around on the platform. He looked and dressed and sounded like an Indian. He asked who I was and where I was going, and I answered that I had put my mother-in-law and the others on the train to Darbanga, and that from there they would go to Sirsia. I also told him who I was and that I would be going from Raxaul to Patna with Meena. He asked if I were going to Patna to meet B.P. I told him that I didn't know B.P., and so I wasn't going to see him.

He then asked me where I was going to spend the night. It was around 8 p.m. then. I told him that although there were people who I could stay with I was going to find my own place because I didn't want to bother them. He then told me that he had a place and asked me if I wanted to stay there. When I enquired about who was there, he said his old mother was there. So I said okay, thinking that he was being kind to me. Meena and I went to his place. It happened to be a hotel on the Nepalese side of the border. Its compound was surrounded by tall barriers made of bamboo.

He took me in, told me that he would come back the next morning at eight to help arrange my tickets, and left. As he walked out, however, he locked the main gate behind him. Now, I was scared. Meena slept, but I didn't, I just sat there thinking—how was I going to escape from this place? I was sitting outside. Then, very late at night, I heard the sound of bangles. It happened to be the bangles of a maid who had just come to the hotel and started doing her work. I went inside and saw her doing the dishes. I then asked her how and where one was to go if one needed to urinate in the night, since the gate was locked from the outside. She showed me a hole that she had made in one corner of the barrier and told me that that's where she comes in and out from. I then stayed there all night. At daybreak, I woke Meena up and told her that we were going. Leaving all our luggage there, taking only the letters, we escaped through that hole.

There was an office of the Nepali Congress in Raxaul, so I went there and told them where my luggage was and asked them to fetch it for me. They went and brought it to me. I then purchased the tickets and boarded the train. And then that man arrived at the platform. He asked me if I had got my tickets and all. I told him yes, and then the train took off. So much for him! He then filed a report—I later realised that he was not an Indian but a Nepali CID man—the result of which was that I was later arrested in Kathmandu!

I first went to Patna and met B.P. there. We stayed ten days there, with D. N. Pradhan. For ten days Jaya Prakash [the Indian socialist leader] still didn't come, so B.P. said he would carry the letters to Nehru and Jaya Prakash, but I refused his offer. Bua had told me to give the letters directly myself, not through intermediaries, and to give B.P. the letter intended for him after I had delivered Nehru's letter. I was also carrying a letter for Jeev Raj, but he also was not there. Since we didn't have much money, Bua had told me to ask for my expenses from Jeev Raj, but since he hadn't arrived by the time we had to leave we asked B.P. for money, but he gave us only Rs 100 IC [Indian Currency].

Then we went to Calcutta, where we thought we would find Jaya Prakash; Mahendra Bikram[3] was there, and we met him. In the meantime he and Jeev Raj had started another political party. I delivered a letter to Mahendra Bikram that Bua had written, and I also asked him for a loan. He gave me Rs 400 and said that I didn't have to repay it, it was a kind of present to Tanka Prasadji. B.P. also came to Calcutta, and again asked for the letters for Jaya Prakash and Nehru, but I refused to hand them over.

Then we went to Banaras where I waited for Jaya Prakash for eighteen more days, and still he didn't turn up. We stayed with Diwakar Bhaju. Krishna Prasad Bhattarai [Prime Minister, 1990-1] also used to come morning and evening at B. P.'s request, asking for the letters, saying he would take them. Then we (Meena, a Praja Parishad member whose code name was Chirkabhai, and I) went back to Patna, where we stayed in B.P.'s flat. He invited Jaya Prakash to his house, and when he came I finally gave him the letter. After reading the letter Jaya Prakash asked me what Bua's education was. He said, he's written such a long letter, but it's all about the country, and nothing about himself.

The next day we were invited to Jaya Prakash's house, and he asked if I wanted to say anything more. I said no, everything was in the letter. He also asked if I wanted to deliver the letter to Nehru myself, or if I wanted him to take it to him. I said I wanted to go myself. He asked if I wanted to go now or later, and I said now. After that Jaya Prakash made all my travel arrangements, made an appointment with Nehru for me, etc. He bore all my travelling expenses, and provided us with an escort. In Delhi we stayed in Jaya Prakash's house there. In those years rice was a delicacy in Delhi, and as Meena was not used to eating *roti* [unleavened bread], it was hard for her. We looked

---

[3] Mahendra Bikram had helped Tanka Prasad buy the cyclostyle machine.

for rice everywhere. We almost missed the train for Bindavasini [a pilgrimage place] looking for rice. In the evening also we went around looking for rice at hotels, but it was hard to find.

We went to see Nehru in Parliament House, Room Number 11. When I saw Nehru I didn't say much. Bua had written an eleven-page letter to Nehru. Eleven pages! He read it in front of me. The letter to Jaya Prakash had been fourteen pages long [see appendix two]. They were very thick! He asked me if there was anything else I had to tell him. I said no, there wasn't anything else, that everything was written in that letter. I think I took eleven letters in all, but now I remember only nine people I delivered them to. Besides Nehru and Jaya Prakash, Bua had also written to Ganesh Man [leader of the Nepali Congress after the 1990 movement], B.P., Matrika Babu [M.P. Koirala, first non-Rana Prime Minister], Surya Babu [Surya Prasad Upadhaya, a minister during the 1950s], Jeev Raj [founder-member of Praja Parishad], Mahendra Bikram [who bought the duplicating machine in Calcutta], and Pushpa Lal [founder of the Communist Party of Nepal]. I delivered the letters to all of them. Pushpa Lal, Jeev Raj, and Mahendra Bikram were in Calcutta, the rest were in Patna. B.P. and others gave me the letters that they wrote Bua in response.

It was illegal to do all this, but the police didn't really catch me until I arrived back in Kathmandu. I stayed behind in Sirsia while Meena and Shanta returned to Kathmandu to go to school. I sent the replies from India with them. Later I returned to Kathmandu. In different groups all of us returned to Kathmandu—Meena, Shanta, Mithi, Bua's second mother, and Sanima. In those days you had to go into India to get somewhere else in Nepal, so we took the train to Raxaul, then the Nepali train from Birganj to Amlekhganj. From Amlekhganj, we took a bus on the dirt road to Bhimphedi. Then we walked for two days to reach Kathmandu, spending the night at Kulekhani, before crossing the Chandragiri Pass [which leads into the Kathmandu Valley]. Meena rode in a *doko*, while Shanta and second mother-in-law rode in an *olinkath* [an open palanquin]. Meena was ten years old, Shanta eight. They could walk a little bit of the time.

Soon after our return I heard that there was a warrant out for my arrest, and I decided to go underground. Ram Hari's wife, Ram Hari's daughter, Ram Hari's brother-in-law, and I—we all went to Ram Hari's uncle's place in Lubu, south of Patan, where we thought we would be safe. That's near Godavari, at the southern edge of the valley [several hours walk from Kathmandu]. We went in the morning. The same afternoon, however, Ram Hari's uncle's wife, without realizing it, brought the CID man who was searching for us to our hide-out. That is, the person whose house we were hiding in, accidentally brought the CID directly to us!

What happened was that as a result of the CID report, a warrant had been issued for my arrest. They had discovered the replies to our letters from Bua in the *theki*. Therefore they knew about the letters I had taken to Nehru and others. But I had not told Ram Hari's uncle about the warrant. When his wife went out to market, she met two men on the road who enquired about me, and since I had not told her about my activities and the warrant for my arrest, she innocently told the men that I was staying with them. She thought that they must be friends of mine and took them to the house, and that's how I was caught.

When the CID person arrived, he told us that he had come to fetch us. He said that if we were to return and ask for forgiveness, they would set Bua and the other prisoners free. I told the man that he must be a CID man. He then told me to keep quiet and come downstairs. So we did, and then left to walk back to Kathmandu. When we arrived at the prison in Patan, they took Ram Hari's wife away. They didn't recognize me, however, and thinking that I was just any other person they let me go. Ram Hari's wife had her second daughter, Padma, with her. (She now lives next door to us.) Ram Hari's wife told me that she wanted to keep her daughter with her because she didn't want to be by herself in that prison. Thus mother and daughter stayed in prison and I left.

By this time, there were police searching for me at my place in Battisputali. So, not knowing what to expect, I went underground in the house of a man I knew in Baneshwor, one Murali Thapa. He had been a peon [unskilled office worker, errand boy] in my father's Sanskrit school. In those days Baneshwor was considered remote from Kathmandu. There were no big roads connecting the two places, just trails and fields. I stayed underground for a week. After that, I didn't want to stay underground anymore. How many days was I to stay underground? What was I to do?

At the end of that week I went home, at about 7 o'clock at night, to Thamel. I told my father that I couldn't stay underground forever, and that I would go report at the gates of Singha Darbar. I was scared, and I didn't know what they would do to me, but I thought it was better to go, rather than always be on the run and hunted down like

1. Janardan, Tanka Prasad's grandfather

2. Tanka Prasad's father, Tika Prasad, at his writing table

3. Tanka Prasad, his father and his office staff. Biratnagar, c. 1920

4. Tanka Prasad and his father, Tika Prasad

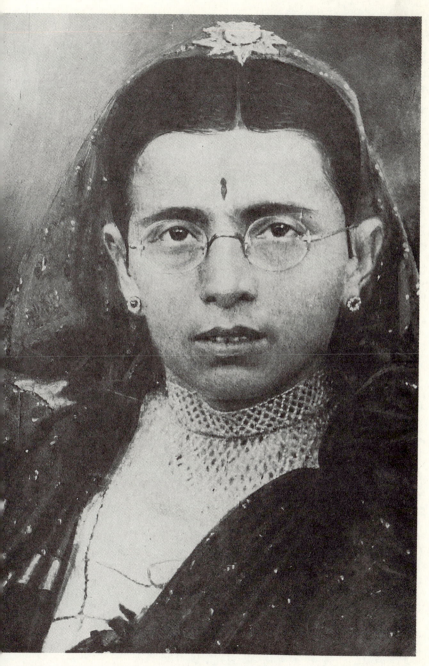

. Tanka Prasad's birth mother. Possessing normal vision, she poses with glasses
purely for cosmetic effect

6. Tanka Prasad and his second mother

7. Tanka Prasad posing with hunting rifle and two tiger cubs

8. Rewanta Kumari and Tanka Prasad's nieces.

9. Tanka Prasad, manacled in iron chains from his
neck to his ankles, in Singha Darbar in 1940 or 1941.

WATCH NEPAL NOW!

THIS HORRIBLE PICTURE WAS SMUGGLED OUT OF NOTORIOUS KATMANDU JAIL
This photograph, smuggled from inside the notorious Katmandu Jail, show Shrees Govinda Prasad Sharma, T. P. Sharma, twice-elected President of the Nepali National Congress, C. P. Sharma and Ramhari Sharma. For the last seven years, these gallant fighters for freedom are condemned to pass the rest of their lives in the dark, dingy and damp cells of the jail. Note the inhuman way they are kept chained and fettered. Should India betray Nepal's gallant fight for freedom against the tyrannical rule of the Ranas?

10. Tanka Prasad and his three prison mates for ten years. The surname Sharma is used generically for Brahmins in Nepal. The picture was published in the generally leftist Indian magazine, *Blitz*.

11. Tanka Prasad and Rewanta Kumari shortly after he was released from prison

12. Prime Minister Tanka Prasad and his cabinet. Left to right: Chuda Prasad Sharma (Foreign Affairs, Agriculture and Forestry); Purendra Bikram Shah (Defense); Tanka Prasad Acharya (Prime Minister and Home); King Mahendra; Gunja Man Sardar (Finance, Industry, and Commerce); Bal Chandra Sharma (Education and Health); Anirudra Prasad Singh (Law and Justice).

13. State visit of Premier Zhou Enlai. The two Premiers have an animated discussion while those on the sidelines, including the King and Queen, look on with apparent envy. Such public, peripheral positioning of royalty became unthinkable during the 1960-90 Panchayat period, when the King and Queen were always

14. Prime Minister and Mrs Acharya

15. Tanka Prasad and Rewanta Kumari in their bedroom, 1991.

16. Tanka Prasad and Rewanta Kumari in 1991.
(Photos 16 and 17 by Stephen Swan)

17. Tanka Prasad, 1991.

18. Tanka Prasad, Rewanta Kumari and all their children. Front :
Krishna (Tanka Prasad's distant relative); Second row : Kushumakar,
Tanka Prasad, Rewanta Kumari, Pushpa; Third row: Mallika, Shanta,
Bachhu (Tanka Prasad's distant relative), Bir Bhadra, Meena, Angira.

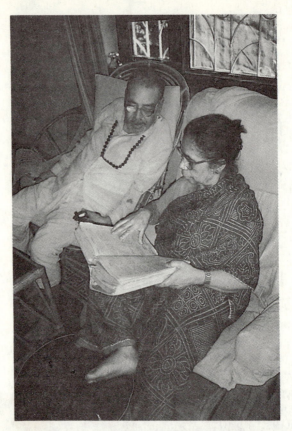

19.   Rewanta Kumari reading aloud from the
      Mahabharata to Tanka Prasad, 1989

20.   Tanka Prasad stamp issued.

a dog. I was much more anxious about Bua than about myself, and I was ready to bear the punishment or imprisonment if it came. My father told me not to go. I said I'm going. I said I neither want to stay underground, nor do I want to be escorted by the police; I'm not going there with the police tagging along, I'm going alone. My father repeatedly told me not to go. But my father's father, my grandfather, told me that it was okay to go. And so, at 10 o'clock the next morning (it was during the month of *Shrawan* [July-August]), after having my morning meal, I went to the gates of Singha Darbar.

They asked me who I was. I said, I am so and so, and I came because I have heard that you are looking for me. Then they took me inside. Once inside, they interrogated me. They had captured the pot which I had smuggled letters to the prison, and had brought it to Singha Darbar. It wasn't my letters they detected, but the letters Bua had sent saying that he had received all of mine and Nehru's and the others' letters. They showed me the pot and said that letters had been smuggled in it. I denied it, but they insisted, placing the pot right under my nose. Placing the pot in front of me as evidence, they accused me of taking letters in and out of prison. I finally said yes, I had done that. They asked me what the contents of the letters were. I told them that I didn't know how to read, so I didn't know what was written in them, I only brought them in and out as per instructions.

In this manner they continued to interrogate me. I was in the midst of the interrogation when the police arrested Chuda Prasad's wife, who arrived escorted by four policemen. They arrested her because she too had been implicated in the illegal correspondence. Even by 5 o'clock that day the interrogation was not finished. They therefore wanted me to come back the next day. They told me that since I had come to the gates by myself, voluntarily, I could leave on my own, but that I should come again the next day. Then they let me go. They sent Chuda Prasad's wife home again escorted by four policemen, one of whom stayed at her house to guard against any attempt at escape! I went back the next day and continued through more interrogation the whole day.

One of the things they asked was whose daughter I was. I told them I was Kedarnath Aryal's daughter, Pitambar's granddaughter. My grandfather used to work at a Rana house, at Dharma Shamsher's [a son of Bir Shamsher]. Dharma Shamsher was a Jangi Lath, one rank lower than the commander-in-chief, at that time. My interrogator was

Hari Shamsher, Juddha Shamsher's son and King Birendra's maternal grandfather. Sardar Som Prasad, Subba Upendra Purush, and a lieutenant were also among my interrogators. After I told them whose daughter I was, Hari Shamsher said to me, 'Pandit Pitambar has, throughout his lifetime, served the Ranas and earned his bread. How could you, who have grown up under him, do this?' I asked him what I had done. He said to me that it was not anything else but the fact that I had said that I would not honour the Maharaja.[4] I told him that it wasn't me who was saying it, rather that mother nature herself was saying it through me, that the time had come to change these institutions. They then let me go. However, I was on parole. I had to go and report at Singha Darbar once every month. They required this of us until our husbands were all released from prison, which happened only after another year or two.

When I went to make my parole report the next time, they had brought Chirkabhai there. Chirkabhai was the code-name we had given to one of the members of the Praja Parishad. His real name was C. B. Raman. They took me to him and asked me if I knew him. I told them that I didn't know him, that I had no idea who he was. Then the lieutenant who had taken me inside exclaimed, 'Oh my god, this means trouble!' Actually, Chirkabhai had gone with me to India to deliver the letters, but if I had said I recognized him it would have been an open-and-shut case against him. When I said I didn't recognize him that upset the whole prosecution case. After delivering the letters I had returned to Sirsia (near Janakpur), but Chirkabhai returned directly to Kathmandu, where he had been caught and jailed.

It was hard writing letters to Bua in prison. We tried all kinds of things. We had discovered that if you write with lemon juice, the writing is invisible to the naked eye. To see the writing you have to hold the paper over a fire and warm it up. The same is true if you write with *phatkiri* [alum]. I never sent letters written this way, but I did receive them and warmed them up so I could read them. I always wrote with ink, but Ram Hari's wife used to use alum and lemon juice.

[4] Maharaja was the term for the Rana Prime Minister; by contrast, the King is Maharajdiraj, or King of Kings.

Legal difficulties

Toward the end of Bua's time in prison I also had to fight a court case over some land in the Tarai. As long as my second mother-in-law was alive, there were no problems. I had gotten along with the second concubine, Ganga, alright too; she had been hired as a servant, and was very sweet. But she passed away shortly after I was married, and then Indumati (the third mistress) came. She was more difficult, because she had come from the beginning as a mistress, not as a servant, and she created lots of problems. Indumati filed a court suit against me in Jaleshwar, the district headquarters of Mahottari, after my second mother-in-law died, in *Shrawan* [July-August], 1950. She had nineteen ropanis of land that was already in her name. Another twenty-one *bighas* was in Bua's second mother's name, and Indumati wanted that too. She claimed everything, and wanted nothing to go to me.

So my second mother-in-law's sister (Sanima) and I went to Jaleshwar to fight the case. We were staying at some friend's house when towards the evening they threw us out, telling us we couldn't stay in their house. This was a distant relative of Bua. They used to let us stay there, but after Bua's second mother died, they wouldn't let us stay there anymore. Bua's first cousin was also in Jaleshwar, as Inspector of Police. He was the one who told them not let us stay there. We tried to stay at another house. There too, we were not allowed to stay. I went to three different houses one after the other, but none of them would let me in. Finally, I went and stayed at a Kalwar's; a Kalwar is a low caste in the Tarai. They were not supposed to touch the water we drank. I don't know why they are considered so low; they used to grind mustard and other kinds of seed for oil. They are Muslims, and they eat rodents, such as mice. At the Kalwar house only the wife was there, the husband was out. She too told me not to stay. 'My house will be confiscated by the government, don't stay here', she said to me. I told her to let me stay one night on the porch. I told her that I would rebuild her house for her if the government destroyed it, and I asked her to let me stay for one night. So we slept on the porch of her house that night.

Early the next morning I took all my bedding, etc. and knocked on the Bada Hakim's [Governor of the district] door. I was really angry, and I said: 'What have I done that I am not welcome in anyone's house? If you want to arrest me, go ahead and do it. I am at your door. Otherwise, what is this? I cannot find one home that I can stay in. What have I done?' He replied to me saying, 'So, people don't want to let you stay with them, what can I do about it?'

I then went to the office where the case was being handled. Even there nobody would speak to me. Fortunately, we had connections with two men working there. One was a subba related to Ram Hari. The other was a clerk, some distant relative of Bua. So he took care of the papers. The land was in my second mother-in-law's name, and we wanted to transfer it to my name. Now, since the mistress had filed a suit claiming the land, we could not do so right away. Indumati had said since our property was confiscated she should be sole inheritor. I got the use of the land, but not the title. They gave me papers which said I could use the land, but not own it, and then I returned to Kathmandu.

The case continued until Bua got out of jail. When he got out he agreed to let her have the nineteen *bighas* that were in her name, and he kept the twenty-one *bighas* that were left from land my father-in-law had bought from the government in an auction. Since we had nothing but the land when he got out of prison, we had to gradually sell off that land in order to have enough money to live on. Bua's father had originally bought 101 *bighas* of land in an auction. That was *jamindari* land—that is, he had the responsibility of collecting taxes for the government from tillers on associated lands for which he had *jamindari* responsibilities. He sold eighty *bighas* and spent all the money in Banaras within three years. The nineteen *bighas* of land in Indumati's name he had bought privately, at a different time.

After Bua's father died Indumati lived in Janakpur and rented out her nineteen bighas, but she always complained about not having enough. She sold some of it and eventually moved to Kathmandu where she stayed with her brother for a while. Much later the money that she got for the land was put in a fixed-rate deposit bank account in her name, but with Bua as sole inheritor, and she got the income from that account.

She had trouble getting along with her brother, so we took her in with us again. She was always complaining to Bua about the rest of us, telling on people and trying to get people to quarrel all the time. Late one evening, at about 11 o'clock she had a big fight, I do not remember with whom, but she was pretending that she was about to leave. Bua was trying to restrain her. She had created many scenes like this before, threatening to leave. The children thought her behaviour was demoralizing. Finally on this night Meena said, 'Either

she stays in this house or me, and that is that'. The next day we arranged
for her to go to her brother's place, but he wouldn't take her either,
and she went to a hostel at Pashupatinath. There also she quarrelled
and subsequently returned to her brother, who inherited her fixed deposit,
to perform her rites when she died.

Tilak Shamsher was the name of that Bada Hakim [see page 149-150].
Owing to wartime [World War II] shortages, he went to different villages
to distribute salt and other items that were rationed. He came near
our village, so my mother-in-law and Sanima and I went to fetch our
quota. His wife was sitting on a cot, and he said 'Look, Maya, this
is the woman who says she can rule the country'. Then he said to
me, 'Can you, bajai [here, female Brahmin]?' I said, 'Why not, this
ruling is being done by people, and what can be done by some people
can also be done by other people'.

Reflections

In the beginning of my life with Bua I was but a little kid. I was twenty-three
when he went to prison. He would not tell me anything. He wouldn't
tell me about their operations. I didn't know anything. At first he also
didn't write me from jail. Then after two years I wrote a letter and
sent it with one of Ram Hari's wife's letters, and then he started writing
to me. In the beginning I had no knowledge of politics, but later on
I began learning from the Congress and from books. The more I learned
about it, the more I felt I should do something for the country; and
if not for the country, at least for Bua. If I wouldn't actively support
him and his work, it wouldn't be right, and I would feel bad in my
heart. I had a deep urge to do it. I never had any fear. The more
I did it, the more I wanted to do it—I didn't know what kind of force
was driving me to do that. It never occurred to me that I could be
jailed. I was very much influenced by the female Indian revolutionaries,
like Laxmibai, Vijaya Laxmi Pandit, and others. I had read what they
had written. Later I also read a book about the Rani of Jhansi. I used
to get these books from members of the Nepali Congress. They were
mostly in the Tarai, across the border. I got books from their offices
in Jaynagar and Darbanga. I had to go through Jaynagar on the way
to Bua's house in Sirsia [because of lack of roads, one frequently had
to travel from one part of Nepal to another by crossing over into India,

taking the train up or down the border, then reentering Nepal], so I stayed there too.

For the first couple of years Bua was in prison I really could not bring myself completely to believe that he would ever be released. For about the first two years I felt that this was just how it was. After the first two years I started reading political books, books about India, about independence. It was after reading such books that I became a little more aware of what politics was all about. After that I felt differently. I realized that such things happen in the world and started feeling that he would eventually be released. After that, I believed in my heart that he would come out, that he would not have to spend the rest of his life in prison.

When he was in jail there was a lot of hardship, but I never felt that he should not have been a politician, or wished that he had been something else instead of a politician. No, I never felt that. I don't know why, but I never felt that. Well, for the first couple of years after his imprisonment I felt that maybe he should have done something else, but in two or three year's time I began to understand things a little bit and then stopped feeling that way. When anybody told me he would never get out of prison I would never believe it, I would always say that he would. When I used to say that Bua would come out and I would bring him home from the prison gates in grandeur and covered with garlands, Sanima would thrust out her lower lip, meaning that she didn't take what I was saying seriously. And my second mother-in-law would say that I was just saying these things to console her, and she wasn't sure whether she would ever see him again or not. I brought Vijaya Laxmi Pandit's book (her life-story) and read out a section of it where her daughters had proclaimed, 'Mother, as long as you are in jail, we will not let this flag [the Indian flag] be pulled down.' I used to read this to Meena and Shanta, to educate them about the political world. Later, I also used to read a book written in Hindi called *Great Women of the World*.[5] It had stories about people

[5] *Bishwaki Mahan Mahilae* (*Great Women of the World*), was one of her favourite books. It consisted of brief biographies of Kastur Ba (Gandhi's wife), Sarojini Naidu, Vijayalakshmi Pandit, Amrita Shergil, Mahadevi Varma, Rajkumari Amritkaur, Kamaladevi Chattopadhyay, Radan Edjang Kartini, Eleanor Roosevelt, Helen Keller, Pearl Buck, Annie Besant, Madame Curie, Madame Matesari, Madame Chiang Kai-shek, Madame Sun Yat-sen, Catherine Breshkowaski, Joya Kosmodeminskaya, Jane Adams, Evangaline Booth, Lady Mountbatten, and Khalida Adib Khanam.

like Helen Keller. I admired her very much; her stamina and courage were so remarkable.

It would be good if at least one of our sons would go into politics, like Bua. At least one of them has to continue what Bua started. Let him go to prison if he has to. For one thing, the prison will not be like it was then, when Bua was in jail. The cell in the Golghar where they kept him was eight feet big. He had to sleep, eat, excrete, and do everything else in that one room. These days it's not like that. When Bua was released and when he became the Home Minister, I went to take a look at the prison-cell that he had stayed in. I felt very unhappy when I saw it. How could he have stayed in such a place for ten entire years?

When I knew that he was going to be let out of prison I went and waited at the prison gates four or five days before he was to be released. I learned about the release from rumours that would pass around at demonstrations. There were lots of others too, packed in the Tundikhel, waiting! There was great activity on the Tundikhel, lots of speeches, etc. It was very exciting, since Tribhuvan had already flown to Delhi. The Congress people would tell me what would happen, what would become of the Ranas, so I was filled with wonder and pleasure that he was coming home.

During this time I used to organize strikes and demonstrations, I shouted slogans, I organised political activities, going around on foot and in jeeps. Everyone was on the streets, including Mahila Sangathan [Women's Organization] members. Everyone knew the prisoners were going to be released soon, and they had a lot of respect for those who had been jailed. I never thought that he would be Prime Minister, although many people were talking about it. I didn't have any interest in what kind of government job he might get or not get. I was just happy to have him back after so long a time.

I had deep feelings about it. While he was in prison I was kept busy during the day taking care of the children and my second mother-in-law and Sanima, or visiting my *maiti*, or being involved in political jobs. But at night I was very lonely and felt nostalgic about my days with Bua after we got married. I felt depressed and hopeless and insecure. I wasn't clear about what would happen in the future, whether he would get out, or what would happen if he did get out. I just accepted life as it came every year. After so many years of separation, when I heard he would be released, I felt as if I had suddenly become alive again, that I was being reborn. Then my feelings gradually changed and I began to feel more secure and happy. I had seen pictures of him, so I wasn't worried about not recognizing him. People had made drawings of him and smuggled them out. And we had been in frequent correspondence too, since on the two days a week (Fridays and Mondays) that I took things to the jail, I also sent him letters. So I wasn't worried.

Once he came to the prison gates, we came home together. That was on 10 *Magh* 2007 (23 January, 1951 AD). Well, there was no home actually, since I was staying at his sister's place then, so we went there. I saw him first from a distance; he didn't come to me immediately because there were so many people around him, he had to give speeches, etc. There was a long procession to Itam Bahal [north of Thamel], there were more speeches, and Khadga Man Singh sang a song about freedom he had composed in prison. Finally we came back together in a car.

Chapter 9

Tanka Prasad's Return to Politics

While we were still in prison, our friends on the outside were becoming very active. Ganesh Man and B.P. Koirala and many others were organizing in India, staging strikes and armed raids in the Tarai. On 6 November 1950, King Tribhuvan sought asylum in the Indian Embassy. He could do nothing else. The Ranas had decided to put Ganesh Man (who had been caught again) and Sundar Raj Chalise and others to death, after they had been arrested and charged in a plot to kill the Rana Prime Minister and other high Ranas during the Indrajatra festival, so they wanted King Tribhuvan to sign the death warrants. If he had stayed he could not have avoided it. By seeking asylum, Tribhuvan helped save their lives. Previously, in 1941, in the case of Sukra Raj and the three Praja Parishad members, the Ranas just executed them without any royal warrant. I know this because when Pitambar Subba read Ram Hari and me the sentence of death prescribed for us and the four martyrs, we asked to see the King's official stamp (*lalmohar*) on the paper. There was none.

Although the Indians had signed a treaty with the Ranas just three months earlier, the Indians agreed to give asylum to King Tribhuvan because they were afraid of the Ranas in the sense that the Ranas had the support of the British and had sent a delegation to China seeking assistance. Therefore, in the mind of the Indians, Nepal could provide a suitable stronghold for all the Indian princes to move against India.

But the Indians also wanted British approval to give shelter to King Tribhuvan. A British mission came to Nepal to find out whether there was much public support for King Tribhuvan or not. Our family members, such as my wife and Ram Hari's wife and many others, helped organize a demonstration of around 30,000 people at Gauchar [literally, 'cow pasture'] airport (it was our first airfield) in support of King Tribhuvan, chanting 'Long Live King Tribhuvan!', and other slogans against the Ranas. This convinced the British and the Indians of the support for King Tribhuvan. On 11 November the King and his family flew to Delhi (except for one of his little grandsons, who the Ranas then proclaimed as the King!)

This brings up the question of why Nepal was saved when all other Indian states were absorbed into the Republic of India. Firstly, because China would have surely objected (China considered Nepal their *chilli* garden[1]). Secondly, Nehru thought there would be no harm in letting China conclude a treaty with Nepal, since he thought it would not be difficult to make Nepal one of India's states in the future. Nehru was willing to allow Tibet to become a buffer state between India and China. He would have been successful in his plan if he had not aroused Chinese suspicion by bringing the Dalai Lama to India. Later, when I was Prime Minister, the Chinese invited me to China in retaliation.

After King Tribhuvan flew to Delhi the Ranas were willing to release us—their hand had been forced, and they no longer had much choice. But they wanted to keep Khadga Man Singh in jail, because they always regarded him as a criminal rather than as a political prisoner. They wanted us to say that he was a criminal, but we refused, and this delayed our release for three or four days. But finally, we all walked from the jail to the Tundikhel.

Not long thereafter the Indian Ambassador's private secretary came to me and told me that the king wanted to see me. So Chuda Prasad, Khadga Man Singh, and I went to Delhi, where we met the King. B.P. Koirala and M.P. Koirala were not allowed to see him because Nehru didn't trust them. Even then, B.P. was of a mercurial nature: he was a disciple of Jaya Prakash Narayan, who had broken away from the Indian Congress—that's why Nehru didn't trust him. The leading role of the Congress in the late 1940s brought the King closer to the Koiralas, but he could not confide in them as fully as he could with the Parishad people. I went to see M.P. Koirala, but he showed no interest in holding political discussions with me; he even appeared to be deliberately ignoring me. The King said that he wanted to see us because he was implicated with us and he was one of our comrades [laughter]. He added that when he returned to Kathmandu we should

---

[1] A phrase implying a subordinate position; the contrast is: small garden:minor crop::large fields:major crops.

visit him in his palace, so together we could make our plans for the future.

Negotiations took place between Nehru and the King. In India the King was just like a man in prison—he was kept in Hyderabad House. He had to do everything through Indian channels. Of course there were elements, such as the Ranas, who would have wanted to kill Tribhuvan at that point. It was mainly for his protection that the Indians took such measures.

The King wanted to oust the Ranas completely and not accommodate them at any level in any capacity. India was prepared to let the Ranas continue to rule but with modifications, so the 'Delhi Compromise' was forced on us. The Indians were in a hurry to compromise with the Ranas, who were trying to strengthen their position with British and Chinese support. The Ranas invited British officials to Nepal and sent a high-level delegation to China. The King wanted to discuss this with me, but by the time I arrived in Delhi it was too late, and the King had to accept the compromise.

We were angry with the Ranas, but we had to put on a conciliatory face towards India, suggesting that everything was going smoothly and peacefully among us. At the time of the Ranas, the British controlled Nepalese foreign policy and defence. Indians tried their best to inherit this legacy from the British, but they were unable to. I had a quarrel with them about this. I said 'Nepal has a right to become completely free, and if we are a colony we are only half-free. We must be completely free. We are not going to obey you in our foreign policy and defence'. Such quarrels went on for a long time. I shudder to recall those days.

The first government after Tribhuvan returned to Kathmandu, on 18 February 1951, was a Rana-Congress coalition, with Mohan Shamsher continuing as the Prime Minister, and there was no point in inviting our party to join it. Also, the Nepali Congress thought that since they had come to power through insurrection, other people had no place in the politics of Nepal. We wanted to join the Nepali Congress while retaining our name, Praja Parishad, within the Congress. This arrangement would have been similar to that adopted by the Socialists led by Jaya Prakash Narayan inside the Indian National Congress, but B.P. was cool to the idea. He wanted to show that we did not matter much. The Congress had played dirty tricks on us in the past too. After his release from prison in 1947, Jeev Raj Sharma went to Calcutta and wrote a booklet on the Praja Parishad which was destroyed by Congress people. Not a single copy of it could be distributed. Congress people feared such publicity would attract their workers to the Parishad.

Later that same year, in November, when M.P. Koirala headed a new government, the first non-Rana dominated government, he called me to the palace and offered me two seats in his government. I considered the number inadequate and rejected his offer. I told him that we did not go to jail in the hope of being ministers and prime minister, but that we started our work only because there was no one to speak against the exploitation of the Ranas, and to work against them. Therefore, I told him to form his own government, and I came back from the palace.

During the time I was serving my life sentence in jail, there was nobody outside who could run the Praja Parishad and conduct its activities, though two or three people communicated with us. At the same time, the Nepali Congress based in India had started its activities. So, those who were outside, even if they had been in the Praja Parishad, also joined the Congress. They thought that the Nepali Congress was doing what needed to be done, and if the Nepali Congress was working, then there was no need to engage in similar activities in a separate party. We Praja Parishad members had several meetings with Congress people, so we could work together. Our biggest disagreement was over foreign policy, towards India. This made us decide to work separately. There was extensive support for Praja Parishad, especially in the Kathmandu Valley.

After 1951 the Praja Parishad was reorganized in a country-wide network. We had workers in all the districts. We wanted to fight for poor peoples' rights, and we led the struggle for 50-50 sharecropping. Similarly, in 1954 we led the untouchables into Pashupati, thereby opening all temples to them. Sometime during the 1950s we changed the title of the head of our party from President to General Secretary, because that was the pattern of the socialist countries. Later we changed it back again. You see, I was by conviction a socialist. The Nepali Congress also claimed to be socialist. But we saw that there were people in the Congress who could never be socialists, such as Subarna Shamsher Jang Bahadur Rana. The Nepali Congress was full of Ranas and Shahs and people like that—big landlords. We had to fight against the landlords, not fight with them on our side. We also chose the hammer and spade as our party symbol.

In 1951 we also formed joint plans with the Peoples' Democratic Front, which was composed of nine groups. I was Chairman of the Front. When Matrika became Prime Minister he banned the Communist

Party, which was part of the Front. In 1954 we went together with the Congress Left and the Nepal Jana Congress, who merged with the Nepal Praja Parishad. After a dispute with Bhadrakali Mishra, who had become its Chairman, we reorganized the Praja Parishad in 1957.

I was released from ten years in jail in 1951, and I was imprisoned again the same year, while Mohan Shamsher was Prime Minister in the Rana-Congress government. The Praja Parishad had called a strike in the city. It was about general disorder over a football game inside Singha Darbar. The gate was closed and police started beating the people. It was not fair. So we called a strike and the strike was complete. On that account we were put into jail. At that time B.P. was Home Minister in the Rana-Congress government.

At first I was put in the same cell that the Ranas had put me in earlier—the Golghar. There were many other active democrats there with me, like Rishikesh Shah. We were kept there for two or three days. Then we were put in the Bhadragol Jail, adjacent to the Central Jail but separate from it. We were there for one night. And we could not sleep because of bugs [laughter]. You would be amazed, there were so many bugs. Then the next day we were transferred to Jawalakhel [a part of Patan], where we were kept under preventive detention, what amounted to house arrest. We were kept in a compound that had belonged to Juddha Shamsher, near the zoo; we stayed in one of the outbuildings. We were there for about a month and a half.

Our treatment in jail was the same as the Ranas had given us. B.P. Koirala had just come to power as Home Minister, and he had made no changes. He did try to give us political leaders special rations of food, such as milk and oranges, but I refused to accept them. I said that whatever we got should be made available to all the prisoners.

Many of our guards in Jawalakhel belonged to the Liberation Army [see below] and one of the guards was about to use his gun against me [laughter]. Luckily I was saved. What happened is that one of my fellow prisoners was Agni Prasad Kharel, who entertained ambitions of becoming Home Minister. I told him that the Home Minister would have to know English, and since Agni Prasad didn't know English, he would have no chance of getting that post. It would have to be cleared with Nehru, who wouldn't agree to it. He got furious at this, and one of the guards who was loyal to Agni Prasad raised his gun to shoot me. The rifle fired, but fortunately Rishikesh Shah and others pushed the rifle away, causing the bullet to harmlessly ricochet off the ceiling. Then they helped calm him down.

I wasn't given a definite sentence, I was just put there for an indefinite period. I thought I might stay in jail for many years again. But B.P. Koirala put us in jail for a month and a half, and before he could do anything more he was sacked. If he hadn't been sacked he might have kept us on in jail [laughter]! I don't think he was a democrat, you see; by temperament he was an autocrat. My wife went to see him and said to him, how come I was put in the same jail where the Ranas had put me? He responded by saying, 'There? Really? I don't know'. When I got out there was a big procession for us [laughter].

Sometime before 1953 we organized a peasant's movement in Mahottari for reforms in tenancy rights. In those days tenants used to get seven parts of what they produced on the land, while landlords got nine parts. We demanded a half-half division of the crop. We were successful, and the landlords had to give in.

After 1951 Indians had advisors in every department of the government. We protested against that. When Matrika became Prime Minister he banned the Communist Party. Then an Indian military mission came to Nepal, and we protested against both these actions. In those years Indians did whatever they liked in Nepal. For example, Tribhuvan Rajpath began being built without any agreement.

In 1954 an Advisory Council, an unofficial parliament whose members, representing all political parties, were nominated by the King, was formed. Praja Parishad had about eight people on the Council. The Council functioned for about a year.

Between 1950 and 1959 the Praja Parishad grew very fast. In the 1959 elections we put up forty-five candidates. Only four won. I also contested the elections but was defeated. The main reason we lost is that we were a nationalistic party; I was a staunch nationalist, and we fought on a nationalist platform. Since we were fighting for the poor, the rich wouldn't donate to our cause, and we didn't want foreign funding, so we had very little money and lost. In contrast to other parties the Praja Parishad had no wealthy supporters, either inside or outside the country. We had only Rs 12,000 to spend for all our candidates. King Mahendra had given us Rs 300,000 for party activities when I was Prime Minister, but this had been spent by the time of the elections. The larger part of the Rs 12,000 came from the sale of my own printing press, and the rest of the money was raised from party members. Unlike the Nepali Congress and the Gorkha Parishad, the Praja Parishad did not give a single farthing to the voters. The Nepali Congress had money and won a majority; Gorkha Parishad had money and won about fifteen or sixteen seats. Everything depended on money. Even though we didn't do well in the elections, our workers didn't give up. Until 1960, when all parties were banned, we were still active. After that I got high blood pressure, and I've continued to have high blood pressure ever since. Now also the Praja Parishad has not forgotten our national responsibility. We are trying to organize ourselves slowly. We hope that its nationalistic, democratic viewpoint will be understood and followed by the people.

The Congress had money from India, but also probably some American money too. That I don't know, it's very difficult to say. The Congress, through B.P.'s connections with the Israelis, also had support there. The reason that B.P. was known in Europe was because Jaya Prakash Narayan had introduced him to international socialists there. So when he went there, he had contact with the socialist leaders of Europe, as well as of India. But Nehru didn't like it.

I did not depend on any Indian leaders; I had contact with only one Indian party leader, P.C. Joshi, the first President of the Indian Communist Party, and no others. I went to Allahabad in 1952 and met him there. Rishikesh Shah was also there. I addressed a public meeting Joshi had called on my account. There was great pressure from Indian independence leaders on Nepal at that time, and I opposed it. I, or rather we, thought we must do our job by ourselves, and not rely on the support of others. From there we went to Delhi and met Nehru. The All-India Radio had branded K.I. Singh [who had led the Liberation Army against the Delhi Compromise King Tribhuvan had engineered] as a *dacoit* [bandit], and we opposed that characterization. Nehru believed it. When I talked to Nehru, I said K.I. Singh was not a killer or a looter or a dacoit, and Nehru was reasonable about it. He told me he had heard all this through a 'collector' [a government bureaucrat] in Gorakhpur. He said he would investigate it, and the next day the radio called K.I. Singh a 'rebel leader' of the people of Nepal.

K. I. Singh and the Liberation Army (Raksha Dal)

The Raksha Dal (Liberation Army) had been organized in India and brought to this country under K.I. Singh's leadership. Most of the members of the Raksha Dal came from Burma, where they had been members of the INA organized by Subash Chandra Bose.[2] It was much more a militia than a political organization, and they had carried on with armed struggle even after the settlement in Delhi. Then the Indian troops came into Bhairawa in the Tarai, as they could do according to the 1950 treaty, and suppressed it. K.I. Singh said that the Indians turned around and slapped his face. He was imprisoned in Singha Darbar, where many of the guards and others were members or supporters of the Liberation Army. They were not happy with the Congress government.

We heard that there was discontent in the Liberation Army because they were not getting their regular pay and were asking for something more, which could not be fulfilled. At the same time, there also had been discontent on the outside, as some Ranas had gotten together and were planning a conspiracy against King Tribhuvan. They approached me many times to lead it. I refused.[3] Then they turned to K.I. Singh. A few days later his Liberation Army (Raksha Dal) attempted a coup.

One day at two o'clock in the morning (I was staying at my sister's house then) I heard the sound of horses' hooves. I thought that maybe they were people of the Nepali Congress who were returning from a party and perhaps drunk [laughter]. So, I didn't give it much thought. When I tried to turn the lights on there was no electricity, so I went back to sleep. Early next morning, one of my party men came to me. He said that everything is finished, K.I. Singh finished everything, all the ministers are taken into custody, what shall we do now, what is our duty? I told him to go back home.

At that time, there was still the custom of a curfew, signalled by having a cannon [*top*] fire every evening on the Tundikhel at 9 p.m., after which people could not go out again until it was fired again the following morning. The curfew had been imposed decades before by the Ranas, and was stopped around 1952 or 1953. So, after the morning cannon was fired I went out. When I reached near the *charkhal adda* in Dilli Bazaar,[4] I went up, very fearfully, to a group of Liberation

[2] Subhas Chandra Bose led the Indian National Army, which was allied with the Axis powers during World War II; the Liberation Army joined forces with the Congress in their armed attempt to overthrow the Ranas.

[3] Tanka Prasad may have been perceived, as a politician out of power, as a likely coup leader.

[4] The *charkhal adda* was the centre of government offices during Rana times; the building still contains government offices. *Char* means four, *khal* refers to the place where gambling with cowrie shells takes place, and *adda* is office. Presumably the building originally contained four such gambling rooms.

Army guards and asked one of them, 'People are saying that K.I. Singh has captured everything. Is it true, *dai* [older brother]?' He responded, a little sharply, 'Why are you asking? He's captured everything!'

Then I went to Puskarnath Uprety, one of our party members who had spent five years in jail, and Basudev Prasad Rimal, a relative of mine. When I told them what had happened, they said that perhaps I had only had a dream. I told them, no, come out and see. So we went out. And in Dilli Bazaar I found Shivaraj Pant (he's now a member of the Rashtriya Panchayat). We went by way of Kamal Pokhari and proceeded towards downtown. By then there were quite a lot of us, quite a sizable number, about twenty-five or thirty people. When we reached Kamaladi, a truck came from the opposite direction, and we heard a 'halt'. We halted.

The truck was full of Liberation Army men with guns and all that. K.I. Singh had sent them. Agni Prasad Kharel, who I'd been in prison with briefly in Jawalakhel, was also there. We halted and he yelled out, 'Hey, is there any Tanka Prasad or Man Mohan Adhikari [President of the United Marxist-Leninist Party following the 1990 democratic movement and Prime Minister 1994-5] there?' I came forward and I said 'Yes, I'm Tanka Prasad Acharya'. [laughter]. He told me to get in the truck and sit down on the front seat. I told them that to inform Man Mohan we must go to his party office, the Communist Party office, downtown. Then we went straight to his office in Naradevi. At the Communist Party office there was a man called Gauribhakta, who was Man Mohan's wife's oldest brother. I asked him where Man Mohan was. A few days before I had warned them that they might all be arrested and that they should therefore be careful. So, Manmohan was in hiding. I persuaded Gauribhakta to take me to him. He took me to Man Mohan and I said, 'Look, Agni Prasad Kharel—he was the self-styled commander-in-chief of the *kanda* [incident]—has written this letter which says that Man Mohan and Tanka Prasad, both of them, must come'. And I said to him, 'Why don't you come? I am going. Whatever is to be done, I will see it. If you don't go, you will be against it'. Then Man Mohan said 'Alright, you go, but I will not go'. Then I returned to the Liberation Army people. I told them that Man Mohan was not home.

We continued on, and when we reached Bir Hospital we stopped.

Agni Prasad and the others were trying to get a man from the hospital. When he came we saw that he was Tek Bahadur (a Thakuri). We knew that in 1950 he had been a CID [Central Intelligence Department] agent responsible for informing the Ranas about us, about the activities of the Praja Parishad. When he came and sat in the truck I became suspicious—I thought that this thing is not right. The truck then took us to Singha Darbar. From the inner gate of Singha Darbar, Ganesh Man Singh was coming. He had also been taken prisoner. He was recruited to talk with the King. Ganesh Man told K.I. Singh that he would not go alone, that I should be ordered to go with him [laughter]. When I met K.I. Singh, he told me to go to the palace with Ganesh Man. So, both of us went to Narayanhiti Darbar [the royal palace] and met with the King. I said to the King, 'Your Majesty, K.I. Singh has sent a message of reconciliation. What is in your mind?' He said, 'First tell him to lay down his arms, then only we can talk. Before he lays down his arms we are not going to talk with him'. I said, 'Whatever Your Majesty has said I will convey it to him'. Then Ganesh Man and I went back to K.I. Singh at Singha Darbar.

K.I. Singh had slung his rifle over his shoulder. But I saw that the chiefs of the Liberation Army units were slowly slipping away. I saw that this was not going to be successful. I thought, we must get away from here [laughter].

Then we sat with K.I. Singh, and he wrote down five points—joint government of all parties, five-year plans, and so on. I saw that they were good points. I said that I would take his points to the King, and at the same time I told him, 'Look, we are surrounded by state troops outside, so don't stay here, go.' I told him without letting it be known to others. He said, 'Yes, I'm going. I'm just waiting for those of my comrades who are in Nakhu Jail'. That's all he said.

I went back to the palace and told the King that these are his demands. The King said that he must first lay down his arms and only then can all these things be considered. He said to tell him that first he must lay down his arms. That was quite right. So, we came back again to Singha Darbar. By then, K.I. Singh had already slipped away. His comrades from Nakhu had already come, and they had slipped away by way of Tripureswar Road. And we, like idiots, thought he was still there! Agni Prasad Kharel was there. He asked for me, so I went and asked him what was up. He said to me, We have to have our demands met, the government should be turned over to us, understand? I said okay and left.

Then gunfire broke out between Singha Darbar and the other side of the Tundikhel. Where could we go? We wanted to hide. We went into a canteen in Singha Darbar, because we were also very hungry [laughter]. We went there and had some food and waited until the gunfire ceased. After that, we tried to get out of Singha Darbar. Then some people in the Liberation Army started saying that Ganesh Man should not be released. They wanted to imprison Ganesh Man. That was not good. Then Puskarnath Upreti said, 'If you let him go I will bring Ganesh Man back to you when you want him, it will be my responsibility.' Finally they let Ganesh Man leave. And with a white flag on the car we drove away [laughter].

We reached Narayanhiti Darbar. It was already 5 p.m., and it was cold since it was the month of January. The king said to us, 'Now don't worry, K.I. Singh is already gone, you please sit and have some food here' [laughter].

Conspiracy Theories

In my view, all this was a conspiracy of Mahendra, Hari Shamsher (his father-in-law), and other Ranas, a conspiracy which arose because they did not like Tribhuvan, for two reasons. The reason for bad feeling between Mahendra and his father might be that Mahendra felt his father was too pro-Indian. Also, the Ranas were all anti-Indian at that time. But in reality Tribhuvan was not pro-Indian. He had no choice but to lean a little towards India, because everything—his escape, his return to power—had happened with India's help. The declaration that was drafted in India said that he would hold elections for a constituent assembly that would result in a republican system. This Mahendra did not like. Tribhuvan had no worries about turning Nepal into a Republic, because he did not like his eldest son Mahendra. He thought that if he had to give away power it might as well be to the people instead of giving it to those conspirators and rascals [laughter]. That obviously Mahendra did not like, since he would have lost his power. And so he conspired against his father.

The reason the Ranas disliked Tribhuvan is that he had objected to Mahendra marrying Hari Shamsher's daughter, Ratna Rajya Laxmi. Thus Mahendra was not happy with his father because he did not want him to marry the girl of his choice. She was Hari Shamsher's daughter, and the sister of the late Queen, Indra Rajya Laxmi Devi

Shah. King Tribhuvan was of the mind that there should be no matrimonial relation between the Shahs and the Ranas. But King Mahendra, the then Crown Prince, insisted. He even threatened to resign from being Crown Prince if he was not allowed to marry Ratna. So with much difficulty he was allowed to marry her, on 10 December 1952. King Tribhuvan did not attend the marriage ceremony. This could be one very plausible reason for tension between them.

Thus Hari Shamsher again became the father-in-law of Mahendra. He was the main instigator behind Mahendra's attempted coup. It was rumoured that Hari Shamsher sold a golden *thal* [plate] to finance the Raksha Dal [Liberation Army]. It was common knowledge—you see, everybody knows this. And Hari Shamsher was subsequently banished from the country. It may not be believed by some because they did not see it with their own eyes, but Hari Shamsher was driven out of the country. He lived in India for two years. I met him in Lucknow. He told me that he had been banished from Kathmandu, and that he wanted to return, but he needed permission from the King to do so.

I think these are the two factors that prompted Mahendra to act against his father. Now, how can one deduce that he had conspired against his father? K.I. Singh went to Tibet. Then Mahendra became King, after which he tried very hard to bring K.I. Singh back. So K.I. Singh came here and there was a big reception in his honour. It was King Mahendra who held the reception. We were also fooled. We also took part in his reception [laughter]. They put him up at Hari Shamsher's.

When you look at all these things, the circumstantial evidence is intriguing. It is said that when K.I. Singh came from Tibet he had two suitcases full of Indian notes (they weren't given to him by the Chinese) amounting to several lakhs. I don't know what the Chinese said to him after he reached Tibet. The Chinese perhaps did not favour him much. They just gave him asylum, that's all. Where did he get all that money? When I consider all these things, I have a suspicion that Mahendra was involved. I cannot say this for sure because I did not see it with my own eyes, but from circumstantial evidence I conclude that K.I. Singh was fully instigated by Mahendra and Hari Shamsher.

At the time of the coup he had been placed in detention at Singha Darbar by the Congress. The main reason why the coup failed was that K.I. Singh was not well-informed about the coup at the time. The Raksha Dal worked without his consent. Mahendra was behind it all.

Mahendra probably realized that unless he had some people to assist him, to stand by him, it would be difficult for him to run the state. So, he sought refuge in the Ranas. It's true, too. Now the Ranas are doing quite well. Whatever happens to the people, whether they are happy or not, the Ranas don't care.

K.I. Singh could have created chaos if he had wanted to, because he had some arms. But he also knew that this was a palace conspiracy, so he couldn't be eager to take part in it. He had actually instructed his followers not to go to the treasury or the banks. He was not a bad man, but these people who wanted to use him for their purpose made him look dishonest, a bad man. K. I. Singh himself was not bad. He was a public man, but here a public man gets little attention. Here success come to one who by hook or by crook makes money and gives presents to the King. During my Prime Ministership King Mahendra wanted me to form a ministry with K. I. Singh, which I refused. I told him that I could not go together with that man and asked him to forgive me for refusing. After having given K. I. Singh a lot of lifts King Mahendra eventually made him Prime Minister.

This is the story of K.I. Singh. It represents only my suspicions, and it hasn't been confirmed from other sources. No one has yet dared to write it, but the truth must come out.

Home Minister

I was offered a cabinet position many times but always rejected it because of disagreement on major policies with the leading constituents of the governments formed at different periods. However, during the second Prime Ministership of M.P. Koirala, King Tribhuvan pursued me intensely to join the Koirala cabinet. In view of my sentimental attachment to the King I could not reject the offer, so for ten months in 1954-5 I was Home Minister in the government headed by M.P. Koirala. I knew I would have difficulty working with him. The focal point of difference concerned relations with India. I was not prepared to allow any Indian interference in Nepalese affairs. Eventually even M.P. had difficulties with the Indians. They badly rebuked him for accepting, without prior consultation with India, the U.S. offer of wheat for the flood-stricken people of Nepal.

I had a quarrel with M.P. Koirala and wanted to resign. M.P. was surrounded by people who wanted to make money. And he had no command over his followers. He could not command even the Liberation Army. The Prime Minister had the Liberation Army chief work through him, not me, and also the Home Secretary didn't come to me. I complained to the King that since nobody came to me, why was I needed? I asked him to please allow me to resign. The King said that I should not resign, so I did not. Then he called them to the palace and reprimanded them, and they started working through me. Eventually M.P. asked the King to relieve me or accept his resignation, and I was disgracefully removed from the cabinet. I was not even given a chance to tender my resignation. I would have taken the initiative in doing so, but I considered it unnecessary since Mr. Koirala had already tendered his collective resignation and its acceptance was expected any day. Don't ask me what we quarrelled about. As Bernard Shaw said about Mahatma Gandhi, 'How dangerous it is to be too good. How dangerous it is to be too honest'.

During my time as Home Minister I looked after home affairs, including the police. At that time the police were mostly members of the Liberation Army. The Liberation Army consisted of people who had been given arms in India and other places and had come here with B.P. Koirala, Subarna Shamsher, and others, when the Congress was fighting from India to overthrow the Ranas. There was quite a big lot of them.

I had the chore of turning the Liberation Army into the police force. That was a very hard thing to do. I had to do screening, i.e., assign posts according to abilities. At that time there was a man called Yakthumba, who was the chief of the police, and he was regarded as very dangerous. He was from the Limbu tribe. Since many people in the Liberation Army were Limbus, they could do anything at his bidding. That's why he was regarded as dangerous. This police force had a separate station in Sri Mahal, their headquarters. Before Yakthumba, when B. P. Koirala was Home Minister, Nara Shamsher [executioner of the four martyrs] had been the Chief of Police.

Yakthumba came to me and asked me to let him stay until I had reorganized things. I said okay and gave him some assurance. I said, 'Hey, you Police Chief, I will make you ambassador' [laughter]. He agreed, so I asked King Mahendra to please send Yakthumba on a diplomatic mission, which he did. He made Yakthumba Consul General of Burma. He made a lot of money there, but I don't know where that money is. He was surrounded by money-hungry people. The Home Secretary was also transferred while I was Home Minister, so his family was not happy with me, they were very angry with me [laughter].

Prime Minister

My first son was born the day that M.P. Koirala resigned (and me with him). The second son was born the day I was called to form a ministry [laughter]. The morning that my second son was born [8 *Magh* 2012; 21 January 1956], I was called to the palace. What happened that morning was that at 4 a.m. my wife said she needed a nurse, and I went to the town to get one. When I came back with her and my friend Chuda Prasad, my wife had already had the delivery. About an hour later, Sher Bahadur came and informed me that the King wanted to see me. I was rather surprised, you see. It was 8 o'clock in the morning, and I couldn't think of a reason why the King would want to see me. I thought I might be in some trouble! [laughter]. They took me there in the palace jeep.

We sat, King Mahendra and I, in a small meeting. And he said, 'Tanka Prasadji, we want you to form a new government. Four of the seats are for you. I will keep three seats'. I was very much surprised. I thought that perhaps the king would head the cabinet and others would be taken in. I thought something along that line would perhaps be the case. I couldn't say no, because I thought being in a political party and being asked to form the government, it would be a great weakness on my part to say no, you see [laughter]. So I said 'Yes, Your Majesty'. Bal Chandra Sharma was the president of my party then.[5] The King said, 'What would Bal Chandra Sharma say?' The King was by nature a questioning man. I told the King, 'Your Majesty should call him and ask'. Then he said, 'Alright, will you please bring him, saying that the King wants to see him'. So I took Bal Chandra Sharma with me to the palace the following day. The King said to Bal Chandra Sharma, 'Mr Sharma, if I make your Tanka Prasad Acharya the Prime Minister', [then I knew that I was going to be Prime Minister], 'what would you say?' He said, 'Yes, that is alright'. He had to say yes [laughter]. And he also insisted that he should be included in the ministry. I said that was alright.

The King had three of his own people in the cabinet. One was Gunja Man Sardar [General Nara Shamsher had tried to force Tanka Prasad to implicate him in the Praja Parishad activities during the 1940

---

[5] As part of the process of merging his party with the Praja Parishad (as Bhadrakali Mishra had also done), Bal Chandra Sharma had been offered the Presidency of the party; Tanka Prasad remained as a member of the executive committee.

interrogations], who had served the Ranas and was quite an efficient hand in administration; another was Purendra Bikram Shah, a kinsman of the king and also a capable man; the third was Anirudra Prasad Singh, who is now the Chairman of the Raj Sabha [Council of State]. The four on our side were myself; Chuda Prasad as Foreign Minister; Bal Chandra Sharma as Education Minister, and Pashupati Ghosh as Communications Minister.

Foreign Relations

When I became Prime Minister Nepal was still a closed country. Besides India, we had no diplomatic relations with any country except Britain and America. And the relationship with America was sort of a secondary one. The United States first had relations with India, and through India they had relations with us. What you call this kind of relationship I don't know [laughter]. This was because Americans thought that Nepal belonged primarily to the British, and after the British left, they thought that Nepal belonged primarily to India. And they used to treat us accordingly. I always argued that Nepal should be as independent and sovereign as India, not its satellite state.

Foreign aid began to come to Nepal in a somewhat regular way from the time of my premiership. There was a famine in about 1954, when I was Home Minister, and people were dying of starvation. The Americans came forward generously. That was the beginning of American aid under PL 480,[6] although they had been active in Nepal since 1952. Indians had constructed the Tribhuvan Rajpath, but for their own militaristic interest because China was advancing towards our northern border. It was not built with our interest in mind.

I was Prime Minister when King Mahendra's coronation took place. Until then we did not have much aid from any country. King Mahendra asked the Americans to give us five million rupees to beautify Kathmandu for his coronation. All the roads were dirt, there were no parks, etc. Representatives from many countries came for the coronation.

One day during this period I was sitting beside the Ambassador from India, Gokhale, when he suddenly asked me, did the King think he could get aid from the Americans without the Indians' consent?

[6] Congress passed Public Law 480 to enable countries like India to pay for American agricultural products with soft currencies.

It was the first time that I came to know about the money Mahendra had asked for. At that time the Americans could not give us aid directly. They had to come through India. I did not say anything at that time, but I was deeply hurt by the Indian attitude towards us.

Then I directed the local newspaper *Samaj* to print a rumour that China was going to give millions of rupees to Nepal as aid. At that time you must remember China and America were like cats and dogs. The paper said that China was giving us twenty-four million rupees. It said that Russia was also giving us money. This flustered the Americans, as I intended it to.

At that time there was only a branch office here of the American Embassy in Delhi, and an American by the name of Howard Houston who was the chief of aid there attended the coronation. He came to me and asked me if there was anything we wanted from them. I asked him how we were supposed to talk to the Americans. He asked me what I meant by that. I told him about my talk with the Indian Ambassador. What the Indian Ambassador had said to me was that the King had asked the Americans for five million rupees in aid, but how did we expect to get money from the Americans without India's permission? This statement continued to prick and annoy me. So I asked Houston why I should talk to him, and I said that I would rather talk to the Indians because in order to get something from the Americans I had to talk to the Indians first. This is what the Indian Ambassador had given me to understand.

After that, Houston became a little concerned, and he was even more disturbed when he heard that China and Russia were giving us aid. He returned to India, and when he came back to Nepal he told me that we could ask them for any kind of aid. I said to him that they should first decide whether Nepal is an independent country or not, and only after that decision had been made would I ask for aid. Then he went back to Delhi again.

At that time the American Ambassador to India was Chester Bowles, I think. He had a charge d'affaires, a very tall man, who came here and said to me that he had come directly from Eisenhower. When I asked him what message he was carrying, he said that he was sent to Nepal to tell us that the United States did regard Nepal as a completely independent country. I gave him my thanks [laughter]. I asked him whether he had visited the King or not. He said no. Then I told him to go to the King and give him Eisenhower's message. After a few days I went to meet the King and asked him whether the American

Charge d'affaires had visited him or not. He said yes, and that the Charge told him that America regarded Nepal as an independent nation.

Then talks about aid started, after which the United States established something called Regional Cooperation. They were still not prepared to have a separate embassy here. Under the name of Regional Cooperation they suggested a project of road construction. The cost was to be shared by Nepal, India, and America. Americans had also agreed to help build a railway line from Raxaul to Hetauda, but the Indians didn't agree, saying that their share would be too costly for them to bear. Therefore the line did not materialize. Later, the Indians were also opposed to the Kathmandu-Kodari [from Kathmandu to the Tibetan border] highway. But King Mahendra replied that communism would not come to Nepal by taxi, on four wheels. A few roads did get built here and there. This is how Americans began coming in.

In 1956 the Americans also came up with a plan to build a road linking Kashmir to Tibet. Some part of the road had to pass through Nepal, e.g., from Raxaul to Hetauda and through some places in the eastern part of Nepal. I agreed to the plan. Tenders were invited and the contract was concluded. But then I resigned from the government, so I do not know what happened afterwards, but it was never built. I also initiated a plan to build a road in the east that would go up the Sunkosi and link the Kathmandu Valley with the eastern Tarai. There is a mountain called Tinaru in Sunkosi. Our plan was to take the road across that mountain up to Janakpur. I don't think American aid has achieved anything very substantial, except their contribution to malaria eradication, which was very important.

When I was Prime Minister, Paul Rose, the head of the American aid mission, came to me and asked me to sign within three days a thick pile of papers authorizing an aid agreement of three million dollars. I was furious at being given such short notice and said I would need more time to study them before signing. I was worried because on the one hand we badly needed the aid, and on the other India was vigorously trying to obstruct the aid agreement with the US. Rose begged me to sign them at once, otherwise he would lose the allocation from Congress. I jokingly asked him if he regarded me as his orderly, but I finally and reluctantly signed the agreement. I told him that the next year I expected to have plenty of time to read the papers first. He assured me that this would be the case, but by the time of the next agreement I was no longer Prime Minister [laughter], so I don't know what happened the next time around.

During most of the Rana period Nepal had diplomatic relations only with the British, and by the late forties only India and the Americans had been added to the list. Then when I came to power, I tried to expand them. I tried to build good relations with the Americans. I met Mr. Bunker, the Ambassador in Delhi accredited to Nepal. Later I met his wife [Carol Laise, who served as US Ambassador in the late sixties] too, since he married her here [laughter]. I had quite a nice relationship with him. Other Ambassadors I did not have as much familiarity with. But relations with the Americans during my premiership were very good. They have written letters to me praising my efforts to improve our relations. I have no prejudice against them.

Three days after I assumed office I outlined in very clear terms my foreign policy objectives in a public meeting. The King did not raise any question about my statement, which meant that he did not disagree with it. But later he faced pressure from different quarters, including, significantly, bureaucrats from our own Ministry of Foreign Affairs. The Foreign Secretary asked me to consult the King before I issued any foreign policy statement.

I opened relations with other countries, such as the Soviet Union, Japan, China, Switzerland, and Egypt. When I opened relations with the Soviet Union, the Indians were very angry with me. I didn't tell the Indian Ambassador I was going to do that.

In the area of foreign relations, when I was Prime Minister I also brought up the idea of a Federation of Himalayan States. When I spoke to the Bhutanese Minister, it was quite all right with him. But after I spoke to the Sikkimese Minister he reported our conversation to the Indian Ambassador. The Indian Ambassador was very angry with me. That was during King Mahendra's coronation.

I wanted the development of my country. So from the beginning I said that whoever gives me assistance for the development of my country, I was prepared to take it, whether America, or China, or the Soviet Union, or India, or anybody else. India came forward with aid first. We are grateful to whichever country has provided us aid, but it must be utilized properly. The only option for Nepal is to promote public sector enterprises. Little benefit may accrue in the beginning, but that will grow. The Americans have invested a lot in Nepal. If they had invested it in public sector enterprises we would have gained a lot by now. Yet when a difference of opinion arises between them and us on the public vs. private issue, then we are branded as communists. As for myself, I am a bit to the left, but that does not mean I am not a democrat. The aid givers should put aside their bias against public enterprise and give direct aid to improve our agricultural and basic industrial condition.

In fact, we have been trying to encourage both public and private enterprises for a long time, but private enterprise has not been very effective. Once I had a talk with an American diplomat from the embassy. He told me that America had done so much for Nepal. They had provided training for manpower development and so on. I told him that the only thing that the Americans had taught us was how to take bribes.

Whoever comes with plans to help us reach this goal is our real friend. The only true friends of Nepal are those who would help Nepal in such sectors as food research, basic necessities, etc. However, unless Nepal can stand on her own feet in these matters no one can help her.

There was one journalist named Armstrong, editor of *Foreign Affairs Journal* in America, who wrote that Nepal cannot be an independent country, that she has to depend on India particularly in military matters. Such was the attitude of the Americans at that time. Because America had some kind of conflict with the Chinese then, they wanted to see Nepal aligned with India, so that we would fight jointly against China. But fighting against the Chinese through Indians did not take place. That was their wrong assessment. That made a very bad impression on the Nepalese as well as on other countries.

It was pitiable that the Americans should think that if there is a tussle between India and China, Nepal should act as a satellite of India. The Soviet Union's attitude also was that Nepal and India should unite against the Chinese. Therefore it was difficult to formulate our foreign policy so that Nepal would not be aligned with any country. It is remarkable that being sandwiched between two such big countries we have been able to remain independent. The reason is that our needs have been very few, and we could meet our clothing and food requirements from our own production. We had no need of sophisticated items. That is why we were able to survive. Now, if we could just continue to fulfill our food and clothing requirements, there would not be any need to kneel before anybody.

Nepal concluded a treaty with China during my tenure as Prime Minister. In 1955 Sardar Gunja Man was head of the King's Advisory Council; D. R. Regmi was also a member of it, handling foreign affairs. During that period a Chinese delegation came to Nepal to establish a treaty. The King and Regmi suggested a treaty on the basis of Pancha Sheel.[7] The Chinese went back without concluding a treaty. In 1956, when I was Prime Minister, the Chinese returned to Nepal and proposed a treaty which would be limited to Tibet-Nepal relations, not relations with China as a whole. At that time Tibet paid Nepal an annual tribute of Rs 10,000. I told them that the treaty should be about Nepal-China relations in general, and based on the principles of *Pancha Sheel*. When Nehru was requested to sign a treaty with Nepal on the basis of *Pancha Sheel* he said, who agrees with the principles of *Pancha Sheel*?

The Nepalese team, consisting of Kesar Bahadur and Nara Pratap, drafted a treaty with the Chinese. The Chinese wanted us to give up the Rs 10,000 annual tribute, but Purendra Bikram Shah and Gunja Man, King Mahendra's representatives in my cabinet, wanted to keep it. They talked to the King about it, and he in turn asked me and my cabinet colleagues for our opinions. But Purendra Bikram and Gunja Man and I were the only ones who went to see him about this. The King didn't want to give up the Rs 10,000 either, so Nara Pratap and Kesar Bahadur went to the Chinese and asked if they would sign the treaty with a provision that Nepal continue to be paid Rs 10,000 annually. The Chinese would not agree to such a treaty. I told the King I agreed with the Chinese position and said I was leaving the palace to go home. The King said he would contact me about it. When I got back I told my wife that this is it, my premiership is over. At 12:30 a.m. I went to sleep. At 1 a.m. the King called and told me to go ahead with the treaty. I called a cabinet meeting the following morning at 8 a.m., at which the treaty was approved, and it was subsequently signed. That's how China came to recognize Nepal as a sovereign country.

State Visits

After we opened relations with China I went there on a state visit. Mr. Ulan Fu, leader of the Chinese delegation which attended the coronation, extended the invitation to me. When I told the King about it, he approved since this was our new approach to foreign policy, but he feared critical reaction from India. The Indians were furious. The Indian Ambassador, Bhagwan Shah, said I should visit Delhi first. I

[7] 'Five Principles' enunciated at the 1955 Asian-African Conference in Bandung included respect for territorial integrity and sovereignty, non-aggression, noninterference in internal affairs, equality and mutual benefit, and peaceful coexistence.

refused. Then he said that Nehru could come to Kathmandu to see me, since the Indians were determined to show that Nepal could do nothing without their prior approval. Again I refused. I told the Indian Ambassador that I had received the invitation from China first, and that I should therefore visit there first. I said when I came back I would go to Delhi. I accepted the Chinese invitation myself.

Everything in China was so big—airports and such. Nothing of ours could measure up to theirs. So, a little bit of inferiority complex comes upon you [laughter]. And there was Mao Zedong. An Emperor of China! We had heard about Chinese Emperors. Now, he was the emperor, but even more than an emperor. The evening of our arrival in China we were called to see him. He came outside his residence to receive us. We sat as two separate groups—on one side he with his ministers and on the other, me with my wife and our friends. His bald head glittered in the lights of the room. You get awed, feeling as though he is a deity [laughter]. But the way he spoke! He was a simple man. He didn't speak English. He said that he was learning four words a day. I said to him, 'Look! If you continue to learn four words a day, then in a year you will have command of the English vocabulary'. [laughter]

He introduced his ministers to me. As he introduced them he said, 'This one is of the Christian League, this one of the Buddhist League, this one of this and that one of that. People of all different beliefs! But we cannot let them go', he said, 'because all of us, together, have to reform China.' Then he said, you know, 'This one here is a Mongol. He is an invader. He gave us a lot of trouble too. We erected that huge Chinese Great Wall to keep him out. He is a crook. He might arrive in your country. But don't worry, we are in between and we'll never allow such people to come to you' [laughter]. He talked in such a humourous way that all of us started laughing.

Then he said, 'Today the imperialists want to perch on our head. If we shake our head even a little bit they become angry. Look at the British in Egypt. Egyptians want independence, but the British don't give it. This is the kind of work imperialists do', he said. Mao Zedong also said to me that we must emancipate women, that women are a big help. It has been happening in various places. But I feel that some have gone to extremes. You must go the middle way [laughter].

Then I said, 'There is one thing I am worried about. We have made a border agreement with you. In the agreement it is written that only the traditional line will be acknowledged. It is very difficult to pinpoint that traditional line (we had a map). I'm worried that something might happen later. In our country there is all this rumour by the opposition party [the reference is to the Congress Party] that we have sold Nepal to China (K.I. Singh was one of the rumour mongers). What will happen?'

He said to me, 'Look, our country is very big, your country is very small. If a little bit of ours goes it will not harm us, but if a little bit of yours goes it will be very harmful to you. You should not worry about it at all for twenty years. As long as we are alive you have nothing to worry about. But after we die, we cannot guarantee this [laughter]'.

He talked in such a humuorous manner and made us feel so comfortable that we had no need to feel any inferiority complex. We talked with him very freely. We were very assured. That talk about twenty years is remarkable. Exactly twenty years later he died.

I was also impressed very much by Zhou Enlai. He was very, very gentle. He never wore the attitude of being the Prime Minister of a big country. Never! He was a very simple man. I said to Zhou Enlai 'Look, we are such a small country. You are such a big state, how can you treat us on equal terms? It is only for the time being perhaps that you are treating us on equal terms'. He said, 'How big is Japan? The Japanese captured us. Size doesn't make any difference. It is man who counts. It is man's mind that counts, not man's number. Do not worry'. It was from such statements that he initiated the slogan, 'Big Nation Chauvinism'. He meant that this concept should be resisted and abandoned; what matters is the spirit of the people, not the size of the country. Zhou Enlai had been in France, you see. He had stayed in France, so he knew French. And even English. When the interpreter could not translate the way he wanted it, Zhou Enlai would interfere and correct it [laughter].

On my way home I went to Japan too. At the airport I said to the Japanese that we should be admitted to the United Nations. I also told them that in Asia, Japan is the pioneer of industrial development and other things, and that Japan is a country which we regard as a guide to our future paths. I also carried a message for the Japanese from Zhou Enlai. The message was that China was prepared to open trade relations with Japan. With all these developments, the Emperor became happy with me. Later, they conferred on me the Order of the Rising Sun. Very beautiful! When I was in Japan on my state visit they gave me a transistor radio, which was probably the first transistor radio to reach Nepal. King Mahendra was interested in it, so I presented it to him. Later on he gave me a National Panasonic radio, which

I still have. It was very difficult at that time for the Japanese. Food scarcity and other things, such as the pressure of population, were problems. So their Foreign Minister asked me to give a statement saying that Australia should give land for Japanese to settle down. I said, how can I say this? For 200 families I can give you that; come to my country, and I can give you land for 200 families, I told him. If somebody had taken me up on my offer to house 200 Japanese families in Nepal, it would have been very rewarding today. We would have had Japanese aid, their technology, but it didn't happen.

After returning from China I visited India. My delegation included Ram Hari, my wife, and one of my nieces as personal companions. I found Nehru to be a very sympathetic human being. People said that Nehru was overbearing, but I did not find him so. He didn't send me a congratulatory telegram when I became Prime Minister, but at heart he was quite a good man. At the state banquet in my honour in Delhi my niece (my sister's daughter), my wife, and I were sitting next to Nehru and his daughter, Indira, and others. My niece had no experience using a knife, fork, and spoon, whereas my wife had, since she had already travelled to China and Japan, and besides we had organized a training course in such etiquette at the Royal Hotel to learn modern ways. Nehru noticed my niece's difficulty, told her just to eat with her hands and ordered his own cutlery removed. He started eating with his hands, and then we all followed suit.

We also visited Mohan Shamsher [the last Rana Prime Minister] and his two brothers who were living in India. Before we started the Praja Parishad I had gone to see him to suggest that some reforms be made. He was Commander-in-Chief at that time. My main reason for going to him back then was that I hoped to exploit, for the benefit of reform, some differences that I had heard existed between Mohan Shamsher and the Prime Minister, Juddha Shamsher. Nothing came of it, and Mohan Shamsher eventually became the last Rana Prime Minister. We had lunch with him and his two brothers, and I urged them to return to Kathmandu. I said they would be well-received, but they said they were comfortable in Bangalore, so they stayed there until they died.

Domestic Policy

Domestically, the nationalization of forests took place when I was Prime Minister. It was one of the most important accomplishments of my regime. We also organized the Planning Commission. Establishing the Rastra Bank was also a very important move, because until then our foreign exchange deposits were in the hands of the Reserve Bank of India. Until we had our own independent banking system we had no control over the economy. One could exchange Nepali currency and Indian currency from private vendors on the streets.

I also passed the Civil Service Act. Previously the authorities, mostly ministers, appointed or dismissed civil servants as they wished, at their will. And the future of the civil service depended largely on the whims and interests of the men who hired. By the Civil Service Act, ministers were prevented from doing such things. Anyone who was dismissed had the right to appeal to the court. So the Civil Service Act was a great check to such arbitrary actions.

There were still great problems with *chakari* and corruption. So much *chakari!* When I passed that Act, I had to go seven days regularly to the palace in order just to satisfy the palace secretariat. They objected to it very much. At last they said to include them in the civil service. I said alright. Then they agreed, and I passed the legislation. So there is less *chakari* now than there was. Formerly one could expect a colonel to be appointed directly from a *havaldar* [a non-commissioned officer], you see [laughter]. *Chakari* could raise a man abruptly from dust to heaven.

When I was Prime Minister I got *namaskars* [respectful greetings], yes, but no *chakari*. I hated *chakari*. If somebody wanted something, they would come and tell me and if I could do it I would say okay, but if I could not do it, I would say no, it can't be done. I would not accept any *chakari*. I met with everybody who came to see me. It's true that a poor man says a lot of *hajurs* [an honorific term of address], but you must not make them feel self-conscious.

When I was Prime Minister I saw the King very frequently. Not every day, but every alternate day. He was very busy. If I wanted to meet him I could telephone him right in his room. If it was a big decision, I would first talk to him, but day to day affairs I decided myself. I consulted him on decisions such as opening diplomatic relations with other countries.

In those days the King had no direct access to the national treasury.

He was paid a monthly allowance, but anything beyond that had to be approved by the cabinet. King Mahendra asked for Rs 25,000 to build a wall around the Gokarna forest, on the grounds that it was government property. My cabinet agreed. When that proved to be inadequate he asked for another Rs 20,000, which we again granted. Still it was not enough, so he asked for more, this time saying that we could deduct the balance from his royal allowance.

Resignation from the Prime Ministership

The story of my resignation from the Prime Ministership is a long one. The King declared in a palace announcement over the radio that he had to dissolve my government because I could not arrange for the elections. But four months after I resigned they reached a decision to have elections for a parliament and not for a constituent assembly. I am often blamed for wanting elections for a parliament instead of a constituent assembly, but I should make it clear that I stood for a sovereign parliament. It is not quite obvious whether I was asked to leave office because I could not arrange for the elections, or whether the King had difficulty in deciding what the elections should be for. The ballot boxes had already been ordered, the voters' lists had been made ready, and other preparations had been made. Actually I had said that the elections should not be for the constituent assembly, but the Nepali Congress had not agreed with me. The King remained silent. I talked to him about this election many times, but I never got a good response from him.

Earlier I had told the King: 'Look, Your Majesty, we are very much in the clutches of the Indians. We have to free ourselves. If Your Majesty cannot do so, then two or three Prime Ministers must come forward and sacrifice themselves. So, I think I should run the foreign policy. If anything unpleasant happens, then ask me to go away. I will go'. The King said okay. When I started to run the foreign policy myself, I initiated relations with China. Although the Chinese and our government had already decided to open diplomatic relations, they had not been formalized. What I had in mind was to open this country to the world. I also invited the American Ambassador to India to open a residential embassy here.

At this time an important Chinese delegation came here. Because they spoke my name with familiarity and because I had developed friendly relations with them, the palace wanted to show the Chinese that I was an insignificant nobody and to show the Indians that the Chinese had come here just to meet me and that the Nepalese people were against it. Therefore they arranged a big demonstration from the house of Lok Darshan, the King's own secretary, on the grounds that the price of rice had gone up too high in the market. It had been one *mohar* (fifty paisa) for a half kilo then. The following day I realized what was going on, so I went to the palace and told the King, 'If you had wanted me to leave the office, you could have told me so straight away, and I would have resigned. There is no need for you to arrange this sort of propaganda'. He said, 'Alright then, you resign'. I went back to my friends and consulted with them, and the next day I resigned.

When Sardar Gunja Man got wind of this, he invited Mani Babu [Tanka Prasad's long-time friend and editor of the Nepali-language newspaper *Samaj*] to his place and said to him, 'I hear that Tanka Prasad is going to resign. Although I do not know what has happened between him and the King, even if the King has told him to resign, this is not the right time for him to do so. It won't be good for the nation, it will drag her one step behind. Maybe you can make him understand. Try to make him understand'. Mani Babu said, 'I'll try to convince him. But if he has already decided to resign, there is nothing I can do'. Gunja Man said, 'Mani Babu, what the consequences of Tanka Prasad resigning are, those you'll eventually see with your own eyes. I am not going to live for long. And it's not that I oppose his resigning from the office because of fear that I'll have to go then too. It's because it will not benefit either him or the King. The present situation is such that even if the King asks him to leave, he should tell him that it is not the right time for him to go. You'll understand this later. I've asked you to come here just to tell you this. See what you can do about it'.

When I talked to Mani Babu about Gunja Man, I said that although he was not a member of my party and was a royal appointee, within my government he had supported me and stood by me more than even my closest friends and associates. He was a patriot. When we decided to establish diplomatic relations with China, India said that the talks with the Chinese should include Indian representatives. Nobody dared raise his voice against this proposal; everyone kept mum. It was only he who resisted from the beginning and succeeded in not letting the

Indians in. You can imagine what the consequences would have been if we had allowed the Indians to take part in those discussions.[8]

The Indians felt that I leaned too much towards the Chinese, you see. This compelled the King to get me out of the cabinet. He wanted to show the Indians that he was not pleased with me. So, he had to engineer all this show. My government was dissolved on 14 July, 1957. It had the longest tenure of any of the post-Rana and pre-Panchayat governments. King Tribhuvan had told me about Mahendra, that he will cause you trouble, and put himself in trouble too.

Not long after I resigned, a huge non-cooperation movement was organized collectively by all the political parties, including ours, to hold elections. In Birganj I had made a speech, when I was Prime Minister, saying we should have elections for a parliament instead of a constituent assembly, because it was not consistent to have a constituent assembly in a country with a King. I was worried that a constituent assembly could adopt a constitution which would abolish the Kingship and make Nepal a part of India. In those years Indian influence was extremely strong in Nepal. B.P. filed a case in the Birganj court against me for making that speech, but the case was dismissed on the grounds that everyone had a right to express his [their] view[s]. Afterwards the Congress accepted the principle that the elections should be for parliament.

[8] Tanka Prasad's version of the election issue, and the information on Gunja Man, is from *Samaj*.

Chapter 10

Life as the Prime Minister's Wife
Rewanta Kumari

My grandfather had a great grudge against the Ranas, so he liked Bua's getting into politics. He always asked me to tell Bua to be patient, that he would win, and he always gave me courage and inspired me. He worked at Dharma Shamsher's [a son of Prime Minister Bir Shamsher] house, as their *purohit* [family priest], so he went there every day. But he never took any of us there. Other *purohits* sometimes took their families to their patron's houses, but not my grandfather. He would say, 'I have to go because I have to work in order to feed you, but you don't have to, so why should you come?' Once he went with Dharma Shamsher's widow on a *Char Dham* [four places] pilgrimage to India. They included Jagannath [near Calcutta], Rameshwaram [on the southern tip of the Indian subcontinent], Dwarka [on the western side], and Badrinath [in the Himalayas]. When he came back he said, 'I went traipsing after that widow to do the pilgrimage, but wherever I went there were only stones and stones, no gods'. Dharma Shamsher's son was Ekraj Shamsher. My grandfather was also annoyed with him, and when he came home he would say 'moro' [from marnu, to die], a kind of curse. He didn't like the supercilious way the Ranas treated him and attempted to make him feel servile.

In 1947 or 1948 the first radios arrived in Nepal. Only Ranas could have them. We weren't allowed to have them. Ekraj Shamsher had a radio, and my grandfather told us that Ekraj would play his radio with the door closed so that grandfather couldn't hear. Since my grandfather's grandson-in-law was in jail, he was not supposed to hear outside news. Later in the evenings, he used to sit at the end of the balcony and listen to the radio in another Rana house across the street.

In 1950 one of my neighbours brought a radio to our house and we used to listen to it. By that time things were loosening up.

Only once did grandfather say anything at all negative about Bua. One of my aunts [father's sisters] had TB and spent two years in the sanatorium. While she was there her husband did not remarry, but when she got out she came and stayed with us in Thamel. Then after she was cured her husband brought another wife to his house. At that point grandfather got very upset. He said he had married his daughters and granddaughters into well-off and respected households, but that one brought ruin on himself because he didn't have any sense, and the other got himself in trouble and into a big house (i.e., jail) because he had too much sense.

Nobody really discussed politics in my own home when I was growing up. My father and uncles were mostly government employees. My third uncle taught English at Trichandra College for a year and a half, and then died. My second uncle worked as a clerk in some government office. My first uncle also studied Sanskrit. As government employees they refrained from discussing politics, which was a risky thing to do. So, they used to talk about Sanskrit literature, but not politics. My introduction to politics was through Bua's example.

It was not easy being a politician's wife, whether Bua was inside or outside prison. His political engagements took all his time, and I had to take care of the children and manage the household single-handedly. He had very little time for the children or me. For example, when our second son, Kanchhu, was born, Bua didn't even come home for a few days. Well, that is a long story. The day Kanchhu was born Tanka Prasad became the Prime Minister. We were staying at his sister's house then, in three of the rooms. Holding the Prime Ministership means having lots of visitors, and there was no place to put them, so he went to stay in Sital Nivas, the government guest house. I had just given birth to a baby, so I couldn't go [because of her polluted state after giving birth]. He had just become the Prime Minister, people were surrounding him all the time, and he didn't come home at all. Counting Kanchhu I had three small children under the age of four, and I had to take care of them single-handedly.

On the eleventh day of a child's birth, there is what we call the *Nwaran* celebration, where we do *puja*, and 'come out' from the seclusion we observe because of our polluted state. You see, the mother and child cannot come out into the sun for the first eleven days after a birth. Then on the eleventh day, you pray to the sun and come out into the open. At that time the father has to be present. The father has to put the child on his lap and give him or her a name. But Bua had not come home for nine days, so on the tenth day I sent him an invitation card to attend the *Nwaran*. I sent him an invitation card along with coconut and betel nut [substances typically accompanying formal invitations]. Then he finally came.

Kanchhu was born at 5 o'clock in the morning, and at 8 o'clock that morning Bua became Prime Minister. He suspected something when he left the house, because the regiment came, made a military formation, and saluted him right in his sister's house.

At the time he became Prime Minister, I was happy; it was all joy. The first three or four months he was Prime Minister I didn't go anywhere, to any functions, because of the new-born baby. Then later I started going out. I never stayed at Sital Nivas, only he stayed there. Then after fifteen days we rented a house in Pani Pokhari belonging to a man who had been our neighbour in Thamel. I moved straight to that rented house in Pani Pokhari. However, it was too small, so we moved again, this time to Arvind Shamsher's house in Kamal Pokhari; he was looking for a tenant, so I went to see it and thought it would be adequate and moved there.

As the Prime Minister's wife I was busy looking after people. I was so surprised, I didn't know how to feel. I was proud of Bua and of my new role. After attending parties, seeing bigshots visit the house, I felt I had become an important person too. I didn't worry about not having our own place, because Arvind Shamsher's house in Kamal Pokhari was big enough, and the government paid the rent on that house. As far as house servants are concerned there were Mithi (who had been with me already for about eight years), a cook, and a nurse-maid for the kids; the nurse-maid herself had a daughter. And since Bua was Prime Minister, there were always peons [unskilled office workers] and guards around.

When Bua became Prime Minister I met many people, either at parties and functions or at our house, since people were constantly coming to see Bua about their various problems. No one ever tried to bribe me. I never really engaged myself in such matters and, therefore, nobody talked to me about such things.

I met many different political leaders of other countries. When we visited India, when Bua was Prime Minister, Nehru recognized me and asked, aren't you the same person who delivered that letter to me? I also met Mao Zedong, Zhou Enlai, and others. At that time, they were sympathetic towards Nepal and its political leaders. They were nice people.

My favourite was Zhou Enlai. In that place of six hundred million people! He remained unchanged even when Mao did change. He remained the Prime Minister from the time of the revolution until he died. He was popular among all his people. Otherwise he might have changed too. I also met Madame Sun Yat-sen. I couldn't converse with her, since I don't know English. So, when you go to other countries you meet people, sit around, return home, that's it!

I like going to other countries. It's fun. I would go again if I got the chance. I have been to North Korea also. That was a nice place too. But of all the foreign places I've been to, China was the most impressive. In terms of discipline and development, it is China. Nepal and China began developing their countries back to back. We started in 1951, and they started around 1949. We went there in 1956. They had already advanced incredibly. Here in Nepal, we don't have anything even today.

In Japan too there was so much development, but Japan was a developed place from the start. I went to Japan also when Bua was with the government. We went to China and Japan during the same trip. During the Panchayat period I supported Bua's views on the need for democracy and freedom. I did not have much chance to see the King or Queen in those years, though Bua would occasionally meet with them and speak his mind.

We talked to the King and Queen together in 1980, at Thulo Babu's wedding. I don't remember how he addressed me, but the Queen called me *tapai*. They wanted Bua to be Prime Minister. I don't remember exactly what Bua said, but the King asked me if I would support the Panchayat system. I said, sarcastically, that you consider us outside the Panchayat system, when we are actually in it. Whereas you consider those who are corrupt and exploit poor people, to be inside the Panchayat system! Those who expose and criticize the corrupt ones, they should be considered to be more a part of the Panchayat system than those Panchayat officials who exploit and cheat others. He only smiled.

Chapter 11

Food, Clothing, Shelter, Education, Health
Tanka Prasad's Political Views and Activities

Government

I always thought of Nepal as a separate country, because it was not under the direct rule of the British. Even as a small boy I felt that; although it was not well articulated, there was a consciousness and feeling that we were a separate country.

I have been thinking about what sort of government might be good for this country, and I think the best would be an intellectual aristocracy. Not an hereditary aristocracy but an intellectual aristocracy. Plato says that a state run by a philosopher king is the best system. But it is very hard to find a philosopher king. A philosopher king will never happen—that is only Plato's dream! I've thought a lot about whether a philosopher king will do or not. I've decided that because of the people that would work around him, he would not do. The king might be a philosopher, but his aim cannot be philosophy. He would be surrounded by people with whose assistance he has to run the state. From whomsoever he takes assistance, they will start earning money, and the corruption will start there.

I have read much about socialism and communism, I've read this and that and very many things. I had to know different philosophies and different political systems that are prevalent in the world, so that I would be able to say which one is the best for Nepal. Unless I have studied different philosophies and methods, how could I say which one is fit for Nepal?

Whether one wins or loses, whatever it may be, there should be democracy. In a democracy there are different groups, different ideas, and if one set of ideas and people cannot rule, another will come which can. There are two types of democracy: one is bourgeois democracy, and the other is proletarian democracy [laughter]. Yours is bourgeois democracy. My preference is not exactly proletarian. I am in the middle. I always prescribe the middle way [laughter].

I have also studied Fabian socialism. According to it one should come to power by voting, and only after that should one start nationalizing private property little by little. The owners would be compensated for their property. This is one good way of having a bloodless revolution. What the Fabians did was to form a labour party. Bernard Shaw, Laski, Harold Wilson were all members of the party. They opened the London School of Economics. Some members of this party even reached parliament by fighting elections, but they were not able to accomplish their goals.

Therefore, so far as property is concerned, no owner is ready to sacrifice his property until he is forced to. If the propertied class agrees to sacrifice some part of its interest for the upliftment of the poor, that would be best. According to the communists, the propertied class will never make such sacrifices unless it is forced to. By contrast, the Fabians wanted socialism through a democratic way. The question here is, how much force to apply?

Nepal is on the threshold between feudalism and liberal democracy. What I call feudalism is owning land and having some political power attached to it. Looking back now, I think we worked far in advance of the feudalism of our time. We started our political work very early. At that time there was no consciousness of such things, but we are now slowly advancing.

At that time we were more backward .than a feudal system. We call it the time of *Jangli Raj* [Jungle Government]. There was not so much human habitation then. Only the outer fringes of the Tarai were inhabited and cultivated. And even here in the Kathmandu Valley there were jungles. Very few people were here. The Ranas lived in the valley, and the gentry also. They bought land in the Tarai and used to get revenue from that land. Newars were here, with their religious scriptures and all, such as Tantra, but from a philosophical point of view they are not enlightened. Not even the Brahmins are. A European has written somewhere that Hindus are hypocritical. It's true, Hindus are hypocritical. They speak of high ideas, you see, but in behaviour and all that they act so lowly. Some European has written this, but I agree with him [laughter].

The commercial bourgeoisie had just begun to rise. I can't say whether democracy will come through merchant capital or not. Only when there is industrial capitalism will the question arise of a revolution through the proletariat. In Nepal, too, if you want to do something for the poor, you have to force the propertied class to sacrifice some of its interests for the benefit of the poor. In our opinion there should not arise any such situation where much force would be needed.

The middle class character is that they want the status quo. They do not want to take risks. Nothing will happen unless one takes risks. While fighting a fascist one must take risks. Lenin's elder brother, Alexander, was implicated in a conspiracy to assassinate the Tsar. He was determined to plot against the Tsar. And when people knew about his brother's hanging and all that, they got scared and started moving away from him and his family members. And then Lenin said, 'Look! This is the character of the liberal bourgeoisie' [laughter]. But this lady, Aquino [President of the Philippines], you see, got inspiration from her dead husband and carried on his work instead of retreating from it.

Huntington says that governments rule by consensus. What do you mean by consensus? I have not been able to understand thoroughly what is meant by government by consensus. Some say it is a consensus of three—executive, judiciary, and legislature—and by the concurrence of these three, the government becomes one. Some say it is by the concurrence of the people themselves, that is, the middle class, not the lower class or peasants. So there is no representation of different classes, and government functions by the consensus of the middle class. Which view is correct? In Nepal the king says the government is by consensus [laughter]. He says, *Lok Sammati*, which means People's Consensus.

My slogans are only five. They are: food, clothing, shelter, education, and health for all Nepalese. If somebody can fulfill these five essentials, that will be enough for the time being. To bring about that, one does whatever one has to do. Therefore, in Nepal, unless you force the wealthy people to look after the poor, or develop a mechanism to collect funds for the benefit of the poor, there is no other way to uplift the poor. Even if some country gives us the necessary aid, the exploiters would exploit it, and the people would not benefit from the aid.

Modernization

We do not want a sophisticated society; we can not afford it, and also it is not good for us. The main thing that is plaguing Nepal at present is the modern sophistication. We want everybody to be well fed and well clothed, etc., but modern sophistication does not allow it. We want TVs, cars, fashionable clothes, etc., but when the middle class like us starts thinking in this way, how can we serve the people? I lead a simple life—a thatched house would do—but do Nepalese want such a life? We must sacrifice all these sophisticated luxuries if we want the well-being of the mass.

If we had followed Gandhi's teachings and copied his way of life, i.e., lived like a common man and consumed only the barest necessities, we would have been able to do something for the masses. All this building going on in Nepal is a waste. We don't need skyscrapers. What we need are solid houses for villagers to live in, and a library in every village. I am not an out-and-out Gandhian, but I think he was basically correct in his philosophy. If he hadn't been killed he could have continued developing his ideas. Gandhi would have adopted other means of being self-sufficient instead of, for example, the spinning wheel, if the country had already passed that stage. But we have not been able to follow Gandhi's way of life. Instead, we have been living the life of comfort and at the same time trying to bring the masses to our level, and that is not possible.

It is terrible the way China is now being Americanized—people wanting western fashions, men wearing neck ties, prostitution developing. The Chinese should be Chinese and not try to be like the Americans. It is not good, and they can't afford it. Compared with China and India, we are a small country of no importance.

People say China is turning away from communism, but I do not believe them. China is just trying to lure the Hong Kong Chinese capitalists, American Chinese capitalists, and other Chinese capitalists from all over the world to bring their money back to China. The Chinese are only trying to remove the fear of the Hong Kong people that if China takes over Hong Kong all their lifelong efforts and their wealth will be lost.

The Americans think that their colonies will grow everywhere according to their own pattern, but that is not the case. The circumstances are not the same everywhere. Americans had enough land and other natural resources. They had and still have so many opportunities, and they think the others do too.

But in Nepal there are very few opportunities, and few people who are rich enough to invest in industries or business. Most of the existing Nepalese private enterprises at present are owned by Marwaris [Indian merchant group]. They seem to be Nepali, but in fact they are not. They repatriate whatever money they have earned to India. They are just like the merchant in Shakespeare's 'Merchant of Venice'.

Marwaris are hated because they are money lenders, merchants, and they cheat people. Newars do the same thing, but not as much as the Marwaris. They say that the Chinese also are traders and that they do the same thing, but we have no experience with them. Traders are hated everywhere. Jews are hated because they are money lenders. It is ironic that so many great men have been Jews—Einstein was a Jew, Christ was a Jew, Karl Marx was a Jew, Freud was a Jew [laughter]— yet they are persecuted.

The thing is that in a country such as ours there is no need for PhDs. We do not need so many high qualifications; what we need are practical minds. Universities of America and other countries provide us scholarships for MBA and other high degrees, but there are not many industries in Nepal which can use the sophisticated skills of an MBA or such. My daughter wants to go to the US to study nutrition, but I'm opposed to the idea. What is the need of studying nutrition? The problem is how to have enough food for everyone, and studying in the US won't solve that problem. The main contribution of the West to Nepal has been baked bread and bathrooms [laughter].

There are very few people who understand the problems Nepal is facing right now. There are so many hidden talents in Nepal, but there has not been any machinery developed so far to identify and exploit those talents. Instead the government sends people to different countries to learn skills. One *havaldar* [a non-commissioned officer] traced the whole blueprint of the Kathmandu-Kodari highway, which the Chinese followed afterwards. That is, there are hidden talents in Nepal, and it would be cheaper to exploit them than send our manpower to other countries.

There is no hope for this country because we don't recognize our skills and resources, just Gurkhas. The Nepalese people are foolish. For example, a man may be quite ordinary, but if he becomes a Gurkha soldier, he gives such a snappy salute, 'Yes Sir, Saheb!'. The army, the police, they are all so loyal to the King. There is really no alternative to the King. One has to be a military leader before one can be a political leader. This is why the King usually wears an army uniform when he tours the country. B.P. was supposed to be an alternative, but he was a Brahmin and the troops didn't respect him. People get the government they deserve.

The *saheblok* [Hindi; the sense is 'big shots'] come here and spend a lot on their own comforts. When the Indians built the Tribhuvan Raj Path [the first road from Kathmandu to the Indian border], they first built houses for themselves, then they built the road. Some of the houses could be used for maintenance workers and equipment later, but there were still too many houses to be used. The Chinese only make temporary rest houses, and then take them away whenever they finish their work.

America

I have read somewhere that in America a Spencerian ideology was followed in the past—i.e., survival of the fittest, or to quote a proverb, 'Every man for himself, and the devil take the hindmost'. But politicians did not stick to this ideology, and they did many things for the benefit of the public. Otherwise, Americans stick to the idea that all property should be privately owned, and that only those who are the fittest should survive, leaving the weaker ones to die. I do not know very much about America, but I think the older generation of Americans may still hold to that belief.

These days it is difficult for countries to have any connections with Americans. Suppose an American gets killed here, then the whole blame would come on our entire country. And perhaps Reagan would just start taking action against us [the reference is to a retaliatory American raid on Libya]. Reagan sits there and claims that even if one American dies he will destroy the entire world. That's not right. Reagan has become quite arrogant. A powerful nation does not really give much consideration to weak nations. Gadafi himself is quite something too. He can support terrorists, and act through them. Then these terrorists cause the common American people to suffer. Reagan's anger was directed towards Gadafi, but Reagan wanted to teach a lesson to other Libyans also, claiming that they too were Gadafi's supporters. The poor innocent people were killed and he was teaching them a lesson. This is too much! They were innocent people. This is the arrogance of power.

A different example is the Iran *kanda* (incident). Iran took American hostages. Then there arose the question of American power. Carter was in a spot. If he attacked, it would be counted as an invasion. So he could not attack. He tried many ways to free them, and they were freed in the end. But in the minds of the people, there was implanted the thought that even such a worthless country as Iran was able to insult them and make fools out of them.

I liked Jimmy Carter. I said to Carter's wife that we liked Carter. Under him America started supporting human rights, and the UN fanfare for human rights was started. He has done all the work in a peaceful manner. He handled the Middle-East problem quite well. We are grateful to him. I did not get to talk to him at length directly, but I got to talk to his wife. I said that the welfare of the common people was not valued. She agreed.

But Carter made a big mistake in Nepal. When Jimmy Carter came here, the King introduced everybody, and we shook hands. The King did a very clever thing by introducing us dissidents to him. That impressed Carter very much, that our King was such a democratic fellow. Of course, Carter thought that the King was so liberal. But it was all a show, just propaganda, and Carter didn't realize that. One should not go to a foreign country and just spit out something without understanding everything [Carter issued a statement praising Nepal's human rights record]. What did Carter see when he came here and went trekking? He saw everyone was going about on their own, everyone had clothes on, and all that. What did he deduce? He figured there is freedom here, and that it wasn't like what the Shah did in Iran. But it is not necessary to be so cruel here, and yet be autocratic.

The people in America are not just of one kind. They are of many different kinds. Some have come from England, some from France, some from Spain, some from Germany, etc. So it's a mixture. As such, all are not of the same thought. There are fair-minded people too. My daughter also says to me, Bua, you tend to eye everyone with the same view, you should not do that. For example, there is Mondale, a democrat. He wants reform. But Reagan is a crook! [laughter].

H.G. Wells has written, 'Ignorance is the price of pride'. In the preface of the book *New Machiavelli*, he wrote that the world had committed such great crimes. In America also, the aboriginal population, whom we call the Red Indians, was eliminated. Do we think that it will go unavenged? It will be avenged.

There was one American Ambassador here named Douglas Heck. I used to visit him, and he also used to call on me. We used to have long talks. He was very much afraid of the communists, and I used to tell him that he need not be afraid of communists. Because unless there is a great calamity, communists can't do anything. There are two major communist countries—the Soviet Union and China. But they turned to communism only after two world wars. Therefore, one need not be afraid of Nepal turning communist at this juncture. If the Soviet Union helps the people in Nepal just as they helped the people of Afghanistan, the country might turn communist, but there is no possibility of the Soviet Union helping us on that scale.

Monarchy

The King might have been considered an incarnation of Vishnu in the past. But with the spread of education, the veneration for the King is fast evaporating. I think the idea of the king as a reincarnation began in the olden days when he was described as an incarnation of Vishnu in order to ensure obedience from the people. It was tactical and expedient to do so. When you say Raja, Raja means an incarnation of Vishnu, and they won't disobey a Raja. It is only a myth, but it ruled the country. Now people have ceased believing in such things. Prithvinarayan [eighteenth-century founder of present dynasty of Kings] is considered a reincarnation, but not for people like us, not for people who are educated. That belief is for those who are completely uneducated. He was a conqueror, and he was considered a superman. He really was a superman [laughter]. Tribhuvan and Mahendra subscribed to the idea that they are incarnations of Vishnu only in a ritualistic way. Otherwise, by conviction they never believed in it themselves. The same is true of Birendra.

As for the future of the monarchy in Nepal, whether it is a monarchy or a republic or a democracy, whatever it is, it all depends upon its achievements. If a monarchy can accomplish something for the people, then it will have a long future. If the King cannot do that he will also have to go. If a republic can perform service for the people, it will remain. Otherwise even it will go. It depends on deeds and achievements.

There were many princely states in India, but all disappeared because of selfishness; Indian Princes were very selfish, their life was luxurious, and so when people with modern ideas came in, the people became enlightened and started believing in new things. Even in Europe monarchs were not very enlightened. Louis XIV said, 'I am the state'. [laughter].

Formerly, India did not support the King, but now Rajiv Gandhi, perhaps, thinks that there is no need for interfering in such a small nation like Nepal, and that they can get whatever they need without interfering too much in Nepalese affairs. Our economy is such that we have to depend on India even for our daily necessities. Therefore, India's assumption is that eventually Nepal has to bend to its will.

As for the present King [Birendra], to tell you the truth, people are losing faith in him fast. If a person cannot fulfill his own promises, then there is no ground for keeping faith in him. If the King were overthrown, anybody could take over. The army can take over or India might come and take over. The Chinese will not come for it, but India might. If the army takes over, Nepal would become a military kind of state, like Pakistan. A military takeover here would not be good.

From the liberal point of view, King Tribhuvan was far better than the other two. It seems that the more educated the Kings are, the less liberal they are [laughter]. But what does education mean? In our Sanskrit teachings, it is said that if a man is educated he becomes quite modest and liberal. I have watched Birendra grow from his childhood. King Birendra was quite good in the beginning, but people around him corrupted him. He was even prepared to give us democracy, but afterwards people around him who were interested in making money in his name, gaining benefit in his name, they corrupted him—the mother, wife, everybody corrupted him. Personally I think this man is not so bad. Sometimes those around him have given him bad advice, but he himself is a good man, there is no doubt about it.

The King is a tyrant. For instance, now the government has to reduce our currency by twenty-five rupees per hundred Indian rupees, i.e., a 14.5 per cent devaluation of the Nepalese currency against Indian currency. And during this time the King goes to Hetauda [on his annual tour of the country] and spends millions of rupees. He is squandering money like anything. The masses have to suffer from this. The middle class does not suffer so much.

The King can't accurately assess the needs of the country, because he is surrounded by too many sycophants. By all appearances the King is an honest man, but in actions the wife seems to have more influence. She is greedy, and someone characterized her as an 'emerging Imelda'. But otherwise she is very fit to be a queen.

As an illustration of liberal attitude, King Tribhuvan used to address me as *tapai* [see Chapter 7, footnote 4]. King Mahendra also addressed me as *tapai*, but King Birendra addresses me as *timi*. The palace people have taught him to call us *timi*. I did not like being called *timi*, but since I could do nothing about it, I just let it pass. Sometimes when he addresses me as *tapai* I am surprised. When the King came to Sano Kanchhu's [the youngest son's] wedding he tried to avoid using any pronoun with me. He sometimes used *timi*, but in general he avoided using either *timi* or *tapai*, sometimes by using impersonal forms of the verb, and sometimes by speaking English. Addressing us as *timi* is a palace conspiracy in order to make the King unpopular. He was taught especially by the Ranas around him to address us Brahmins as *timi*. The Ranas wanted to humiliate us in all possible ways, because they were angry with us for being one of the main causes of their downfall. Before 1950 the Ranas also used to address us as *timi*, while they used to address others as *ta*. After 1951 they started to address us as *tapai* [laughter].

When King Birendra came to Sano Kanchhu's wedding we talked for a long time; he was supposed to stay twenty minutes, but he stayed forty-five. He was very courteous and polite. The Queen didn't come, so I told him I thought maybe she had an allergy to me.

I don't know what Dipendra will be like when he becomes King. After all, he is a descendant of a Rana. I never expect the people's good to be served by royalty. You need the people themselves, you must have the people's son. This fellow [meaning the King] cannot see what goes on below him. You haven't seen his circle—all Rana families, Rana exploiters. He sits in the middle of that circle. The King doesn't know what I feel and how I maintain myself and my family. If he doesn't know even my circle, how and what does he know of the lower class? In whatever circle you are, that circle's consciousness comes to you!

Mao Zedong has correctly said, 'If you want to develop the consciousness of the proletariat, you must go and live with them'. Similarly, if you want to develop the consciousness of the peasants, you must go and live with them. You cannot actually live with them, but you must go around from time to time and see how they live. You cannot grasp the consciousness of the lower class by just sitting in the palace, by just moving among women in powder and lipstick. Only a son of the people can bring that consciousness! He can move anywhere he likes, even to the lowest strata, and develop consciousness. Mao Zedong said that so very beautifully, I appreciate that very much.

The King should go out without letting other people know he is the King. He should go incognito. He did this once or twice in the beginning, but that is not enough. He is always surrounded by guards and generals. Only give me two people who can be trusted, and let him go with me, I will take responsibility for his security. I will take him! Who else will do it? Nobody will do it!

Politics

We Nepali political leaders sometimes fight, but we are not deadly enemies. We subscribe to the same ideology, you see. Nepali Congress people are social democrats, I myself am a social democrat, and Regmi is a social democrat. In India also, Nehru called himself a social democrat, as did his daughter, and his grandson also says that he will adopt the socialist pattern. Here it is just a matter of leadership, not ideology—we are all social democrats. Leadership and getting power—that is the personal factor. Social democrats are not successful. The palace plays us off against each other.

For example, M.P. Koirala [first post-Rana Prime Minister and Prime Minister in 1954-5 when Tanka Prasad was Home Minister] was formerly my political rival, but now my daughter is married to his son. You see, when you take a side, when you have a party, then you have to fight with the other parties. So, you become partisan, but you can still be friends. That's quite natural. On the other hand Gorkha Parishad was the Ranas' party, and they were our bitter enemy.

The communists of Nepal are just the representatives of the lower middle class. They are not real communists. They can not advocate that their fathers' property be distributed among the landless. Marx, Lenin, and Mao were also from the lower middle class. They were able to afford a hand to mouth existence. And also, unless India turns communist, it will be very difficult for Nepal to turn communist.

When Nehru said that he is a socialist and he wanted socialism in India, then the Americans considered Nehru their enemy. John Foster Dulles said that whoever was not America's friend was America's enemy. That was such nonsense. However, Nehru was never a communist, he only had some sympathy towards leftist programmes. He was not a communist out and out. In other countries, too, Americans made the same mistake and supported tyrants.

We have a story about Hirandya Kasipu, who was a demon. He

had asked for, and received, a boon from Brahma. The boon was that neither on water nor on land nor by any man could he be killed. Even all the gods from heaven could not do anything to him. Then he had a child born to him called Prahlad, who started praising Vishnu. Hirandya Kasipu tried to kill him, his own son, but he couldn't. At last, he drew his sword to kill his son and struck a pillar. From within the pillar appeared the Narsingh *avatar*, or incarnation. The Narsingh *avatar* is an incarnation of Vishnu as half lion and half man. What Vishnu did, in his Narsingh form, was to put Hirandya Kasipu on his lap and kill him with his own claws.

This is just an educational story. Whether it is literally true or not I don't know. But the moral is that if there is nobody from outside to do any harm to you, then from within you there springs up the tendency to destroy yourself.

The Roman Empire went this self-destructive way. So did the Byzantine Empire, and the Persian Empire, and other empires. And then the British Empire—such a big one—went this way. We were told that it would never go, but it did. And now it's the Americans' turn! [laughter].

Fighting tyrants is not easy. One has to go through all sorts of trouble and hardships to do so. But we did it. What made it so difficult was that the Ranas were supreme here, with the support of the British. The British were interested in recruiting Gurkha troops, and the Ranas permitted them to recruit troops. The British had nothing to say about what happened to the Nepalese public, so the Ranas could do anything they liked. But even then there was some restraint. The British kept some restraints on the Ranas.

The trouble now is that there is no one to keep restraint on the ruler. I identify the King with the Americans. Reagan supports this fellow [the King]. There are nice Americans, and we are glad to associate with them. But these people of the State Department who come here? We hate them. If Americans cease to support this fellow, the next day the government would fall. But the Americans just try to court the King.

This is very unlucky for us. We supported Americans like anything; we knew Americans were for liberty. They fought for liberty, and we thought they would fight for liberty for others too. Those Britishers who went to settle in America later fought against the British with the same ideal, liberty—no taxation without representation, etc. But we were wrong. Everywhere we see they just want a strong man, like

Marcos or the Shah, to look after their interests. They will allow even a tyrant to prevent communism from spreading.

I don't know very much about Stalin, but so far as I can tell, at that time everybody tried to destroy Russia—Britain, France, and other countries as well—all bourgeois countries tried to destroy him. To handle it he had to take stern measures to protect himself and his country. Churchill said that those whom Stalin killed were traitors. During the war also he killed many people.

In politics if one goes against the principles one has to kill. The Ranas also killed. They killed their own brethren. Jang Bahadur's brother, Ranodip Singh, was writing 'Ram, Ram, Ram' [God, God, God] in the evening when they tore down the whole door, thrust a gun in, and shot him. And Bir Shamsher, he killed Jang Bahadur's sons and took the reign in his own hands. All this sin. It's all from being *jangli* [of the jungle], that is, barbarian [laughter]. Jang Bahadur was the only good Rana. It's true he killed many people to take power, but they were rascals anyway and deserved their fate.

Women

So far women have not be able to take much advantage of modern developments. But women have always been important. In our scriptures it is said that Brahma, the creator of the universe, while explaining the process of creation says that he needed women, so he initially split into two parts [laughter]. Although in practice the position assigned to women is very low here, it is not so according to the scriptures. We worship women in the form of Kali, Durga, etc. They are not ministers, but Durga and Kali mean more than ministers [laughter]. There were a lot of women members of Praja Parishad after 1950. The situation of women will change, but in such matters we must be very careful. We must go the middle way. I think China and Russia also would do better if they took the middle way. And America also would do well if it chose the middle way [laughter]. And in reforms also, you must go the middle way.

The thing is, the situation of women is bad, specifically in the hilly regions. Here in Kathmandu, I think most women are satisfied with what they have. Here, women have joined different kinds of services. My daughters and daughters-in-law all have responsible jobs. The problem is not so bad here. The problem exists specifically in the hilly regions and also in the suburban areas.

About the women's movement, who is doing it, that I don't know. People come here from other places and gather people and claim they are doing something for the women. They come and go, but what have they really done? Nothing! This work has to be done by Nepalese women themselves, and then it will be fruitful. These days, there is something happening. But there is one catch! Men do not do household work, things like picking up cow-dung, cooking, etc. Women have to do it. From morning till night women take care of the household. What needs to be done is to have men share the household responsibility. This can be done, but only if the government gets involved. Our government has no interest!

Legally, you cannot have more than one wife now. Before, polygamy was allowed, as a result of which women remained very suppressed; a woman was afraid that her husband would bring in another wife. These days, you can't have more than one wife, which has given women a little more freedom, and men also are a little more hesitant. You cannot marry another wife so you have to remain with the same one. This has, to a certain extent, resulted in better treatment of women.

Napoleon said that there are two reasons why a man may divorce a woman: adultery and barrenness. In this respect Nepal follows the Napoleonic code [laughter]. We do not have so many divorces now. Among the Brahmins, the divorce rate is very low, because a Brahmin girl is not entitled to divorce. So, she has to stay with her husband. Even if I take another wife, my wife will remain. She may not stay with me, but she will not take another husband. Our King has a wife, and according to rumours has gotten interested in another woman, but he has not been able to have a second wife [laughter].

Sherpa women can have more than one husband, that's their traditional system of polyandry. This is because the number of men is greater than the number of women. So, women are allowed to have multiple husbands. Here, it's not like that. Here, I think the number of women is greater than the number of men.

It is affection that binds a husband and wife together. It is affection that gives you pleasure. If you are staying together only for sexual purposes, it's no use. Sexual purposes vanish afterwards. And what then? When you are faithful to one another, then affection grows. And that affection itself is a very desirable thing. If you are devoted to your woman then she will be bound to be devoted to you. If the wife is devoted then the husband also must be devoted, and eventually they can develop that affection. This devoted life is such a great pleasure, you cannot find it in any other thing. The failures are due to wanton passions, you see [laughter]. It is very difficult to control passion. If you see a beautiful girl, then naturally your mind goes to her [laughter]. I asked my wife if when she sees a beautiful man, her mind goes to him. She says no. She says that her parents told her that I am her husband and that she cannot just eye another man. Her parents impressed that on her mind. So she says that her mind does not go to another man. But I can't say that for myself. If I saw a lovely girl, my mind used to wander to her [laughter]. Beautiful things, you see, one likes to see beautiful things. Even now, when I see a beautiful woman, I like her, but not from a sexual point of view, just from the point of view of beauty. When I see a very beautiful girl, I would like to marry her to my son [laughter].

Caste

Politics also brings about social reform. The two are interconnected. Social reform brings changes in one's political ideas, and these ideas in turn bring about changes in social values. The caste system is going out of fashion in Nepal. Brahminism had already weakened by the time I was growing up. Among the well-to-do people, who observed Brahminism? They did perform *puja*, but Brahminism in its strict sense was observed by only a very few people. My family was not so strict. We didn't eat chicken, that was prohibited. But we ate tomatoes, onions, garlic, mutton, and goat. I learned about other castes when I came in contact with them. Two of the concubines of my father were Tamangnis [laughter]. The third one was a Chhetrini.[1] When I got out of prison I had no wish to go through any kind of *puja* to restore my caste, even though some people, including my father-in-law, were apprehensive about eating with me. In prison I read the *Gita* many times; in my opinion that was my *puja*.

Even the orthodox people in the hills have started to mix up more with low-caste common people. In Nepal caste is no communal problem, though in India it is still a problem. Religion was never a hard nut

---

[1] The Tamang are a Tibeto-Burmese speaking ethnic group found mainly in the hills north of the Kathmandu Valley; Chhetri is the second-highest caste, after Brahmins. The suffix 'ni' feminizes unmarked nouns generally taken to be masculine or neuter.

to crack here in Nepal, because with the political and social reforms, the religious superstitions and the old beliefs also went away.

When we thought of political reform fifty years ago, and in the intervening years, we wanted a socialist pattern of government. In Nepal we had to think about this caste system. What we wanted was not to force people to abandon their prejudices. At present one can see people from different castes—e.g., Brahmins, Chhetris, Vaisya, Sudras, eating together in restaurants and hotels, and mixing with each other in the market place. So what we foresaw was that when the society advanced, the caste system would automatically go away, and then we would not need to force a new system on the people. There was the problem of untouchables not being allowed into Pashupatinath temple. In some temples, e.g., in Gujyeswari, the lowest caste (Pode) is made the priest of the temple. I was the one who led the untouchables inside Pashupatinath in 1951. There was a big opposition against my move, but I did not give up my efforts and led them into Pashupatinath. After that I went to King Tribhuvan and asked him to create an avenue to represent untouchables in the cabinet. He replied that I was already a representative of the untouchables, so what was the need of others? [laughter]

Today people do not mind the untouchables going inside Pashu-patinath. There has been a change in social attitudes about the un-touchables in the last fifty years. People have not changed these attitudes, but the age has changed them. In the British Embassy there was a cook from the lowest caste. People had to go to the Embassy and dine with the British Ambassador when they were invited there, and the low-caste cook served the food [laughter].

Progress

Compared to fifty years ago, there has no doubt been progress in Nepal. But whether that progress is nature-made or man-made is very difficult to deduce [laughter]. Morally it is worse. We have some values, but now people have started ignoring them. We also have some family traditions, but all that, everything is going. I do not say that we should preserve all of them, I only say that the good ones should be preserved and the bad ones should be discarded. The joint family [parents, sons, and their wives and children living as one economic and residential unit] is a good institution and should be preserved.

Whether there is more bribery and corruption now than fifty years ago, what to say? The whole society seems to thrive on bribery, although the peasants and manual labourers do not take bribes. Look, the only honest man who lives on his own labour is the peasant. Others are all extorters [laughter].

Someone came to see me and very proudly said that he had not exploited anybody so far, and that he was a very clean man. I asked him how he had not exploited. He said, 'I work for the government, I get my salary, and with that salary I maintain my family'. I said, how much do you get? He said Rs 2000. I said to him, what is your qualification to get that Rs 2000 [laughter]?

The king gets how many lakhs [one lakh = 100,000] or crores [one crore = 10,000,000] a month, and from where? Is that not corruption? For what does he get that much? And even secretaries get so much. It all comes from extortion. The government gives the salaries, but the money comes to the government through extortion. Now, more than from extortion, the government gets the money from foreign aid.

Pension

Ganga Lal's wife gets a pension, and I think Dasarath Chand's step-mother got a pension; Dharma Bhakta's father got a pension, and his wife got some land. Ram Hari and I were also offered land in the Tarai by the Political Sufferers' Committee, as were others, but we didn't take it. A friend had given Ram Hari twenty-eight *bighas* of land, and a friend of mine had more or less given me some land too (he sold it to me at such a low price it was like a gift), so we felt we had already gotten land and it would be wrong to accept more.[2] When I resigned as Prime Minister, King Mahendra said I should take two lakhs of rupees then, but I did not take it.

Myself—I am entitled to get Rs 1500 pension. That was awarded by the cabinet, from the government budget, in 1969. Now I get Rs 4450 per month. It was Meena who spoke to the King about my pension when he was here a year ago for Sano Kanchhu's wedding. She said

[2] The friend was Purendra Bikram Shah, Defence Minister (but not a member of Praja Parishad) in Tanka Prasad's cabinet. He relates that he once complimented Tanka Prasad on how smartly dressed he was. Tanka Prasad replied that he would have to live by selling his clothes as soon as he was out of the government. Mr. Shah vowed then that he would not let Mr. Acharya starve as long as he lives (Interview with Betsy Goodall, 6 May 1970).

it was a shame to the nation for her father to have to live on such a meagre amount. At the time it was given, in 1969, Rs 1500 was a respectable sum, and you could even save a hundred or two hundred rupees a month from it. But it is nothing now—a clerk's salary. The amount I receive now is adequate, but even from that sum we can't save anything.

Honesty

Only very few people can observe honesty, because it is very difficult. Particularly in a society such as ours, which is poor and has a tradition of corruption in high places, it is very difficult. The reason I never took any bribes is also because of tradition. My father never took bribes, and I wanted to follow his good example.

You must first define what honesty is. The World Bank's Vice Chairman, Hopper, came here and talked to me. I said, 'We are not responsible for the loan that Nepal has taken from your bank'. He was taken aback. I said to him, 'Why are you surprised? Whatever you give us as a loan is all drained away. The Panchayat people take it, to feed the Panchayat people. I wouldn't have objected if they had even improved their own land and raised some cattle, that would at least have been an asset to the country. But they do not do that. They spend that money drinking and merry-making. And we are not going to pay back your money' [laughter].

There is only one element in this world which is honest, otherwise all the others are not honest. That honest element is the peasant. They produce, they sell, and whatever they receive they get for their own labour. And that is why here peasants are poor—because they are honest. In America, peasants are not poor [laughter]. Here, only the peasants are honest. Others are all dishonest, exploiters, and swindlers [laughter].

There was a movement in Russia that was called the Narodnik Movement in about 1905. In that movement they said that only people who participate in production are honest. Office workers and intellectuals are not honest and should be driven out. That was the movement.

Activities During the Panchayat Period

I started a weekly paper here called *Himalayan Current*. I can't exactly say when, but it was sometime after Mahendra's takeover, after 1960.

It was an English weekly. I haven't had much practice with English, so I can't write too well. The chief editor was Barun Shamsher Rana. Barun Shamsher writes well, you see, so we used to write the paper—Barun Shamsher, Kirti Nidhi Bista, and I.

This is what happened: I wrote to King Mahendra, saying that there is no paper here worthy of the name. So, Your Majesty, there must be a paper in English for foreigners. You must help it. Do you know what he did? He started *The Rising Nepal* and called on Barun Shamsher to become the editor of that paper. So, Barun Shamsher was editor of *The Rising Nepal* for some time. My plan was destroyed. We had no money, so we could not continue our own paper.

Once I went to the King and said that something should be done for those who had suffered politically under the Ranas. This was in 1963. The King said to give him a list of names, and I gave him a list of 700 names. He asked me to be Chairman of the Political Sufferers Committee (in 1956 Ram Hari had been Chairman of it). I said no, it would be a thankless task. But my wife said to me, 'it was you who got all these people into politics, now you should speak on their behalf'. You can say no to the King, and you can say no even to God, but you can't say no to a good idea from your wife. I didn't support the Panchayat at any time. In the beginning, in 1961, I told King Mahendra I would support his direct rule for a limited, fixed time, but not indefinitely. The King did not agree, so I left the National Guidance Council. The Panchayat system is an organization of feudals. Members of the Panchayat have some land, and they become Panchayat members just to get political power. One good feature of the Panchayat system is that it has a unit in every village, whereas no political party in the past could have dreamed of such a vast organization. I was never formally offered the Prime Ministership during the Panchayat period. But at the time of Thulo Babu's [Tanka Prasad's oldest son] and Sabita's marriage, the King asked me what I wanted to support the Panchayat system. I told him no good work had been accomplished in the Panchayat; let it do something good and only then will I support it.

At the time of the referendum (1979-80), King Birendra talked to a number of political leaders, including me. I went to see him at his retreat at Nagarjung. We had a long, four-hour meeting. I advised him that we should have at least two political parties. I also said that he should assess the situation properly and realistically and get out from under his wife's influence. I also said that members of the royal family should either give up doing business or give up the royal titles. I also told him that people talk about 'Commission *Tantra*', meaning that members of the royal family get huge commissions for being the critical connection between government and private concerns on the leasing of contracts.

Thus, I accepted some assignments in the beginning, but later refused all offers, either because I disagreed fundamentally with the Panchayat system, or in some cases because of protocol. I was not willing, as an Ambassador, to work under a Foreign Minister junior to me in politics. I did serve on the National Development Council, which was just a council presided over by the King; all the secretaries and ministers were on it plus four or five who were outsiders at the time, like myself, Pashupati Shamsher, and others. We used to hold meetings and such. I left it because I found it boring and useless. In 1963 I served on the National Guidance Council until I resigned from it, and in 1972 I served on the Land Reform Commission.

In the mid-sixties B.P. wrote to me and said since I come to India occasionally, why didn't I come to see him in Banaras. So I did. I told him that his idea of an armed movement relying on young kids was doomed to failure. The Nepal army was large and strong, it was not like the situation in 1950. I told him he could not win by violence, and that he should come back to Kathmandu and we could stage a joint non-violent movement. He agreed, but at that point Girija [his younger brother and Prime Minister after the 1991 elections] walked in. B.P. explained what I had said, but Girija had something else to do and left. After a few days the Okhaldunga incident took place [an uprising which was quashed by the army], when a number of people were killed, and after that the idea just fizzled. The change that has just taken place [1990-1] is also the result of a non-violent movement.

Politically, the most significant thing I did in my life was to distribute leaflets and do whatever I could against the Ranas. It was the urge of nature, not our urge, I think. That means it was the urge, the propulsion of nature to make us do that [laughter]. We were only a few people, and the political consciousness was very low in Nepal. Even then we did something.

But my most significant accomplishment in life is that my wife gave birth to three sons and four daughters [laughter]. That also is political [laughter]. I educated my children, you see, and now they are competent people. And for the country, what better contribution can I make? [laughter].

Chapter 12

Breaking the Bonds of Tradition
Rewanta Kumari's Political Activities

These days, many women are involved in politics. Before, there weren't many. In *Mangsir* [November-December] of 1947 we formed the Adarsha Mahila Sangathan (Ideal Women's Organization). In the beginning, there were four of us: me, Kamini Koirala (first the wife of Kamaksha Babu, now the wife of Rudra Giri; Kamaksha Babu died, and in 1949 Kamini married Rudra Giri; they call her Kamini Giri now and she's still alive); D.N. Pradhan's wife Hemlata Pradhan (she's dead now); and D.P. Pariyar's mother, Dhana Kumari. The four of us started it. I got to know them when they came to meet their husbands and relatives who had been jailed in Jaleshwar; they all stayed in Jaleshwar with me. Later we became more friendly. Among us, they made me the Chairman (*Adkhachya*). Hemlata was responsible for finance, and I think Kamini was the publisher. The Ranas didn't know about it. How would they know?

We started the Mahila Sangathan when I was in the village, in Sirsia. The Nepali National Congress's office had opened in *Mangsir* [November-December] of 1947 in Jaynagar, in India. That's across the border from Janakpur. The Ranas wouldn't have allowed such an office to be opened in Nepal. Even in India the Congress could not operate freely until the British left. People from the Congress in Jaynagar told me that something like this should be done, and asked me to do it. We talked about establishing a Mahila Sangathan there, and so we started it. The purpose of the Mahila Sangathan was to help women. Women suffered a great deal.

Our Mahila Sangathan office in Jaynagar was part of the Congress office, but we also had our own separate office in Janakpur. The Ranas found out about it only later. In the beginning we didn't put up any sign marking our office. In the mornings I used to gather the village children and teach them there. At that time, when we went around looking for prospective members, people were scared of us, they would not meet with us. When we tried to give them pamphlets, they would run away. If you went out on the street and tried to give a pamphlet to someone, they would turn their heads and not take it. I would go up to people walking on the streets and try to give them pamphlets, but they would not take them, they would be scared and just run away. They didn't say anything, they just ignored us or ran away, as if some wild animal were after them.

The pamphlets said that women should be independent. We had pamphlets saying that women should not be treated the way they were being treated. Since none of us could write very well, members of the Congress Party wrote them for us. We had printed the purpose of Mahila Sangathan, our agenda, everything, in those pamphlets. The pamphlets aren't around anymore. We also pasted up our pamphlets—not only ours, but political posters put out by the Nepali Congress too—on bridges and on the outside walls of railway stations, and places like that.

I wasn't scared of distributing the Mahila Sangathan pamphlets. If I was scared, why would I have distributed them? We used to do our pamphleteering work in the night. There was a fear of being caught, but if the fear had been too great, I wouldn't have been able to do all that.

It wasn't so difficult to undertake these activities, but at that time you had to do things underground. That means we couldn't really accomplish anything, we couldn't really do anything very significant. At that time, the Ranas were in power, and everybody was scared. People were even scared of talking to me. We had printed a membership receipt, and if we went and asked them to become members they would be scared. A handful of Tarai women from the village had become members, but what could they really do? They weren't much help. Bua heard about our activities in starting the Mahila Sangathan. He said it's good, he said we have to do it.

Later more women participated. At that time there weren't many literate women. There was only a handful of us. As time passed, people became more aware and literacy increased. Also, the Ranas were thrown out of power. That made working conditions easier, since workers didn't have to stay underground.

After starting the Mahila Sangathan in Jaynagar I came to Kathmandu. In Kathmandu, Ganesh Man's wife, Mangala Devi, started a women's organization and called it Nepal Mahila Sangathan. We had named our organization Adarsha Mahila Sangathan. We had begun ours in 1947, and Mangala Devi began hers in 1948 sometime during the rainy season. I attended meetings of her organization too, and she had asked me to head it, but I said no, because I was already working in the other one. I didn't feel right about chairing both organizations. I did help Mangala organize, and they would always invite me to their meetings, and I would attend them, but I did not become their chairman or a member. In 1949 or 1950 Pundya Prabha Devi Dhungana, daughter of the poet Lekh Nath, formed the Akhil Nepal Mahila Sangathan [All Nepal Women's Organisation]. Now there were three different organizations. We wanted to form one big organization, which we thought would have more clout, so ours and Pundya Prabha's organization were merged. Mangala Devi kept hers separate. We had somewhat different ideas and therefore wanted independent organizations.

I quit working in the Mahila Sangathan in 1958. The reason is that they wanted to have a demonstration in support of Congress then; Bua's government had just been dissolved, so I thought we should stay out of politics. That's when I stopped being involved in those activities. The national Mahila Sangathan under the Panchayat system was opened by Prince Himalaya's wife in 1969. She wanted all the organizations to be merged. I was the Treasurer of it at first, but later I dropped out of it.

Mahila Sangathan calls me frequently, asking me to come to meetings, but I don't often go, either because Bua doesn't want me to, or because I don't feel like going. They talk about how much they've done and are doing, but I don't see many real accomplishments. They are all educated and talk a lot, but I don't see anything concrete. There are so many women who really need help, those who are poor, etc., and every time someone calls on me asking for help, I send them to the Mahila Sangathan, but nothing seems to come out of it—they don't get jobs, etc.

I think it is possible for women in Nepal to get equal rights eventually. Later, yes. It will be difficult now, but in succeeding generations it will happen little by little. I think it's possible for a woman to become Prime Minister of Nepal. Of course, why not? If it's possible in other countries, why not here too?

Chapter 13

We Come Like the Water and go Like the Wind
Tanka Prasad's Religion and Philosophy

Rousseau said that man is born free but is everywhere in chains. This is false doctrine, and most of the world lives under it. In the US there is too much freedom, there has to be order and restraint too. Life is very complex, you see. Freud is to a very great extent correct. There are two or three instincts which work in man. One is self-preservation, which is a very strong instinct. Another is the sexual impulse, which is also strong. Another is for prestige and for money. Money is a common goal because in order for two people to live together they must have money. And again for yourself, you also must have money. Besides that there is a thirst for knowledge. Thirst for knowledge also is a strong impulse.

As for the relation between religion and Marxism, don't ask me this question! [laughter]. Because sometimes I become completely Marxist, you see, and sometimes I become entirely religious. This is my dilemma. I am not free of it yet.

I know about materialism and its chief proponent, Karl Marx. I have read Lenin also. Most of their points are valid, but I could not become a complete materialist. I could not agree with them on some points. That life is only material I do not agree. There is something beyond which we can not see or even conceive of.

Idealistic philosophers are also not very consistent. I have read Bergson's *Elan Vital*. Bernard Shaw has also written a book, *Back to Methuselah*, and I've also read *The World as Will* by Schopenhauer. I do not agree with them, neither do I accept materialism completely.

I have read a lot about philosophy. I have read Hindu philosophy, Soviet philosophy, Greek philosophy, and many other kinds. I have many books about philosophy, by such writers as Kant, Schopenhaur, Nietszche, Voltaire, Plato, Karl Marx, Engels, Lenin, Mao, and other authors. I got many of these books from India when I was young. Being a socialist, I had to read Marxism, and I've read Lenin. Plekhanov I have not been able to read because of a shortage of time, and also because I wasn't sure whether it was useful or not.

I became interested in philosophy because I thought unless one has a philosophy one can not think in a proper way, or in other words see things in their proper context. It gives you an outlook. Religion is a commandment which you have to obey. You can not question it. A ritual is mostly filled with action, but philosophy is for thinking. But one must follow either a religion or a philosophy. Unless one follows either of the two he can not see things in their proper light.

Religion and philosophy are highly correlated. Religion without philosophy is not sufficient, and every religion has its philosophical basis. Therefore, when I read a religious book I also try to understand the philosophy behind it. Christ gave instructions on what should be done and what must not be done, and also on his father in heaven, who will see what you have done. He did not philosophize. The same is the case with the *Koran*. Mohammed gave instructions and did not philosophize.

There is not much difference between the Christian god and the Hindu god. We call god what Christians call 'father in heaven'. I always speak with respect about Christianity. I revere Christ. I have learned the *Bible* the same as I have learned our holy scriptures. The great religions are the same everywhere. Christianity, Buddhism, Hinduism, Islam, are not so different from one another if you look at them in an impartial way. I revere the Buddha as much as I do Vishnu. I don't differentiate between the Hindu, Christian, and Muslim gods. The whole universe is permeated by God—the gods of different religions are all the same. Only foolish fellows manufacture the differences. If the King were to convert to Buddhism, nothing would happen. The King can be anything—Christian, Buddhist, Hindu! Nevertheless I would rather be cremated than buried. The *Bible* says that on the Day of Judgement everyone will be resurrected, but I wouldn't want to stay that long in a grave, just to be resurrected. I'd rather be cremated.

Somebody asked Gandhiji what new thing he had given to the world. He replied that he had discovered or taught nothing new. He just tried to lead the people on the old righteous path. You can search every nook and corner, from Aristotle and Plato—all the areas have been covered by one or the other writer. There is nothing left to be discovered, and there is nothing new to be given to the people [laughter].

It is the social movements that count, not religious ideas. I have read books on American liberalism. Since I have to talk and deal with Americans I must learn their system. Liberalism is an old system. It was brought by the English settlers to America and was adapted according to the new environment. So American liberalism is also an old theory adapted according to the requirements of modern times.

What matters in religion is the philosophy, not the rituals. As for ritual—I don't believe in that. I look at what the philosophy is. Marxism is a philosophy. Buddhism is a philosophy. Hinduism is a philosophy. There are different philosophical systems in Hinduism—six systems, the famous six systems. One of the systems is materialistic. I suffer from *Bhakti Marg* [the path of religious devotion]. I have not seen God, but even then I think that there is some power who is moving this world. That is *Bhakti Marg*. That gives you pleasure also.

My father could not understand any western language, so he did not know about western religion and western philosophy. As a Hindu he was a very religious man and used to conduct *puja* for two hours a day. He also directed me to conduct *puja*, so I used to conduct *puja* for one and a half hours a day. Once I asked him why he worshiped stones. He replied that it is not that he worships the stone. The stone in fact is just an object to concentrate his mind. It is not the stone that he worships, but some higher thing that he worships. It is difficult to concentrate unless there is some object before your eyes on which you can concentrate. In our religion stone worshipping is a very primary step. There is no need for stone worshiping in higher stages of Hinduism.

My wife performs rituals in the *puja* room. I do too, but not these days when I'm not well. I sit on my bed and pray. I also used to do *yoga* for three or four hours a day. The whole atmosphere in the *puja* room is different. Saying my prayers in my room is quite different from saying my prayers there. That is the reason for praying in the *puja* room—the atmosphere. When you go to a church, the atmosphere is quite different. Nowadays many people probably don't go, but they probably went when their fathers and mothers compelled them to go [laughter]. Our *kuldeuta* [family deity] is Bajrajogini [the goddess of a temple near Sankhu, at the northeastern edge of the Kathmandu Valley]. Many generations ago, when we were in Banaras, our *kuldeuta* was Bindavasini. The Bindavasini shrine is a little west of Banaras, just beside the famous mountain—Bindyachal. We found out about this only recently when one of my cousins had gone through family records and discovered this fact. When we came here, my forefathers adopted Bajrajogini in Sankhu. Our *Ishta Deuta* is Dakshinkali [a temple south of Kathmandu]. The *Ishta Deuta* is the deity whose *mantra* you have learned.

I told my son that even though he does not believe in rituals he must do them. Everybody naturally does whatever he likes, but he must also sometimes do some things which he does not like. Suppose you are put in a very difficult position in which you are not happy and you have to do something which you do not like, then what will you do? Even though you don't like it, nevertheless you must do it, and you must develop such habits in your childhood. Nobody is put in a situation where he can do only what he wants to and nothing else.

Ram Hari and I, when we were in jail, reasoned and reasoned and reasoned about reincarnation, you see. Daily we reasoned, but we could not reach any conclusion [laughter]. How can one know about such a thing? We lived like hermits in prison. We tried to find out what is the truth, but we never found it. I was going to tell the world and my friends, that if there is a God, he is very hard to get at. Maybe there is none [laughter].

I was always a very devout Hindu. When I went to jail, there were some Buddhists there also, so I started reading Buddhist literature. In Hindu philosophy it is said that there is *atma*, or spirit, indestructible *atma* which guides everybody. But in Buddhism, there was no mention of *atma*, and Buddhists don't accept the *atma* philosophy. As Hindus we place all our faith and all our hope in God, so when I heard that there was no God I underwent a very painful experience. Then I started reading both the Buddhist and Hindu literature thoroughly. Ultimately I found that there was no difference between Buddhism and our philosophy. After reading Buddhist literature I gave up all religious rituals. And Buddhist literature also gave me the chance to read Marxist literature open-mindedly. I don't find much difference between Buddhism and Hinduism, only that Buddhism proceeds to the ultimate truth differently. We both have the same goal, but somehow we reach it differently.

People from Europe and America come to visit Pashupatinath, but they are not allowed inside the temple. They get annoyed with this. But there is a reason for excluding them. Formerly, people used to deposit their valuables in the temples, e.g., at Somnath and many others. When the Muslims came here, they saw all the riches of the country lying in the temples and looted them several times. Therefore, from then on people started not allowing foreigners inside the temples.

Christ was born in a cow-shed, and therefore Christians should respect cows, rather than killing them. All killing is bad, as both Buddha and Gandhi said. I was a vegetarian for the ten years I was in prison, and for two more after I came out. Although families of the Newar prisoners brought them water buffalo meat and offered some to us, we didn't eat it. We asked our families not to send us meat. Nowadays I eat goat and chicken, but not water buffalo.

I would like to write a story along the lines of *Animal Farm*. In it, animals would gather on the Tundikhel and discuss how evil people are, killing so many thousands of animals. They would start a new religion, but they wouldn't be able to accomplish anything.

Once, when I was invited to dinner by the Russian Ambassador I was not eating meat you see, as I had become a vegetarian once again for five years. I had given up meat because one time when I was walking towards Kamal Pokhari I saw the carcasses of two animals while butchers were in the process of slaughtering a third. I thought it was too horrible, and I started hating it. 'My brother', the Russian Ambassador said, 'you are in politics, and you need strength for that. Without strength, how can you carry on in politics?' In this way he persuaded me to eat meat once again.

Formerly I was an optimist, but now I am a pessimist. Although I am a pessimist, I do not completely give up on worldly affairs. I must do it, anyway. But I have no faith that any permanent pleasure will come from the pursuit of worldly things. There is none. The most important thing to do is to follow your dharma.

In Hinduism, a man goes through four stages: *Brahmacharya* [student], *Grihasthashram* [householder], *Banaprasthashram* [forest-dweller], and *Sanyas* [renunciation of all worldly pleasures and interests]. I am nearing *Sanyas*, you see [laughter].

Hinduism cannot be reformed! Look, whoever is capable of taking just what he wants from Hinduism for himself can do that. It is a matter of selection. Whoever doesn't need it won't take from it; whoever needs it can take from it. Take the *Gita*, for example, B.P. Koirala has written that the *Gita* is not useful for worldly purposes, or something like that. I think he did not read it, he probably only heard about it. He thinks he's higher than Lord Krishna. But the *Gita* is a compilation of many systems, six or seven systems. From my boyhood I have read the *Gita*. It is written in the last paragraph of every chapter of the *Gita* in which *yuga* (era) that particular philosophy originated. There are four *yugas*: *Satya Yuga*, *Treta Yuga*, *Dwapar Yuga*, and our present one which is *Kali Yuga*. So, Hinduism is not just one thing; it is a compilation of many yugas, many beliefs. You can also take a materialistic point of view from it. Krishna says, if you leave aside all *dharmas*, different beliefs, and only devote yourself to me, I will relieve you from all sins; don't worry, just devote yourself to god. He said people can take him any way they like—as a monkey, as a snail, anything—since god is everywhere.

Religion is such a powerful thing. People want to know what there is after life. We are all in search of a life after death. What is there ultimately? Ama and I have a quarrel going on now. She wants *moksha* [release from rebirth] when she dies, and I want rebirth as a saint or a warrior. I want to be with her whether she goes to heaven or hell, so I've told her that when she dies I will grab hold of her sari and she can pull me with her [laughter].

About life after death I have no decisive position. But if there is no life after death, there is no need for religion—absolutely no reason for religion. There may be a social function for religion. You need religion so that people know what to do and what not to do. Before, there were hardly any police here, about twenty-five to thirty of them. Priests ruled the society. Only police will not be enough [laughter]. Even now, when one dies here, a scripture called *Garud Puran* is read to the people, in which it is written that if you commit this sin you'll get such a punishment after death, and if you do that sin you'll get a certain punishment, and so on. It's all what is called 'inventory', but it is effective especially among uneducated people. You can make formulas and then teach them and make the people behave accordingly. You can formulate some codes for social conduct. So formerly, a *pandit* used to rule, not the police. But these days, the police rule, not the *pandit* [laughter].

In the sense that the church is regarded in your country, there is no church here, there is no exploitation. In your country there are a lot of people who go to church. What are they guided by? By what is said in the church by the bishop or archbishop [laughter]. The difference is that in your country the boys and girls are compelled to go to church, either by a mother or by a father. Here, it's not like that. If you go it's alright and if you don't go that's alright too. Even the Chinese, in their heart of hearts have sentiment for religion. That's what I think. So do the Russians.

I once said to the Russian Ambassador, 'In your country, nobody perhaps goes to church'. He said no, that his mother herself goes to church. Many people go to church. Even the young people are going these days, he said. The Soviet Union conducted such a stern anti-religious campaign because the position of church and religion was very strong, and it was very difficult to overcome it. But they overthrew it. If it had not been necessary, then there would have been no need of doing so.

There are so many scientists working to find out what the ultimate is. I've read *Einstein's Universe*. Einstein didn't write it himself, somebody else did, but Einstein read the book and said it was an accurate portrayal of his views. He was thrown out of school three times [laughter], but he turned out to be the greatest scientist of the age. When he was sick and lying in bed, his uncle gave him a compass for recreation. When the compass needle moved, he wondered how it functioned, and that aroused his inner genius. And when he recovered he started learning.

I say, listen, science can teach you the relation between things. But science doesn't teach you how to utilize them, where to use them. Einstein said that science can tell us the way the world is, but it can't decide what we should do—for that we need religion. He also said we can never reach the ultimate truth, there are some regions of enquiry that will never be known. When he looked at the stars in the sky, he shed a tear over the wonder of it all. 'We come like the water and go like the wind'—Omar Khyam said that. The mystery of where we come from, where we will go—these are all painful thoughts. My age (seventy-six) is calculated by the sun's movement, but what is my real connection with the sun? I believe Darwin was right about evolution, but how it all could have happened seems mysterious to me. I sometimes feel like Goethe's Faust, who said that he had read everything, all different philosophies and so on, and at the end he felt he was right back where he started.

Chapter 14

Religion and Philosophy
Rewanta Kumari

My parents were religious, everyone at home was religious. I lived with them, so I too became religious. I do *puja* to many gods, sometimes it is to one, sometimes it is to another. But the one I pray to most regularly is Narayan. Laxmi Narayan is the same as Vishnu and Laxmi. At my *maiti* in Thamel, also, we used to pray to Laxmi Narayan. Here too I have kept images of Laxmi Narayan in the prayer room. I also worship Narayan in the form of a *shaligram* [black ammonite fossil] we keep in the prayer room. A proper *shaligram* should have four spirals on the fossil, and it should not be broken open (you can see the fossil through a hole). It should be small enough so that you can hold it in your fist. Generally only Brahmin men who have had their sacred thread ceremony worship *shaligrams*, and women are not supposed to do *puja* to *shaligrams*. But Bua didn't want to do it, so he asked me to.

My belief in *shaligrams* is strong. Once someone robbed the *puja* room in our present house. We had several silver utensils in our *puja* room, which the thief must have seen. One night I thought it would be good to let the gods have some ventilation, and I left one window open. That night someone broke in and took all the silver things, plus a 150-year old *jantar* [carved eight-pointed star, auspicious in Hinduism], but they didn't take the *shaligram*.

After the *puja* room was broken into, we tried to find out who did it by consulting a *gubaju*. To do this you take soot produced from an oil lamp, mix the soot with the oil, then rub the mixture on the palm of the hand of a pre-puberty girl. Then you look at the palm while the *gubaju* recites something, to make a picture appear in her hand, which will clarify what happened. In our case we got Beena [Meena's daughter] to go to the *gubaju*. After the mixture had been smeared

on her palm, a picture appeared there of an old man with a beard
and a stick. When he appears you ask him what happened, and then
he shows what happened by causing the scene to be re-enacted in
your hand. He disappears, and the scene is enacted. In this case Beena
saw three men come to the house with a ladder. Two went up the
ladder to the roof, where they tore open the window screen on the
puja room window. One man went into the room and took valuables
and wrapped them in the cloth I use during *puja*, one waited outside,
while the third waited at the bottom of the ladder. Beena could see
the three men, but she couldn't identify who they were. A young boy,
a cook from Radha's [Ama's younger sister] house stood behind Beena
and also saw these figures in her hand. Later Beena tried to look again,
on her own, but she couldn't see anything. Since she couldn't identify
who the thiefs were, we couldn't catch them, and even if we could,
such evidence wouldn't be admitted in a court of law. Where it would
be useful is if you saw someone you knew, then you could go and
tell them, and they would feel guilty about it.

The prayer room is on the top floor, away from disturbances and
children running around. I pray there about one and a half hours in
the morning, before my morning meal, and a half hour in the evening,
before supper. Before worshipping I have to first light the lamp and
worship Ganesh. Then I invoke all the gods, including Brahma, Vishnu,
(in the form of Laxmi Narayan), and Maheshwar [Shiva], in a copper
vessel filled with water, flower petals, and milk. It's easier to worship
and please Brahma and Shiva, but it's harder to worship Vishnu. But
I would go through all the suffering and difficulty of worshipping Vishnu
because it's more meritorious that way. That was always our own family
tradition.

I also believe some sages have great powers to predict the future.
In 1941 a *Gurumaharaj* [Hindu sage] from Dang came to Thamel. He
had left home when he was eight years old and become a holy man.
I went to see him to ask what the future would bring. When I asked
him if Bua would be released from prison (he had just been jailed
the year before), he said that for eight years there would be no question
of his getting out. In the ninth year they would talk about it, and
in the tenth year he would be released [subsequent events followed
this chronology precisely]. I asked whether I would have sons, and
he said yes, there will be two sons [she had three] and I will have
a happy household. I asked what will happen to my daughters (I had
only two then). He said Meena will not marry in Nepal [she married

in Russia], and at the age of sixteen she will be famous [this prophecy was not fulfilled, but she was a member of the Nepali delegation to an international women's conference in the Soviet Union at that age]; Bua's second mother was there, and he told her that she would not live long as a widow [she outlived Bua's father by two years].He returned to Kathmandu in 1953, when I was pregnant with Thulo Babu. This time he predicted I would have a son, and also one more daughter. When he returned for the last time in 1960 I took everyone to see him, including the children. He said he himself had almost died twice, and the third time he would not survive. He looked at me and said (without my telling him) that I had three sons, one more than he had predicted. He predicted that I would not outlive my husband but that I will survive to the age of seventy-five.

I have made many pilgrimages. First, when Bua was in prison, I went to Gosainkunda, up to the lake where I bathed, prayed, and spent one night and then returned. I have also been to Manokamana in Gorkha. When I was in Banaras I visited Bed Byas, Adi Kesab, and other pilgrimage spots. I have also been to Bindabasini in Banaras. There is a *Bhagwati* [deity] called Uchhet Bhagwati in Madhubani—I went there. I have been to Bagdwar, the source of the Bagmati River. Out of the four Narayans in Kathmandu, I have been to three of them— Changu Narayan, Ichangu Narayan, and Bisankhu Narayan. The one I have not been to is Makchya Narayan, near Thankot.

I have gone to Swayambhunath many times. There's a temple to Saraswati and one to Durga. I worship there and at the Buddhist shrines also. I've been to Boudhanath too, but just to see it, not to worship. I've gone around the stupas there [Hindus and Buddhists frequently worship or visit each other's holy places].

The guardian deity of this household is Tara, in Sankhu. I have been there many times. The guardian deity of my father's household is Kali, in Gorkha. I have been there once.

Each deity has his or her own *mantra*, so different people follow different *mantras*. *Gayatri mantra* is for all Brahmins. It's usually passed from father to son, or from older to younger brother, or it can be accepted from a *guru*. Since each deity has its own *mantra*, I gave Kali's *mantra* to my daughters-in-law. On Bua's side our deity is Tara, and her *mantra* is the *mantra* Bua would give to his sons.

I love to go on pilgrimages. When Bua was in prison, I went to the Bagmati Jatra, which takes place here in Kathmandu. It always starts on the day of the new moon in Jesth [May-June]. There is a lake a little further down from Dakshin Kali, where pilgrims bathe. That's where we started, and the rest of the pilgrimage consisted of following along the Bagmati River, walking on the bank, till we reached its source. We did not return home for fifteen days after we started. We stayed in Dakshinkali, bathed there, and proceeded to Chobar, where we bathed and spent the night. We also bathed at five or six places along the way. From Chobar we came to Baneshwor, bathed and stayed there. After that, we went to Rajrajeshwari Ghat, then to Arya Ghat, then to Surya Ghat, then to Gauri Ghat. In this manner, we bathed at different places each day. Sometimes we bathed sixteen or seventeen times in a single day, and sometimes only once or twice a day.

When I went on the pilgrimage, we bathed in two places the day we stayed in Gokarna. The day we stayed in Pashupati, we bathed sixteen times on our way from Rajrajeshwari Ghat to Arya Ghat. On the way from Arya Ghat to Surya Ghat we had to bathe in seventeen or eighteen places. And then, on the way from Surya Ghat to Gauri Ghat, we had to bathe in about ten or twelve places. After a day was over we had to spend the night at the last place we had bathed. We couldn't go anywhere else. The next morning a Brahmin would pray with a large water-vessel in front of him, then put it on his shoulder and start the day's journey. We all followed him. We bathed, prayed, then bathed at another place, and so it went. The pilgrimage ended in Bagdwar, on top of Shiva Puri, the source of the Bagmati. The water comes out of a stone tap there, which is carved like the mouth of a tiger. Similarly, the source of the Vishnumati river is from the naval of a reclining Vishnu located in a cave.

As for eating during those fifteen days, we fasted in the morning, and then cooked and ate at night. We had porters for carrying the necessities. There was a total of twelve hundred people. But of the twelve hundred, eight hundred were bathing pilgrims and four hundred were porters. There were two of us who shared one porter. In those days it was cheap; we paid him one or two rupees per day, plus meals. On the day we reached Sundarijal, I started menstruating and, therefore, I had to return from there [because the pilgrimage could not be continued in her impure state]. The others continued the next day to Bagdwar and then to Sankhu. From Sankhu the pilgrims had to go back to Pashupati to pray and perform a sacrifice before they returned home.

Sanima and I went together on this pilgrimage. It was a delightful trip. Bua didn't know I went. I felt very tranquil and comfortable being part of this kind of mass movement of worshippers. The religious feeling made me go, the serenity of mind you can get from these things. Also, I was bored and lonely, being all alone without Bua.

My grandfather had not wanted me to go. He was worried that I wouldn't be strong enough to walk along the rivers and on their sandy banks, rather than on good trails. Nevertheless, I managed to get away by telling him that I was going to stay with my maternal grandmother in Chabahil. I didn't write to Bua about it, because there was no point in doing so. If he had been here I might not have gotten to make that pilgrimage, because he might not have allowed me to go.

Later on, Bua and Sano Kanchhu [youngest son]and I made a pilgrimage tour of south India. We went to Rameshwaram, Dwarka, Tirupati, and Balaji. Another time, Bua and Sanu [youngest daughter]and I visited Jagannath, in Orissa, and Kamarukamachya in Assam. Bua made these itineraries. He would just decide all of a sudden that we should go, and we would go. Bua and Shanta and I made still another pilgrimage to Hardwar. I also went to Badrinath with Shanta's family.

During the years Bua was in jail, I worshipped in the morning, but not at night. I recited the *Bhagwat* in the morning, and in the evening I just did the *rudrachha* beads [repeating a *mantra* with each bead]. When he became Home Minister I was so busy in the house that I didn't have time to go to the *puja* room, so I just read the *Bhagwat*; instead, Sanima did the *pujas*. Deep down I felt a little guilty about not being able to perform the daily *pujas*, it made me feel uncomfortable. But there are other times also when you don't do *pujas*—e.g., during pregnancy, and for ten days after birth, and after a death in the family. No relative on the male side within seven generations can do *pujas* during these pollution periods. After the naming ceremony on the eleventh day, we bathe and then we can all do *puja* again. So, it is not all that unusual not to do *pujas*.

In our family everybody follows their own way of worship or eating. Once when Sanima was worshipping *Chandrama* [the moon] Meena told her that Americans had walked on the moon, so what was the point of worshipping it? Sanima replied that this was her moon, not necessarily the moon the Americans had walked on. Sanima always cooked her own rice [*swayam pakya*], to be sure of its purity, until she was bed-ridden with a severe back problem. Then she was willing to eat whatever the cook prepared. She died of a heart attack in 1970.

Before I cook a meal in our house I always take a fistful of rice and put it into an empty pot. I do this every day, and after about a month or so several pounds of rice accumulate. At this point I give it away to someone, usually a Brahmin man or woman, or a *jogi* [ascetic], or just to someone who is poor and needs it. Before, when we had wood fires, I would put a token amount of anything cooked into the fire, but you can't do that nowadays with kerosene stoves. I would also give some food to cows, crows and dogs, but since there are few cows or dogs around here I don't do that any more. But I do still feed crows and pigeons every morning, in addition to putting the fistful of rice aside for a guest.

You don't have to go out of your house to be a saint. In order to get enlightenment, it is only necessary to be detached from all the people and material things around you. But if you stay at a particular house and live there with your children, grandchildren, husband, and so on, you get very involved with them. Even if you want to sever that attachment, this illusion in life, you get more and more dragged into it, like sinking into quicksand. For example, if a man is in love with a woman, and you tell him to stop loving that woman and yet remain with her, that is very difficult to do. To get away from your house would be as difficult. To do that kind of meditation, or to get that kind of enlightenment while staying in the house, is very difficult to accomplish.

I don't think about the past or the future; I just try to do the best I can with whatever my present job and responsibilities are. I act in the present, according to my past experience. I don't care about the result, or what others think, or what people thought in the past, as long as I feel I'm doing the right thing.

I don't know anything about science. If you don't understand something, you can't voice an opinion about it. I don't feel anything about men being on the moon; if they got there, they got there. I feel the same about TV. As for watching it, if the programme is good I like to watch it, but otherwise I get bored and don't usually watch TV.

If I could live my life over again, I don't know how I would live—anything could happen. People are forced to bend according to environment and circumstances, which make people do what they do. Circumstances have led me to do whatever I have done in my lifetime, and if they had been different, who knows what I would have done? I cannot say. I have not even gone to school, I just learned a little bit of reading and writing at home. I don't know what I would have done if I had studied more. Circumstances have made me capable of this much. But yes, I always wanted to study, if I had only gotten a chance. I asked Bua so many times to teach me, but he only taught me a little bit, the little bit of English I know. So, the one thing I would do if I lived my life again would be to go to school, to get a proper education.

Chapter 15

She is Me and I am She

Tanka Prasad and his Family

My wife made a very important contribution to my career. I cannot live without her for more than a few hours [laughter]. I lived without her for ten years in jail, but the spirit was quite different then. In our arranged marriages we grow to like our partners gradually. My wife is more than an angel to me. We are inseparable. There are only two people in the world: I and my wife. As Krishna said in the *Bhagwat*, referring to Radha, 'she is me and I am she'. She is much braver than I ever was. She did all she did for me plus she bore seven children. She is all in all to me.

Sometimes Ama and I quarrel, but the next moment we make up [laughter]. Before I went to jail, we didn't quarrel. Now, we quarrel every day [laughter]. Before, you see, women could not quarrel with their husbands. It was a matter of etiquette. Now, it is nothing to quarrel with me [laughter]. We quarrel about nothing in particular—say, if I want the window closed and she wants it open. You see, she always wants a cool atmosphere. In the cold season also she wants to keep the windows open. Twice, I saw her opening the window. We compromise by opening it half-way [laughter]. I have to cover myself with a blanket.

We quarrel, and again in two minutes we make up [laughter]. She has nobody else to depend on, I have nobody else to depend on. So we make up our differences very soon. I cannot remain silent for too long, you see, so I start talking to her. I make up quickly with her. Otherwise we cannot stay together [laughter].

If I had other women to look at, then the quarrel would not be easily made up [laughter]. I have no other woman to look at, and she knows it. Whatever I have, she has it. I have no secrets from her. So long as you are young, you follow separate paths. As you grow older, your paths become one. I have no fear of her leaving me. Her religion has bound her to me. She can't go away from me. So I can trust her with whatever I have. When I was Prime Minister, as well as before and after that time, I could have had relations with other women, like some of the Ranas and others. But I never did, because I was completely devoted to my wife.

She takes care of all my needs. She is more mindful of health than I am, which sometimes results in quarrels. I used to smoke. Then the doctor told me I shouldn't smoke anything at all, so my wife acts on the doctor's advice and is very strict about it. But I still smoke a cigarette if I can sneak one. I also used to smoke the *hukka* (water pipe). Once I had a pack of Marlboros. I had just opened it and taken out a cigarette when my wife appeared out of nowhere and confiscated it and the whole pack.

My wife has never pressed me for a good living, and for a glorious living, never. To me, she's very remarkable, and for her children also she's remarkable. Meena respects her very much, and so do the other children. My boys and girls observe the discipline of the house and have no bad conduct. It is due to her that the children are so well-behaved.

Ama exemplifies perfectly the Hindu ideal of hospitality. Just last week a group of people from the Tarai arrived here at night and needed a place to eat and sleep. She gave them Kanchhu's house, where they cooked their food and spent the night. For Hindus, if someone comes at night, one should take them in.

There is a story in the *Mahabharata* about hospitality. There were four Brahmins—a man and his wife, and their son and daughter-in-law—living in the middle of a very bad draught. The famine was so bad there were only barley stalks left to eat. The man went out to get something for his family to eat, and brought it home. They were all ready to eat when there was a knocking at the door. They found a Brahmin there who hadn't eaten for six days. The father wanted to give his share to the Brahmin. His wife said no, that she would give him her share. So they both gave him their portions. Still the Brahmin was hungry, so next the son and the daughter-in-law gave him their shares. His hunger couldn't be satisfied even after all his hosts had given him their portions of food. Actually the man wasn't a Brahmin, but Dharma Raj, the God of Justice, disguised as a Brahmin, and he was very pleased at the generosity of this family. So in response he took them all to heaven.

Meanwhile, a mongoose in the house had seen everything that had happened. He ate the little bits of *jutho* (leftovers) that had been spilled by the Brahmin. This caused half his body to turn to gold. Then he tried to turn the other half to gold. He heard that Yudisthar was having a great sacrificial celebration, or *yagnya*. Even Krishna was there. The mongoose went to the *yagnya* and flopped around on the ground, trying to turn his other half to gold. Yudisthar thought this was strange behaviour. The mongoose told him that since it was Yudistar's *yagnya*, and since it was such a big *yagnya*, he thought he would be able to change his other half to gold. But it wasn't working, so what was the use of this *yagnya*? the mongoose asked.

But the four humble Brahmins gave from their hearts, they made a genuine sacrifice. The *yagnya* was not a real sacrifice, it was just a fancy, big celebration. Therefore big, lavish occasions are not good. The moral is that you should give humbly to people in real need, not indulge in great, ostentatious displays.

Hospitality is a great ideal. Formerly, one could travel in the hills, all across the country, without any money, because wherever you were, someone would feed you if you were hungry. People are so money-minded nowadays that that may no longer be true.

Family finances

Since I was arrested and jailed I have never been very well off. When I went to jail my father had 101 *bighas* of land in Mahottari. My father died while I was in prison, and one of my father's concubines, who was very young when my father died, took possession of the land that he had left, and I was left with nothing. Some land he had sold, some he had given to others, and only twenty-one *bighas* of land remained. How much is the cost of that land now, do you know? Sixty thousand per *bigha* [laughter]. If I still had that land now, I could have had two cars [laughter].

I was penniless when I came out of prison. There had been one house in my name in Kathmandu, in Sifale near the Black Bridge, with eight *ropanis* of land. But the Ranas confiscated and auctioned off all that property—the house and the land—when I was put into prison.

I bought forty *bighas* (about sixty-five acres) of land in the Tarai from my friend for a very nominal price long after I resigned from the premiership. It was more of a gift. But I had to bring up my seven children—they had to be educated, married, etc. We had no house of our own, so I had to build a house. I had no other source of income to cover all these expenses. So I sold my land bit by bit. Now there is not one inch of that forty *bighas* of land left. I had full faith in God. I thought that if I remained honest and served the people, then there would be no dearth of provisions or money for me. But now I'm a proletarian. So it was useless to believe in God [laughter].

I rented living quarters ten times. I had to shift ten times, you see. And my wife said, what is this nonsense, always shifting, always shifting, we must have a house. Then, without my knowledge she went to Queen Ratna. The Queen told her to select a house to buy. I was not here then. At that time one could not buy a house worth living in for less than fifty thousand rupees. So my wife said that to the Queen. They were willing to give us only twenty thousand. By that time I had come back to Kathmandu. I said to the Queen's secretary, 'At twenty thousand rupees you cannot even have a horse stable [laughter], so you keep the money. When I earn some more money from other sources, then I will ask you to hand it over to me. Then I will select a house and buy it.'

The secretary was angry and asked me how I could say this, considering that it was the Queen who had offered it. I told him that even though it was the Queen who had offered me that and I was very thankful to her, it would not buy a house. So I told him to keep the money with him because if it came to me, I would just spend it. This went on for three days. On the third day I thought I should not act in such a way and my irrationality vanished. So my wife went to fetch the money.

I thought that I would not buy anything here, but rather go to the Tarai and settle down there. But my wife didn't agree, and we bought this land on which we now live. We had only twenty thousand rupees. When we inquired about the price of the land, we found we could buy two *ropanis* for eighteen thousand rupees. All of my friends also pressed me to buy it, so I bought it for eighteen thousand rupees.

In my absence my wife started laying the foundation with the remaining two thousand rupees. With two thousand rupees she started laying a foundation! [laughter] This put me in a dilemma as to what to do. I had borrowed a tractor from the National Trading Corporation on loan. What to do? This woman, my wife, had put me in a dilemma. So I sold the tractor for Rs 34,000. I gave that money to her, and with that money the lower story of the house was completed. I only recently finished paying off the loan of that tractor.

Our house is made with only mud between the bricks, not mortar. Then for only Rs 2000 we had the whole outside cemented, as protection against deterioration from the weather. The inner plastering and other such things, my daughter Meena took care of. I sold some of the land a man had given me in the Tarai to build the second story, and the tin roof which covered it. Recently the tin roof was removed, and replaced by a cement roof. For that I sold two *katha* of land, and my sons also chipped in to put up the new roof.

My wife built the house, not I [laughter]. I wanted to go away with the twenty thousand to a village in the Tarai and build quite a nice hut there and live there [laughter]. Later, when she was supervising the construction activities in the building, I used to go from room to room interfering with everything she was doing. She finally told me to sit in one place and do something else and not to bother her. So for some time I sat in a room and wrote poetry or translated others' poetry, such as Sanskrit poetry or the *Rubaiyat* by Omar Khyam. Later, sometime during the 1970s I also took up painting, but after I painted one picture I realized I had no talent and gave it up.

My relationship with my children differs from child to child. My mother worried that since I was short, and my wife was short, that our children would all be short. But Meena is the only one who is very short. When Meena was born, I imagined that she would be like Asoka's [third century Emperor of India] daughter. She works in Nepal Rastra Bank [the central bank], but she is not a bureaucrat. She devotes her energies to the development of the country. It would be good if she goes into politics. I would like to see her further her father's mission. She exhibits momentary anger sometimes, but about trivial subjects. She has never disregarded my feelings, with the exception of when she married a foreigner. Since marriage with a foreigner was not permitted then, the King asked me what to do. She was already in love, so it would have been unfair for me to have denied her permission. She knew her own mind, and I could not have insisted against her wishes.

We married off Shanta early, and she lives with her family. My other younger children have just started their careers. My youngest, Sano Kanchhu, is very fun-loving. Sometime during the early 1980s Sano Kanchhu played a trick on Regmi [a friend from boyhood and fellow-politician]. Regmi, Surya Prasad and I had been talking about plans to start a joint movement against the Panchayat system. Regmi called when I was out, and Sano Kanchhu told him that the police had taken me away and that he didn't know where they had taken me. The news spread like wildfire, and Regmi and Surya Prasad Upadhyay and others packed up their things and made ready to flee, thinking that the police would come for them too. Then the Home Minister also heard about it and was surprised, because he hadn't given any order for me to be arrested. When he called and realized what had been going on the joke was over.

One thing I am very scared about is my children's illnesses. I am particularly scared of hydrophobia, since our servant's seventeen year old daughter, who had grown up in our house, died of the disease. I was very upset at the death of Mithi's [the Acharyas' servant for forty years] daughter. The doctor gave her seven injections, and I told him he should give another series, for a total of fourteen, but he thought seven would be enough. Afterwards I drafted a memorandum stating that Nepal should request a foreign doctor to give us advice on rabies. There were so many different ideas floating around about how long to observe the dog after it had bitten someone, how many injections to give, etc. I said it was a serious problem and we needed to get correct information about it.

Chapter 16

Family Life

Rewanta Kumari

Meena was my first child, but before her I had a miscarriage four or five months into my first pregnancy. I did not know I was pregnant. My aunt and I were both pregnant at that time. We had some stomach problems and went to a *vaidya* (homeopathic doctor), who gave us medicines. I took them since I didn't know I was pregnant, and therefore had a miscarriage. That was in 1933, and I was told that it was a male baby. When Meena was born four years later it didn't matter to me whether my baby was a girl or a boy. Either was perfectly alright, especially if it's the first-born. Normally, when you have a lot of kids and they are all girls, you wish for a son. But why worry when you have just given birth to your first baby simply because she is a girl?

Meena was born in our house in Sifale. Bua was at home then, and his second mother and Sanima were also living with us. When I was pregnant with Meena, Bua would say that he would send our child to England to be educated, and if it was a girl he would make her like Bhrikuti, who went from Nepal to China and converted China to Buddhism. When I was pregnant with Shanta he didn't show so much interest, because he was so involved with politics then.

Shanta was born two and a half years after Meena. Meena was born in 1937, and Shanta in 1939. Even though I already had a girl, I did not particularly wish for a boy the second time. However, Bua and his second mother did express the concern that there was no son. The reason they were worried was that my mother had given birth to nine girls before a son was finally born. So everybody was concerned that it might be the same with me, that maybe I too wouldn't bear a son. Almost all of my sisters had died. But I never felt that my children would die. I never worried about that.

Giving birth was not difficult. We took it for granted that women had to be pregnant and give birth. Other activities went on as normal. Although we were financially strained we lived a happy life. I remember one incident involving a big *suntala* [orange/tangerine] tree in our next-door neighbour's yard in Sifale. The *suntala* used to be very big. Our neighbour would not even let us buy some from them. The day before *bhai-tika* [see page 16], Bua, Sanima and I went and stole a whole lot of *suntala*. We then divided them up, and we each had twenty or twenty-five *suntala*. On the day of *bhai-tika* I went to my parent's place in Thamel to put *tika* on my brother and left my share of *suntala* in the cupboard. The next day I returned home. That day I was not feeling too well; I had pains, and then in the evening Shanta was born. Then Sanima thought that she might as well eat my share of the *suntala*, since I was not supposed to eat them after giving birth.[1] But when she opened the cupboard she was amazed to see that they were all gone! What happened was that I had consumed all those *suntala* myself after coming back from Thamel in the evening, before my cramps got really bad! All of us had a big laugh about it.

I treated Sanima as a mother-in-law. Everyone thought that's what she was. As long as she was alive, she assumed all responsibility in looking after the house. I didn't have to do anything. She did the shopping, fasting, *pujas*, everything. She never got fed up with children, and they all liked her very much. Beginning with Babi (the third daughter), all my children called her 'ako ama' ['the other mother', *ako* being a child's mispronunciation of *arko* (other)]. She took them to bed with her. If we came home late at night, after a party, and took Babi away from her bed, Sanima wouldn't even know, she would be fast asleep. Sanima gave so many nick-names to our children, which were always appropriate. Meena became *Rhunchi* [one who cries]; Thulo Babu she called *Haure* [direct and quick-tempered]; Shanta was *Lavar Pare* [advocate of the underdog]; Kanchhu was *Kunte* [cute face]; Babi was *Hajuri* [respected, loved]; Sanu was *bhukuli* [chubby]; Sano Kanchhu was *gokarna* [naive]. Sanima was not educated and so didn't understand some things about the outside world. When she saw a foreigner, she thought she should speak Hindi to make herself understood. Therefore she spoke Hindi to Victor (Meena's Russian husband), thinking he could understand it.

---

[1] 'Cold' foods should be avoided during the ten days of birth pollution, or during any time of sickness.

Meena was a healthy baby, but Shanta was always sick, and she used to cry a lot. With Bua gone and Shanta always sick and crying, I used to get irritated and slapped her a little some times. I was preoccupied with so many worries in my mind at that time, for example the time Meena got lost.

In 1939 just after Shanta was born, there was a *jatra* [fair] in Thamel near the Bhagwan Bahal. That year it was in *Magh* [January-February], and Meena and my sister, Radha, wanted to go see it. So I took them and let them watch from a neighbour's window. Since I had left Shanta alone at home, I went back to check on her. After some time Radha came home by herself, and I asked her where Meena was. She said she was still at the *jatra*. I went to look for her but she wasn't at the neighbour's house. I didn't know what to do. I stood there on the square and tried to look around. One of the neighbours came and asked me what had happened, and I told him that his *bhanji* [niece] was lost. He went to look for her, and after half an hour found her and brought her back. He explained that he saw an old man with a *doko* filled with vegetables on his back and Meena under his arm. Meena was kicking and crying. The neighbour grabbed her from behind and took her; he asked the old man where he was taking her. He said she was alone in the street, crying, so he picked her up and carried her. I asked Meena why she went off alone like that. She replied, 'You went one way, Radha *didi* [elder sister] went the other way; I tried to find the way home and got lost!'

And then, fourteen years after Shanta was born, I had my third child, and she too was a daughter—Babi. Babi was born in 1953, two years after Bua's release in January, 1951, after ten years of imprisonment. Babi is fourteen years younger than Shanta. Even then I was not bothered about whether it was a boy or a girl. I wasn't troubled! After spending ten long years thinking that he might never be released and then finally seeing him released, and then bearing a daughter! No, I wasn't worried at all. She was God's gift to me. I was very happy.

But people around me were concerned. My husband was upset, Sanima was upset, and people who came to visit us would say, in a disappointed tone of voice, 'Oh, it's a girl'. I used to get mad at them and reply that having a baby after thirteen years of the life I had led was the important thing, and that whether the baby was a boy or a girl didn't matter, because she was more precious to me than anything. I said, 'Why do you get upset—you do not have to marry off my daughter'.

Two years after Babi was born we had our first son, Thulo Babu.

He was born the day the government in which Bua served as Home Minister was dissolved. Then eleven months later, our second son arrived. Oh, of course it's difficult to raise little kids so close in age. Actually there were five children of around the same age. When Babi was two, Thulo Babu came. Then when Thulo Babu was not even one, Kanchhu came along. And when Kanchhu was two years old, Sanu was born. Sanu was born the morning after we married Shanta off. And when Sanu was eighteen months, Sano Kanchhu came along. So, all five were around the same age. I gave birth to all my children without medical assistance, just people like Sanima helped. I was being taken to the hospital to give birth to Sanu, but she was born in the car. I was going to the hospital because it had become more fashionable, and because the house was in turmoil after Shanta's wedding. Sano Kanchhu was born feet-first, but even then I had no professional help, because there was no one at home, except for the older lady who lived in the other part of the house. Thirty-six days before my last child was born, Shanta gave birth to our first grandchild, Rita. We moved four different times during this period.

It wasn't so expensive to bear and bring up seven children in those days. At that time, the fashions and demands weren't yet like what they are these days. There wasn't so much inflation either, things were quite inexpensive. And also, having all these children after my husband had been in prison for ten years! It was all happiness, not trouble. If he hadn't been in prison so long we might have had more children, or maybe we wouldn't have. Who knows? I was never afraid Bua might take another wife or concubine. When Bua was Home Minister, Indumati came to visit us and brought a woman with her whom she introduced as her sister. Bua had been gone for a while, and when he came back he asked me, why do you allow her to stay here? Only then did I learn that she was not Indumati's sister and that much earlier Indumati had tried to arrange for her to be a concubine for Bua, when he was staying in Thankot at the hotel his father had started there. She was trying to do that again, and Bua said she should leave. Then she and Indumati both left.

When it was time to send Meena and Shanta to school, Bua was still in prison, so I sent them myself. I taught both of them the ABCD's; I taught them whatever I knew and then put them in school. I was sad that I had never had a chance to go to school, so I wanted my daughters to get this chance. Meena was three and a half years old, and Shanta was one when he went to prison. Meena was in the seventh grade, and Shanta was in the fifth grade, when he came out of prison. He stayed in prison for ten years, and by the time he was released many people had started sending daughters to school.

Meena and two of my nieces [Tanka Prasad's sister's daughters] went to study in Gandhi Ashram, Ajmer, in 1951. That's somewhere in India, I'm not exactly sure where. Well, I wanted her to go and learn, so I sent her. Nevertheless, after eighteen months all three returned, complaining that the facilities weren't very good and also that the food was bad. So Meena continued her studies in Kathmandu in Padma Kanya School and did her intermediate degree from Padma Kanya College, an extension of the same school. She used to study all the time, and sometimes when Bua wanted her to do some household chore, she wouldn't do it and then he would threaten to throw away all her books!

Meena got her BA Honours degree from Delhi. Queen Ratna gave us enough money for Meena to study for two years in Delhi, after Meena wrote her requesting it. She took half of it for the first year, and the other half we kept in the bank here. At the end of one year we had spent the other half of the money just on our expenses, so Meena had to write the Queen for more money to get through the second year. King Mahendra had also given Bua a car and Rs 25,000 after he resigned as Prime Minister, but we had to sell the car because we couldn't afford to maintain it and the driver, and besides we needed the money. Our expenses were very high during that period, because we had to incur the cost of marrying off both Shanta and Bachhu, a distant relative staying with us.

Shanta did not want to continue in school. She studied until the ninth grade, but she was not so studious, and when asked, she was glad enough to quit studying and get married. Meena, on the other hand, said she didn't want to get married, she wanted to continue studying, so I let her study. But I had to convince my husband, who was more conservative in these things. He wanted to marry off both Meena and Shanta, but Meena was vehemently against it, and I supported her in this. After returning from Delhi, Meena went to the Soviet Union for further studies. At first we did not worry that Meena would leave Nepal because we did not even know that she had applied for the scholarship to Moscow. When she came back from Delhi, a scholarship to Russia had been advertised. She filled out an application, took the examination and all that without telling us—she didn't even tell us that she was going to Russia. Then she told us what she had done and that she was going. She didn't tell us she was going for six or seven years, she told us it was for only three years.

When she got the scholarship to go to Moscow my husband didn't want to send her, so I had to convince him and argue with him. He was worried that after many years it would be hard to marry her off, but I thought, if she wants to study we should let her study. When Meena was nine, he had written from prison that he was worried about how I could marry her off, since I had no resources for something like a marriage. I told him that he shouldn't worry about her marriage, that for the moment we should just worry about educating her. I regretted so much not being able to study and to get a good education. Then she went to Russia. She wanted to go study, so we said alright. She was gone for six years.

After a couple of years in Moscow she wrote to us that she was getting married. She had applied in Moscow for permission to marry a Russian and to keep her Nepalese citizenship. In those days Nepalese women automatically lost their citizenship if they married a foreigner. The King was informed about her application, and there was an enquiry from the palace asking whether it was alright with us or not. Even the King asked us. 'Your daughter says she's getting married there, what should we do, permit it or not?', he asked us. Without the Nepal government's permission, she could not get married. So, Mahendra asked us about letting her get married. If we were to tell her not to, it would be against her wishes. That wouldn't have been right on our part, it would have hurt her.

When she got married in Moscow, Bua blamed everything on me, saying that it was because I didn't let him marry her off here in Nepal that she got married in Moscow. Before she went to Moscow he kept on insisting that we should get her married. But I said if she wants to study we should let her study. So when she got married in Moscow, Bua told me it was all my fault. Meena does say that I let her study, that I was the one who educated her.

When Bua heard about Meena's marriage, he worried so much he didn't sleep for three or four days. I also thought it would have been better if she had married a Nepali. For two years Bua didn't write to Meena, but I wrote her. After some months I sent some things to her with Gopal Prasad Bhattarai when he went to Russia. When he came back, he said he thought that Victor, her husband, was a good man, that he could mix well with others.

When Meena returned home with her husband and daughter in

1966, it was not at all uncomfortable for us. He got along with us very well. We never had to treat him differently simply because he was a foreigner. He would eat whatever we ate. He never needed anything different. All we had to do was cook him a little bit of meat differently, and he was all happy. He was very easy to get along with.

Bua didn't pay much attention to our children until after his retirement from active political life. That's when he started taking a more active role with them. Then the death of Mithi's daughter, Malati, intensified that interest.

In addition to our own children there were many other people who stayed with us off and on over the years. When Meena was born, my second mother-in-law's younger sister, Sanima, and her father came to live with us. She had been widowed at the age of fifteen. Her in-laws had also died, and they had no sons to take care of her or her father. They lived in our house, but they had a separate kitchen. They were from Dhading [a district west of and adjacent to Kathmandu Valley]. She helped take care of Meena and carried her around. My maternal grandmother also lived with my parents in Thamel, because she had no sons, and my mother was the only surviving daughter.

Then there was Bachhu. She was a grandchild of Bua's father's oldest brother (a granddaughter from his fourth son). Previously our flat and theirs had been in the same house in Battisputali. That was before Bua got out of prison. Bachhu and her parents were staying in the lower flat, and we were in the upper one, in the late 1940s. In 1953 Bacchu's mother died. For about three years after the mother's death, the father and daughter stayed together. Her older brother had disappeared sometime before. She had an older sister who was married. Then in 1956 the father abandoned her and went to the forest in Gokarna to live, as a hermit. Somebody brought me the news that the daughter was by herself in Battisputali, that the father had left her. Her father did not have a house, and her mother was already dead. I told the man who brought us the news to bring her to our place, and thereafter she remained with us. She was about thirteen or fourteen then. So, she came to stay with us around June of 1956. We brought her to our house and looked after her. We married her off from our house too, in 1959.

My father died young, in 1959. He had asthma. When I took him to our family doctor, he said his lung had already been perforated and had healed itself. He said that as long as the scar on the lung was intact he would live, but that the moment we saw blood coming from his mouth, we would know that the scar had ruptured and that he would die.

My father came to visit me just eight days after I had given birth to Sano Kanchhu. We had arranged for Bachhu's marriage, so he had brought a water pitcher and huge brass pot (to wash the feet in, during the marriage ceremony) and was going back. I asked him to take a rickshaw, but he said it wasn't far and that he could walk. He said, 'One can't always hire a rickshaw, so I'll just walk'. That night he vomited blood. We called two doctors, who treated him, and said he was better. But on the seventh day after he vomited he died. When he came to see me I asked him if he wanted to see Sano Kanchhu, and he said don't disturb him, since he was sleeping. So he never saw him.

My younger brother was still young then and couldn't take care of my mother. So when my father died I brought and kept my mother and my brother at our place. That was in 1961. Then, in *Phalgun* [February-March] 1966 I arranged for the marriage of my brother to a girl from Baneshwor. In *Baisakh* [April-May] I sent my mother, brother, and his wife back to Thamel to live. Actually, mother continued to stay with me and would only sometimes go stay with my brother and sister-in-law. She was with me when she was dying.

My mother became partially paralyzed in *Asar* [June-July] of 1970. I took her to the hospital where she stayed four or five days. After that she was never able to get up and walk around again. Probably she had a brain haemorrhage. One side was paralyzed, and one eye was useless. Then I brought her home. During *Dasai*, on *Panchami*, she was talking alright, and I gave her some *malpua* [a kind of sweet] to eat. Indumati was also with us then, and she took the *malpua* to her; my mother wanted more, but I said no. The next day when I came down after my *puja* at about noon, my mother was losing consciousness. I asked if I should recite the *Bhagwat* [stories of Krishna], and she grimaced, and I felt very bad. But I did recite it. She was getting worse. Nobody was at home; the masons were building Padma's house, next door, and I went and asked the workers to help me carry her outside. Then I called the *Ghate Vaidya* [the doctor at the *ghat* (platform) by the river who pronounces someone dead] in the evening, and he said that I should take her to Pashupati. We took her there, and they did the *das dan*.[2] Then I came home, while my brother stayed

---

[2] Literally, *das dan* ('ten prestations'). This refers to the ritual in which Hindus give

at the *ghat*. The next day nothing happened, she was in a coma. The third day I stayed there all night. The following morning I came back home, and I was going to do *puja* after my bath when I got a call saying that my mother was getting worse and to come back to Pashupati. Bua said he would also come, and to wait for him, but by the time he had finished his *puja* and we went, she had died.

Another person who stayed with us was Kedar, the grandson of Bua's father's oldest brother. He recently died of cancer. He stayed with us for about two or three years.

Another grandson of his father's oldest brother (a grandson from his youngest son), called Krishna, stayed here too. His story is like Bachhu's, in that his father died when he was very young. His mother left Krishna and went off with another man. Until 1956, when he was brought to our house, he was raised by his mother's sister. He stayed with us for seven years. I sent him to school until he passed the S.L.C., then he got a job in Nepal Rastra Bank. The Bank posted him to Birganj, and he continued to stay there. In 1960 Krishna married, but it was his aunt (his mother's sister) who married him off. They found a girl for him, Bindhu, and they came to live with us after their marriage. They stayed about two years after the marriage, and gave birth to their first baby, a girl, while they were with us. They stayed with us until 1962. Then Bindhu went with the baby to her *maiti* when we moved to Bua's sister's house, because once again we could not find a house big enough for the money we had. When Bindhu wasn't with him he was having an affair, so I wrote to Bindhu immediately and said to come back right away and not let Krishna out of your sight. He built a house on the land we gave him in Birganj and lived there with his family. Five years ago he changed jobs and moved to the Food Corporation, in Kathmandu. He lives nearby with his family now. He visits us every day. He has two sons and two daughters, and several grandchildren by his daughters.

With so many outsiders it may get a little crowded sometimes, but if it does, what of it? The little orphans, your own kin, where do you tell them to go? They have nobody. It wasn't very difficult to manage. I wouldn't have brought them into our house if it was going to be difficult!

Another person who has stayed with us for a long time is Mithi.

water and *kush* (sacred grass) and money (some coins on a plate) ten times to someone of a higher status, whether religious, such as a family priest, or social, such as to the wife-receiving family from the wife-giving family.

Mithi has been living with us for more than forty years. Her name is Mithi, but sometimes we call her *Lati* [*Lato* (or its feminine form, *lati*) is a general term used for people who have difficulty speaking well, because they are deaf or mentally retarded], since she can't speak very well. I didn't know where she came from, but one day in 1947, in the month of *Paush* [December-January], she arrived at the door of the house I was staying in and squatted down in front of the door. I was living in Battisputali back then and was in need of a servant. I thought she was a beggar and gave her some money. She took the money, went and bought some snacks, and came back and sat at our door and ate the food. Then I asked her if she wanted to stay with me. She nodded affirmatively. She could not speak. I asked her whether she would steal, and she again nodded affirmatively; when I asked her if she would not steal, she still nodded yes. She started speaking a little only later, but at that time she could not speak at all. When I took her to Janakpur and gave her a better diet (milk, meat, etc.), she gradually learned to speak. Going back to her arrival on my doorstep, I asked her what she would do if she stayed with us. She made gestures to say that she would do the dishes. I asked her what caste she was; she nodded 'yes' to whatever caste I asked about. If I asked if she was a Brahmin, she nodded yes; if I asked if she was a Damai [low-caste tailors], she again indicated yes. She nodded yes regardless of what I asked her. But I let her stay.

Later I discovered that she had been married and that her husband's house was in Gokarna. She had run away from home; she hadn't liked her house in Gokarna because it was only a small thatched hut and her husband was very dark. She would refer to him as *kalo* [black]. One thing about her was that she would refuse to go anywhere outside of our house. That was because since she had run away, she was afraid of being seen by members of her household. We needed to get water every morning from outside the house. So, she would go very early in the morning, and rush back with the water, even though the water tap was very close to the house. Then, she would not even look outside the window, she was so scared someone might see her. In 1949 we left the Battisputali house for Mahottari with Mithi and both girls and Sanima and my mother-in-law. But before we could leave the Valley we had to stay for two or three days in Indrachok with Bindhu, my cousin [mother's brother's daughter], because my second mother-in-law was ill with flu and had a high temperature. Bindhu's husband was also in politics. We then went to Bhimphedi, where we again had to spend three or four days on my mother-in-law's account. Somehow, Mithi's father-in-law and brother-in-law tracked us down in Indrachowk and came there to get her. When they came, she locked herself up in a room, she was so afraid that they would take her back. She didn't want to go. Finally they left, content that she was staying with us and in good hands. But we had to give a written commitment that we were taking her with us. Even later, her mother-in-law came to get her. But she still wouldn't leave us.

She has a son, Mahadev, who stays with us too, and we are taking care of him and educating him. His father was a cook we used to have here. Now he stays in Birganj, farming on the one and a half *bigha* of land we gave to him. He is married to another woman and has other kids from her. They all stay with him, except for one son, Asok, who has recently come to help take care of our *buharis'* [daughters-in-law] children. Actually, before Mahadev was born she had another son by another man who was staying in our house; that son was one month older than Kanchhu, but he died less than a month after he was born.

Between her first son and Mahadev she had a daughter who was six months older than Sanu. Her name was Malati. Her father was a soldier who was stationed with us as a guard when Bua was Prime Minister. When we discovered Mithi pregnant with his child, we sent her with him to his house in the hills. But passersby brought me news that she was begging on the road, and that the guard's first wife in the village had kicked her out along with the child. We sent somebody to bring them back to us, and since then they have been with us. Malati was raised here and was a playmate to my children. She had to do some work, but even so I never felt that she was an outsider; rather she seemed like a member of the family.

We sent Malati to school, and she was in the ninth grade when she was bitten one day on the way to school by a dog infected with rabies. She didn't come back home right away. She went to school first, and when she returned home we saw the wounds and blood and asked her what had happened. She told us, and we sent her to the hospital. She took seven shots for seven days. After the seven days, we told the doctors that she still had the wounds and, therefore, she should get some more shots. They said that the wounds were in her legs, and so seven shots were enough. This was in the month of *Chaitra* [March-April]. In *Baisakh* [April-May], she insisted on getting married to a young man she had met. We had found a young man for her to marry, but she wanted to marry the man she knew, so we married her off, gave her furnishings for her new house in Gokarna, such as pots and pans, mosquito net, etc. Five months later in *Bhadra* [August-September], she died. She died at the age of eighteen due to rabies.

After she died we went to visit her husband. At first we weren't sure what she had died of, and entertained the possibility that her husband might have had some hand in her death. Later it was confirmed that she died of hydrophobia. I was very upset over her death and couldn't talk to anyone for two or three days. She was beautiful, even though she had smallpox marks on her face.

I've already mentioned that we did not have a home, that anywhere we stayed the landlord would sometime or other ask us to leave. It was twenty-six years from the time I got married till the time we built this house! I was like a cat, moving my kittens, as our Nepali proverb says [*biralole chaura sareko*]. First I stayed in Sifale, then in Battisputali. While Bua was still in prison his second mother died, in 1947. After that, I moved out from the Battisputali flat. I left all my belongings at his sister's place and went to stay with my parents. Sanima stayed at his sister's house. Then we moved to Kamal Pokhari, and within Kamal Pokhari itself we moved four or five times. I went to stay at his sister's house three different times. When Bua was released in 1951 I was staying at his sister's place. Then, in *Aswin* [September-October] of 1953 we moved to Dilli Bazaar, where we lived for about a year and a half. After that, we again went to live with his sister. We kept a separate cooking hearth, although it was in the same attic. It was when we were there that my husband became the Prime Minister in 1956. We had only three rooms there, with long lines of political people visiting everyday. After that he went and stayed at Sital Nivas [official government guest house]. I couldn't go there because I had just given birth to my second son, so I remained at his sister's for about fifteen or sixteen days. Then I too went to Maharajganj. We stayed at a house in Pani Pokhari. But that house was too small for us so after about fifteen days we moved to Arvind Shamsher's house in Kamal Pokhari. We stayed there as long as Bua was with the government. After that we moved to Laxman Dittha's house in Kamal Pokhari in *Shrawan* [July-August] of 1957. I gave birth to Sanu and Sano Kanchhu in that house. We stayed there for nearly five years.

And then in 1962 we went to stay at Bua's sister's house once again. It was pretty crowded with so many people: I had five kids, plus there was my mother-in-law, my brother, Sanima, Mithi, and a cook, and all of us moved into three rooms of Bua's sister's house. It was difficult. Bua and I stayed in the original room where we had stayed before, and Sanima and the others stayed in the other two rooms. After staying there for six months we moved to the house of a Pandey (from Biratnagar) which was also in Kamal Pokhari. After that we came here, to Baneshwor. Before we built this house, we stayed at a house a little further up the road from here.

So, we needed a house, and in about 1964 the Queen called me and said that Mr. Tanka Prasad had said that he didn't have a house, and she asked me what we had done about it. I told her that we couldn't really do anything, all we were doing was moving from one place to another, that we didn't have a house. Then she told me to look for a house. I asked her what the cost of the house should be. She said about ten/twelve thousand rupees. But where could you get a house for ten/twelve thousand? I searched at many different places. When I sent in the price of Rs 45, or 46,000 for a house, they did not buy us one. Much later, in 1966 they gave us Rs 20,000 to build a house. It was with that money that I bought this plot of two *ropanis* [eight *ropani* = one acre] of land that we have now, for Rs 18,000. Bua was against buying the land. He wanted to use the money to pay rent on the house we were living in then, and just continue living there indefinitely.

Meena also came back from Moscow with her husband and daughter in 1966. She came in *Shrawan* [July-August] and started working for the Rastra Bank in *Bhadra* [August-September]. Six months later she took a loan of five thousand rupees from her employer, and it was with that money that we laid the foundation of this house.

We had a little bit of land in Barharawa, near Kalaiya in the Tarai. That had been sold to us at a very low price by Purendra Bikram; he was called a Sahebju, some branch of the Royal family who had been under a kind of exile from Kathmandu. We had taken a loan from the government and bought a tractor to farm that land, but we sold the tractor and used the money to put a roof over the house. We didn't completely pay off the loan on that tractor until just a couple of years ago. We just kept paying a little at a time, but now it's finally all paid off!

Well, in the beginning Bua was of a mind not to build a house in Kathmandu but rather to go and stay in the Tarai, and settle there. He wanted to go and spend the Rs 20,000 in the Tarai. But I did not agree. I told him that I would stay here even if I had to live in a hut! He got angry at me because I said I wanted to build a house here, and he left Kathmandu. So, I started building the house without him! He went to the Tarai with some men to farm. I stayed behind looking after the kids and overseeing the construction of this house. Someone helped with one thing, another helped with something else, and the first floor of the house got erected. One person gave us the wood for the door and window frames, another brought us the iron, and so on. After the first floor was done, we moved in. Then, little by little, the second floor was constructed, but not until much later.

Finances in this household have always been a problem. I take care of all the household expenses myself. That can be difficult! But, though it's tough, one must do one's house work, so I do it. It's difficult because once in a while there are arguments. Sometimes, there is not enough money to go around. Now I'm turning over these responsibilities to my daughters-in-law.

We have a big household, with my three sons and their families. I wish all my sons would stay together in one place as long as I live. Now, what should I say? I am sure nobody will stay together forever, but deep down inside I want them to stay together as long as I live. Meena wants to move into her own house too. I told Meena also to stay in this house as long as I live, and then move out after I die. But she wouldn't agree. I told her she is all alone now, where would she go, but she says she'll go anyway [she built her own house nearby, where she now lives].

We are happy now. There have been many difficulties in our lives, but we are together. If Bua and I have arguments, they are about this and that, and this and that. There's no saying. Sometimes this, sometimes that. When we make up after a fight, it just happens automatically. For one or two days you feel bad, but you say these things happen, and things get back to normal. During a fight, he does all the talking; I keep silent.[3] The one thing I like least about Bua is the way he flies into a rage and says whatever is on his mind, which includes abusing other people by calling them all kinds of names.

---

[3] Sometimes Ama does talk, and she chides Bua sometimes. When Ama chides him, he will stop talking. But she is loathe to admit this.

Chapter 17

Our Changing World

Rewanta Kumari

In my parents' home, they used to say that a Brahmin should not eat onion, garlic, tomato, chicken, or eggs after marriage (or after the sacred thread ceremony for boys). It was okay to eat them if you weren't married, when you weren't expected to observe caste rules, but not if you were. I started to eat tomatoes only much later, after my marriage, somewhere along about 1941, after Bua went to prison. I still don't eat chicken and eggs, but I eat onion and garlic now. I started to eat onion and garlic after Bua came out of prison, after 1951, when I began moving around more and meeting other people.

I don't like the taste of these foods that much. If a dish is made only of onion, for example, I don't eat it because I don't like it. But if they just add onion and garlic to some other dish, I'll eat it.

It probably was originally considered a sin for Brahmins to eat these foods. They used to be referred to as 'forbidden food'. An orthodox Brahmin should not eat rice that has been touched by a person of another caste or receive water from a person of a low caste. Until 1947 I observed these restrictions. Before, I wouldn't eat any food except that which I myself personally cooked. Even in the Nepali Congress office in Jaynagar I cooked my own food. But it became increasingly inconvenient and difficult to refuse food from these Congress people; it was awkward. There everybody else would eat, and they started complaining about my not eating. Then Bua was in jail, and I told myself that he's eating, so I might as well eat too! Also, I read that it was permissible to eat food cooked by others, and that even in the *Mahabharata* there is no prohibition against taking food from others. In the *Ramayana* Ram happily ate food presented by a low-caste woman, who tasted it first for him, whereas Laxman grimaced and threw aside the berry she offered. Later when Laxman was hurt by Ravana's son, Indrajit, he could be revived only by a life-reviving drug that grew out of the berry Laxman had discarded. Hanuman brought the plant and revived him. So I changed my eating habits.

I don't drink tea anymore. I used to when I was younger, but because of a bleeding ulcer, I stopped. It's been about twelve years now since I stopped drinking tea. I don't eat chilli peppers either. I don't eat anything hot or sour. I can't—I get stomach aches if I do! I have an ulcer even now, so I have to watch what I eat. Even a little diversion from my routine causes me pain.

When I was little, I would eat in my Newari friends' houses. When I got older I stopped, because after marriage you aren't supposed to. Later on, with my involvement in politics, I had to go to the homes of various castes and eat there. But until 1951, if I went to the home of someone in Kathmandu whose caste was other than Brahmin, I would eat only snacks, not rice and *dal*. It was only after 1951 that I started eating anything anywhere. Well, in the very beginning I did feel a little bit uncomfortable doing that, it took a little bit of adjustment. But then I became used to it.

Once Meena went with me to the Congress office in Jaynagar when I ate there. I told her not to tell anyone at home that I was eating there, because my in-laws should not know about it. But Meena squealed on me. Indumati, the concubine, was able to coax her into telling on me, by giving her four annas [one anna = one sixteenth of a rupee], and she told my mother-in-law. Fortunately, my mother-in-law did not say anything. Indumati caused a huge scandal in Sirsia by trying to bring a panchayat case against me because of my breaking caste dietary rules. She wanted me to be decasted so that I would be disinherited, and then she would inherit Bua's father's property.

She brought the police and tried to get them to arrest me because I had eaten beside a *Damaini* [female member of the *Damai* (tailor) caste]. The *Damaini* was D.P. Pariyar's mother, Dhana Kumari. The day Indumati made her accusation I had gone to bathe in the river, and when I returned there were four policemen waiting for me. They asked about the people who were staying with me, then left. Dhana Kumari had been staying with me, but by the time the police came she had moved on. I found out from an acquaintance, the manager of Janakpur Ram Mandir [temple dedicated to Ram], that Indumati had made this accusation. I went to stay at the Congress office in Jaynagar for a week until things cooled off, otherwise I would have been arrested. I wasn't angry, because I knew Indumati was uneducated and ignorant and therefore bound by old traditions, so I didn't feel anything. I took pity on her. That was in 1948.

In my *maiti*, they didn't find out about my new eating habits then. They didn't know for a long time. They found out only after Bua got out of prison. After Bua got out of jail, when we went to my *maiti* to eat, my natal family had to eat with us, out of decency, but they were uncomfortable doing so because Bua had been decasted after the trial. I was by implication also tainted, since I ate his *jutho* [polluted food. A high-caste Hindu man leaves a small amount of food on his plate after eating; his wife then adds her own helping to it and consumes it all], so it was an awkward situation. I didn't believe he needed to have a special purifying *puja*. Others were embarrassed to bring up the subject, since it entailed so many bad memories and unpleasant experiences.

There have been changes in many other customs since I was little—for example pertaining to menstruation. It is the custom to remain apart from everybody else for the first four days of your menstrual period. You can not touch anyone, you can not touch food that others eat, you have to eat separately and clean your dishes separately. Then on the fourth day you bathe, clean your dishes, and dry them. Only on the fifth day can others eat what you touch. Actually, you can touch children, but that's all.

The very first time you get your period, you have to remain apart from others, enclosed in a dark room, for twelve days. All four of my daughters—Meena, Shanta, Babi, and Sanu, went through it. You know, when you get your period for the first time you cannot even see the male members of your family. You have to hide yourself. You can't look at men during this time. It was said that the life span of a man becomes shortened if he is seen by a woman during her first menstruation period. You cannot see the sun either, so you sit all day with the curtains drawn. You bathe on the fourth day, the eighth day, and then on the twelfth day. On the twelfth day, after you bathe, you pray to the sun and then only can you come out and see everyone. I went through all this myself.

My daughters have had somewhat different experiences. Well, Meena and Shanta were kept in a dark room for twelve days, yes [the room has to be in a house not frequented by the girl's male relatives]. But not Babi and Sanu. Babi was having an SLC exam then, and we couldn't keep her in a dark room for twelve days just for that, because if we had she would have had to drop the exam. Also the society was changing, so we didn't think it was so important anymore. Sanu probably also had a similar circumstance, but I can't remember what it was.

During your second period you should be secluded for eight days, and during the third for five days. Actually, even Shanta was let out to take an exam on the fifth or sixth day of her second period. Babi and Sanu didn't stay secluded the full twelve days, but they did move out of the house, because you aren't supposed to look at your father and brothers during that time. Babi stayed with the neighbours, and Sanu stayed at Shanta's.

It is a good thing that women are now studying, working, asking for equality, etc. Before, when women weren't doing such things, so many women had so many hardships. Even today, after all that has happened, there are still so many women who have hardships, who suffer a lot.

I just read in the newspaper today that some Nepali woman got married, and then her husband took his wife to Calcutta and sold her for seventy thousand rupees. Somehow this woman managed to reach an organization of Nepalese residing in Calcutta, and they brought her back. But the person who brought her back, without knowing it, brought her back to the same people who had sold her. A school teacher and another woman were involved in selling her.

There are many differences in Kathmandu and in Nepal generally between the present and how things were fifty years ago. Some things are better now, while some things were better then. What is good about today is that there is freedom. Well, actually, freedom is present and absent at the same time. How can you claim there is freedom when you can't really voice your opinions? But, then again, how can you say there is no freedom now when during the Ranas' autocratic rule nobody could enter the ruling body, nobody could open their mouths. At least today the common people are there too, they have at least a little bit of authority, at least some rights.

What was good then was that the Ranas had a systematic management. Today, Nepal has become a land of no regulations. The Ranas were very systematic in what they did. Yes, they preyed on the poor, and they did not do anything towards developing the country, and they just accumulated riches for themselves. But their discipline, their management had a form. There was not so much inflation. There used to be no bribery, like today, in offices. Oh, sure, bribes went on here and there, but nothing like today. The Ranas would punish anyone other than themselves if they found out that the person was taking bribes.

There are many differences in my life between now and forty years ago. Forty years ago, there were difficulties in every direction. We didn't even have a roof over our heads. I couldn't even see my husband.

Compared to when he was in jail, my life is wonderful now. When Bua was in jail, I didn't know what would happen. Sometimes the prisoners would go on the rooftop of the Golghar, and people would be able to get a glimpse of them. So if I found out that he was on the rooftop, I would run to the prison gates hoping to catch a glimpse of him. But they would actually put up curtains at the gates knowing that we would be able to see them on the rooftop, so that I never got to see him. Back in 1941 they even refused to let Meena go in naked to see him.

When I think of all those things, the hardships of those days, I am happy today. I have a house, my children are grown up, that's all I need. I have everything. There was a time when I could not even see my husband, there was no place to stay, out of the two daughters one was with her grandfather, the other one was here. The unhappiest event of my life is the day he was jailed. The happiest day of my life is when he was released from jail after ten years and four days of imprisonment.[1] Now at least we have a home. I am in my home with children and grandchildren. What more can I ask for? Isn't it great for me now?

Now I have everything.

---

[1] From interview in *Samikshya*, 17 *Paush*, 2038 (1981).

Chapter 18

Practitioners and Practice

How did this otherwise unexceptional Brahmin, from a conventional urban, middle-class Hindu family, come to confront the overwhelming power arraigned against him, reconstitute the political discourse of his time, and successfully transform an ideology into practice? What he did, why he did it, and how he managed to pull it off, with the vital support of his wife, I try to clarify in this chapter.

To a certain extent Tanka Prasad accounts for his life in terms that were predicted for him at birth, when his horoscope forecast that he would become either a *Raja* (King) or a *Jogi* (Saint). Both those influences, he said, fought inside him, making him combative.

The combativeness to which he refers is illustrated in his initial, audacious provocation of the Ranas. The pamphlets (Appendix 1), which he wrote single-handedly, with their tropes of sweat and blood, claws and chains, the imperatives of sacrifice and fighting for freedom, illustrate his daring, unrelenting challenge to the legitimacy of the Ranas' power. The first pamphlet shows the fundamental level of his attempt to change the political discourse of his time. He not only used abusive, uncompromising language towards the rulers, but he also utilized the pronoun *timi*, normally used only for children, servants, or those with whom one has an intimate relationship, to refer to the Ranas. This outrageous, unthinkable rhetorical device added to the effect of a challenge so basic that it conceded nothing to his opponents; for the time being they retained their political power, but Tanka Prasad was already eroding their symbolic capital.

His were fighting words. The political, economic, and military resources of Nepal were concentrated in the hands of the Rana family, who lived in pseudo Greco-Roman palaces behind high brick walls, separating them from the rest of the population. Life was so tightly controlled that Nepalese citizens needed passports to travel in and out of the Kathmandu Valley. Modern facilities for education, health, transportation, and communication were essentially non-existent. Tanka Prasad's wording left no doubt that the Ranas were responsible for the miserable state of the country, and that he intended to change things.

Tanka Prasad waged a two-pronged war, and his other pamphlets were directed not at the Ranas, but at what he called his Nepalese brothers. In these pamphlets Tanka Prasad appealed simultaneously to two things: a generalized (and generally Western) sense of political and economic justice, and a Hindu concern with religiously and morally correct consciousness and conduct. He does not hesitate to chide his countrymen to take what we would now rather anaemically call a pro-active stance *vis-à-vis* the powers that towered menacingly over them. Again, the appeal is to self-interest as well as to religious exhortation and reflects the mixture of his ideological training: as a Hindu and as a student of revolution, influenced by assorted strands of the Western political and philosophical tradition.

All this makes clear that he did not deploy the 'weapons of the weak'.[1] There was nothing subtle about his rebellion—no malingering, no foot dragging, no irony, no dissimulation, no hidden transcript. Such out-and-out revolutionary movements as Tanka Prasad attempted are not common. Not without reason did Scott observe that revolutions do not often work out very well for those who start them. And there certainly is no resemblance to Kondo's (1990) part-time Japanese workers who accommodate their superiors so much while resisting them that she is driven to doubt the validity of the whole notion of resistance. Scott's and Kondo's important and perceptive analyses need to be supplemented by world-historical cases such as those of Tanka Prasad, whose rebellion, far from being subtle or everyday, could be described as reckless and romantic, even suicidal. His stance reminds one of John Wayne, who, told that things aren't always just black and white, replied, 'well, I say, why the hell not?' Tanka Prasad is an inconveniently traditional and modern person to write about in these post-modern times.

Let me qualify the sense in which Tanka Prasad is not a good candidate for post-modern man. At the level of general assumptions about either Hinduism or democratic socialism or any other 'ism' to which he

[1] Scott, in his seminal work *Weapons of the Weak: Everyday Forms of Resistance*, writes about marginal groups in Malayan society who employ traditional modes of resistance to subvert authority. By contrast, Tanka Prasad's modes of resistance, though rooted in tradition and informed by Western philosophy, are those of a privileged class. For a South Asian view similar to Scott's see Ranajit Guha *Elementary Aspects of Peasant Insurgency in Colonial India* and *Subaltern Studies I-VI*.

subscribed, Tanka Prasad's convictions were a constant anchor in his course of action. He did entertain all sorts of de-centered doubts at the level of action on any given issue, especially after he was released from prison and had to oppose King Tribhuvan (and especially his son and grandson, Mahendra and Birendra) on one issue or another. As he himself said, he wavered in his philosophy. But his doubts did not restrain him from resolutely blazing the trail that he did, because his populist, nationalist, democratic core ideology never changed. When issues were black and white, as they tended to be in the beginning, he did not hesitate to call them that way.

What, then, were Tanka Prasad's traditional roots? His account sets forth his middle-class, Brahmin, somewhat pampered background. The stories his mother told him from the *Ramayana*, tales of Krishna, and so on constituted a body of ethics for him and provided the security he felt in his environment and who he was. As he says, it is not the literal truth of these stories that stayed with him, but rather some of their core values, such as truth, honour, and courage.

The second part of his education came from exposure to liberal Western political ideas, absorbed from various Western thinkers, and even the example of Napoleon (who, coincidentally and ironically, was one of Weber's favourite examples of a charismatic personality) plus the illustrative and on-going case of the Indian independence movement, which embodied and played out many of these ideas.

His attitude toward the monarchy illustrates some of these braided ideological strands. His pro-palace stance was rooted partly in his appreciation, and in King Tribhuvan's case, genuine affection, for what the Crown had contributed to the history of Nepal. Kings had a legitimate role to play in the cultural world he was born into. He was also profoundly influenced by his early exposure to English history and the rise of a democratic, constitutional monarchy there. It was an epiphany for him to read in a history textbook that it was not just the English King who ruled, but others too, especially as the Industrial Revolution, empowering some classes at the expense of others, resulted in bourgeois democracy. And finally, on a more strategic level, he was keenly aware how dangerously vulnerable to an Indian take-over his country would be without a unifying national symbol.

One other crucial component of his development needs to be emphasized: the perceived injustice to his father done at the hands of the Ranas. This episode embittered Tanka Prasad very much, radically altered his life-style (because his father had to sell their house and some land to raise funds to repay the stolen money), and 'struck hatred' in his heart against the Ranas. It was the anger that this incident caused, combined with earlier Hindu values and later European ideas, that pushed him over the edge and into the revolutionary role in which he cast himself. Things like *chakari* (ritualized obsequiousness, inscribed on bodies and postures), and the sheer injustice of Rana rule, he said, drove him to want to overthrow them. As in Gandhi's case (Erikson 1969), an incident he experienced as a young man concerning his father was a crucial component in his subsequent development.

The target of his revolt—the autocratic political system—was narrowly drawn. He was never in revolt in a more general way against his culture (e.g. Hinduism) or society (e.g. the caste system). He said, 'We in Praja Parishad had little interest in Arya Samaj. They just wanted social reforms, whereas our main objective was political reform. They did not believe in icon worship or caste, whereas we did worship icons. We accepted people of all castes, but we didn't specifically disavow caste as such, the way they did'. At a personal level, he rejected the aristocratic, high caste tradition of taking concubines, as his father had. Rather than revolting against his culture, he contested it mightily, promoting a version of it which he thought was truer to its ideals.

Finally, and not so obviously, Tanka Prasad came from a tradition of political violence. The Rana family had itself come to power ninety years before as the result of an extremely bloody massacre of noblemen and courtiers, the so-called Kot Massacre. Furthermore, there had been a history of intrigue and power plays within the Rana family during their reign; because the Prime Ministership passed from older brother to younger brother instead of from father to son, the temptation of a younger brother to do away with an older brother was sometimes too much to resist. Of nine Rana Prime Ministers, only four died peacefully in office (Regmi 1950). Thus, what made Tanka Prasad's challenge unique was not the idea of overthrowing the Rana Prime Minister, although that was unprecedented for someone from a segment of society outside the circles where such cabals were hatched. What was unprecedented was his call to abolish the entire system of hereditary family rule (at least the non-royal part of it) in favour of a democratic, constitutional monarchy.

Thus the cultural tradition presented to Tanka Prasad was both constraining and enabling. The constraints are all too immediately apparent: the repressive institutions of the extremely harsh regime he and his friends wanted to change. The Ranas did not, to understate the case, suffer suggestions for political change gladly.

Enabling were his indigenous cultural heritage and the radical European and American philosophy he had read about. Tanka Prasad speaks frequently and admiringly of these Western writers and their impact on him; their substance was in any case well-known and common-place among independence- and revolutionary-minded politicians in the sub-continent over the last century or two. The indigenous ideological and sociological foundations of his thinking were less obvious but equally powerful.

Brahmins have held hegemonic ideological sway ever since they were established as the peculiarly godly caste. As a group they have dominated Hindu discourse, even when they have been on the religious defensive, as they have been over and over again, in the face of challenges from forces as diverse as Buddha, *Bhakti* (devotional sect) movements, and Ambedkar, the leader of the untouchables. Tanka Prasad's case falls within this ambit of Brahmanical supremacy, but with some Nepalese idiosyncratic twists.

One of the traditional Brahmanic options has been that of the man-in-the-world giving up his caste, and even his family, for the life of the *sanyasi*, the world renouncer—what Dumont calls the individual-outside-the-world (Dumont 1970:46). It is through Hindu society's world-ly ends—*dharma, artha, karma* (roughly: duty, profit, pleasure)—that, paradoxically, the Brahmin revitalizes and legitimates the social order, providing it with an intra-societal critique, while devoting himself to his own liberation.

Even when renunciation is not actually practiced—and it is not much pursued by Nepalese Brahmins—it remains a laudatory ideal. Brahmins brought with them to Nepal their moral and religous primacy and made it stick even to some extent among those on the tribal fringes of mainstream Hindu society. The special role of Brahmins is central to the construction of power and agency in Nepal. Even among those Tibeto-Burmese groups who are not part of the Hindu tradition Brahmins are recognized for their religiosity and intellectual preeminence, although these attributes may be counterbalanced by such qualities as avariciousness and duplicity.

Tanka Prasad was raised in this tradition, both in the license he was given as a child and the rudimentary learning that was his birthright. At the same time his literacy in a generally illiterate society gave him access to the ideological armaments of the West. The result was a cultural innovation: rather than renounce the world at the end of his life, he denounced the world at the beginning of his life. Even when brazenly defying the political powers over him, his voice carried the diffuse authority and legitimacy his Brahmanic status conferred on him. The Ranas could not excecute him, much as they would have liked to, not just because it was illegal, but because it would have been too great a sin to have done so. It is no accident that subsequent political leadership of political parties in Nepal have been disproportionately Brahmins, a fact which leaders of various so-called Mongoloid, Buddhist, and Tibeto-Burmese movements in post-1990 Nepal have pointed out with alacrity, anger, and anguish.

In addition to his ideological background and the outrage he felt from the injustice done to his father, the idiosyncratic quirk of leadership needs to be addressed. Although he was not a high aristocrat he was, like most revolutionaries anywhere, from the middle-class, and the imperiousness that came along with the high caste and relatively high class position he occupied were important ingredients in his own cultural self-confidence. Being to the manor born, he talked to and dealt with the Ranas the way he did because he had had plenty of practice in the commanding way he treated others—his father had been an effective role model in this respect. Even as an old man he continued to use the pronoun *ta* (even more familiar than *timi*) to talk to adults like taxi drivers, not out of disrespect but out of downright imperiousness. And he was known for his intermittently autocratic, irritable, demanding demeanour towards his wife, children, servants, and the unfortunate anthropologist occasionally caught in the withering crossfire.

Tanka Prasad's thinking takes a more practical turn in recent times. Regarding the future of the monarchy in Nepal, for example, which he had always strongly supported, he said it all depends upon its accomplishments, echoing Balzac's sentiment that you can do without a king, but not without your dinner.

I have characterized Tanka Prasad and Rewanta Kumari as playing lead roles in the political and social drama of their times. That they were not mere members of the chorus is crucial. Through the struggle to reinterpret traditional symbols of authority and power and recast their meanings, Tanka Prasad began an ongoing process that, altering his culture forever, made possible, and continued into, the democratic elections of 1991.

What has resulted from this human action in the world is a traditional system transposed to a new and different key. The result was not, as

Marxists might envision it, and as Tanka Prasad would have liked, a transformed economy, but a radically altered polity, and an enhanced supply of 'symbolic capital' available to empower his comrades and their countrymen. Domination still exists in its peculiarly Nepalese forms—caste, ethnic group, gender, class, region, religion, occupation—but new dominators have emerged, power has become vastly more diffuse, and the centrality of traditional asymmetrical relations is now widely and actively questioned rather than passively assumed. Characterized negatively, political change was failed reproduction (Sahlins 1981). Put positively, a social transformation took place, an example of the creative, restructuring aspect of life as people rediscover and reinvent their cultures in the changing historical circumstances of our postmodern, postcolonial, post-traditional world (Marcus and Fischer 1986:24).

Tanka Prasad's strong religious orientation in part motivated and certainly sustained him throughout his struggles, as it did in Rewanta Kumari's case. He contested religion (after all, the Ranas were also Hindu) and adapted it to novel political ends, but he never saw any contradiction between his political beliefs and action and his religion. It would be more accurate to say that Tanka Prasad never doubted anything in his cultural tradition because he interpreted or reinterpreted it in such a way as to make sense of it all. Liminal he was not, in part perhaps because the influence of foreign ideologies came only from the printed page—he never talked to an European until after his release from prison in the 1950s. He was not a general-purpose social reformer. He simply wanted to change some specific aspects of his tradition—particularly those concerned with power. Culture here thus is not essentialist, but historical and emergent, 'the ever-changing outcome of a confrontation of discrete interests with shifting contexts and empirical constraints' (Sax 1990: 506).

Tanka Prasad was instrumental in recreating and fundamentally restructuring the tradition he inherited, but not through pragmatic, short-term, self-aggrandizing 'moves'. He illustrates Ricoeur's point that a major asset of utopian thinking is to preserve a distance between the present and the future, by making a gap between a system of authority claiming legitimacy and the population's actual belief in that legitimacy (Ricouer 1986: 179, discussed in Fox 1989). Tanka Prasad was motivated not only by immediate problems to be solved, but by images and ideals of what is good and proper—in people, in relationships, and in conditions of life (Ortner 1984). For Tanka Prasad these images and ideals were foregrounded in the public arena—above all in politics.

For Rewanta Kumari they figured in the domestic realm—the home. Politically, Rewanta Kumari was a reflex of Tanka Prasad. As supporter and smuggler, but never as sycophant, she sacrificed far beyond what was expected even from a subservient Hindu wife (her sufferings parallel Sita's in the *Ramayana*). She sustained him in his struggles when she could as easily have withheld or withdrawn her support. His life and accomplishments depended on the fusion of her life with his.

Founding the first women's organization in Nepal represents only the end-point of a long process of unmaking and remaking her own traditions. Thrown on to her own minimal resources for the ten years her husband was imprisoned empowered her and realigned her life and values. She had no option but to become the father as well as the mother of her children. She took risks and changed her own way of life from what both her parents and her parents-in-law—and in some respects even her husband—had raised her to follow. Rather out of the temper of her time, she fiercely defended and promoted the education for her own daughters which she had been denied. When her oldest daughter became the first Nepalese woman to marry a European, requiring the King's assent to allow her to keep her Nepalese passport, it was her mother who stood by her and supported her out-of-caste and out-of-country union. Rewanta Kumari remained as devotedly Hindu as she had always been, but aspects of her life as a Brahmin, such as those pertaining to diet and commensality, changed fundamentally. She remade her life and culture at least as much as Tanka Prasad did his.

Just as Tanka Prasad's courage and fearlessness in action had native roots, they also had indigenous clients. The only payoff he dared hope for was justice, welfare, and freedom for his countrymen, unlike those other much more famous exemplars of Nepalese bravery, the Gurkhas and Sherpas, who do what they do for handsome Western wages. At the simplest level Tanka Prasad, like Nate Shaw (Rosengarten 1974), just wanted to right what he considered to be wrongs. Put another way, he aptly exemplifies Barrington Moore's assertion (1978) that 'people must perceive and define their situation as the consequence of human injustice: a situation they need not, cannot, and ought not to endure. By itself of course such a perception is no guarantee of political or social changes to come. But without some very considerable surge of moral anger such changes do not occur'.

Anger is one thing, 'pulling it off' is another. I have assumed in most of this book that Tanka Prasad was successful, but it is not transparently clear whether his revolution ended in success or failure or somewhere in between. In the short term, with his comrades executed and he himself serving a life sentence in prison, Tanka Prasad's revolution could not have failed more ignominiously. No matter how intense his anger, it needs to be emphatically pointed out that were it not for the collapse of British rule in India, which conveniently provided the burgeoning Nepali Congress Party a sub-continent in which to organize, operate, and attack the Ranas, he would have spent another forty years in prison. In the medium run, the verdict is more mixed. On the one hand, Tanka Prasad was released after spending ten years in jail, to eventually become Prime Minister; on the other hand the by-then-sprawling democratic forces suffered a thirty year eclipse after the royal takeover of 1960.

The relatively happy ending is the highly successful multi-party revolution of 1990 followed by the 1991 election of a democratic government headed first by the Congress Party, followed by a Communist electoral victory in 1994. This new system, including the King as a constitutional monarch, built on what Tanka Prasad and his associates began in the 1930s. The 1990 movement, like Tanka Prasad's original rebellion, succeeded only because of the way the increasingly democratic world was turning outside the borders of Nepal. It took time for the hegemony Gramsci and Williams have talked about to crumble, but when it did it imploded spectacularly. What Tanka Prasad had contested as a voice in the wilderness became common political currency. Even in the beginning Tanka Prasad did not bring all this about single-handedly, of course, and in many respects his story is meant to stand for those of his like-minded comrades, both those of his own generation and those who quickly came out of the woodwork in droves, and who now have saturated the political landscape in Nepal.[2] The problematic he posed as an individual became a collective ideological answer.

I have attempted to avoid the problem of treating history as a 'process without a subject'[3]—and its close relative, that of the 'cultural dope'—by making human agency, as manifest in the words of these supra or

---

[2] The internal politics of this resistance is mentioned only briefly here, in Tanka Prasad's occasional references to his rivals, and in Appendix 2. For the importance of this and other theoretical problems in resistance studies see Ortner 1996.

[3] E.P. Thompson (1978) in 'The Poverty of Theory and other Essays' is critical of social theory (e.g., Marxist models of process) which neglects or minimizes human agency and the importance of the human subject in history. The lack of a biography of Tanka Prasad, let alone Rewanta Kumari, is exemplary of this lacunae in Nepalese historiography.

subalterns (depending on the point of view)[4] the centrepiece of this social transformation. All social transformations, whatever the structures of their conjunctures (Sahlins 1981), depend on the operations of agents. Agents—micro elements working in a macro matrix—are neither particles of matter whose actions are determined externally, nor little monads guided solely by internal considerations. They are the products of culture and history, of historicized culture. Tanka Prasad's and Rewanta Kumari's own pasts combined with their presents to give them all the tools they needed to do what they did, producing an ontological complicity between them and their world. The cultures they could not accept as they were enabled them to make culture. Refusing to be laced into trans-historical strait-jackets, their histories empowered them to make history.

What anthropologists call practice theory is not so much a theory in any formal sense as a set of approaches which emphasize the non-deterministic alternatives available to people, allowing for a wide range of responses of actors to their experience, whether they be those who occupy the extreme poles such as Tanka Prasad or Kondo's Japanese factory workers, or Scott's peasants, who fall somewhere in between. This aspect of human life which Bourdieu, indulging his 'somewhat decadent desire to say complicated things' (1990: 139), calls the habitus, emphasizes not just the social and political systems which structure what we do, but also the way in which, reacting to them, we make and remake those structures. Tanka Prasad and Rewanta Kumari picked their ways through their habitus, altering it while it simultaneously expanded them and their options. They both manipulated, and reinterpreted important parts of their habitus—their traditional *dharmas* which, despite all the changes worked in them, remained just that—traditional.

A practice approach gives us a clearer picture of both the genesis of modern Nepalese political and social life, and the reproductive, generative, intentional lives of Tanka Prasad and Rewanta Kumari. Another way of saying that the habitus can give rise to new structures is to say that it is 'an infinite capacity for generating products—thoughts, perceptions, expressions and actions' (Bourdieu 1990:55)—all of them historically and culturally rooted, so that they are no more unpredictably novel than they are precisely replicative. This setting of limits may be apparent to an omniscient observer blessed with the acuity of hindsight. From the point of view of their opponents, who held all the chips, Tanka Prasad's and Rewanta Kumari's actions were quite unpredictable.

---

[4] See Spivak 1988 and Coronil 1994 on the question of whether subalterns can speak.

Bourdieu admits that habitus is only durable, not eternal, and the Acharya case demonstrates the limits of gradualism. Given the rapidity with which the whole house of cards eventually collapsed, one might argue that the Rana Prime Minister was really only an Asian Wizard of Oz in his Emerald City of Kathmandu. But the fact that he was a Wizard with heavy artillery at his disposal is not a trivial qualification.

The details of Tanka Prasad's life do not support the notion that there was something predetermined about it—his horoscope notwithstanding—that the structure of the times made it come out the way it did. On the contrary, the series of random lucky and unlucky accidents illustrates Bourdieu's contention that "Nothing is more misleading than the illusion created by hindsight in which all the traces of a life, such as...a biography, appear as the realization of an essence that seems to pre-exist them (1990:55).[5] At any stage of his life things could have gone otherwise than they did, but measured against the slings and arrows of everyday life, his search for a moral fulcrum remained steadfast.

Nor should Tanka Prasad's case be taken as evidence for a resurrected voluntaristic, Great Man Theory of history. The point is neither that the Nepalese political system was on a collision course with the rest of the world anyway, which it was; nor that eventually someone else would have done what Tanka Prasad did anyway, which is certainly true; nor that no one had thought or done such things before in his cultural universe, which is also true. The view that 'only individuals matter' can be dismissed outright (Lukes 1977). I assert more modestly only that agency is not epiphenomenal and that intentionality is a key component of culture. The point is simply that as things turned out, Tanka Prasad and Rewanta Kumari were the ones who did it in their time and their place, and they did it their way.

Tanka Prasad's insurgency was, like any insurgency (Guha 1983), a motivated and conscious undertaking, whose praxis was constituted by will and reason, not a spontaneous and unpremeditated occurrence. The issue is not the routine one of a powerful person acting over someone who would have acted otherwise if power had not been exercised (Giddens

---

[5] Bourdieu elaborates the point further: 'The genesis of a system of works or practices generated by the same habitus...cannot be described either as the autonomous development of a unique and always self-identical essence, or as a continuous creation of novelty, because it arises from the necessary yet unpredictable confrontation between the habitus and an event that can exercise a pertinent incitement on the habitus only if the latter snatches it from the contingency of the accidental and constitutes it as a problem by applying it to the very principles of its solution...' (1990:55).

1979), but rather the anomaly that someone without power acted as if he had it. I have accordingly paid less attention not only to structure, or to the rules of the game, or to strategies and tactics to manipulate the rules (Barnes 1980:301), and more to looking at what it takes to break the rules and start a new game.

Tanka Prasad was not afflicted with liminality, nor was his resistance based on models of Hindu heroes, because Hinduism is singularly short on heroes, except for the divine sort. What charisma Tanka Prasad did have, apart from the hereditary charisma of his caste, affected his opponents more than his followers; after all, it was the former, not the latter, who thought he was endowed with supernatural powers, and in the 1959 elections he did not even carry his own neighbourhood. The norms he promulgated did not lie outside existing social norms, they were just innovative reformulations of them, the creation of a political will that made work 'what is structurally barely possible' (Cardoso and Faletto 1979:176).

Tanka Prasad was unique only in thinking what he thought and doing what he did at the time he thought and did them. His actions mirror Magritte's self-portrait, Clairvoyance, which shows the artist looking at an egg, while painting on his canvas not the picture of an egg, but of a bird. That is, Tanka Prasad saw a future-oriented logic to practice that few others at the time could see. While his case may be extreme, that is no reason to dismiss it. Human beings frequently do something like this in a more quotidian, small-scale fashion, a la Scott or Kondo—contesting the incoherent spots in their cultures, nibbling at the edges of them, pushing them where they can. Anthropological views of human agency have too frequently and uncritically resembled that of the hero of Camus' *The Stranger*, who at the end of the novel said that in the long run one gets used to anything. Even Kondo's resisters are more inventive than that.

It is sometimes asked, in reference to Gandhi: what would have happened to him if he had resisted the Nazis instead of the British? Tanka Prasad's case suggests he would have been executed without fanfare, just as Tanka Prasad would have been but for the quirk of caste. Tanka Prasad's case also illustrates what is now a commonplace: the existence of internal as well as external colonialism. There were no foreign villains for Tanka Prasad, an anticolonialist without a colony, to throw out, only certain of his own countrymen. Both his ideology and his actions became increasingly built on the contradictions and tensions inherent in being simultaneously a revolutionary and a staunch monarchist and an uncompromising nationalist, committed both to Hinduism and to a modern democratic state. Therefore in later years the views of this supra-subaltern were not always consistent, a fact predicted by his horoscope and one which he would be the first to recognize. He would probably also have agreed with Aldous Huxley's aphorism that the only completely consistent people are the dead.

I have tried to formulate a concrete, intimate view of the creative, active, inventive capacity of these agents, and the fullness of lives that reacted sharply to their autocratic times, making their own history—practitioners going about their practice. Decontextualized notions of agency and power lose what we most need—actual cases of doers doing all the doing that they do indeed do (Ortner 1984). Put another way, if you want to understand agency, consult your local agent. Gandhi said, if there is one convert to a cause, you can add zeros to the one and the first zero will account for ten and every addition will account for ten times the previous number. But if no one makes the first move, multiplicity of zeros can only produce more zeros (Fox 1989). Nepal today is what it is, rather than something else, in some small measure because of the moves Tanka Prasad made first, and the way Tanka Prasad and Rewanta Kumari practiced their lives.

Appendix 1

Tanka Prasad's Anti-Rana Pamphlets (1940)

Note: Pamphlet 1 is translated into English here for the first time. The others were translated by the British Embassy at the time they were produced in 1940. The original Nepali versions have long since disappeared, but the translations were found in 1985 in the India Office Library in London by Mr Rishikesh Shah, who turned them over to Tanka Prasad.

PAMPHLET 1

EDICT

Attention all you Ranas! In order to free the Nepalese from your tyrannical claws, to promote education through the enforcement and development of the cultural heritage of our fellow citizens, to make the Nepalese people one of the most civilized in the world, and to let the glory of our nation shine in every direction for thousands of years, you[1] may know that a party called Nepal Praja Parishad has been born.

Ranas! Although circumstances gave you the opportunity to perform noble deeds, instead you became the slaves of your selfishness, and instead of contributing to the progress of the people, you have sucked their blood and tried to make your sons and grandsons rich. Think yourselves, how blind your selfishness has made you. Even such evil deeds do not burn your insides [kalejo, literally 'liver']. The same people who entrusted their freedom, security, esteem, and national progress and cultural development to you, you have robbed of their wealth, turned into slaves and taken their retardation as your development, denigrating their honour—these are the despicable acts you have been performing. You have no aim other than to make the people blind and to loot them of their possessions. You want their families to die for a single grain, so that you can quench your

---

[1] Tanka Prasad addresses the Ranas as 'timi', thus giving the Nepali a cheeky, brazen tone that the English translation lacks; see chapter 7, footnote 4.

thirst for debauchery through their sweat and blood. Ranas! It is surprising that you still dare to go to Pashupatinath and Guheswari to offer your prayers. No, this cannot be so. What you are doing is only pulling the wool over the peoples' eyes. One who respects God will also fear him, but where do you show any fear of God? Within the clutches of your evil claws, one crore [one crore = 10,000,000] human beings has been inflicted with suffocating poverty. But even then your claws still reek from the stain of their blood. Ranas! Recently again you have shown the picture of your unbridled selfishness. You sent the army to help the British, but sending the army to help someone is such a momentous measure—who did you ask before you made that decision? What benefit can we derive from getting entangled in the war in Europe? What achievements did the Nepalese people get when you sent the army to help the British in 1914? You were the sole benefactors. You could deposit ten lakhs [one lakh = 100,000] rupees in the bank every year. Now that Germany has captured Paris, you are seized by the fear of a German victory, and in order to assuage your fear, and for your own personal gain, you have turned the Nepalese people into slaves and stripped them of everything.

But No![2] Now you still hope to maintain your autocracy and to suck the peoples' blood. The characterization of your tyranny even Brahma with his four mouths cannot describe.

Ranas! Don't think that your sins will not be disclosed. You will definitely pay the penalty for your cruelty. This is the law of god. The catastrophic autocracy you have perpetrated will ruin you. Just wait till the people open their eyes. You will definitely face disaster, because then your force and swords will be of no more avail to you than trying to disperse the clouds simply by blowing with your mouth. You still have time to repent. Hope you will not lose this opportunity.

President,
Nepal Praja Parishad
9 *Asar* 1997 [22 June 1940]

[2] The Nepali for this phrase is 'hoina, hoina'.

PAMPHLET 2

O! Nepalese Brothers! A few days ago a notice was issued to the Ranas which you will have received and from which it would be clear to you as to what is the aim of the Nepal Praja Parishad. The members of the Parishad are firm in their determination to stand against the Ranas' swords to liberate the people by giving them proper education and to bring the country forward in progress. Brothers, come and follow the brave warriors who are ready to shed their blood for your sake. How long will you remain sitting bound by the Ranas' chains? How long will you remain half naked and half fed? Have not you known the reason of your great poverty? If not, understand it is the avarice of the Ranas for money, which has reduced the country to beggary. It is the Ranas who have thrown your independence into the rivers of their self-will; have made you slaves and enjoy themselves on the money earned by your sweat. They make you run to their gates and treat you worse than dogs. They claim that they themselves are the administrators of justice, but really they are robbers. It is about 100 years since they have been ruling, but what have they done for your improvement? Where is your hard earned money? It is deposited in their names in the banks of London and New York. You—unfortunate brothers—you do hard labour, but the benefit is enjoyed by the oppressors. You do not get food and are pressed down under poverty. Even then if you do not open your eyes, whom do you blame? Your luck, your stupidity and cowardice are to be blamed. Now wake up, friends, and relate reasons of your poverty by raising your voice against these oppressors. Ranas are sinners and great atheists. They have no fear of God in being traitors to you.

Brothers, rise and shake off your impotency and establish unity among yourselves. The brave warriors of the Nepal Praja Parishad are going forward and you should follow them. Surely right will eventually be victorious.

One who uses force in disregard to the above principles is the arch enemy of the society. His object can not be anything else but to swindle the society of its wealth, then to keep it under the clutches of abject slavery and ultimately to grind it in the millstone of torture. To allow such an enemy to stay at the helm of the Government, even for a moment, is not only a great obstruction but fatal to the prosperity of the society—and such is the condition of the Nepalese society, under the Ranas' rule.

It is the first and foremost duty of every individual to wipe out the very existence of such an enemy so as to preclude any possibility of its revival.

If this is not done the condition of the society would be the same as that of an innocent man under the clutches of tyrannical rule. It is safer to live in a jungle among bloodthirsty wild beasts than to live in a society governed by such an unscrupulous ruler.

Brothers! rise up and try to free yourself from the fell clutches of such robbers. You are human beings! Respect humanity! It is better to die in the fight for freedom than to rot in the bonds of slavery. This is the law of humanity.

Lord Krishna says "O! Son of Kunti rouse up and fight. If you fall go to heaven but if you win you attain salvation."

President,
Nepal Praja Parishad

PAMPHLET 3

O! Nepalese Brothers! Come out of the darkness into the light. Give place to reasoning in your brains and see what is happening; how great evil can result from seemingly insignificant mistakes of society. Government is neither the individual property of anybody nor is it anybody's patrimony. It is a limb of civilized society. It is an institution whose duty is to enforce the laws made by a society. It should therefore be in accordance with the wishes of the society. Law is simply a tie among the members of a society; therefore, none but the society itself has the right to formulate it. A society which does not possess this right cannot be called independent. It is in this case either a state under some foreign element, e.g., India under the British, or under the slavery of a few tyrants, e.g., Nepal under the Ranas.

A king or governing body is a servant of society and his duty is, as said above, to enforce the laws of the society and to impart justice to the people in accordance with the laws.

Its main duty is to protect the society from foreign hostile aggression and also to protect the liberty of the people and to look to their moral and economic prosperity. Any action of the Government which is not justified by the laws is arbitrary. To aspire for something more than what is delegated to it by the laws of the society or to take greater remuneration than that allowed by the society becomes a source of inconceivable evils. Just imagine what would happen if a person to whom you have entrusted your entire wealth for good or bad betrays you. Under such circumstances the primary duty of the society is to mete out suitable punishment to such treacherous ruler or Government for his crime. As a ruler is the servant of a society, any action of his which is against the wishes of the society, is a crime.

As regards the Nepal Praja Parishad, people ready to join the Parishad in sacrifices for their country can easily trace the whereabouts of the Parishad. But it should be borne in mind that anyone looking for a ghost will not find God.[3]

President,
Nepal Praja Parishad
12th *Asar* 1997 [25 June 1940]

---

[3] That is, anyone looking for us with bad motives in mind (i.e., the Ranas) will not find us.

PAMPHLET 4

O! Youths of Nepal! It is not necessary to relate the atrocities of the Ranas among the educated youths. But it is a matter of regret that though they are aware of the fact, they are themselves ready to be pressed along with their illiterate brethren under the steam roller of the Ranas' oppression instead of up-lifting them. It is not that the youths lack courage. They are merely incompetent and incapable.

Brothers! The reason of your incompetence and lack of self-respect is the oppressive rule of the Ranas. The Ranas have kept you under their power for the last three generations and have impressed in your heart their domination in such a way that you do not dare to raise your voice against them—not even at this time when the smoke from the fire of the World War has foreshadowed their misfortunes and they are quivering with fear from head to foot. Think for yourselves! How deep rooted in your heart is the Ranas' thraldom.

Brothers! It is a great pity that the Nepalese people who live subjugated by them should be allowed to exist. They are not ashamed to run after the Ranas' cars or to remain hanging about their gates even if kicked by them. Who should hold the reins of Government? The Ranas' sons are born Colonels and Generals but for a job of Rs 40 you, even after passing the B.A. degree, have to run from door to door where *Atphaharias* [Ranas' gate-keepers] push you aside. Even that sum of Rs 40 is considered excessive for you whereas big allowances for Rana families are not so. What sins have you committed that Jackals should rule in the territory of the Tiger?

Brothers! Your sins are clear that you have forgotten how to serve your country. For service self sacrifice and bravery are required. You consider yourselves to be in comfort.

Appendix 2

Tanka Prasad's Letters from Jail to Jaya Prakash Narayan and Bishweshwor Prasad Koirala

Tanka Prasad's letter from prison to Nehru is not available. When I asked if it was similar to his letter to Jaya Prakash Narayan, Tanka Prasad said, only half-humourously, 'No, in the letter to Jaya Prakash I was a socialist, and in the letter to Nehru I was a democrat'.

> Sri Jaya Prakash Narayan, Patna
> Long Live Nepal! Long Live Hind!
> Hon'ble Friends,

It would be better to introduce ourselves before writing anything. We are members of a socialist organization called Nepal Praja Parishad, established in Kathmandu in 1936. Nine years have passed since we have been somehow leading our life enduring the harsh rules of Nepali jails. You must have known many things about us through the workers of the Nepali National Congress.

We had long desired to write a letter to you, but we had failed to do so because of our inability to find a person who could deliver it to you. It is only after being inspired by the special needs of the situation prevailing here at the moment that we are writing this letter and sending it to you by resorting to a clever tactic.

The way you and your party have helped us in our public-awakening is very commendable. For this, we and our country will always remain grateful to you. We are confident that you will continue to show whole-hearted readiness till the last in resolving our problems in the same way as you have been helping us from the beginning.

The type of slackness that has emerged in the politics of our nation today is a matter that is worth pondering by us. What is the cause of this slackness? How can it be removed? We are writing to you in this letter about these very issues.

Thanks to your assistance, the Nepali National Congress had achieved great successes at the beginning. But in the end we failed to derive benefits from these successes owing to the immaturity and personal ambitions of its leaders. You know full well about the rift that took place within this party. Had either of the two factions marched ahead in the field of action taking into account the true welfare of the people even after such division, something would have happened by now. But this was not acceptable to our leaders. They thought that everything could be accomplished without facing any risk simply by raising an uproar while living in India.

Sacrifice and self-restraint are very effective means to attract the common people toward oneself. This, of course, has a special significance in the case of people who have grown up in the Indian spiritual culture. From the materialistic viewpoint also, there can be no firm determination without sacrifice. Policies cannot be properly brought into practice and defended in the absence of firm determination. And it is like a day-dream to wish to gain success without properly putting into practice and defending policies. The leaders have first of all to gain the trust of the people while undertaking tasks relating to a people's movement. For this, they should consider defending their policies as a very necessary task. In our opinion, the slackness that has emerged in the people's movement here is the bad consequence of the blunders of the leaders of the Nepali National Congress, in particular Sri Bishweshwor Prasad Koirala. Two years ago, when the Nepali National Congress had first launched its movement, the people here had begun to show full respect and trust toward it.

You also know how they had followed him. But later he lost his reputation among the Nepali people. The reason was that after he was released from detention because of his illness (the Ranas had perhaps released him on your request), it would have been appropriate for him if he had come back here to salvage his policy of Satyagraha and told the government that either it should keep him in jail together with his colleagues (who had been arrested along with him) or fulfil his demands. But instead of defending his policy, he stayed on in Delhi and began contesting against Dilli Raman Regmi for the post of President. Consequently, the Nepali National Congress split into two factions. This provided a good opportunity to the government. It sent its agents to infiltrate the Congress and thus further aggravated the division as far as possible. Dilli Raman was a person with a lust for power. Even then, Sri Koirala should have understood the situation and let Sri Dilli Raman remain in the post of the President for some time, and he himself should have come here and told the above-mentioned thing to the government. You can imagine how he would have gained public trust and how Sri Dilli

Raman would have been unable to work against him if he had done so. It was because of this single blunder that everything went wrong, and the people began to say that Sri Bishweshwor Prasad Koirala had caused slackness in the movement and also a split in the Congress by accepting a bribe from the Ranas. It may be true that the Ranas themselves had spread rumours to this effect, but the common people had no alternative but to believe them inasmuch as the main leader of the movement had gone to India after being released, while his colleagues and workers were (still) detained. Even persons of integrity began to believe these rumours. When he came here recently, we wrote to him about this blunder. In reply, he said that he did not wish to risk his life.

When asked to state why he had come back this time, he wrote that he had come back here to form a joint front against the government. But that this was not true became clear after an enquiry. Workers in the capital had tried very hard to end the rift in the Nepali National Congress between Sri Koirala and Sri Dilli Raman. But these efforts failed to produce any satisfactory result. Disappointed at this, the workers thought it better to stand on their own feet. Accordingly, they appealed to the people to open a new organization to be known as the Nepal Praja Parishad. Sri Koirala had, therefore, come back here with the objective of bringing to his side the Satyagraha that was planned to be organized here, or hampering it. But his desire could not be fulfilled inasmuch as workers here were very angry with him and were determined to launch the movement.

In the meantime, we were corresponding with each other. We had written to him: 'People's trust in you is declining. Please return to India this time without doing anything. Not all the activities will come to a standstill simply because of your arrest. You play your role, the rest will be taken care of by Nature. A people's movement does not depend on the strength of or rely on one single individual. You should be prepared to repent your past blunders. The government had announced that it would enforce a new constitution from the beginning of the new year. But it has not yet done so. What you should have done was to arrive here on the prescribed date and start your activities. There is still an opportunity. Raise your voice from somewhere here in protest against the false announcement of the government. It does not matter even if you are arrested, inasmuch as you would have then played your role'. But this advice failed to have any effect on him. Why would he want to risk his life? But when he was about to go back, the government arrested him and detained him in an isolated jail.

Meanwhile, political prisoners lodged in Central Jail No. 2, where the workers of the Panchayat movement were being lodged, shouted slogans in protest against the atrocities by the captain of the Jail. They were then subjected to indescribable assaults by the government. A total of 142 persons sustained injuries, and a total of fifteen persons, including eleven of them and four of the old colleagues of Sri Bishweshwor Babu, are still being detained by the government in a hell called 'Golghar' in Central Jail No. 1. We, Tanka Prasad and Ram Hari, were detained in that hell for a period of two and a half years, and Khadga Man Singh was detained there for a period of eleven years. We have now been shifted to No. 2 because of the need to create a vacancy there.

A few days later, Sri Koirala also began a hunger strike. Two days before starting the hunger strike, he or one of our friends sent a letter to us here asking for sympathy and support. We, on our part, made arrangements for that. Eight persons started a hunger strike here in his support. Meanwhile, the Nepali National Congress announced the launching of a Satyagraha movement from 1 June. Sri Koirala perhaps met Mohan Shamsher on the nineteenth day of the hunger strike. We learned later that Mohan Shamsher had asked him to stop the proposed movement. On seeing the prospects of his release, Sri B.P. Koirala had written to his friends to stop the movement. In any case, he was released. Explaining the reason why the movement had been called off, the Nepali National Congress had a statement published in newspapers. It said, 'Since parleys are being held between the government and the Nepali National Congress, there is a need for a peaceful atmosphere. The movement has therefore been called off for a few days.' Sri Koirala left for Patna immediately after his release.

On reaching there, he published a statement which said, 'The Nepal Government maintains a satisfactory attitude toward political workers. After my release, I do not see any ground to continue my hunger strike,' and so on. Now tell us, what one would think about him when he issues such a statement on reaching there even after knowing about the suffering caused to political prisoners on 31 March 1949, and the ill treatment being meted out to them by the government even now. Was there no ground for him to continue his hunger strike even though the government had fulfilled none of his demands (for the fulfillment of which he had staged a hunger strike)? He departed from here without even informing those eight persons who were staging a hunger strike to express support and sympathy with him that he had broken the hunger strike.

Later, when he reached Delhi, he said, 'I am sure that the Nepal Government will do something within a month. I am fully confident that our decision to call off the movement will prove appropriate. The Nepal Government is truly eager to introduce some reforms. I am optimistic about this, and am sure that the government will make such effort,' and so on. To what extent the reactionary Mohan Shamsher and his brothers who, because of their low-level lust for power, compelled their elder cousin, Padma Shamsher, a reformist, to give up his post, will be eager to do something for introducing reforms aimed at public welfare is something that even ordinary people can understand. Let us assume for a while that Sri B.P. Koirala intended to accomplish his mission by so flattering the Nepal Government. But our heart does not allow us to believe this. This is so because Sri Koirala knows full well that Mohan Shamsher, a crafty diplomat, is not someone who will be trapped by his sweet words. What should one say about Sri Koirala and the Nepali National Congress? They said while calling off their movement that parleys were being held between them and the government. But when the government later contradicted this, they failed to give any reply whatsoever. Finally, the talk of parleys too proved false.

Sir, should a responsible national organization like the Congress engage in such falsehood and make mutually contradictory statements without any hesitation? Such acts will only undermine the trust built among the people. Our leaders perhaps do not know that this is a people's movement and that the trust of the people is essential to operate it. He committed a blunder this time also in regard to the issue of defending policies. Was it appropriate for him to leave for India after being released without the fulfillment of even a single demand? It is true that he was being lodged in an isolated jail and that he was suffering a lot. But for this he should have approached the government and got himself shifted to some other better place within the jail. The matter would have been different if he had been released along with all other workers of the Nepali National Congress who were being detained. We believe that it would have been appropriate for him if he had left for India after the government did something in exchange for the calling off of the people's movement.

Not all activities come to a standstill simply because of the arrest of the leaders of a people's movement. On the contrary, their influence continues to spread outside invisibly in a more effective way. The people began to trust him once again when he was arrested this time also, and perhaps a section of them even became ready to participate in the declared Movement of 1 June. What else could be the basis for a people to judge the virtues of a leader and follow him if he did not make a real sacrifice? By this we do not mean to say that a leader should risk his life everywhere.

We know full well that not everything can be accomplished through crude sacrifice. Even then, such sacrifice should be made whenever necessary. Otherwise, nothing can be accomplished even through all-out efforts. We have already stated above that one cannot achieve success without properly applying one's policies. This calls for a sacrifice. Moreover, a confusing policy cannot have its way among the people. One has to approach them with simplicity and true sympathy. In addition, there should be enough consistency in the statements of the leaders. A leader should avoid making mutually contradictory statements at different times. What they should do is to make measured statements so that the people may understand them and act upon them. Their brain is not well trained to establish a relationship between quickly changing statements.

All this was about Sri Bishweshwor Prasad Koirala. We have no good news about Sri Dilli Raman Regmi either. It is being heard that he issues statements at press conferences from one place. He had long ago demanded from Lucknow the formation of an interim government. If anyone can oust a despotic government that has been ruling for the past 100 years simply through such paper challenges from abroad, there is no need for a confrontation through large-scale preparations for a revolution. Be that as it may, the reason why it is necessary for us to write to you about Dilli Raman Regmi is that he is perhaps a member of the Indian Socialist Party and that whatever he does is believed to have been directed by you. It is because of his relations with you that he still enjoys some reputation here despite his repeated blunders. But how long can he remain worthy of the trust of the people in this manner?

At the moment, people have great trust and respect for you. Our people are inclined toward a revolution because of their very precarious condition and the way you socialist leaders have raised your voice for the fulfillment of their political needs in the meantime. All this makes us think that the influence of the Indian Socialist Party will continue to spread in our country for a long time to come. But the way B.P. Koirala is committing blunders is very dangerous for this. People here are very angry with him because of his present activities. We deeply regret that political activities on the people's side in our country have already begun to give rise to bickering among their leaders. They aspire to become leaders, but they do not know that it is the leaders who have to come forward to risk their life at times of crisis.

Now we wish to tell you that just as you have done the favour of helping us in our affairs, you must also maintain a watch over the activities of the leaders of the Nepali National Congress and try to bring them to the right track. We do not say that Sri Koirala has done so because of evil motives. This is perhaps due to some change in his own attitude. If so, he can come back to the right track. We have no personal dispute with him. He has done us good, and we hope even now that he will continue doing so. But personal interests should have no place before the national interests. That is why we have been compelled to raise the above-mentioned issue leaving aside our gratitude toward him. We regard you as our honorable colleague and well-wisher. Perhaps Sri Koirala also considers you to be such. In such a situation, he must not feel that we have done anything bad to him by presenting his shortcomings before you in order to make him mend his ways.

So far as the organization is concerned, had the leaders of the Nepali National Congress moved along the right track, it would have become a very big organization by now. The people are prepared to enter into a new era. Their economic condition is very poor, and they are clearly opposed to the present rulers and their polity.

In our opinion, the organization that will be formed here now should be based upon socialist principles. It may be said that since a conscious proletariat has not yet emerged here, there is no possibility of the establishment of a socialist organization here. The examples of Bukhara and other countries in the north, however, show that wherever in the world it has been possible to carry out the principles of socialism, these have been enforced by relying not upon the conscious proletariat but upon a strong party organization and the strength of a few persons who have gained knowledge of those principles. In the Soviet Union itself, it was possible to enforce socialist principles for the first time on the strength of a party. If anyone says that it is wrong to do everything by relying only upon the strength of a party, then it is all right. But so long as the fight with the enemy continues, and so long as the significance and realization of one's principles do not penetrate into the nerves of the common people, they are of limited use as a weapon. Our people today have two paths before them—socialist and capitalist. From the perspective of the historical process, one phase begins only after another. But does it matter if we take the path ahead through a short-cut, taking advantage of the situation prevailing in the country? This task can best be accomplished by taking over state power on the strength of a party. We will then not only have the strength of a party, but also the support and sympathy of the masses for our task. The Nepali National Congress should move ahead at this juncture with this fact in mind. When we wrote to Sri Koirala about this, he said at one place in his reply that there was no possibility of any socialist activities in our country. At another place, he said that the Nepali National Congress too could become a supporter of socialist principles in the future. At yet another place, he strongly denounced groupism. It may be that he too is a supporter of socialist principles and may eventually take the Nepali National Congress toward socialism. But what we mean to say is that our future will be molded to a large extent in the manner the leaders instill consciousness among our innocent people. If anything goes wrong now, it will not be possible to resolve the problem later in any way; you will remain a socialist, but the country will be trapped in the whirlpool of capitalism, as is the case with Nehru and his Hind now. That is why we say that we should have an organization based upon socialist conscious-ness immediately.

As for our present programme, we believe that there should be a movement in the cause of civil rights as well as for the release of political prisoners. So far, no single organization has become so strong in our country as to launch an effective movement single-handedly. That is why all existing organizations should launch a movement jointly. We have written to all in this connection. We have also written to Nehru for his sympathy and support. We are sending the letter through you. Please forward it to him if you think that this will serve some purpose.

We wanted to write a lot about the Indian Socialist Party but could not do so for lack of space. So we content ourselves with whatever little we are able to write in these columns.

First of all, we would humbly like to ask the reasons for the apparent failure of the Indian Socialist Party to make good progress. Yours is a revolutionary socialist party. We think that even if a party with faith in socialism eventually gains majority support by following constitutional means, there is no guarantee that the capitalists will not set up an aggressive fascist party in India, as in Germany and Italy, and try to suppress us by all possible means. If we have to be ready for a fight in any circumstances at any moment, why not start adopting revolutionary methods right now? However, the Indian Socialist Party does not seem to be so actively engaged in revolutionary activities. But people like us who are in jail have no way to know much in this respect. In any case, we would say to you that the Indian Socialist Party does not seem to be as active as demanded by the present situation.

We know that you are opposed to the communists. It may well be that the communist parties in several countries are merely platforms for Russian propaganda. It may also be true that they want to expand the Soviet dictatorship throughout the world. If all this is true, then we too hate them. But the problem that we must consider seriously is how to check the advance of communism in the country. Communism is a very powerful movement. If any group of leftists can demonstrate enough dynamism and influence as a reaction to the conservatism of the capitalists, who are opposed to economic equality and to the sinister manoeuvers of the orthodox religious sects which back them, it is the communist party. It is as fanatically and mercilessly hostile to its enemies as the capitalists and their backers. The communist party not only offers a new economic model to the people suffering from the old order, but also a sense of satisfaction to them in the form of a new faith. Communism is not only a creator of a new socio-economic system, but also stands as a faith in its own right. The workers of a communist party are imbued with indomitable enthusiasm and dynamism. It is a sheer mistake to think that communism is spreading in the world solely on the strength of Soviet funds and expertise in its operation.

The entire poor masses of the world are being attracted by the idea of economic equality. It is communism that has been able to foster this idea by giving it the form of an international ideology. For the time being, however, communism may not be able to gain in strength in India. You are also witnessing how communist influence is growing in eastern countries. If you wish to check the growth of communist influence in India, then you too will have to demonstrate the same degree of dynamism and fanaticism in the form of a faith as the communists do, motivate your followers for a crusade against capitalism, and capture the reins of government from the capitalists, and then introduce a socio-economic system which is as good as or even better than the one propounded by the communists. Only then can you check the growing influence of communism.

We are getting some insight into your difficulties. A solid front is essential for overcoming such difficulties. We can therefore tell you that our own country can become a solid front for you if you can encourage our movement and help us to make it successful. Through this front, you can work steadily for the propagation of your ideology in India also.

At the moment, in India the government is in the hands of Nehru and people like him who visibly love poor people. We therefore believe that no one will obstruct us if we do something here now. However, if we miss the present opportunity and the reins of India's administration passes into the hands of the puppets of capitalists, we will not be able to do anything here in the name of socialism. We, therefore, desire that change should not come about in this country just now [*sic*]. To this end, you should help us to the best of your capacity.

For several days [*sic*] we have been confined in jail. We are quite shut out from the outside world. For this reason, some of our views as explained above may appear erroneous. We request you to send us a letter pointing out those errors and suggesting the path that we should follow. There are many omissions in this letter. This was unavoidable because of lack both of space and time. Finally, we apologize to you for all those omissions, and bid good-bye.

Yours,
Tanka Prasad Acharya, *et al.*
Kathmandu Jail (Kal Kothari)

To,
Bishweshwor Prasad Koirala,
Nepali National Congress

Dear Friend,

Your actions have dismayed us to an extent which beggars description. You are aware of the atrocities the regime is perpetrating on political prisoners here. How then did you dare assert that 'the government maintains a satisfactory attitude toward political workers?' On what basis did you also say that 'the government is making efforts to introduce some reforms?' We fail to understand what sort of policy you are following now. We wonder if you have made such statements to save your own face after having come out of the harsh conditions of jail life. Far from describing the atrocities committed by the government, you have praised the government.

Since last year, people had begun to look upon your motives with suspicion. But we did not give any importance to these suspicions. But we felt greatly hurt after we became aware of your latest activities. We have written to Babu Jaya Prakash Narayan also about your actions. Whatever you may think of it, you appear to me to be a great materialist who does not have the slightest regard for truth and seeks to fulfil his selfish interests by any means. But you will be left nowhere if you follow such an approach. From the materialist viewpoint also, one must defend and adhere to one's policy. Once you went on hunger strike and wrote to us for support and sympathy. In response, eight political prisoners here also launched a hunger strike. But the moment you reached Patna after being released by the Ranas, you issued a statement declaring that there was no more ground for continued hunger strike. Is it proper to forget your fasting comrades in this manner? Did you consider these hunger strikers to be your puppets? The government has not fulfilled any of your demands. Politics is not just an art of deceitful behaviour. You should bear this point in mind. On reaching there, you started claiming moral victory. But here, the government is forcing your followers to sign documents of confession. What sort of moral victory is this?

How is one to describe the scores of mistakes committed by you? To err is human, of course. Moreover, we do not say that you alone are in error. But I am constrained to say that there is a lot of difference between motivated or calculated error and an error arising from immaturity of thought. If any person commits an error out of immaturity of thought, he has to admit it, as otherwise it may prove as fatal as motivated or calculated error. It is said that our leaders rarely acknowledge their mistakes. That is why it is said that 'it is not right to compel the popular and eminent leaders to admit their errors'. You may feel offended at these words, but you will have to bear responsibility for your actions after involving yourself in national tasks. We do not want to use harsh words in describing each other's attitude. We eagerly wanted to meet you and hold talks with you. But for several reasons, our minds are now separating from each other. We are sad for this.

Finally, even now we would like to advise you to pick up the correct road and resume efforts to form a joint front for launching a movement for securing civil rights. We have written to Sri Regmi, Sri Mahendra Bikram, Sri Gopal, etc. also in this connection. You should try to bring us all together and secure our support and then launch a movement. We cannot just keep waiting for generosity from the Maharaja and other high-ranking officers. Wise men like you must realize that groups with mutually opposite interests cannot expect generosity from each other.

Yours,
Tanka Prasad Acharya, et al.
Kathmandu Jail, (Kal Kothari)

Appendix 3

Thanka Presented to Tanka Prasad on his Seventy-fifth Birthday

The Enduring Leader of Democracy
The Esteemed Sri Tanka Prasad Acharya!

The active role that you played in the political field to bring democracy to the country, by ending capricious family rule, will be remembered for a very long time in the history of Nepal.

In 1936 AD it was due to your inspiration and encouragement that those eternally memorable martyrs, such as Dharma Bhakta and Dasarath Chand, uniting under one conception, established an organization called Nepal Praja Parishad, which descended onto the battlefield of struggle. You caused many young people to actively join this organization and taught them to be dedicated to the nation. People who know that you started a political organization at a time when it was a big crime just to talk about one's fundamental rights, venerate your courage and bravery. At that time, being Chairman of Nepal Praja Parishad and receiving sympathy from the father of the nation, the late King Tribhuvan, you succeeded in building solid support in a very difficult struggle to establish democracy.

Image of Gallantry!

In 1940 AD during a lawsuit that was being tried against your political workers in Singha Darbar, you were transported from Jaleshwar to Kathmandu, bound in fetters and handcuffs. At that time, without paying any attention to the torture that you received on your arrival in Kathmandu, you imparted a sense of boldness and endurance to your friends who were imprisoned. On your arrival at Singha Darbar, the Rana Generals became increasingly anxious as the prisoners displayed more boldness and fortitude, and the judges were daunted by your brave and clear-cut testimony. Although living under a sentence of life imprisonment with many friends, you did not abandon your commitment to politics. It was your worldly power that did not let you lessen your rationality and endurance to continue that commitment. It was these qualities and sacrifice that inspired the youths to establish the Nepali Rastriya Congress (later Nepali Congress) in 1946 AD, in Calcutta, and also to accept you as its first Chairman.

Impartial, Conscientious and Able Administrator Acharyaju!

In the short period of your Premiership, you showed administrative farsightedness in establishing the foundations of modern administrative organizations, which are running smoothly and systematically due to your influence.

Emblem of Nationality and Dedication!

The valuable foundation that you built to advance the Nepalese value of freedom and sovereignty, by making Nepalese foreign policy distinguished in the world, based on the five principles of co-existence, removed the chains that had closed the door of Nepal. Everyone knows that your praiseworthy aim is only to expand the nationality and dignity of the nation's people.

Abundance of Honesty and Simplicity!

As an honest citizen of Nepal you never promoted your own self-interest. Being a fervent opponent of corruption, how much your experienced mind has been worried by the immoral and disgraceful conduct and selfish attitude of high officials emerging these days, is known only to those well acquainted with you. The pronouncements and activities that you undertake in order to promote the welfare of Nepal and her people are enthusiastically received by the Nepalese people.

A nation cannot develop without democracy. Nepal cannot progress by depending only on foreigners and without standing on her own feet. To think of developing the country through the ununified power of the people is only an illusion. In the same way, if there is no consensus concerning democratic power, the fountainhead of development cannot erupt. That is why it has been your clear conception that unity and political organizations are the essence of national development.

Let Nepal always avail itself of your leadership. We hope that we get the chance to celebrate your one-hundredth birthday, like the Diamond Jubilee of today, and we wholeheartedly wish you good health and a long life.

Commendation Programme
Acharya Diamond Jubilee Celebration
Committee
Basantpur, Kathmandu
Monday, 24 November 1986

Appendix 4

Tanka Prasad's Speech at his Seventy-fifth Birthday Celebration

(From *Charcha*, 16 *Mangsir*, 2043)
[1 December, 1986]

For celebrating my seventy-fifth birthday with such warmth and enthusiasm today, I would like to offer all of you my special gratitude. The esteem which you have bestowed on me today is not for me alone, but also for the brave fighters who ascended onto the field of struggle for the sake of democratic principles. I hope in the future you will establish a culture which will respect those who deserve it, and not only me.

Arresting the Nepalese people and Nepal, keeping them in darkness, and calling 'ruling' actions which fulfilled their and their families' selfish needs, maintained the Ranas for one century. It was I and my friends who warned them and raised our voice for the sake of democracy. Our organization, Nepal Praja Parishad, made a public announcement that it would abolish the Rana regime and struggle to establish democracy. At the same time, Martyr Sukra Raj Shastri and many other intellectuals were denouncing the Ranas through social and religious methods. I feel that the steps they took and their activities were not less courageous, and hence we should also accord the same esteem to them.

Today I remember our brave martyred friends who, fighting for the establishment of democracy and against autocratic family rule, climbed the stairs leading to the noose smiling, and who, with bravery and smiles, received the bullets. But we have not yet been able to fulfill the dreams the martyrs dreamed, and it is our duty to make those dreams come alive. In our faith they sacrificed their lives, and if we can not do anything, it means we have let them down. What I want to suggest by this is the need to reflect upon the present situation of Nepal. Today we have been deprived of our main political rights. The same political parties who brought an end to the Ranas' autocracy have been banned now.

The last twenty-five years' experience has already proved that there can not be any development in a country where there is no organized opposition party, and where people have been deprived of their democratic rights. The country can only develop in a definite way if the politics and the economy are entrusted in the hands of the peoples' representatives. Today's need is people-oriented politics and a nation-oriented economy.

In Nepal, if there is any slight hint of development at the government level today, it is because of external help. And now since the external help has been withdrawn, so has democracy gone. Reliance on others yields such consequences. Foreign nations do not care whether there is democracy here or not. All they want from Nepal is the fulfillment of their selfish needs. Therefore, regardless of whether it is a question of economic development, or of democracy, we have got to achieve it by standing on our own feet. And hence, the time has come for all of us Nepalese to draw our attention to the following points:

1. Preservation of nationality. But nationality should be for the sake of all the Nepalese people, and not for the selfishness of some two or four families, which is not at all a true nationality.
2. Abolition of autocracy and the establishment of democracy, analogous to the policies and principles adopted in civilized nations.
3. Bringing an end to feudalism. A system should be established in which every citizen gets enough to eat, has clothes to wear, and shelter, and at the same time has access to education and medical services. This system must be established by the joint effort of the Nepalese people.
4. Any person involved in anti-national activities such as blackmarketing, smuggling, etc., should be strictly punished.

Appendix 5

Tanka Prasad's Letter to the Chairman of the Kathmandu Nagar Panchayat on the Occasion of Martyr's Week in April 1989

(Published in *Samaj*)

Mr Sharda Prasadji,

Dear Sir,

You have invited me to participate in the programme to celebrate Martyr's Week. I thank you for that. However, where is there a place of esteem in this Panchayat System for the ones who sacrificed their lives fighting for democracy? This I have not been able to understand. The late King Mahendra had said that this change was to be for a few days only, but decades have already passed since he passed away, and this system is still prevailing. The name of democracy was not allowed even to be uttered during the time of the Ranas, and today also it is the same. It is only because there are foreign embassies in Kathmandu, and because of some different conditions, that the name of democracy can be uttered. But it is strictly prohibited to speak of political parties, there is an effort to suppress and silence history, and corrupt historians are involved in this. People do one thing and call it something else, and your attempt to make me participate in such activities is unsuccessful. Because my health also doesn't allow me to participate, I am unable to come.

Sincerely yours,
T. P. Acharya

Appendix 6

Extracts from an interview with Tanka Prasad by Harihar Bihari, entitled 'What is the Senior Politician Doing?'

(Published in *Saptahik Bimarsha*, *ca.* 1989)

'So what if the Rana regime has faded away, their descendants still occupy high ranks and are still powerful. They are still conspiring and suppressing freedom fighters to get their rule back. Not only anti-Panchayat people, freedom fighters, and leftists, but they can not even tolerate Panchas who want simple, small reforms. Panchas who are no longer in power have also become second class citizens. In such a situation, what purposes does Martyr's Day serve? It's only the anti-democrats and those who are corrupt who celebrate Martyr's Day. Because the embassies are here, because this is the capital, and because of the fear that the Panchayat system will be unpopular in foreign countries, they allow the name of democracy to be uttered here, but not outside Kathmandu. That is why I did not participate in Martyr's Day. They sent me an invitation, and I gave them a written refusal. I wrote everything clearly in my reply. Why should I go there and show my face among a bunch of scoundrels? After all, I would not be allowed to speak my mind, and the things I do speak about, the reporters are not allowed to publish. Was this the dream the Martyrs had?'

He got very emotional while speaking, and tears rolled down from his eyes. After a while he gathered himself together and said he wouldn't mind going to prison again, he had no fear of prison.

'I will not cease to speak even if they imprison me. This partyless system must be removed from the Panchayat system, and the right to organize political parties must exist. If I have freedom of speech, it doesn't mean I will speak about anything I want to. I will not speak against the King anyhow. Nobody should think ill of the King. The monarchy is very important for the sake of the security, protection, and national unity of the country. I have frequently drawn the attention of His Majesty to various things which I have seen need improvements. He himself is aware of the situation the country is in. And I have been telling him frequently that we can not do without democracy if we think of the benefit to the nation, the King, and the people. What else can I do? I am old now, and my health is failing. Chuda Prasad, who was younger than me, has already died. How much longer can I live? I thought I could at least eat better after the raise in my pension. But forget about eating better, towards the end of the month I don't have money even to buy medicine! If am in a situation like this, what must be the condition of the others who struggled for democracy? The Panchas have robbed the nation and can do whatever they want, as if the nation were their own property! Almost forty years have passed since 'democracy came', but people are still dying of starvation here. If it goes on like this the Basic Needs programme will never meet its goal in twelve years. You will never get your rights by begging for them. Nobody got their rights by begging for them in this world...'

Appendix 7

Excerpts from Speeches on the occasion of the Eighty-fourth Birth Anniversary Celebration of Tanka Prasad (3 December 1995).
The speakers run the entire gamut of the ideological and organizational political spectrum in Nepal.

Man Mohan Adhikari (Prime Minister 1994-5 and President, United Marxist-Leninist Party (UML)

Tanka Prasad was the first person to organize a political party with the goal of establishing democracy and constitutional monarchy in Nepal. His movement of the 1930s was the seed from which modern Nepal grew. He gave leadership to the first generation of political activists. He always stood for his principles. He never consented to doing politics from outside Nepal. And with his inspiration I stayed in Nepal. He was always of the view that success can be had only when the Nepali Congress and Nepali Communists join forces in a movement within the country. Eventually that was what we had to do in the 1988-9 (BS 2046) movement. His contribution in bringing together the Nepali Congress and the Communists is unique. He was always concerned for the smallest details of human rights violations, and his door was always open to all people, irrespective of their political beliefs. Many human rights meetings were conducted in his garden when no one was willing to offer space for such meetings during the Panchayat era. We should all follow his example and work for the political stability of the country.

Krishna Pahadi (President, Amnesty International Nepal)

Tanka Prasad fought for human rights and made history in the 1930s before the establishment of the United Nations and general acceptance of the Human Rights Convention.

Daman Dhungana (Nepali Congress, former Speaker of the Parliament)

Tanka Prasad was the first political leader to lead youth against the Ranas sixty years ago. Four met martyrdom under his leadership, and this sequence of events led to the BS 2007 (1950-1) revolution. Like Bhanu Bhakta, the *adi purusha* [founding father] of Nepali literature, Tanka Prasad is the *adi purusha* of modern Nepali political history. He was a revolutionary and a great patriot throughout his life. He took courageous steps as Prime Minister in designing Nepalese foreign policy. His door was always open to all political workers during the Panchayat era, whom he inspired to work for the re-establishment of democracy in the country.

Pashupati Shamsher Jang Bahadur Rana (Rastriya Prajatantra Party, holder of several ministerial posts during the Panchayat era, Minister for Water Resources in coalition government, 1995-, and grandson of Mohan Shamsher, the last Rana Prime Minister)

Tanka Prasad was a great freedom fighter. His contribution to this nation is enormous. He gave direction to Nepal's foreign policy during his Prime-Ministership. His patriotism was reflected in the non-aligned foreign policy that he embraced during his tenure as Prime Minister of Nepal, and which is still appropriate for Nepal. Due to its geo-political situation, the non-aligned foreign policy will remain the best course for Nepal so long as the nation remains a sovereign state. We took inspiration from his patriotism, honesty, and his incorruptible character. Nobody can question his honesty during his Prime-Ministership. I first met him in 1969 and became a frequent visitor at his home. His life style was very simple. I considered him my guru. He was a living martyr till his death.

Matrika Prasad Koirala (several times Prime Minister, former President of the Nepali National Congress Party, and leader of the Janata Parishad)

I was a government employee when Tanka Prasad started the freedom movement against the Rana regime in 1940. That was a dark period for Nepal, when there was no individual identity. People were recognized only by the post they held in the Rana government. It was at that time that he showed his bravery by challenging the Ranas. I heard about the movement from General Migrendra Shamsher, son of Babar Shamsher. I had accompanied the General on a hunting trip. Tanka Prasad was the first person to inspire people to fight for democracy and individual rights against the Rana regime.

Appendix 8

Shah Kings (1769-present)
and
Rana Prime Ministers (1846-1951) of Nepal

Shah Kings

Name of King	Year when		Died	Age at death	Years of Reign
	Born	Ascended the throne			
Prithvinarayan Shah	1723	1743	1775	52	32
Pratap Singh Shah	1751	1775	1777	26	2
Rana Bahadur Shah	1775	1777	1806	31	29 (abdicated 1799)
Girvan Juddha Bikram Shah	1797	1799	1816	19	15
Rajendra Bikram Shah	1813	1816	1881	68	31 (abdicated 1847)
Surendra Bikram Shah	1829	1847	1881	52	34
Crown Prince Trailokya	1847		1878	31	
Prithvi Bikram Shah	1875	1881	1911	36	30
Tribhuvan Bir Bikram Shah	1906	1911	1955	49	44
Mahendra Bir Bikram Shah	1920	1955	1972	52	17
Birendra Bir Bikram Shah	1945	1972			

Rana Prime Ministers

Name of Prime Minister	Born	Became P.M.	Died	Age at death	Years of Reign
Jang Bahadur Rana	1817	1846	1877	60	31
Ranodip Singh		1877	1885		8
Bir Shamsher J. B. Rana	1852	1885	1901	49	16
Dev Shamsher J. B. Rana	1862	1901	1914	52	1
Chandra Shamsher J. B. Rana	1863	1901	1929	66	28
Bhim Shamsher J. B. Rana		1929	1932		3
Juddha Shamsher J. B. Rana	1875	1932			13
Padma Shamsher J. B. Rana		1945			3
Mohan Shamsher J. B. Rana		1948			3

Appendix 9

Marriage and Kin Ties between the Rana and Shah Families

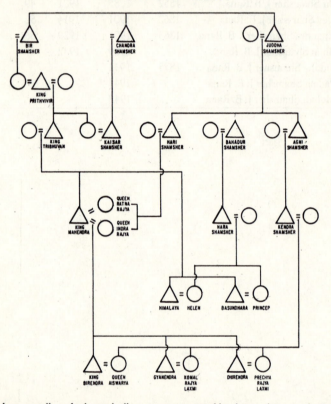

The chart partially and selectively illustrates marriage and kinship ties between the Ranas, who monopolized the Prime Ministership from 1846 to 1950, and the Shahs, who have controlled the Kingship from 1769 till the present. It shows only the more recent connections and omits most polygynous marriages and concubinage. For example, King Mahendra's oldest son, whom he fathered by a Newari woman, is not shown.

Note that both King Birendra and Queen Aiswarya are great-grandchildren of Prime Minister Juddha Shamsher J. B. Rana (her father and his mother are first cousins). King Birendra is also related to Juddha through his father's side: his step-great grandmother is Juddha's niece. Note also that King Mahendra's brothers were married to the daughters of Nara Shamsher, who executed the martyrs and interrogated Tanka Prasad.

Appendix 12

Chronology of events in the lives of Tanka Prasad (TP) and Rewanta Kumari (RK)

(ages indicated in parentheses after events)

Year
B.S. (AD)

1969 (1912) TP born in Parasi

1973 (1916) TP moves to Bishalnagar

1975 (1918) RK born in Kathmandu

1976 (1919) TP moves to Bara

1981 (1924) TP moves to Biratnagar

1983 (1926) TP moves to Sifale; teaches Ram Hari

1984 (1927) TP attends Darbar High School

1985 (1928) TP and RK married (TP 16, RK 10)

1986 (1929) TP's mother dies; Ganga (second concubine) dies

1990 (1933) RK's miscarriage (RK 15, TP 21); TP meets Dasarath Chand in Kalaiya, sees Dharma Bhakta on King's Way

1991 (1934) TP's father opens Bhimpedi Hotel

1992 (1935) TP meets Dharma Bhakta in Bhimpedi

1993 (1936) Praja Parishad founded

1994 (1937) Meena born (RK 19, TP 25); TP and Dasarath Chand go to India

1996 (1939) Shanta (second daughter) born

1997 (1940) pamphleting (*Asar* (June-July)), TP goes to Banaras; Praja Parishad officers chosen (*Bhadra* (August-September)); TP arrested (10/29, ca. *Kartik* 13), TP goes to prison (Jan 1941) (RK 22, TP 28)

1998 (1941) RK lives at Kancho Baje's; Meena goes to Sirsia to live with her grandfather in *Shrawan* (July-August); RK and Kancho Baje go to Banaras in *Mangsir* (November-December)

2003 (1946) RK returns to Sirsia

2004 (1947) TP's father dies; RK founds Mahila Sangathan; TP elected President *in absentia* at first Congress meeting; India achieves independence from England

2005 (1948) RK moves to Battisputali, Mithi arrives on RK's doorstep

2006 (1949) TP's second mother dies; RK smuggles letters to Jaya Prakash Narayan, Prime Minister Nehru, B.P. Koirala and others

2007 (1950) RK lives in *maiti*; court case over land with Indumati; King Tribhuvan given asylum in Indian Embassy; TP released from jail (1/17/51); TP and RK live at his sister's house (RK 32, TP 38)

2008 (1951) Meena (14) goes to India to study; Raksha Dal Mutiny (1/22/52), K.I. Singh flees to Tibet

2009 (1952) Babi (third daughter) born in 1953

2010 (1953) family moves to Dilli Bazaar; TP serves as Home Minister for ten months (2/18/54)

2011 (1954) Thulo Bhai (first son) born in 1955

2012 (1955) family lives at sister's house (1956); on 21 January 1956 Kanchhu (second son) born; on 27 January TP becomes Prime Minister; China (second son) born; China trip; family lives in Kamal Pokhari (Arvind Shamsher); (RK 37, TP 43)

2014 (1957) TP's Prime Ministership ends in July; family lives in Kamal Pokhari (Laxman Dittha); TP's older sister dies

2015 (1958) Sanu (fourth daughter) born the day after Shanta (second daughter) is married at the age of 19

2016 (1959) RK's father dies; Rita (first granddaughter) and Sano Kanchhu (last son) born; B.P. Koirala becomes first elected Prime Minister (RK 41, TP 47, Shanta 20)

2017 (1960) Meena (23) to USSR for M.A.; TP Chairman of the Land Reform Commission (1961); King Mahendra imprisons entire cabinet and initiates 30-year Panchayat system

2018 (1961) TP issues statement that, "It is time the people got their fundamental rights."

2019 (1962) Beena (Meena's daughter) born; Acharyas live in Kamal Pokhari (Pandey)

2020 (1963) TP Chairman of National Guidance Council

2023 (1966) Acharyas rent in Baneshwor; palace gives Acharyas Rs 20,000 to buy land; Meena returns from USSR

2024 (1967) TP demands organized opposition in the National Panchayat and public access to its sessions, right to criticize government policies and hold public meetings, and release all political prisoners

2026 (1969) TP chairs first meeting of human rights association at his own house

2027 (1970) RK's mother dies; Sanima dies in July

2029 (1972) TP Chairman of Land Reform Commission and Vice-Chairman of Political Sufferers' Resettlement Committee

2031 (1974) TP organises national convention to discuss national economic and political problems; convention cancelled by government's refusal to allow use of public places, including TP's own house, for such meetings (1975)

2034 (1977) Government prevents publication of TP's Martyrs' Week speech (March 10) demanding civil rights and popular democracy

2036 (1979) After tour of countryside TP issues statement (April 6, 1978) describing deep popular frustration that could erupt any day; in May, weeks after his April 6 statement, widespread rioting leads to announcement of national referendum on the Panchayat system

2043 (1986) TP's 75th birthday celebration (*Mangsir* 9; November 24). TP and other political leaders issue joint statement condemning massive civil rights violations by the government

2045 (1988) Amrita (great granddaughter) born to Beena; Chuda Prasad dies (1989). TP joins other political leaders in demands for lifting ban on political parties, freedom to hold peaceful public meetings, release of political prisoners, and condemnation of human rights abuses by government

2046 (1989) Umesh (first grandson) marries

2047 (1990) Children born to Rita and Umesh (grandchildren), and Sano Kanchhu (youngest son); two-month agitation for multi-party political system succeeds on April 8; King Birendra becomes a constitutional monarch

2048 (1991) Elections to national parliament held on May 12; Nepali Congress wins with small majority over Communists; Praja Parishad is registered political party but fields no candidates

2049 (1992) TP dies on April 23, of cardiovascular failure

2051 (1994) Communists form the government after electoral victory

Bibliography

Acharya, Tanka Prasad. *Statements and Speeches*. Kathmandu: 1980.

Adhikari, Krishna Kant. *A Brief Survey of Nepali Historiography*. Kathmandu: Sahayogi Press, 1980.

Bakhtin, M. M. *Speech Genres and Other Late Essays* (ed. C. Emerson and M. Holquist; trans. by V. W. McGee). Austin: University of Texas Press, 1986.

Barnes, J.A. 'Kinship Studies: Some Impressions on the Current State of Play'. *Man*, vol 15:2, 293-303, 1980.

Bihari, Harihar. 'Jetha Rajnitigya Ke Gardia Hunuhuncha?' ('What is the Senior Politician Doing?') *Sapthahik Bimarsha* (*Weekly Discussions, ca.* 1989, Nepali weekly newspaper).

Bourdieu, Pierre. 'The Biographical Illusion'. Working Papers and Proceedings of the Centre for Psychosocial Studies, no. 14, 1987.

—— *The Logic of Practice*. Oxford: Polity Press, 1990.

—— *In Other Words*. Oxford: Polity Press, 1990.

Bruner, Edward M. 'The Opening up of Anthropology' in Edward M. Bruner (ed.) *Text, Play, and Story: The Construction and Reconstruction of Self and Society*. Washington, D.C.: The American Ethnological Society, 1984.

Camus, Albert. *The Stranger*. New York: A. A. Chomp, 1946.

Caplan, Lionel. *Land and Social Change in Eastern Nepal*. Berkeley: University of California Press, 1970.

Cardoso, Fernando and Enzo Faletto. *Dependency and Development in Latin America*. Berkeley: University of California Press, 1979.

Charcha (*Talk of the Town*, Nepali newspaper)

Coronil, Fernando. 'Listening to the Subaltern: The Poetics of Neo-colonial States'. *Poetics Today*, 15:2, 1994.

Crapanzano, Vincent. 'The Life History in Anthropological Field Work' *Anthropology and Humanism Quarterly*, vol. 15:2 and 3, winter 1977.

—— *Tuhami*. Chicago: University of Chicago Press, 1980.

Dale, Stephen Frederic. 'Steppe Humanism: The Autobiographical

Writings of Zahir Al-Din Muhammade Babur, 1483-1530' *International Journal of Middle East Studies*, vol 22, 1990.

Dainik Samaj (*Daily Society*, Nepali newspaper)

Dumont, Louis. 'World Renunciation in Indian Religions', in *Religion/Politics and History in India*. Paris: Mouton Publishers, 1970.

Dwyer, Kevin. *Moroccan Dialogues: Anthropology In Question*. Baltimore: The Johns Hopkins University Press, 1982.

Denzin, Norman K. *Interpretive Biography*. London: Sage Publications, 1989.

Erikson, Erik H. *Gandhi's Truth: On the Origins of Militant Nonviolence*. New York: W. W. Norton and Company, 1969.

Fisher, James F. *Sherpas: Reflections on Change in Himalayan Nepal*, with a foreword by Sir Edmund Hillary. Berkeley: University of California Press, 1990.

Fox, Richard G. *Gandhian Utopia*. Boston: Beacon Press, 1989.

Gadamer, Hans-Georg. *Truth and Method*. New York: Seabury Press, 1975.

Gandhi, Mohandas Karamchand. *An Autobiography or The Story of My Experiments with Truth*. Ahmedabad: Navajivan, 1940.

Gautam, Rajesh. *Nepalko Prajatantrik Andolanama Nepal Praja -Parishadko Bhumika* (*The Role of the Nepal Praja Parishad in Nepal's Democratic Movement*). Banaras: published by the author, 2046 (1989).

Geertz, Clifford. *Local Knowledge*. New York: Basic Books, 1983.

Giddens, Anthony. *Central Problems in Social Theory: Action, Structure and Contradiction in Social Analysis*. Berkeley: University of California Press, 1979.

Goodall, Betsy A. 'Tanka Prasad Acharya: A Political Biography'. Unpublished Ph.D. dissertation, Claremont Graduate School: 1974.

Gorkhapatra (official Nepal government daily newspaper). Interview with Tanka Prasad Acharya, 11 November, 1990.

Gramsci, Antonio. *Selections from the Prison Notebooks*. London: Lawrence & Wishart, 1971.

Guha, Ranajit. 'The Prose of Counter-Insurgency' in Ranajit Guha (ed.) *Subaltern Studies II: Writings on South Asian History and Society*. Delhi: Oxford University Press, 1983.

—— *Elementary Aspects of Peasant Insurgency in Colonial India*. Delhi: Oxford University Press, 1983.

—— *Subaltern Studies: Writings on South Asian History and Society*. Delhi: Oxford University Press, published annually, 1982-94.

Human Development Report, 1995. Published for the United Nations Development Programme. Oxford: Oxford University Press, 1995.

Kondo, Dorinne K. *Crafting Selves: Power, Gender, and Discourses of Identity in a Japanese Workplace*. Chicago: University of Chicago Press, 1990.

Kumar, Satish. *Rana Polity in Nepal*. Bombay and New York: Asia Publishing House, 1967.

Langness, L.L. and Gelya Frank. *Lives: An Anthropological Approach to Biography*. Novato, California: Chandler & Sharp, 1981.

Levi-Strauss, Claude. 'Ten Questions Put to Claude Levi-Strauss', *Current Anthropology*, vol. 31, no. 1, 86, February 1990.

Lukes, Steven. 'Methodological Individualism Reconsidered', in *Essays in Social Theory*. New York: Columbia University Press, 1977.

Malla, Kamal P. *Impeccable Historiography in Nepal, A Rebuttal*. Kathmandu: Educational Enterprises Pvt. Ltd, 1984.

Mandelbaum, David H. 'The Study of Life History: Gandhi', *Current Anthropology*, vol 14, no 3, June 1973, 177-206.

Mathema, Dhruba Bhakta. *Interview*, 31 May, 1989.

Matri Bhumi (*Mother Earth*, Nepali newspaper)

Messerschmidt, Donald A. 'The Hindu Pilgrimage to Muktinath Nepal. Part 1. Natural and Supernatural Attributes of the Sacred Field', *Mountain Research and Development*. vol. 9, no. 2, 89-104: 1989.

Mishra, Chaitanya. 'Development and Underdevelopment: A Preliminary Sociological Perspective', James F. Fisher (ed.) *Occasional Papers in Sociology and Anthropology*. vol. 1. Kathmandu: Central Department of Sociology and Anthropology, Tribhuvan University, 1987.

Moore, Barrington. *Injustice: The Social Bases of Obedience and Revolt*. White Plains: M.E. Sharp, 1978.

Nehru, Jawaharlal. *An Autobiography*. Bombay: Allied Publishers, 1962.

Ortner, Sherry B. 'Theory in Anthropology Since the Sixties', *Comparative Studies in Society and History*, vol 26:126-166, 1984.

—— 'Resistance and the Problem of Ethnographic Refusal', Terrence J. McDonald, (ed.), *The Historic Turn in the Human Sciences*. Ann Arbor: University of Michigan Press, 1996.

Pradhan, Bhiktara. *Nepali Jivani Ra Atmakathako Saiddhantika Tatha Aitihasika Vivechana*. [Principles of Nepali lives and autobiographies and Historical analysis] Kathmandu: Nepal Rajakiya Prajna-Pratishthana, 1987.

Ramanujan, A. K. 'Is There An Indian Way of Thinking? An Informal Essay', McKim Marriott, (ed.), *Contributions to Indian Sociology*. vol 23, no. 1, Special Issue: 'Toward an Ethnosociology of India', January-June, 1989.

Regmi, D. R. *A Century of Family Autocracy in Nepal*. Banaras: Nepal Rastriya Congress, 1950.

—— *Inscriptions of Ancient Nepal*. Delhi: Abhinava, 1983.

Regmi, M. C. *A Study in Nepali Economic History*. 1768-1846. Delhi: Manjusri, 1972.

Ricoeur, Paul. 'The Question of the Subject: The Challenge of Semiology' in *The Conflict of Interpretations: Essays in Hermeneutics*. Evanston: Northwestern University Press, 1974.

—— *Lectures on Ideology and Utopia*. Edited by George H. Taylor. New York: Columbia University Press, 1986

Rosengarten, Theodore. *All God's Dangers: The Life of Nate Shaw*. New York: Avon Books, 1974.

Rousseau, Jean-Jacques. *The Confessions*. New York: Penguin Books, 1953 [1781]

Rudolph, Susanne Hoeber, and Lloyd I. Rudolph. 'Becoming a Diarist: Amar Singh's Construction of an Indian Personal Document', *The Indian Economic and Social History Review*, vol 25, no. 2, 1988.

Sahlins, Marshall. *Historical Metaphors and Mythical Realities: Structure in the Early History of the Sandwich Islands Kingdom*. Ann Arbor: University of Michigan Press, 1981.

Samikshya (Review, Nepali newspaper)

Sax, William. 'Village Daughter, Village Goddess: Residence, Gender, and Politics in a Himalayan Pilgrimage', *American Ethnologist*, vol. 17, no. 3, August 1990.

Scott, James C. *Weapons of the Weak, Everyday Forms of Peasant Resistance*. New Haven: Yale University Press, 1985.

Shachirani Gurdu. *Bishwaki Mahan Mahilae (Great Women of the World*, in Hindi). Delhi: Yug-Prakashan, 1952.

Shah, Rishikesh. *Modern Nepal: A Political History from 1769 to 1955* vol. 1. Delhi: Manohar Publications, 1990.

Sharma, Jeev Raj. 'Nepal Praja Parishadko Samchipta Itihas' ('A Brief History of Nepal Praja Parishad'), *Daily Diary*, 13 Bhadra, 2045 (29 August 1988).

Sharma, Ram Hari (ed.). *Swarnajayanti Smarika (Golden Jubilee Memorial*, in Nepali). Banaras: Nepal Praja Parishad, 2043 (1986).

Snellgrove, David. *Four Lamas of Dolpo*. London: Oxford University Press, 1967.

Spivak, Gayatri. 'Can the Subaltern Speak?', Cary Nelson and Lawrence

Grossberg (eds.), *Marxism and the Interpretation of Culture*. Urbana: University of Illinois Press, 1988.

Srivastav, Kashi Prasad. *Nepalki Kahani* (*Nepal's History*, in Hindi). Delhi: Atma Ram, 1955.

Stiller, Ludwig. F. *The Rise of the House of Gorkha*. Ranchi: Patna Jesuit Society, 1973.

Thompson, E. P. *The Poverty of Theory and Other Essays*. New York: Monthly Review Press, 1978.

Tilak, Lakshmibai. *I Follow After*. Oxford: Oxford University Press, 1950.

Tuker, Francis. *Gorkha; the Story of the Gurkhas of Nepal*. London: Constable, 1957.

Upadhyay, Govinda Prasad. 'Itihaska Pathharu' ('Lessons of History'), series of articles in *Samaj* (*Society*, Nepali newspaper), 2044-2046 (1987-1989).

Upadhyay, Mani Raj. 'Acharyaji Sanga Adha Ghanta' ('Half an Hour with Acharyaji'), in *Samaj* (*Society*, Nepali newspaper), 14 Mangsir, 2044 (1987).

Uprety, Prem R. *Political Awakening in Nepal*. New Delhi: Commonwealth Publishers, 1992.

Watson, Lawrence C., and Maria-Barbara Watson-Franke. *Interpreting Life Histories: An Anthropological Inquiry*. New Brunswick, New Jersey: Rutgers University Press, 1985.

Williams, Raymond. *Marxism and Literature*. Oxford University Press, 1977.

Index